Dear Papa,

hope you

enjoy.

Love Magee

2008

"Kiser's book is highly relevant to what is going on in the Islamic world. Abd el-Kader is the embodiment of the true moral, theological and rational ideas taught by Islam. I strongly recommend this book…" - **Muhammad Ammar Khan Nasir**, Editor Monthly *Al-Sharia*, Pakistan

"I hope and pray we can make Abd el-Kader's life and message more accessible to people in this time when it is so sorely needed. Kiser does a beautiful job of mixing a dramatic narrative with solid scholarship." - **Reza Shah-Kazemi**, editor of *Islamic World Report*, Author and research associate of the Institute of Ismaili Studies in London

"This engrossing and uplifting story of emir Abd el-Kader…could only have been written by someone with a profound knowledge of the French and Arab worlds and a keen sense of the eternal struggle between morality and Realpolitik…" - **Fredrick Starr**, Chairman Central Asia-Caucasus Institute, Johns Hopkins School of Advanced International Studies

"…a masterful rendition of Abd el-Kader… who stands as a giant for the ages, one we could do well to study and emulate." - **Douglas Johnston**, author of *Religion: The Missing Dimension in Statecraft*

"Abd el-Kader is a special gift that comes from the sands of Algeria… Kiser's book is an invitation to discover and pause, appreciating the life of an unexpected hero." - **Andrea Bartoli**, Combie Chair for Conflict Resolution, George Mason University

"Abd el-Kader lived by a chivalric code steeped in the Arab concept of honor. When, in our own day al-Qaeda terrorists claim the title of "knight," it's worth recalling a time when Arab warriors embodied the noblest attributes of knighthood: courage compassion and restraint. John Kiser brings both the man and his world brilliantly to life." - **Steve Simon**, Sabbagh Senior Fellow, Council on Foreign Relations

"… In an era when Islam is feared and widely misunderstood in the West, when we are often told that Islamic values are threatening to our way of life, here is the story of a Muslim hero whose tolerance, humanity and forbearance offer a persuasive rebuttal… This excellent book is both highly entertaining history and a powerful argument for respect and tolerance across religions." - **Kenton W. Keith**, Former US Ambassador to Qatar and Vice President, Meridian International Center Washington, DC

"In Abd el-Kader, Kiser gives us a lens to understand the highest traditions of the Arab Muslim culture…Explaining the importance of Abd el-Kader's voluntary surrender, a French general tells his parliament: "Abd el-Kader is the embodiment of a principle — that of great religious affection…this man has become the living symbol of an idea that moves the masses deeply.' The emir's real value for interfaith dialogue is that he is a devoutly conservative Muslim. In a way, this is who we should be negotiating with." – **David Mc Allister-Wilson**, President, John Wesley Seminary

COMMANDER OF
THE FAITHFUL

COMMANDER OF THE FAITHFUL

THE LIFE AND TIMES OF EMIR ABD EL-KADER

JOHN W. KISER

MONKFISH BOOK PUBLISHING COMPANY
RHINEBECK, NEW YORK

Monkfish Book Publishing Company
27 Lamoree Road
Rhinebeck, N.Y. 12572

Printed in The United States of America.
Book and cover design by Georgia Dent.
Cover art: *Portrait of the Young Emir Abd el-Kader* / Zoummeroff Collection

ISBN 978-09798828-3-8

Library of Congress Cataloging-in-Publication Data

Kiser, John W.
  Commander of the faithful : the life and times of Emir Abd el-Kader / by John W. Kiser.
     p. cm.
  Includes bibliographical references.
  ISBN 978-0-9798828-3-8
  1. 'Abd al-Qadir ibn Muhyi al-Din, Amir of Mascara, 1807?-1883. 2. Statesmen--Algeria--Biography. 3. Soldiers--Algeria--Biography. 4. Algeria--History--1830-1962. 5. French--Colonization--Algeria. I. Title.
  DT294.7.A3K57 2008
  965'.03--dc22
                                        2008020888

First Edition
10 9 8 7 6 5 4 3 2 1

Bulk purchase discounts for educational or promotional purposes are available.

Monkfish Book Publishing Company
27 Lamoree Road
Rhinebeck, New York 12572
www.monkfishpublishing.com

For Pam, David, Anne and Pierce

TABLE OF CONTENTS

ABD EL-KADER'S
CAMPAIGN THEATER
1832 -1847

T. Tepper

HISTORY, ACCORDING TO THE TRUISM, is written by the victors. Yet, it was the victors who paid homage to the moral, intellectual and spiritual qualities that made Abd el-Kader a widely recognized "great man" in the mid-nineteenth century. Those same qualities make him a particularly important figure today for Muslims and non-Muslims alike, as the prejudices afflicting both worlds have changed little in the intervening years. His best attributes speak to all thinking people.

From 1832 to 1869, during the height of his fame, Abd el-Kader's name struck many different chords with Americans, Europeans and Arabs: freedom fighter, chivalrous enemy, holy man, scholar and philosopher-statesman. For some Europeans, French in the main, he was a monstrous barbarian, and to his Arab enemies, a deluded blasphemer, and even an infidel. Only after closer inspection of the emir, while imprisoned in France and later in exile, did the hostile portrayals give way to the more generous ones: humanitarian, saint, conciliator and bridge between cultures.

Around his extraordinary life a whole literature developed in the second half of the nineteenth century that was written by admirers seduced by his cunning and resilience in battle, intellectual range, nobility in action and thought. His critics and enemies left their traces in the works of his admirers, but were not motivated enough to write their own versions of history.

The first generation of writers, and the sources for subsequent biographies, were those who knew him best — military men of various ranks and nationalities. They had either fought him, worked with him during periods of peace or knew him while he was a prisoner in France or in exile. The tablet of tablets for Arab and non-Arab writers alike was written by an Englishman, Charles Henry Churchill. This descendent of the dukes of Marlborough, and distant cousin to Winston Churchill, met with Abd el-Kader for an hour each day for several months during the winter of 1859 to 1860, when the emir was living in French-supervised exile in Damascus. Churchill's *The Life of Abdel Kader, ex Sultan of the Arabs of Algeria*, is an indispensable source used by virtually all later biographers of the emir. Aside from a work by the emir's son,

Mohammed, Churchill's is the only non-Arabic biography based directly on the emir's own words.

When describing the emir's youth, I have relied on the work of an eminent French scholar who has immersed himself in the emir's world as few Westerners have. Professor Bruno Etienne's book, *Abdelkader*, is one of the very few biographies that gives appropriate emphasis to the all-encompassing role of religion in the emir's life, as one might expect in a man whose name means "servant of the Almighty." I am very grateful to have been able to draw upon his informed imagination, aided by his recordings of oral history that are preserved today in bardic song and storytelling.

Lastly, I confess not to have attempted an exhaustive narrative of the emir's life. Rather, I have approached my subject in the manner described by Lytton Strachey when writing about the great Victorians whose lives overlapped that of Abd el-Kader; that is, "to row out over that great ocean of material, and lower down into it, here and there, a little bucket to bring up to the light some characteristic specimen from those far depths…"

GLOSSARY

Agha — chief of a cavalry or infantry unit (military), a district chieftain (civil)

Aman — sacred pledge of protection and hospitality, safety or security during war

Arab — originally, those who live a nomadic life, synonymous with Bedouin

Berber — original non-Arab inhabitants of North Africa, of uncertain origins

Bey — Turkish governor of a province (or beylik)

Bled — the rough backcountry

Burnoose — rough woolen or cotton outer garment with a hood, usually worn in winter

Cadi — a judge

Caid — a tribal leader, military or civil

Caliph — the governor of a Muslim state, successor to the Prophet Mohammed

Dey — a title for the chief bey, first among equals to whom the others paid homage

Douad — a member of the warrior aristocracy

Douar — a small village or neighborhood

Hadith — a saying of the Prophet

Hafiz — someone who knows the whole Koran by heart

Janissary — elite soldiers of the Ottoman Empire, originally captive Christian children

Jihad — struggle or striving in the cause of God; any moral or spiritual effort either against one's lower instincts or in the cause of justice

Kabyle — one of several Berber tribal groups throughout North Africa

Kougoulis — offspring of Turks and native women

League — three miles

Makhzen — tribes that collected taxes for the Turks

Marabout — a holy man or member of a religious brotherhood

Moor — a city-dwelling Arab

Mokaddem — guide or director of a zawiya or a local religious brotherhood

Sharifian — one descended from the Prophet Mohammed

Sublime Porte — The Ottoman government (from the French for "Sublime Gate")

Sufi — a Muslim who seeks a more intense experience of God; member of a religious brotherhood, living under the guidance of a master

Sunna — the acts and sayings of the Prophet

Ulema — scholars of Islamic law

Umma — the community of Muslim believers, predating the concept of the nation-state

Zakat — Islamic tax required of Muslims

Zawiya — a school and refuge run by a Sufi brotherhood

INTRODUCTION

*Such is the history of the man for whom our town is named.
A scholar, a philosopher, a lover of liberty; a champion of his
religion, a born leader of men, a great soldier, a capable administrator, a persuasive orator, a chivalrous opponent; the
selection was well made, and with those pioneers of seventy
years ago, we do honor The Sheik.*

Class of 1915, Elkader High School

"WHAT KIND OF NAME IS THAT?" newcomers ask.
Settlements in the American West were typically
named after Indian tribes, army forts, biblical references or the Old World origins of the pioneers. Iowa is typical. Its
map is speckled with places such as Norway, Rome, Moscow, Jericho,
Luther, St. Anthony, Lourdes, Holy Cross, Fort Dodge, Osage and
dozens of -burgs and -villes. All the more remarkable that there is a
town in Iowa called Elkader.

They call themselves "Elkaderites," which sounds disturbingly like
El Qaeda-ites. But they are neither admirers of Osama Bin Laden, nor
relatives of the Jebusites or Amorites or some other Old Testament
tribe. Elkaderites are unique. Theirs is the only town in the United
States named after an Arab.

The man responsible for planting the name of a distant Muslim
warrior in the rolling farmland of northeastern Iowa came from Utica,
New York. The archives of the Clayton County Historical Society say
Timothy Davis was born in 1794 when Utica was still a rugged wil-
derness, instilling in him "habits of frugality and industry" as well as
"pluck and energy to battle the world." Following the westward march
of the time, Davis settled in Dubuque in 1836, then still the Louisiana
Territory. He practiced law and made a name for himself defending
settlers who were being prosecuted for cutting timber on government
lands. Davis's speaking ability, lively mind and knowledge of international affairs made him a respected local personality whose advice was
sought on diverse subjects.

In 1846, Davis had concluded a business venture with his two law partners to acquire property north of Dubuque. A site on the Turkey River was ideal for a flour mill. Together, they laid out a new town plan centered around the future mill. His partners, Thompson and Sage, gave the honor of naming the new town to their friend.

Davis surprised them. Thanks to *Littell's Living Age*, he had been following from afar the exploits of a "daring Arab chieftain," named Abd el-Kader. This popular digest of the British and American international press had been cheering on the Arab sheik in his long struggle against the French colonization of Algeria. Memories of the American rebellion against British imperialism were fresh enough for Davis to see in the emir's resistance a freedom-fighting cousin. So Timothy Davis, a pioneer spirit, respected lawyer and distant admirer of this resilient underdog, named the new settlement after Abd el-Kader, wisely shortened for American tongues to Elkader.

Fourteen years later, another American would honor Abd el-Kader as a great Muslim and great humanitarian. This time it would be President Abraham Lincoln.

ལ

Emir Abd el-Kader's life was intertwined with two dominant themes of the nineteenth century that we still live with today: the French Revolution and the European colonial grabfest, sublimely hailed as "Manifest Destiny" in its American dimension.

The France that struggled for fifteen years with a minor rebel on the outskirts of the Mediterranean resembled, in certain respects, the United States today. France was convinced of its virtue. And why not? The French were still basking in their post-Napoleonic glory, and their humiliation by Prussian generals had not yet occurred. Its politicians, military officers and colonists believed France represented everything that was best in the world: the highest expression of European civilization, the best armies, the liberator of Europe from feudalism, articulator of the Universal Rights of Man, Christian and Cartesian at the same time, technical, logical, progressive bearer of Christian and republican values. Educated, progressive people everywhere spoke French. In Algeria, France was simply extending the obvious blessings of its civilization. All the natives had to do was give up their backward faith and habits, and learn French.

During the first half of the nineteenth century, European monarchies trembled from the aftershock of a great social earthquake we call today the French Revolution, but at the time, looked more like a dangerous virus: the French flu.

Regicide, anarchy and counterrevolution had begotten the Terror and Bonaparte, and piles of heads. The so-called civilized world today is horrified by scenes of heads lopped off by angry Muslims, forgetting the savagery of its own blood-soaked forbears. France's messy and incomplete march toward Liberty, Equality and Fraternity also needed heads — that of King Louis XVI to start, and then of anonymous thousands collected in baskets like so many fallen apples, the fruit of modern, mechanized decapitation. The picture of France desecrating churches, massacring priests and monarchist sympathizers, producing civil war, terror, chaos and confusion were indelible events stamped for decades into Europe's collective memory, incubated in a devil's broth of war, fear, hunger, hatred, sabotage, fantastic hopes and wild idealism.

Republicanism, Socialism, Communism, Atheism and Bonapartism were all children of the Revolution, crying for freedom from the Old Regime. But freedom, Edmund Burke skeptically observed from across the English Channel, was a strong yet unpredictable force, like a hot gas. Whether it was a force for good or evil depended on how it was controlled and what people did with their freedom. Before he became the great, bloated megalomaniac who exhausted France and consumed its youth, Bonaparte was the great codifier of the new French freedom. From California and Louisiana to Egypt and Turkey, the influence of his Civil Code lives on today as a model of justice and equality.

The Old Regime that disappeared was hierarchical, a world in which one's station in life was defined by birth and one didn't strive beyond it. Society was divided into three estates: the church, the nobility and everyone else. The French officers drawn from the old aristocracy discovered in the bedouin Arabs' structured social relations, warrior ethos, and notions of chivalry and hospitality nostalgic throwbacks to the Old Regime.

The cataclysm that officially ended in 1815 with Napoleon's abdication left France deeply divided for decades over the role of the monarchy, of the Church, of the people and France's place in the scrum of colonial competition. This was the fractured society that Abd el-Kader confronted, first as a chivalrous resistance leader against a bumbling French occupation that began in 1830, then as a stoic and unyielding prisoner in a turbulent, schizophrenic France. Staying, leaving, partial or total occupation were the choices offered in the debates of the French parliament during the 1830s. This indecisiveness helped the emir's cause while he was Commander of the Faithful, but became a curse when, as a prisoner in France, his future hung on the outcome of its domestic struggles.

Imperialists in France glossed the occupation of North Africa as re-Christianizing the holy heartland of the late Roman Empire, birthplace of Saint Augustine and other fathers of the Church. The socialists and anti-imperialists saw the adventure as pure folly that would only lead to a bad end. The settlers who came to Algeria might have made it work — they had 132 years to try — but in the end it was not their Frenchness that did them in, but their superior attitude and contempt toward the indigenous population. Unlike in the United States, whose expanding population and overwhelming numbers steamrolled the Indians, the colonists were always vastly outnumbered by the Arabs. Only a respectful attitude toward people who were different could have made peaceful coexistence possible.

For over forty years, Emir Abd el-Kader was a world figure, admired from the Great Plains to Moscow to Damascus. People of all stations sought him out: first as a wily adversary of a French occupation, later as an unbending prisoner and finally, in honorable exile where he reached the summit of his fame after he saved the lives of thousands of Christians during a rampage in Damascus. The emir's story is about many things, but mainly it is about struggle: struggle against French invaders, struggle with Arabs who rejected his leadership, struggle with humiliation and depression in French prisons and struggle to live as a good Muslim throughout his tribulations.

☙

I am often asked how I learned of the emir and why I became interested in him. Abd el-Kader's story is actually a sequel to *The Monks of Tibhirine*, a book I wrote about Trappist monks in Algeria whose kidnapping and gruesome death riveted France in 1996. Their monastery in the hamlet of Tibhirine lay on the slope of a mountain with a steep cliff face called Abd el-Kader Rock.

Curious about the name, I was told Abd el-Kader was the Algerian George Washington, the father of modern Algeria, who had once directed a battle from the top of the mountain. Abd el-Kader was the first Arab to create a semblance of tribal unity in order to combat the French occupation. But in defeat, I noted a resemblance to Robert E. Lee. He was gracious, magnanimous, respected by his enemies and deeply religious. As I learned more about Abd el-Kader from admiring Catholics in Algeria, I realized that the monks and Abd el-Kader shared a similar view of God, followed similar communal rituals, even dressed alike, and that their faiths found both a real and symbolic fraternity in Tibhirine.

One day a Catholic sister in Algiers gave me a copy of an excerpt from Abd el-Kader's *Spiritual Writings* that she kept handy in her office.

> ...If you think God is what the different communities believe
> — the Muslims, Christians, Jews, Zoroastrians, polytheists and
> others — He is that, but also more. If you think and believe
> what the prophets, saints and angels profess — He is that, but
> He is still more. None of His creatures worships Him in His
> entirety. No one is an infidel in all the ways relating to God. No
> one knows all God's facets. Each of His creatures worships and
> knows Him in a certain way and is ignorant of Him in others.
> Error does not exist in this world except in a relative manner.

No wonder the Catholics in Algiers admired him. Abd el-Kader had enunciated the spirit of Vatican II one hundred years before Pope John XXIII wrestled new, inclusive and revolutionary declarations from the leaders of the Church: The Kingdom of God is bigger than the Church; salvation is ultimately a mystery. Abd el-Kader's God lived in a big tent. No religion possessed God. I liked this Arab's way of looking at his Creator and the different religions.

The French monks in Algeria liked to say: *La richesse, c'est la différence.* We learn about ourselves by taking note of the other. Living amid pious, friendly Muslims, the monks became better Christians. Likewise, Abd el-Kader became a better Muslim by his friendship with Christians while moldering as a prisoner in France a hundred years earlier.

His resilience and ability to cope with defeat, betrayal and despair, and still behave in an exemplary manner, was something I admired. Could I not learn from his life? The term "spiritual journey" has become overused and trivialized, yet who is not on a journey, spiritual or otherwise? Are we not all seekers of something? But are we seeking the right things? How do we get them? What do we have if we do get them? How do we react when life throws unexpected boulders in our path? Abd el-Kader's tradition gave a simple answer. Seek knowledge, for knowledge also leads to right conduct. For the emir, knowledge is of two kinds: knowledge of external things, which he compared to pools of rainwater that come and go, and inner knowledge, the knowledge of the soul, the divine presence within us, which is like a fountain that never goes dry.

After 9/11, an already bad image of Arabs and Muslims became even worse. A "good Arab" or a "good Muslim" story seemed more than ever worth retelling in a world being rapidly polarized around false differences. After the U.S. invasion of Iraq, it seemed to me that the French experience of occupying Algiers — "liberating" it from the Turks, fighting Abd el-Kader for fifteen years while trying to win the hearts and minds of Muslims — offered badly needed knowledge of a world that is new to Americans, yet in its tribal and religious complexity has not changed much since the 1830s.

For France today, Algeria is a world full of bittersweet memories, though mostly bitter; a world of toxic, hate-filled struggles that pitted French against Arabs, Arabs against Arabs, and Frenchmen against each other that lives on today. It is a history that helps explain the deep misgivings of our nation's oldest ally toward America's "civilizing" adventure to uplift people who share many of the same basic values and needs, but whose culture mixes them in quite different proportions.

In addition to Abd el-Kader's, there were wise French voices of that era — minority voices that were overwhelmed by combinations of racism, greed, stupidity and nationalistic arrogance. They, too, are part of this story, one that is merely the opening chapter of a struggle that continues in Algeria today, where the emir's memory is invoked on all sides.

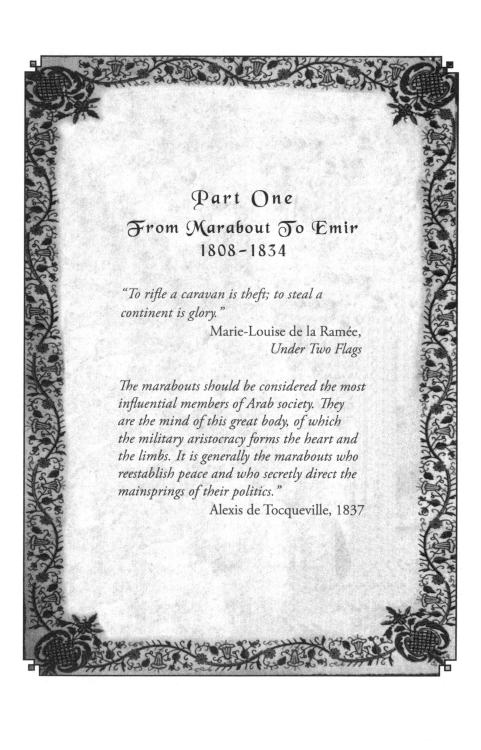

Part One
From Marabout To Emir
1808–1834

"To rifle a caravan is theft; to steal a continent is glory."

Marie-Louise de la Ramée,
Under Two Flags

The marabouts should be considered the most influential members of Arab society. They are the mind of this great body, of which the military aristocracy forms the heart and the limbs. It is generally the marabouts who reestablish peace and who secretly direct the mainsprings of their politics."

Alexis de Tocqueville, 1837

CHAPTER ONE

A General in the Dock

ON FEBRUARY 5, 1848, a short, stocky forty-one-year-old general of the French Army of Africa took the podium before the Chamber of Deputies in Paris to defend his actions. Less than two months earlier, he had taken into his custody the man who had been France's most elusive and dangerous enemy for fifteen years: The Commander of the Faithful, Emir Abd el-Kader. Despite the astonishing military accomplishment his surrender represented, the terms of the emir's capitulation had produced a storm of indignation and criticism in Paris.

General Leon Christophe Juchault de Lamoricière had a brilliant career. As a young lieutenant in the engineering corps, he had been with the army that sacked Algiers in 1830. Three years later, Lamoricière was promoted to infantry captain commanding native Zouave* infantry, renowned as tough, fast marching shock troops. By 1840, at age thirty-four, he had become the youngest lieutenant general in the French army. He also had acquired a reputation for courageous leadership, iron-willed perseverance and an enormous appetite for work. However, the professional envy of others, his too obvious ambition and unorthodox ways made him a frequent target of attack from his enemies in and outside the military.

Lamoricière understood that the French army was unprepared for the new world it had entered. He quickly grasped the importance to the Arabs of that which was fast losing importance in France — religion. He learned Arabic and studied the Koran. Lamoricière didn't accept the conventional wisdom of his fellow officers that fear and intimidation were all Arabs understood. The war was being fought to create a lasting peace necessary for attracting colonists. Harsh, indiscriminate punishment of the natives would not achieve it. Taking the high road

---

* The Zouaves were drawn from the Zouaoua Berbers who lived in the mountainous Kabylia region east of Algiers. These legendary units served France well through WWII. Their dress was imitated by both Union and Confederate units during the American Civil War.

of humane treatment, keeping promises and patiently building trust would accomplish more in the long run than brute force.

These principles, uncommon within the army, gradually won Lamoricière enormous influence among the Arabs and their leaders. By building good relationships with the tribes, he developed an intelligence network rivaling that of the emir himself, who had a famous ability to learn about French army plans and to keep his hand on the pulse of political attitudes in Paris toward the Algerian adventure.

Lamoricière's desire to treat the natives decently, even if only to achieve France's goals, was suspect in the army and among the more racist colonists whose boundless greed he detested. His enemies called him an "Arab lover." They said he was "half Muslim" and an enemy of the Church, when actually he was a devout Catholic who would end his days working in a soup kitchen for the poor. His family coat of arms bore the motto, "God Is My Hope."

In broad strokes, this was the man who marched briskly with dignified self-assurance before the Chamber wearing his Legion of Honor medal over his dark blue jacket with gold epaulets. Before he began his defense, this familiar tanned figure with wavy black hair, d'Artagnan goatee and piercing black eyes surveyed the expectant faces of the deputies. The general's defense was brief and blunt:

> "I have been accused of negotiating when I should have been engaging in operations against the enemy. Do you know what I would have taken if I had done so? I would have captured his baggage train. Perhaps, after further harassing raids, I would have announced that I had taken his tent, some rugs, one of his wives, maybe even some of his caliphs; but he and his cavalry would have escaped into the Sahara. No one can catch their desert hardened horses. If you think it is better for France's interests for him to be in the desert than in Alexandria, it is still possible to send him back (nervous laughter).
>
> "The emir abdicated voluntarily. After throwing all the weight of its valiant armies into Algeria, France finally saw this Arab chief, who had preached and lit the fires of Holy War, lay down his arms and put himself into the hands of our Governor-General. For France this was a triumph that was military, political and moral. The effect this has produced among the

indigenous people is immense and its consequences will be felt for a long time.

"Abd el-Kader is the embodiment of a principle — that of a great religious affection; and in Algeria that is the only kind of political affection that unites the population. This principle manifests itself in Holy War. Religion has the same force as, once, did the principle of legitimacy in France. So much, that by his prestige, his faith, his eloquence, his past victories, this man has become a living symbol of an idea that moves the masses deeply. He represents a great danger so long as he remains in the country."

When he finished, Lamoricière was met with tepid applause and angry outbursts from the deputies: "A representative of France should never have accepted conditions from the emir…He should be treated as a prisoner of war, a defeated enemy…It was a mistake to agree to send him to the Middle East." The majority didn't want to listen to Lamoricière. He knew too much and his detractors knew too little about the man he had finally brought to heel. A marabout's word was sacred, especially if the marabout was Abd el-Kader.

How could the deputies far removed from the realities of warfare against the Arabs know the world Lamoricière had lived in since 1830? Trust had been the key to the general's success. He had won over tribes for France because of his reputation for courage, firmness and fairness. He had shown the Arabs that France could rule better than the Turk. France's enemy of fifteen years had surrendered voluntarily because he had trusted Lamoricière more than the sultan of Morocco, a fellow Muslim. Abd el-Kader's knowledge of the Law and his humanity had convinced him that continuing the struggle against France was no longer God's will.

CHAPTER TWO

Lords of the Tent

GENERAL LAMORICIÈRE HAD TRIED to explain to the deaf parliamentarians in Paris the importance of Abd el-Kader's voluntary surrender. The emir's piety and knowledge of divine law had given him an authority over the Arabs like that conferred by bloodline for European monarchies: legitimacy.

And then, as the general said, Arabian horses were too fast and toughened by years of desert conditioning to allow the softer, clumsier French horses to catch them. For the Arab, love of God and love of horses were part of a single duty. The Koran, God's perfect word, implied a nobler essence for the horse over other animals by calling it El-Kheir, "The Great Blessing." In France, the horse was primarily an object to be sold or bartered. "You don't marry your horse" was a popular expression. The Arab did marry his horse. Divine wisdom and the practical wisdom of the desert were one.

So, let us begin the emir's story with the voice of Lamoricière's fellow officer and veteran of North African campaigns, General Eugene Daumas. Daumas, whom we will meet again later, became something of a military anthropologist of the Saharan Arab. His friendship with Abd el-Kader allowed him to learn much about a culture that rested on two pillars that were becoming foreign to the increasingly urban and secular Frenchman of the mid-nineteenth century: horses and religion.

☙

When I asked the emir about the origin of the Arab horse, he answered with a legend. "God made the horse from the south wind. He said, ' I want to make a creature out of you — condense.' The wind obeyed and condensed. Gabriel then appeared and presented a handful of the new substance to God, who said, 'I call you horse. I make you Arabian and give you the burnt chestnut color of the ant. Men shall follow you wherever you go. You shall be as good for pursuit as for flight; you shall fly without wings; riches shall be on your back.' Then

God put the mark of glory on him — the white blaze on the middle of his forehead. No creature save man was as dear to God as the horse.

"The first man to mount a horse was Adam, but it was Ishmael who was the first to call horses and train the most spirited and beautiful ones. Over time, the horses of Ishmael lost their purity, but one line remained untainted — that preserved by King Solomon, son of David. It is to this line that all Arabians owe their origin.

"This situation came about when Arabs of the tribe of Azed went to Jerusalem to pay honor to Solomon at the time of his marriage to the Queen of Sheba. When preparing to return home leaders of the tribe came to Solomon with a plea. 'O Prophet of God our country is far away and our supplies are exhausted. Thou art a great king; give us provisions that we may return home.' Solomon gave orders that a beautiful stallion be brought from his stables for the Arabs. He told them: This horse is my provision for your journey. When you are hungry, gather wood and prepare a fire. Put your best rider on this horse armed with a sharp lance. You will barely have started your fire when the rider will return with the spoils of the chase.

"Convinced of the value of their gift from the son of David by the quantity of ostriches and zebras killed, the tribe of Azed devoted the horse to stud. It produced a line which they called Zad al-Rakib, or Gift to the Rider, from which all Arab horses today are derived and has been spread from the east to the west by the Islamist conquests..."

The Arab horseman is foremost a hunter and a warrior. The pursuit of wild beasts teaches him the pursuit of men. This Lord of the Tent rarely stays in one place for more than fifteen or twenty days. He goes to the villages of the Tell but once a year to buy grain. For townspeople he has only mocking disdain. He calls the merchants, fattened by sedentary habits, "father of the belly." The horseman by contrast, is lean and muscular, his face burnt by the sun. He has well-proportioned limbs, large rather than small, to which he has added vigor agility and courage. Above all courage. He values courage as the crowning virtue, yet does not condemn those who lack it. He knows it is not their fault if God has so arranged matters.

... These Lords of the Tent have a spirit of the chevaliers of the Middle Ages. He is expected to be wise, generous and courteous. His primary virtue is patience. Seated on his carpet with an air of gentle dignity, he listens to petitioners. This person accuses a neighbor of trying to seduce his wife; that one complains of a man richer than he who refuses to pay a debt; a father demands protection for his daughter whose brutal husband is mistreating her; a woman complains that her husband feeds and clothes her badly and, worst of all, denies her 'her share of God.'

Endowed with wisdom and patience, the chief reflects on the different ways to heal the wounds revealed by his people. He is flexible and applies different remedies for different cases. To some he gives orders. To others he gives counsel. No one is denied his enlightenment or justice. His tent is a refuge for the needy and unfortunate. No one in his camp should suffer from hunger, for he knows the hadiths: 'God will only give mercy to the merciful... Believer, give alms, if only half a date... He who gives today will be replenished tomorrow.'

The Arab warrior is a man of leisure and pleasure. His main preoccupation will be the hunt that moulds him for his sole business of razzia — the art of the sudden raid. Razzia is the lifeblood of the Saharan nomad, from which he harvests glory, vengeance and booty. Glory does not lie in destruction but in plunder....

These stealthy actions take place at different times of day, according to the purpose of the raid. The bloodiest razzias are those undertaken to avenge a killing or the mistreatment of women, and may deploy a force of four to five hundred horsemen, known as a goum. This razzia, called el-tehha, is prepared with great care and use of deception. Once the camp is reconnoitered by scouts riding the strongest horses, the approach is made circuitously, so that, should the goum be surprised by the enemy or its allies, they will be coming from a direction where normally friendly tribes appear. If questioned they will offer a credible alibi for their presence.

The attack is planned for first light, a time when the "women are without their girdles and horses without their bridles." The chief warns his men to kill first the men and kill thoroughly before ravishing the women or plundering tents. In these raids there is usually great carnage of the men, sparing only the farriers, as their work is considered holy. Women, children and wounded are simply left to their fate. In the desert, one is never burdened by prisoners. The victors will carry off tents, Negro slaves, horses, herds if there is time. Other razzias are for booty alone. Excessive cruelty is rare.

Before each raid, the attackers are blessed by a marabout who gives his benediction to the expedition. After a successful foray, there is a celebration to honor the marabouts and the poor. Widows, freed slaves and farriers are all invited to join in the festivity.

Booty is distributed equally among the horsemen of the tribe and its allies. Disputes over the division of spoils are resolved by the mokaddem. He is known for his wisdom, good sense and honesty, for the victors know that disputes over the booty can become violent...

Abd el-Kader might well have been a mokaddem who resolved such disputes, but he was born into a marabout tribe where piety and study were more valued than plunder and glory. His destiny, had it been his to guide, would have been that of a married monk, living a life of prayer, meditation and teaching.

☙

Who, indeed, was this marabout who became a formidable warrior, but in the end put his trust in the word of a French general, believing that submission to France was the will of God?

Marabout. The word confused the French soldiers. Was it a person or a thing? Both, they learned eventually. A marabout is a holy man, a man "tied to religion." It is also his tomb, but may be a 500-year-old oak tree thought by the common people to possess miraculous healing powers. Typically, it is a domed, white-washed mausoleum surrounded by a low mud wall, visited by the poor, frequently women who come to pray for intercession or simply need an excuse to leave the confinement of their homes by seeking the company of someone who is safely dead, but known to have been learned and saintly.

Maraboutism is still widespread in North Africa today, and is strongly rooted in rural populations and among the less-educated believers. Muslim reformers have considered these practices a degenerate form of Islam, full of superstitious and magical beliefs that border on the worship of men. There is no God but God. Idolatry is the supreme sin of Islam. It was into a distinguished marabout family living in the remote Turkish beylik of Oran, in what was known as the Regency of Algiers, that Abd el-Kader was born in September 1808, though some say it was May, 1807.

A cacophany of cries, chants and incantations could be heard from Lalla Zohra's retinue of female relatives and servants gathered in her strong smelling goatskin tent. The most fervent were those of her Negro servant, Mohra. She would be the baby's wet nurse and prayed more loudly than the others for her mistress that this be a boy. Zohra was served a cup of linden tea mixed with clove sticks, thyme and cinnamon to accelerate the contractions. Servants were throwing handfuls of salt in the corners of the tent to keep away evil jinns lurking in the darkness.

"Flap your wings, Oh angel of God, help deliver this child, protect it with your wings, deliver this child," the midwife chanted as she brought a pot of boiling water. Zohra's sister-in-law prayed to their patron saint, Abd el-Kader al-Jilani. "Push, Lalla Zohra! Push!" The head emerged. It was covered with hair, a good sign. "It's a boy. Praise to God. Allahu Akbar! Alhamdulillah!"

The women chanted their prayers louder to give protection against any jinns still floating about the tent waiting to fall upon this newborn creature of God. One of the midwives sneaked off to bury the placenta in a secret hiding place. Afterward, servants brought Zohra a bowl of warm honey to prevent indigestion, followed by a baked pigeon served in pepper sauce with saffron and butter to restore her strength.

Muhi al-Din ordered a ram be sacrificed to renew his pact with Abraham, and then walked over to the womens' tent and took his wife's hand. "I am going to call him Servant of the Almighty, in honor of my mother who once had a dream that told of a grandchild who would have an exceptional destiny." The midwife had prepared seven pieces of cloth, neatly laid across her knees. One by one, she dipped each strip in oil and henna to ritually wash the infant's body. Muhi al-Din placed his hand tenderly on his wife's forehead and thanked her for a job well done. She was happy to have delivered a boy for her husband.

The caids and sheikhs from clans throughout the beylik had come to pay their respects and congratulate Muhi al-Din, the respected head of the Kadiriyya brotherhood. Its influence stretched throughout North Africa thanks to Muhi al-Din's reputation for learning, piety and wisdom — qualities that justified his name, "The Enlivener of Religion." Warring tribes often sought out Muhi al-Din to settle their disputes. On this occasion, more than social politesse was on their minds. This was also an opportunity to talk with their spiritual leader about disquieting things going on in the region.

Across the Mediterranean, Europe was in turmoil. The Christians were fighting with each other and the Turks were anxious about their intentions. People spoke of a great French sultan, called Bonaparte, who had invaded Egypt and won a great victory at the Pyramids. He was said to admire Islam and to have taken a Mameluke bodyguard, but also to have sent spies to reconnoiter the coast of North Africa. The Arabs were unsure if the sultan in Istanbul was willing to defend the faith.

There was also talk of the growing power of the Tidjani Brotherhood, whose influence spread from Laghouat in the Sahara to the province of Oran. Its rebellious leader, Sheik Tidjani, was making things worse with the already oppressive Turkish overlords. The beys wanted peace so they could collect their taxes and lead lives of indolent luxury. These and other concerns were on the minds of those gathered around Muhi al-Din that morning as he sat with his legs folded, working the black wooden beads of his sebha, reciting to himself the ninety-nine divine names while politely nodding as each guest said his piece. Yes, there were many unsettling signs, but only God knows the future. Muhi al-Din had other things on his mind. Now was a time for celebration.

Zohra was the second of Muhi al-Din's three wives. She was well educated for a woman of her time. Not only could she read and write, which was rare even in Europe in the early 19th century, she was schooled in the Koran and the traditions of the Prophet. People called her "Lalla," a title of respect owed to her reputation for generosity, learning and piety. Some Arabs considered her a marabout.

His mother taught Abd el-Kader to read the Koran, to write and to make his own clothes. She showed him how to perform the ritual ablutions that precede daily prayers. They were always in threes: the hands were washed first, then the mouth by gargling, followed by the nostrils, the face from forehead to chin, the arms up to the elbows, then rinsing of the hair from the forehead to the neck, ears inside and out, and finally the feet, beginning always with the right side.

"Ritual purity is half of faith," his mother would tell him. It was both symbol and reminder, a reminder of the other, harder half — to purify one's inner self. To be a good Muslim and become an instrument of God's will, it was necessary to be free of egotistical desires and unruly passions. Zohra also taught him the dangers of mechanical ritualism. He had to pray with his heart and not only his lips. "Don't be like your father's assistant who is like a rooster," she told him. "He knows the hours of prayer but he doesn't know how to pray."

Zohra disapproved of the gossip, erotic conversation and constant tittering of her servants and sisters-in-law. Nor did she like their superstitious ways. She wanted to be sure her son did not believe the foolishness his black nurse Mohra told him about monsters and demons, even if she thought it useful to believe a little bit in demons, particularly those within, and to believe in Hell and the Day of Judgment.

Piety, and learning to fear God, had everyday implications. Life, Zohra explained, is hierarchical and submission needs to be practiced daily, to God and then to each other, according to rank. Each person should submit to the authority above, beginning with the angels and sultans, down to pilgrims and slaves. When before higher authority, one should be silent.

❧

At the age of eight, Abd el-Kader passed from his mother's world over to the all-male world of his father. Circumcision marked the passage, a rite that renewed the original pact of obedience between God and their ancestor, Abraham. Henceforth, he too would practice obedience to God's will.

According to time-honored tradition, the day Abd el-Kader officially entered manhood began with a prayer at dawn. With his palms turned to the heavens, Muhi al-Din beseeched God for peace and protection from idolatry. A ceremonial meal was prepared, accompanied by the sounds of oboes, tambourines and flutes while Muhi al-Din spoke to the elder of each group of guests who had come to honor him. With a slight bow, he thanked each by name, and in sequence, according to age. Afterward, Lalla Zohra's brother-in-law, Abu Taleb, led Abd el-Kader forward to the master of the prepuce as the sisters-in-law and servants cried out their *you yous* and prayers. Abu Taleb held the boy, rigid with anticipation, as the village barber extended the child's foreskin and deftly performed the operation.

Abd el-Kader did well. He didn't cry out. The master sprayed onto the wound a mixture of olive oil and honey he had been holding in his mouth. Afterward, the boy was taken to his nanny, Mohra. She turned him over to the midwife who had brought him into the world. Following custom, she first covered the wound with her saliva and then washed it seven times with butter before sprinkling a fine powder of henna over the cut.

There is another Muslim tradition that says in each century God sends an exemplary man, known for holiness and learning, to counter the natural tendencies of laziness and neglect among believers. Arising from some indefinable source within, Muhi al-Din sensed from the day of his birth that Abd el-Kader was destined to have an exceptional future and gave special attention to his education.

Father now replaced mother as teacher, as tradition required. Abd el-Kader was invited to all-male gatherings to observe, listen and learn in silence. Every morning, Muhi al-Din taught Abd el-Kader the traditions of the Prophet Mohammed, or Sunna, those saying and actions of the Prophet that had been recorded by at least three credible witnesses. Always wanting to know "why," he also studied the commentaries of the great religious scholars who had wrestled with the different meanings that could be extracted from the Koran, interpreted in the light of the Prophet's own deeds and words.

The scholars often disagreed, his father explained, but where there was disagreement and ambiguity, there should also be latitude. Though ambiguity could be exploited by evildoers, and was condemned in the Koran, it was not necessarily bad either. Ambiguity, Muhi al-Din noted, also provided room for growth, flexibility and change. When

Abd el-Kader turned thirteen, he was qualified as an authorized commentator of the Koran and of the hadith, those thousands of sayings attributed to the Prophet. He had become a religious instructor, a *taleb*. His family began to call him by the honorific diminutive, Si Kada.

Muhi al-Din educated his son in the tradition of their patron saint, Abd el-Kader al-Jilani. Their Kadiriyya brotherhood had been named to honor the teachings of this 11th-century holy man. During a pilgrimage to the Middle East, Muhi al-Din's father, Mustafa, had adopted his doctrines. Al-Jilani preached a simple, universal message that attracted not only Muslims but also Jews and Christians: Muslims had a duty to pray for the well-being of all people, not simply for fellow Muslims. He taught Muslims to hold a special place of respect for Jesus Christ. Jesus was the goodness of God and his power of love set him apart from all the other prophets.

Al-Jilani's mission was to save souls, do good works and guide all humanity away from Hell toward the gates of Heaven. When Mustafa returned from Mecca in 1791, he turned Guetna into a center of al-Jilani's teachings and built a shrine in his honor.

A *zawiya* grew up around the marabout at Guetna dedicated to al-Jilani. This school of prayer and study served as a hostelry for pilgrims, students and travelers. As many as 600 students came to study Islamic law during a year, some from Fez and Alexandria. The zawiya was a boarding school, but also a refuge for the poor, the sick and the persecuted. Its handful of buildings clung to a wooded hillside above the warm mineral waters of Oued el-Hammam that irrigated lemon and orange groves in the valley. Wheat was ground in Guetna's windmill and what the zawiya didn't consume was given to the poor. Prayer, study and charity provided the rhythms of life at Guetna.

Abd el-Kader learned about his roots as well. He was a member of the Beni Hachem tribe. Its numerous clans occupied the Plain of Ghriss — an elongated bread basket, rimmed by low-lying mountains, dotted with patches of wheat and olive groves, as well as herds of goats, sheep, and camels, that stretched for fifty miles. Abd el-Kader was not of Hachemite blood himself. According to family genealogy, his lineage was descended from the Prophet Mohammed through the Idriss monarchy that founded Fez and ruled Morocco where his grandfather, Mustafa, had lived. A wise man by reputation, Mustafa was invited by the Beni Hachem to live with them and provide their people with learning and knowledge.

To acquire knowledge, Muhi al-Din catechized his favorite son in the Way of the Beloved One:

> *If you are asked what is the Way, say: It is knowledge, purity of heart and body, patience and having excellent offspring.*
>
> *If you are asked what are the obligations imposed by the Way, say: To not utter evil words, to repeat continuously the names of God, to have contempt for the goods of this world, to fear God.*
>
> *If you are asked by what signs one recognizes people of the Way, say: By their good works, discretion in speech, gentleness, compassion and absence of sinful behavior.*

Mystical knowledge of the Divine Path was important, but so was more down-to-earth knowledge. To acquire worldly knowledge, Muhi al-Din put Abd el-Kader in the guiding hands of his friend, Ahmed Ben Tahar. This versatile scholar was the cadi of Arzew, a small fishing village outside of Oran and an easy two-day horseback ride from Guetna. Under Ben Tahar's tutelage, mathematics, geography, astronomy, philosophy and history were added to the moral and religious foundation laid by Abd el-Kader's parents. Abd el-Kader also learned about plant pharmacology and veterinary medicine, knowledge that would serve him well in the future. The old cadi had Abd el-Kader read Aristotle, Plato and great Islamic thinkers such as Averroes and Avicenna, Ghazali, Ibn Taymiyya and Ibn Kaldun. A collector of books and old manuscripts, Ben Tahar possessed a portion of the *Organon*, Aristotle's great treatise on the nature of the universe that had been translated into Arabic by Muslim scholars.

Si Kada's education was not unusual for a boy born into a marabout family. *The ink of the scholar is worth more than the blood of martyrs* or, *To have knowledge and not use it is to be like a donkey loaded with books,* were sayings of the Prophet that Abd el-Kader learned by heart. Marabouts were expected to be literate and learned and disdainful of material things. Religion and knowledge were considered inseparable.

℘

Adab, or good manners, was an important part of Abd el-Kader's curriculum: when and how to greet others and in which sequence; the right ritual response to a sneeze; how best to control a yawn; when to visit the sick, the poor and one's parents and the proper order for doing so; when to give gifts to others and all the gestures and attitudes that are important for social relations and form the basis of the community of believers. Right relationships between people recognized a natural hierarchy.

Aristocracy was regarded as a law of nature by the Arabs. Breeding produced a natural hierarchy. What was true for horses was true for men. The simplest shepherd knew, "The head is the head and the tail is the tail." Two natural aristocracies existed among the Arabs: marabouts and douads. The former, the French called "the nobility of religion"; the latter, "the nobility of the sword."

Warfare was the profession of the douads. Their specialty was the *razzia*. The douads were suspicious of too much book learning, fearing that an overly refined mind softened the heart in battle. Wealth was acquired by plundering enemies. Their prestige came from their skill in battle and their bravery was measured by how many horses had been shot from beneath them. The douads accused the marabouts of intrigue, greed and hypocrisy. The marabouts accused the douads of violence and ungodly behavior. The charge of ungodly behavior was a powerful weapon among God-fearing men. The more astute French officers recognized in the marabouts' relation to the douad what the Christian clergy of the Middle Ages was to Europe's warring barons: a conscience. Yet, both aristocracies expected from their chieftains courage, generosity and wisdom.

Abd el-Kader didn't share the rapacious instincts of the douad, yet he still learned the arts of war from the universal sport of the aristocracy — the chase. Skill in the chase began with strong horses and good horsemanship. Horsemanship was a core course in his disciplined curriculum. Like other members of the nobility, Abd el-Kader started riding from the day he was old enough to stay on the back of a young colt and the foal got used to carrying weight proportionate to its strength. Young Arab boys learned balance by riding bareback to graze and water their horses.

Tradition taught the Arabs that toughness and docility were the essential qualities of a good horse. Docility came with handling, first at the hands of women whose gentle nature the Arabs believed was calming to a foal; then through contact with people and other animals, and finally, exposure to noise and strange objects. This happened naturally; colts and fillies enjoyed the tent's shelter along with the family menagerie of pet ostriches, goats, gazelles, falcons and their salukis, sleek hunting dogs that resembled greyhounds. Docility made Arab horses easy to mount. They learned to stand stock-still for hours in the desert with reins dropped to the ground.

"A true horseman should eat little and drink little," the Arabs said. Their horses' famous toughness came from conditioning that gradually increased the distances they covered and limited the amount of food and water they consumed. The horse and rider were to become a single personality, each capable of enduring heat and cold, thirst, hunger and fatigue. A good Arab horse could be ridden hard for two days without water. Stamina, courage, agility and an even temperament were the qualities most valued in a horse, as well as the rider. A toughened Arabian could cover 150 miles in a day when pushed.

Days were divided between religious instruction and horsemanship. Mornings were for studying and being quizzed by his father. If Abd el-Kadar was going to rely on the deeds of the Prophet as case history to interpret God's law, then he had to know the chain of witnesses for each of his reported acts or sayings, and know about the reliability of the witnesses used for determining the authenticity of the hadith, and its context. All this study was needed for a true religious scholar to intelligently interpret the law. Horses were the subject of hadiths as well: *The true believer who has trained his horse to shine in jihad shall have the sweat, the hair, even the dung and urine, weighed in the scale of good works on the final day of Final Judgment.* Was that authentic? Could that be valid even if not authentic? Or, *to care for a horse has the value of fasting.* Under his father's prodding, Abd el-Kader's love of horses fed his love of study.

Afternoons, he would go riding with one of several instructors. Young boys were taught to control a horse as they did their hands. They had to master maneuvers that could save their lives in the fray of battle: to stop suddenly at full gallop and spin around after firing their rifles, those "airs above ground" movements — equine acrobatics, essential in a melee, which were taught in the French cavalry school at Saumur, long known by the Arab horseman. Abd el-Kader learned how to ride in a strong wind, to shelter himself between the neck of a horse and the flaps of his burnoose, to navigate his horse over rocky and slippery terrain, and to wave and flap his burnoose to conceal the position of his body when galloping into battle.

Abd el-Kader would disappear into the Sahara to learn the art of surviving in the desert: to make tisane from the mugwort plant to cure fevers and stay alert in the saddle; uses of *bou nafâa*, the multipurpose meadow parsnip the Arabs called "the father of usefulness," and other plants for treating sick or injured horses; the proper times to feed and water a horse; to identify the telltale signs of water under the sand and near rocks. Abd el-Kader learned the names of the tribes and how to identify them from a distance as friendly or hostile from the shape of their tents or by the raptors they used to hunt — eagle or falcon, gray or yellow — and so the endless details that determined life or death in the desert.

At age thirteen, Abd el-Kader was ready to join the hunting expeditions. Unlike the douads, for whom the chase was preparation for hunting men, Abd el-Kader hunted in the spirit of the Arab poet who praised the chase because, "it frees the soul of cares, adds vigor to intelligence, brings joy, dissipates worries, and renders useless the skill of doctors by maintaining the well-being of the body." The hunt built qualities needed for life: intelligence, patience, endurance and courage. The chase taught contempt for danger. Courage was one of the four virtues necessary for moral progress, to which were added intellect, justice and self-control.

Si Kada's quick intelligence, natural piety and questioning mind confirmed Muhi al-Din's belief that his third son had a special destiny. He was better than his brothers at finding water and good pasture, planting seeds, shooting birds, leaping from his horse to slit the throat of a wounded animal and firing a rifle accurately at full gallop. Abd el-Kader could recognize eighteen different types of camels, knew how to efficiently load a mule and find the best route through the *bled*. He could charm the women of the family into agreement when they argued, and could haggle with the wiliest of the merchants over the price of barley. Ben Tahar, the cadi of Arzew, reported to Muhi al-Din that Abd el-Kader was an outstanding student in everything he took up.

ↄ৹

Muhi al-Din knew that the nobility of the sword had contempt for the sedentary life of marabouts and their bookish ways. Yet, he also believed that only with the authority of religious knowledge could Abd el-Kader succeed in carrying forward his teachings — to have faith in the power, goodness and mercy of God; to pursue peace, justice, charity and brotherhood.

His father wanted Abd el-Kader to perfect his public speaking and rhetorical skills, and learn to recite the Koran correctly. The last was of great importance. If his son was to acquire the religious authority needed to tame the tribes, he would have to know how to read the Koran so as to mimic the divine breath that God breathed into man.

Muhi al-Din taught that the human spirit was like an army in battle, constantly exposed to disorganizing forces that are countered only by the discipline of good order and rituals rightly performed. The Koran was the perfect word of God, his father explained, but it had to be recited perfectly to capture the divine energy that organizes the chaos. Man is surrounded by oscillation and random motion. Without the organizing force of ritual, the world becomes unstable.

Muhi al-Din sent him to another zawiya, this one in the provincial capital, run by Ahmed Ben Khodja, a respected scholar and specialist in poetry, rhetoric and recitation of the Koran. When the fourteen-year-old Abd el-Kader arrived in Oran, he was more likely struck by the chaos than the divine organizing energy. He was like the sheltered, if learned, son of a strait-laced country preacher thrown for the first time into the hurly-burly of a big city swarming with temptations and distractions. That, too, was part of Muhi al-Din's educational plan. He knew his son needed to experience diversity and witness the temptations and corruption of the world.

At the zawiya of Ben Khodja, he lived with the sons of Turkish functionaries who governed Oran, the children of douads, as well as Kougoulis — the scorned halfbreeds of the ruling Turks who mated with local women. Ben Khodja warned Abd el-Kader to keep a low profile. The Turks could be abominably arrogant. He was advised to be humble and discreet, and to concentrate on one thing: learn and learn some more.

But he couldn't. Abd el-Kader knew his father wanted him to be more than a bookworm. In 1822, Oran had a population of some 20,000 people. The city bore the imprint of the Jews and Moors who had been chased out of Spain centuries earlier and had brought with them knowledge of metal and leather working, and the plaintive music of Andalusia. Abd el-Kader wandered the streets in amazement.

Everything was new: the noisy bazaars, the colorful potpourri of Berbers, Arabs, Turks, Jews and Kougoulis; the half-moon bay filled with sails of all sizes, its western end punctuated by the large wedge of Mt. Aidour slicing into the sea. He had never breathed sea air before. He was shocked by the filth and stench at the port where he saw barefooted blacks from West Africa and Maltese dockhands staggering like overloaded mules, drunken seamen and ragged beggars who brazenly panhandled. He noticed women shamelessly walking the streets without a veil and with exposed bare legs.

Not content to simply look at all these new and dubious big city wonders, Abd el-Kader tasted the unfamiliar delights of cream-filled pastries and the Turkish baklava served in the homes of schoolmates. Sometimes, he found himself lying on soft silky cushions at a friend's house, being lulled to sleep by the sensual voice of a Jewish songstress warbling songs of a lost Andalusia. But the Koranically correct young man from Guetna found no lasting pleasure in the sensuality of the city. He had been schooled by his father in self-denial.

The impiety all around was incomprehensible. He saw gambling, even by the poor, and the practice of divination of entrails, activities condemned in the hadith. *With drink and gambling, Satan introduces among you the germs of discord... Divination of entrails and fortune telling are acts of the Devil.*

The pious student from tiny Guetna couldn't hold back his disgust any longer. One day, Abd el-Kader blurted out a burning question to Ben Khodja. How, he wanted to know, could the Turks be considered defenders of the faith with their loose living and contempt for the local population? The worldly-wise Ben Khodja listened sympathetically. Then he replied, telling Abd el-Kader of other things to despise — of Bey Hassan's ruthlessness in collecting taxes throughout the beylik, of prostitution and drugs, of the revolts by some of the tribes against the bey for his lack of compassion toward the poor, of the unrest in the eastern beylik of Constantine. The old master's litany of evils was his way of impressing upon the young boy that disorder and godless behavior marked the way of the world.

"Yes, but if you see evil remove it." The Koran was Abd el-Kader's reference in all things.

"Your time will come, but not yet. Evil is powerful. Removing it requires more than your passion and sincerity," his father's friend responded gently.

CHAPTER THREE

Unity and Complexity

ABD EL-KADER RETURNED TO GUETNA toward the end of 1823. He was happy to leave behind the depravity of Oran and his father was satisfied that Abd el-Kader had become more worldly. Muhi al-Din's favorite son also brought back a strong dislike of the ruling Turks who had strayed from the faith in deed and attitude. In the meantime, Lalla Zohra had found a suitable wife for her young nobleman. She negotiated a match with her brother-in-law, Abu Taleb, whose thirteen-year-old daughter, Kheira, she considered suitable. Kheira was beautiful, well-educated, intelligent and from a noble family — their own. Abd el-Kader was fifteen, but already a man. *Wed early, for marriage tames the gaze of a man and guides the conduct of a woman*, said the Prophet.

A great, noisy celebration took place in the Plain of Ghriss. Tribes came from around the beylik to join the carnival atmosphere of snake charmers, acrobatic dwarfs, bards and women singing and dancing to the jangle of tambourines and flutes, all to the accompaniment of joyous gunfire. An old, blind story-teller with empty eye sockets and a cane appeared among the crowd with a monkey on his shoulder. The monkey held a beggar's bowl and people gathered all around: "A penny for the story, a penny for my travel and a penny for my voice and you will know the true story of the marriage of Abd el-Kader and his cousin Lalla Kheira."

> Their first encounter occurred when Si Kada's father sends his favorite son to visit his brother, a marabout in the neighboring Gharabas tribe, to negotiate some business matter. Along the way, Abd el-Kader observes two women by a river. One is a beautiful a young girl, the other, an older woman — her mother or her servant perhaps. The young girl looks up and pierces the heart of the young man with her large, black eyes. At his uncle's camp that evening, Abd el-Kader receives a clandestine visit from the older lady. She comes as an intermediary for the young girl he had seen that day. With a finger to her lips, she gives him three flowers. They were picked by her mistress from

the river bed following their earlier encounter. Her name is Lalla Kheira and each flower is a symbol. One is white, like her body; the second is pink, the color of pleasure, and the third is brown, the color of night and of mystery. She would wait for him by the spring, near the river.

The rendezvous takes place, the servant stands off at a discreet distance. Kheira approaches, modestly at first, her haik still covering her face. The handsome young man takes her hand. Trembling with passion, they embrace, her hands around his neck. Suddenly, Kheira hears a tree branch rustle and sees the hem of a white burnoose. She freezes and cries, "We are lost. We have been seen!"

"Go back to your companion," Abd el-Kader replies with a mysterious smile. "Don't worry."

Abd el-Kader looks into the woods and sees that a member of his uncle's Gharabas tribe had been secretly observing them. Knife in hand, Abd el-Kader chases after him until the voyeur finally leaps into the river, the compromised paramour in hot pursuit. A struggle takes place in the river. Abd el-Kader emerges triumphantly.

The listeners shouted their approval. "Bravo. Our young marabout is a true man. He saved her honor." The monkey collected the coins in the begging bowl as the crowd turned away to watch the noisy, dusty display of horsemanship, music and mock battle known as fantasia.

How good is the bardic memory; how much is embellishment, how much pure fantasy? The story crops up in different accounts of the emir's youth. It is conceivable. Certain, for sure, was his long marriage to Kheira, who would bear him three children. She would be one of four wives, but she would always be first in his heart. Kheira, along with his mother, Zohra, and his sister, Khadijah, would be the three women who sustained him during the black days that were to come.

All three protested Muhi al-Din's decision two years later to continue Abd el-Kader's education by taking him on a pilgrimage to Mecca and beyond: Si Kader was too young; it was too dangerous; he would be gone for two years; he had been married only two years; his older brothers should go first. One can imagine Muhi al-Din respectfully listening to their arguments, yet knowing they were wrong. The education of Abd el-Kader would be incomplete without visiting the great centers of learning in the East. Muhi al-Din reminded his women of the Prophet's words: *Go to China to seek knowledge if you must.* Life in little Guetna was too simple for a son he believed had a special destiny. He wanted Abd el-Kader to witness more of life's complexity. In the fall of 1825, Muhi al-Din and his son joined pilgrims from Morocco who were passing through Mascara to Mecca.

℘

Bey Hassan was worried. The Turkish governor of Oran had received reports that Muhi al-Din's followers had set off for the long and difficult journey to Mecca. Each day since their departure from Mascara, hundreds more pilgrims joined their caravan. There was safety in numbers, but Hassan was also paranoid.

The marabouts were always a problem. Revered and obeyed among the people as guardians of the Straight Path, the holy men were double-edged swords. They were supposed to use their moral influence to keep the peace among the eternally warring tribes and encourage them in their obligations to pay taxes to the Sublime Porte. Yet, they could become just as easily the motors for rebellion as for peace. The Tidjani brotherhood in the Sahara had stirred up trouble a few years earlier. Disgusted by the bey's ruthlessness, its marabout, Sheik Mohammed Tidjani, had led an uprising that threatened Oran itself.

The rebellion had also tainted Muhi al-Din. His brother-in-law, Abu Taleb, had been a sympathizer of Sheik Tidjani. Was Muhi al-Din perhaps plotting an attack under the cover of a pilgrimage? By the sixth day, the hundreds of pilgrims had become thousands, kicking up a moving cloud of dust. That evening, a detachment of Turkish cavalry galloped into the pilgrims' camp in the Chlef Valley with a message. Bey Hassan wanted Muhi al-Din to return immediately to Oran. Muhi al-Din knew he had no choice. Obedience, he had always taught, was the guardian of all the virtues, and the Turkish bey was his rightful sovereign.

His followers thought otherwise. They pleaded with him not to go. Some clutched his robe, others held on to his horse or tried to grab the bridle. "I must go. It is my duty, even if it means my head." Muhi al-Din knew that a bad ruler, even Hassan, was preferable to no ruler, and he had to think of his son's future. He didn't want Abd el-Kader to be tarnished as the son of a rebellious marabout.

In Oran, Bey Hassan received Muhi al-Din with words oozing false friendship. "You know in how much esteem I hold you, my dear Sheik Muhi al-Din. I have been deeply troubled by the things I have heard. You have numerous enemies and I feared you might fall into the hands of the dey of Algiers, as you were just about to enter his territory. My heart was filled with anxiety on your behalf."

"It was to assuage your anxiety, oh exhalted representative of the Sublime Porte, and much beloved caliph — may God protect you — that I responded to your gracious convocation," Muhi al-Din replied matching the bey's insincerity.

Hassan understood he had an influential prisoner who had to be treated gingerly or risk creating new problems for himself. Muhi al-Din and Abd el-Kader were put in the spacious house of a Moroccan merchant. Turkish guards were stationed at all times by their doors. Father and son were allowed to move freely about the city, but always accompanied by guards. They were prisoners. For a year, Muhi al-Din stoically endured his lot. He never complained about his loss of freedom, knowing that his life was in play and anything he said would get back to Hassan.

A battle for Muhi al-Din's life was also going on behind the scenes. Hassan wanted his head. But weighing against his desire to get rid of a potential troublemaker were the arguments of his wife, Bedra. She was a devout woman of strong character and not afraid to oppose her husband. To kill the venerable marabout, she told him, would bring shame upon the bey's own head, possibly a rebellion. Muhi al-Din was a man of God and revered throughout the beylik and beyond. Indeed, he had many devoted followers, including, though unbeknown to Hassan, his own wife. The powerful douad chieftain, Mustafa Ben Ismail, whose Smela tribe collected taxes for the bey was another ally of Muhi al-Din. The bey needed his support to rule. This hardened warrior also urged Hassan to spare the marabout's life and allayed the bey's concerns with lavish gifts.

Abd el-Kader was angry and perplexed. Their detention seemed like an act of divine injustice. After so much preparation, study and prayer to fulfill a sacred obligation,* how could God allow a stupid, brutal tyrant to interfere with His will? "Remember, tests are sent by God to strengthen you," his father told him one day. "Rather than turn away from Him or dare to judge Him, you must realize that He who is the First Cause of all things, also allows his creatures to become muddled in the secondary causes. He chose to give his lieutenants on earth a free will."

The remark made Abd el-Kader think back to the debates he had with his old master, Ben Tahar, in Arzew. He remembered the arguments between the different schools of thought: whether God, the primary cause, intervened in secondary causes; whether man was truly autonomous in the exercise of his will. Yes, it is written in the Holy Book, *God is not unjust towards men; it is men who are unjust toward themselves.* Abd el-Kader used his time in captivity to study. His tutor was Mustafa Ben Thami, the son of the Mufti of Oran who was an accomplished scholar and logician. Ben-Thami would marry Abd el-Kader's sister Khadijah and become his right hand in the years ahead.

Toward the end of 1826, father and son were quietly allowed to leave Oran. This time they didn't return to Guetna. Muhi al-Din feared that yet another horde of pilgrims would join his caravan for the long journey to Mecca. Instead of taking the shorter coastal route, he cut a wide arc to the southeast, over the high arid plateaus, to avoid the possibility of arousing the suspicions of Dey Hussein of Algiers or the bey of Constantine, Achmed Pasha, who was known to oscillate between extraordinary cruelty and extravagant generosity.

But nothing is kept secret for long in the Arab world. Soon friends of Muhi al-Din — holy men, chieftains, and simple believers attached themselves to the column — seeking protection from robbers and tribes who preyed on pilgrims. Evenings were spent around campfires where men told stories, while further apart, the mule and camel drivers chanted their prayers or sung their guttural songs. At each stop, Muhi al-Din told his son about the different religious brotherhoods, their histories, their chains of legitimacy and their patron saints. These lessons impressed Abd el-Kader. Muhi al-Din's respectful manner as he

---

* Making a pilgrimage to Mecca is one of the "five pillars," or obligations, of Islam.

explained the different spiritual variations, helped him to understand his father's modesty and tolerance toward others.

The differences among sects and brotherhoods notwithstanding, Muhi al-Din taught him that only two legacies protect men from straying: the holy book and the instruction provided by the Prophet's life.

෧෨

The pilgrims passed below Constantine, so named for the Roman emperor who made Christianity the state religion of his empire, then on toward Tunis where they would sail to Alexandria. Along the way, Abd el-Kader saw the silent ruins of Thagast, birthplace of Saint Augustine, the son of a Roman father and a Berber mother.

In Tunis, Abd el-Kader met his first Frenchman. Captain Jovas, the boat's captain, spoke a curious patois of Arabic, Maltese and French. It had not occurred to the sheltered Abd el-Kader that knowledge of the world could be expressed in languages other than Arabic and Greek. He asked his father if knowledge was not limited by the existence of different languages. Muhi al-Din reminded him of the holy book of the Jews and the Christians. God punished the people at Babel for trying to unite what God wanted separated. The Koran revealed the same message: *If he wanted a single community he would have made one...He created different peoples and tribes so they would have to learn to get to know one another and to compete in good works.*

"You are going to see places where there are many Christians and Jews. Don't forget they received God's Revelation before we did. Abraham, he was a Muslim," his father explained.

"How could he be a Muslim before Islam?"

"Because he submitted to the will of God. A Muslim is one who submits to God."

"Are Jews and Christians Muslims?"

"Yes, certainly, when they seek sincerely to do God's will. ' ...Thy will be done, on earth as it is in heaven...' is a part of a prayer the prophet Jesus gave to the Christians."

Abd el-Kader discovered in Alexandria a Babel of cultures and religions he had never imagined. There were the multifarious Christians: Orthodox Greeks, Catholics, Armenians, Copts and, amazingly, Christian Arabs. All were different, yet all the same in their adoration of Jesus. The Jews were different from those he knew in the Maghreb, yet similar. Abd el-Kader met Muslims from various schools of legal thinking and ways of interpreting God's word. For several days the young Maghrebin peppered with his endless questions the scholars who had invited his father to meet with them, only to be surprised by the lively intellect of his teenage son.

The pilgrims sailed up the Nile to Cairo. Again, the father introduced his son to the diversity of God's children, even among Muslims. Abd el-Kader met members of various Muslim religious orders who had emigrated to Egypt from Andalusia, once a rich petrie dish of Jewish, Christian and Muslim cultures. They visited the famous al-Azhar mosque, the Harvard Law School of Islam. The influence of this prestigious center of learning and scholarship radiated throughout the Muslim world. But, unlike Harvard, which also began as a religious school to train God's ministers,* al-Azhar never separated God from the law or secular knowledge from religious knowledge.

Word soon reached the viceroy, Mehmet Ali, that a group of pilgrims from the Maghreb were in his city. He was told they were not the country bumpkins many imagined. They were led by the much beloved Muhi al-Din, chief of the Kadiriyya brotherhood who had brought with him a surprisingly precocious son. Mehmet Ali wanted an interview with Muhi al-Din.

This former Albanian mercenary in the pay of the Turks had risen to power by a combination of ruthlessness, political cunning and enlightened curiosity, fueled by a desire to modernize his semi-independent Ottoman outpost. Mehmet Ali had been viceroy for twenty years by the time of Muhi al-Din's visit. He had abolished the oppressive system of taxation, introduced modern factory technology for spinning cotton, built canals and roads, and used European expertise to build a modern conscription army that made him a force to be reckoned with in the Arab world.

Mehmet Ali had recaptured control of Mecca from the puritanical Wahabis, reopened the trade routes to the Sudan and joined the Sublime Porte in a disastrous campaign to put down a Greek uprising in 1821. His fleet had been reduced to driftwood by French and British warships, a defeat that had been a powerful reminder of how far

---

* Harvard College was founded in 1636 as a divinity school; its first benefactor, John Harvard, was a minister.

the Muslim world had fallen behind the Christians. Mehmet Ali was determined to drag Egypt into the modern era.

The Albanian was fascinating. Abd el-Kader was impressed by the viceroy's readiness to listen rather than talk. Mehmet Ali wanted to know Muhi al-Din's views on many different subjects: his impression of Egypt and the other territories they had passed through, his opinion of the Sultan of Morocco, the attitudes of the people of the Maghreb toward the Sublime Porte and his ideas about the intentions of the European powers.

Years later, Abd el-Kader remembered Mehmet Ali's warning to his father. The English and the French wanted to divide up the Arab world. They had started with Egypt and were looking across North Africa toward Tangier. "You, Si Muhi al-Din, are right in the middle."

Mehmet Ali left a strong imprint on Abd el-Kader. As always, the young scholar searched his mental inventory of hadiths to gauge his thinking. *Your era is a reflection of your Sultan; if you want it to be good, be sure to choose a good Sultan.* But there was also the verse in the Koran where the Queen of Sheba tells King Solomon, *When the kings enter the city, they ruin it.* Was Abd el-Kader perhaps thinking that the great historian and philosopher, Ibn Khaldun, was right about the Bedouin? The only free man is the untethered nomad? His secret is the desert itself — clean, pure, harsh, unforgiving and where the voice of God can be heard without the distractions of the city. Did not the prophets come from the desert?

From Cairo they followed in the footsteps of the prophet Moses to Mt. Sinai, where they found hospitality as guests at the monastery of Saint Catherine. For hours they talked with the monks about the unity of God and the diversity of His paths. The monks also insisted that God was one, but three-in-one — a triangle, but still one. They explained that God became human and suffered as a human to show His creatures the face of His love. Abd el-Kader understood that Jesus was to the Christians what the Koran was to the Muslims — direct Revelation. Jesus was the voice of God, made flesh. Jesus Christ was the Way; like the Prophet, an example.

But how could God have allowed his son to be killed? Don't the Christians make a cult of Jesus, a man, making him an associate of God? Aren't they really polytheists? But, if God is all encompassing, all knowing and all powerful, why can't God become a man if God wills it? To these questions Abd el-Kader had no sure answer. Islam had ninety-nine names for God, but that did not mean there were ninety-nine gods. He knew only that God is One. God is God. But like the sun, cannot His light be reflected in different colors?

The Koran revealed that Abraham and his son Ishmael built the Kaaba in Mecca, the great black cube in the center of the sanctuary where the many become one. The diversity of the Muslim pilgrims astonished Abd el-Kader. There were black, brown, yellow and fair-skinned Muslims, men and women, from all over the world: Arabs, Moors, Black Africans, Turks, Persians, Indians, Javanese, and even Tartars and Bukharans from Central Asia. Around the Kaaba, however, they were one: bound together in their common garb of the seamless white gown worn by the Prophet and by their desire to please God.

Once inside the sanctuary after six days of preparation, father and son joined the orderly mass of humanity that spiraled seven times around the Kaaba — swirling gyres whose circumference was nowhere and everywhere. Abd el-Kader remembered the words of his former master at Arzew, Si Ben Tahar: God created order from chaos using geometry. Forms. Plato. Euclid. With geometry, the clever Greeks had measured the circumference of the earth and demonstrated mathematical truths that transcended their imperfect, warped reality. Circling the Kaaba, Abd el-Kader had understood.

They pressed on to Syria. In Damascus, his father arranged for Abd el-Kader to study under the famous sheik Khalid al-Naqshbandi whose Sufi brotherhood had been founded in Central Asia in the 14th century and became widely influential in the Middle East and India. A theme he returned to with the sheik was the same one he had struggled with by himself: how to square the plurality of ways with God's unity. The sheik talked about the different methods of interpreting God's word and the hadiths, the different ways to read the texts and the different levels of understanding, the different approaches to judging the reliability of witnesses, the different forms of behavior that are also righteous. The sheik taught that grappling with complexity and perplexity was a necessary door to pass through in order to discover the meaning that can be extracted from the most important book of all: the book of everyday life.

As always, Abd el-Kader returned to the Koran for guidance. God clearly wanted diversity. Otherwise he would have created one community. But he wanted the communities to compete in good works and in righteousness. But what if one didn't believe — hardly possible for Abd el-Kader to conceive — or if one believed wrongly? Who decides what is correct teaching? When the savants disagree, shouldn't there be latitude in interpretation? At the onset of the Apocalypse, according to the Koran, the world would be divided into factions and sects. When does diversity become chaos? Was it when each does what is right in his own eyes, unguided by the Word? Knowledge was a box whose key was questioning, the Prophet said, and Abd el-Kader had a pocket full of keys.

In Damascus, people talked of the troubled Turkish empire and the corruptness of its officials. Abd el-Kader again recognized the wisdom of his old master, Si Ben Tahar, who told him to pay attention to everyday things, the ultimate textbook from which to learn when properly observed. The arrogance of the Turks was not limited to the Regency of Algiers. They were widely hated. Some spoke of a renewed Arab empire that would replace the Turk. But how? The Arabs were weak and getting weaker. In Egypt and in Syria, Napoleon Bonaparte had shown what disciplined soldiers and superior technology could accomplish. The European powers were calling the ailing Ottoman Empire "the Sick Man." Were there no Arab doctors? Abd el-Kader may well have wondered why not. Would Mehmet Ali show the way?

೧

There was one more tomb to visit. Their Kadiriyya brotherhood's patron saint had been the true goal of the pilgrimage. The Grey Falcon, whose real name was Muhi al-Din Abd el-Kader al-Jilani, had been born in Persia but had studied in Baghdad. He became known for his learning and piety, his sermons, teaching and miracle working. The stories were legion: he lived for twelve months on water only; he practiced levitation and could make himself invisible; flies never settled on his face; he could be in seventy-one places at one time, which is perhaps how he found time to father forty-nine children, the last at the age of eighty-five; he had a special talent for curing epilepsy, such that the disease became unknown in Baghdad.

Al-Jilani taught that men fell into two classes: those who practice obedience to God and those who are rebellious. The former are at peace and happy, doing good deeds in a state of obedient devotion. The latter are those who are in a state of insecurity and misery because the desires of the ego and the flesh dominate in rebellion against God's prescriptions. In each human being, both obedience and rebelliousness are present, but they are unstable conditions. People can change. The good may turn into evil and the evil into good. If purity of heart, sincerity and good deeds dominate, then one's selfish characteristics can be transformed and rebelliousness can be overcome. One who is rebellious but recognizes his errors and changes can be transformed into an obedient servant of God. Like the Christian monks and priests whom the Koran mentions as holding a special place of respect, so too for al-Jilani: obedience, humility and charity mark the good path. Above all, is obedience.

Al-Jilani was loved and consulted by caliphs and paupers alike, and at the time of his death in 1166 A.D., was already recognized as a saint. His tomb attracted worshippers from all over the Muslim world. Located between the Tigris and Euphrates — the two rivers which gave birth to civilization — the city's lush gardens, orchards and bright cupolas must have been a relief to the wind-and-sand blown pilgrims who had trekked from Damascus for thirty days. In Baghdad, the father passed his baton to his son.

Muhi al-Din asked Abd el-Kader to lead the discussions with local scholars and hosts. Soon word spread of the amazing knowledge and intellectual agility of this young Maghrebin who could politely hold his own with the leading scholars of the city. It was said that he was even giving lessons to the graybeards. When asked about his genealogy, he replied as his father had taught him: don't ask about a man's origins, but about his life, his actions and his character and you will know who he is; if the water taken from a river is good, so too is its source.

One evening, Muhi al-Din asked Abd el-Kader to go outside the city to check on the horses and to begin preparations for their long trip home. Soon after, Muhi al-Din fell asleep and had a dream. He was meditating at the tomb of al-Jilani when a huge Negro appeared with a box of dates, milk and honey and asked him:

"Where is the sultan of the West?"

"Of which sultan do you speak?" Muhi al-Din replied. "Here there are only poor travelers who fear the Lord."

"The sultan is the one you sent to care for your horses, the one who one day will lead all the Maghreb with the same solicitude as he shows horses. I will tell you something — the rule of the Turks is soon to end...."

CHAPTER FOUR

The Arrival of the Infidels

WORD HAD REACHED GUETNA by the beginning of 1828. The pilgrims were returning. Their last stop had been in Tripoli to visit the tomb of Mustapha, Muhi al-Din's father, who had died there returning from the Holy Land. A great celebration was prepared by the Hachem to give thanks for Muhi al-Din's safe return and to honor their patron saint, Abd el-Kader al-Jilani.

Fifteen cows and eighty sheep were slaughtered for their homecoming. From around the beylik, streams of people flowed toward Guetna to pay their respects to their beloved marabout. The douads came mounted on magnificent horses, followed by their retinues of slaves and servants. Marabouts and the simple people rode mules and donkeys. The poorest walked. For weeks they came, so many that even the hospitable Muhi al-Din grew embarrassed by the cost of the exuberant welcome-home party. But tradition wouldn't allow him to stop the visits until he had received all the chieftains who wanted to pay their respects. Only then did Guetna return to its studious, meditative ways.

The numerous visitors also caught Muhi al-Din up with the news. Mentioned frequently was the "flyswatter incident" between the French consul and the Turkish Dey Hussein.

♻

The provocation had occurred in 1827 at the annual reception marking the Feast of Abraham, held in the dey's Moorish palace overlooking the port from the summit of the Casbah. Dey Hussein had asked the French consul about the long-overdue debt of twenty-four million gold francs that France owed the firm of Bushnach and Bacri. These two Jewish families had grown from being owners of a small épicerie in Algiers to becoming wealthy international grain merchants and bankers to the dey. The dey, who had supported their claims in the past, reminded the consul that Bushnach and Bacri had supplied wheat to the revolutionary French government when Europe's monarchies were trying to suffocate it. They had financed the feeding of Napoleon's armies. Hussein was annoyed that King Charles X had never responded to his letter proposing a compromise over the back interest.

In front of the dey's entourage, the consul, Pierre Deval, superciliously reminded Hussein that the French king didn't write letters to his inferiors. The offended Turk struggled to control himself before swatting the Frenchman in the face with his fly fan, calling him an "insolent infidel." The consul was recalled to Paris, and, escalating the affair further, the dey made all French citizens leave Algiers. King Charles ordered a naval blockade of the city, explained to the public as a retaliatory measure to restore "French honor." Yet, few people believed it was anything but a pretext for the government to distract a disgruntled public with a foreign adventure. The insult was intentional.

Charles was unpopular. His government had tried to turn back the clock and undo twenty-five years of revolution and reform. The renewed influence of the clergy and of former royalists was disturbing to those who had enjoyed bathing in the fresh waters of secular republicanism. His ministers were not responsible to the parliament. The new, affluent middle class was unhappy — excluded, as it was, from an electorate of only ninety thousand large landowners. The economy was suffering and the government's finances were in shambles. A naval blockade was a warm up to prepare the public for an invasion, one that would require three years of planning.

The case for premeditated aggression was made by the Duke of Clermont-Tonnère, King Charles' minister of war: "There are many ports along Algeria's coast whose possession would be of great utility to France and give us control of the Mediterranean. In the interior, there are immense, fertile plains. Algeria is a veritable El Dorado that would compensate for the loss of our colonies in America." There was also the belief that Algiers possessed the greatest mother lode of treasure in the world — three hundred years of accumulated Barbary loot, ransom for passengers and crews captured on the high seas by corsairs.

A little war to punish an uppity Turk would shore up support at home, burnish the restored Bourbon dynasty's faded glory and, of course, serve the cause of Christian civilization. A coalition was formed. A crusade was announced to root out slavery and piracy, and end the humiliating payment of tribute to this nest of thieves. Its chief rival,

Great Britain, abstained, but France proceeded with the blessing of Austria-Hungary, Prussia, Russia, Holland and the Vatican.

In France, opposition voices became louder as the invasion date drew near. The republican left feared the adventure's real purpose was to get the nation drunk on smoke and gunpowder before the new parliamentary elections took place in July 1830. A glorious little war would also curry favor with the army in case the monarchy needed it to beat down domestic enemies.

In May, the influential *Le Journal des Débats* summarized the counterarguments:

> Let reason try to tell us what we are doing in Africa. Is it to seek glory? What glory is there in attacking Arabs in poorly forti-fied towns that cannons can easily demolish? Can one speak of glory when 35,000 French soldiers face a garrison of 5,000 demoralized Janissaries? Is it for the glory of our sailors in the face of pirates who can't sail a bark? The glory of our officers defeating imbecilic tribal chiefs of barbarian hordes? So, is it a point of honor? But have the insults and impertinences of the dey hurt France? The interests of Christianity? They are non-existent, just as are the supposed acts of piracy.* The expedition will be easy but what will we gain? What is really behind the undertaking? A system of illusions and deceptions which have pushed our poor country to the edge of the abyss. There are bad ministers without a majority in the chambers, without a majority in the electoral colleges who foolishly think they can escape their fate with grapeshot and empty glory.

Neither side, however, was allowed to express doubt about the suc-cess of the mission. To question the capacity of the French soldier was unpatriotic. Had not Napoleon in Egypt, outnumbered ten to one, defeated the Mameluke hordes that vainly threw themselves at his dis-ciplined squares of infantry, whose controlled fire shredded horse and rider into mounds of intermingled flesh?

❧

---

* These had ended for the most part after the Congress of Vienna in 1815.

On May 25, 1830, an enormous fleet of one hundred warships and five hundred and seventy-two supply vessels assembled off the coast of Toulon. They had come from Cherbourg, Brest, Bayonne and Marseille loaded with thirty-one thousand infantry, twenty-three hundred artillerists, five hundred cavalrymen, over a thousand engineers, one hundred and seventy-four cannons, eighty-two thousand cannonballs, four thousand horses, food and forage supplies for four months, forty translators (few spoke the correct dialects), numerous painters, including the great Horace Vernet, and hundreds of sacrificial dogs for testing water.

General Auguste-Louis de Bourmont had been a controversial choice for leading the invasion army. Bourmont had a Catholic royalist's natural revulsion against the excesses of the Revolution — one that left hated priests crucified upside down on their parish doors. Later, he sided with Bonaparte and the Empire. But the night before the battle of Waterloo, Bourmont abandoned his emperor to bargain with the returning Bourbons. He was now in command of the newly formed Army of Africa. To many of his soldiers, however, he was still a traitor.

Dey Hussein was not surprised when French ships appeared off the coast on June 14, just west of Algiers. The place and date of the invasion had been announced months before in the French press. The old maps of North Africa drawn by Napoleon's spies had been put to use by Bourmont's invasion planners. The army would disembark in the half-moon bay of Sidi Ferruch, named after a local marabout.

Turkish cavalry watched French soldiers carrying the Bourbon *fleur de lis* as they came ashore from rowboats that shuttled back and forth like swarming waterbugs. Soldiers kneeled in the soft white sand and sung the *Te Deum*, led by chaplains in long black cassocks. Five days later, seven thousand Turkish infantry and forty thousand irregular cavalry raised from the local tribes charged Bourmont's army on the Plain of Staoueli. Algier's defenders disintegrated in the face of French cannon fire.

On July 4, Dey Hussein sent a delegation to negotiate a truce wrapped in words of unctuous submission. "Oh invincible head of the army of the greatest sultan of our century, God favors you and your banners. But the mercy of God commands moderation in victory. Wisdom counsels mercy as the best way to disarm a conquered enemy.

Hussein kisses the dirt on your feet and repents having broken relations with the great and powerful Charles X."

He offered to make amends for the insult inflicted on the French consul, to renounce the debt owed by France and to pay France for all the costs of the campaign. In exchange, the dey asked to retain his position as ruler and to keep his militia, ships and personal property. "Tell your master," Bourmont replied, "that the fate of your city is in my hands. In a few hours French cannons will reduce the city and the Casbah into a pile of rubble. He must put himself at my mercy and turn over to French troops the Casbah and all the forts in and outside of the city." The next day, the Army of Africa entered Algiers.

Algiers had no more than thirty thousand inhabitants when Bourmont's army descended upon it from the heights overlooking the city. The city had a curious past. In 1516, a local Arab potentate sought foreign protection from the Spaniards who were chasing Muslims and Jews out of Spain. He found assistance in the form of two Greek brothers from the island of Mitylene who had gained fame as privateers. Accepting the flattering request for protection, the brothers consolidated their position by murdering their client and placing themselves under the protection of the Ottoman Turks, whose resurgent new Islamic empire had Christian Europe trembling from Paris to Warsaw. The Sublime Porte dispatched to Algiers a garrison of janissaries* to occupy the important administrative posts in what became known as The Regency of Algiers.

When the French arrived in 1830, Algiers was a mosaic of fifty ethnic quarters and thirty-three guilds that ranged from bakers, potters and tanners to garbage collectors, fishnet makers, policemen and moneylenders. There were 159 mosques, four synagogues for its five thousand Jews, and one church for the Christians. Religion, more than anything else, wove together the complex tissue formed from corporate identities of ethnicity, tribe and tradecraft. It was a society not unlike the one that the revolution in France had recently destroyed, one in which communal identities and rights prevailed over individual rights.

---

* An elite corps composed from captive Christian children, converted to Islam, trained and educated by the state. In the Regency, they represented the summit of the social pyramid.

In the mind's eye of the average European, Algiers was thought to be an unholy nest of filthy pirates and slavers living from robbing and ransoming crews and passengers on ships. To more knowing eyes, it was a little architectural jewel of Turkish imperialism whose inhabitants were quite different from the common view of them. William Shaler, the American consul in Algiers, observed qualities of this white-washed triangle of a city pitched like a sail against the green Sahal Hills that were out of phase with the common, uninformed prejudices toward its inhabitants:

> They are far from being the ferocious barbarians that the term 'Algerines' seems by common consent to imply... I have found them civil, courteous and humane... nor have I discovered in their character extraordinary bigotry, fanaticism or hatred of those who profess a different religion; they profess the Mohammedan creed and fulfill with utmost scrupulousness the rites which it ordains, and as far as I have remarked, without hostility toward those who adopt different measures to conciliate the Divine favor...Domestic slavery in these countries has been of the mildest character, implying rather reciprocal rights of service and of protection, than of slavery...The horrors of the slave market of which so much has been said have no foundation in fact since the suppression of privateering in Algiers (according to treaties of 1815)...

"There is possibly no city in the world," Shaler went on, "where the police are more vigilant and persons and property so secure." So, too, its sinewy alleyways "were paved and generally well maintained." Municipal cleanliness was strictly enforced. Residents were required to deposit their refuse into pre-made slots in the thick ramparts of the city. Every day garbage collectors would come by the walls and transfer the refuse into large baskets mounted on donkeys.

The city was administered through a complex balance of communal powers. Each community lived according to its own customary laws: Turks, Moors, Kougoulis, Jews, Christians (mostly those captured on the high seas for ransom), foreigners and slaves from the Sahara who were freed upon converting to Islam. Each of these corporate organizations elected an intermediary, or *amin*, to the central Turkish authority. The amin represented his community, which had a collective responsibility for the conduct of its own members. Thus, governance rested more on self-policing rather than on the direct use of Turkish enforcement powers. Using the self-regulating powers of traditional communities, six thousand Turks governed a diverse population in an area almost the size of France.

Such was the broth of cultures, races and languages into which France plunged willy-nilly. Bourmont prepared a magnanimous capitulation proclamation to soothe the anxious Muslims. France would "respect the free exercise of the Mohammedan religion; the liberties of all classes as pertaining to their religion, property, commerce and industry will not be harmed; their women will be respected; the commander-in-chief will uphold these commitments as a matter of honor."

One soldier who took the proclamation seriously was a young officer fired with the energy of new ideals for creating a better world, free of class and racial distinctions, guided by reason and Christian ethics. Lieutenant Lamoricière had just been commended by Bourmont. He was the first soldier to replace the red-and-gold embroidered flag of the Turks with the white *fleur de lis*. However, the lieutenant was not the average officer seeking military glory.

The dark-eyed, compact, intellectually curious native of Nantes was born into an aristocratic Catholic family that had been divided by the Revolution. His mother's side was "red." She sympathized with the young, revolutionary republic's unsettling universal principles of liberty, fraternity and equality that had upset Europe's hierarchical order of birthright. Lamoricière's high-Catholic father had been opposed to the revolution's atheist tendencies and its violence against the Church. A natural aptitude in mathematics had won Lamoricière a position in the new, elite École Polytechnique in Paris where he fell under the influence of the mathematician and philosopher, Auguste Comte. He graduated fourth in his class of 104 students and was accepted into the engineering branch of the army.

Professor Comte guided Lamoricière into the new, utopian world of the Saint Simonians. Their rational, progressive faith combined Christian ethics, stripped of the mystery of the cross, with social planning guided by a technocratic elite. The Saint Simonians promoted emancipation of women and equality for Jews and Negroes. They wanted to transform the world through a new morality of love and peace aided by reason and knowledge that would do away with servitude and slavery of all kinds. "From each according to their capacities and to each according to their work," was the dictum that underpinned their doctrines.

The twenty-four-year-old convert to Saint Simonianism was shocked by what he saw in those first days of France's civilizing mission. The ordinary soldiers, like those everywhere, were not concerned with lofty ideas about the unity of races and peoples. More practical needs were on their minds: firewood, water, shelter and opportunities for plunder. Orchards, forests and wainscotting in houses were burned for fuel, mosques turned into stables, palaces and villas became caserns. "Perhaps never, even in the age of the barbarians, has there been an occupation carried out with such disorder as that of Algiers. The hordes of the north who grabbed the remnants of the Roman Empire behaved with more reason and wisdom," wrote Lamoricière's fellow officer, Pellissier de Reynaud, who would also make his career in Algeria and leave for posterity his voluminous memoirs.

No plan for administration had been anticipated. Many Turkish administrators simply abandoned their posts, not knowing if they were expected to serve the new masters and not knowing where to turn. Most simply disappeared when they learned the dey had departed for Alexandria with his family as part of the secret capitulation terms that gave Bourmont and certain officers access to the fabled treasury of the Casbah.

How did the dey manage to leave after submitting so abjectly to Bourmont? "If one tolerates a little pillage," Pellissier explained, "that only serves to cover the big pillage. The big pillage was certainly the treasure of the dey." Hussein's only bargaining leverage with Bourmount was the threat to blow up the treasury containing huge quantities of gold, silver, diamonds, jewelry and merchandise. A value of forty-eight million gold francs was placed on the treasure, which was officially transferred to the French government. Its true value would never be known. Bourmont's officers used compromising documents to light their pipes and otherwise destroyed papers that could reveal the true value of the treasury.

While soldiers plundered the city, France yawned. The Paris Bourse did not respond favorably to the news of the military success, new parliamentary elections went ahead as planned, and the minister president of the royal council opened talks with the Sultan about possibly giving back Algiers. In return, France would keep certain coastal towns.

Upon learning of the fall of Algiers, the tribes, too, were at first indifferent. Invaders had come and gone over the past centuries. Yet most were pleased to see their Turkish oppressors flee. Inactivity and power exercised for too long had gradually ruined a ruling class that once had been admired by the Arabs for its discipline and natural authority.

Now it was the turn of the French. Would they bring stability and order? Or would they remain, as others had, only occupiers of coastal enclaves that were useful for developing trade? What were the intentions of these *franci?* In the past, Spanish and English flags had flapped above the cities of Tangiers and Oran. Algiers had also submitted for short periods to the demands of European civilization. None of these adventures had endured. The tribes watched and waited, unsure of how to react to this new foreign presence on their soil.

A month later, Bourmont received startling news. King Charles had abdicated. A coup to nullify the election results of July 26 had failed. The crown had been transferred to Charles's cousin, Louis-Philippe, Duke of Orleans, who agreed to establish a constitutional monarchy with ministers responsible to the parliament.

Bourmont considered rallying the army to restore Charles to his throne. But his army was in turmoil, divided between royalists and republicans. When a consensus finally emerged, the tricolor replaced the *fleur de lis.* The republican fleet admiral refused to allow the royalist Bourmont to return home on one of his ships, forcing the general to beg a berth on an Austrian brig that was headed for Marseille.

Bourmont left in his wake a trail of mistakes. Once Algiers had surrendered, some of the powerful douad tribes, called *makhzen,* that had long served the Turks, immediately offered their submission to the new boss in town. Bourmont optimistically assumed that all of the Regency would follow. He decided to march inland up to Blida in the foothills of the Atlas, believing he would receive a great welcome from the liberated natives who had suffered under Turkish oppression. Instead, Boumont's column was ambushed in the mountain passes. He assumed he had been attacked by Turks, but in fact, had been attacked by resentful Arab tribesmen.

Like most of the French in the beginning, he had wrongly believed the Turks were the main enemy. He retaliated by expelling the Turks who remained in Algiers, leaving the city without any knowledgeable administrators. This rash action left him with no experienced intermediaries familiar with the languages and customs of their new subjects.

The general's misguided decisions fueled the anxiety of the tribes. Did the *franci* want to rule directly rather than through experienced Turkish administrators whose laissez-faire habits had left the tribes in relative freedom so long as they paid their taxes? Weren't they going to simply occupy coastal enclaves as other invaders had? The punishment of the wrong people and the unusual foray into the interior seemed to present a threatening new kind of presence.

The general was hardly alone in his ignorance. The French knew little of the people, customs and even the geography of the land that Bourmont too quickly imagined himself to have subjugated. Tactical blunders might have been forgivable, but not untrustworthiness. The French general had not kept his word. His glorious proclamation of July 5 had become a dead letter. Muslim property and places of worship were not being protected, and compensation not offered. Nor had Bourmont punished those who had violated his orders. Tribes that had initially submitted in the wake of the quick conquest of Algiers began to have second thoughts.

℘

Chaos spread throughout the Regency while the new government in Paris fecklessly debated the value of the African adventure. The order the Turks had maintained by periodically terrorizing the tribes was followed by another form of terror: anarchy. Warfare among the rival tribes was rekindled, thievery flourished and individuals settled old scores with impunity. No one left his village, marketplaces were empty, goods didn't get delivered and scarcity replaced abundance.

One of anarchy's victims was Bey Hassan, the former jailor of Abd el-Kader's father. Hassan was despised and his authority ended at Oran's city walls. The bey's tax collectors were the powerful Smela and Douair, who had been willing to serve new masters at first. They had urged Hassan to submit after they learned of the fall of Algiers. Like the dey of Algiers, Hassan was willing to recognize French sovereignty and pay tribute, but he wanted to keep his forts and his janissaries. The

French rejected the bey's demand to keep his forts and Hassan didn't have the stomach to resist, notwithstanding the urging of the Smelas and Douairs. His cowardliness lost him the protection of his *makhzen* at a time when less powerful tribes had virtually surrounded the city, suspecting him of plotting to turn it over to the French. In desperation, Hassan sent a messenger to Guetna. He wanted Muhi al-Din to come to Oran.

Abd el-Kader was alarmed by the news. Was this another ruse by Hassan to settle old scores with his father? Muhi al-Din believed it was still his duty to obey the constituted authority in the beylik, however isolated and weak. Indeed, it was Hassan's lack of any real power that made Muhi al-Din confident that he was not going to be ill-treated. If he were, Hassan would be lynched by the Arabs surrounding the city.

A few days later, Muhi al-Din returned. He had received a request from the bey too controversial for him to decide alone. The Hachem leaders were told to come to Guetna for consultation. They gathered in the mosque, where the men sat on rugs in a circle with their feet tucked underneath their monk-like *abayas*. The marabout, Sidi Laradj, occupied the place of honor next to Muhi al-Din. There was also Abd el-Kader's uncle, Sidi Ali Abu Taleb, who had been his demanding riding instructor; his learned brother-in-law, Mustafa Ben Thami, as well as the sheiks from the eastern and western Hachem tribes. Abd el-Kader and his younger brother, Ali, sat apart from the elders. Muhi al-Din allowed a meditative silence to fall over the group before slowly explaining what Hassan had requested.

The bey wanted the Hachem to give him its *aman* — a pledge of protection that, once given, would become a sacred commitment. Hassan would be part of their family. Muhi al-Din spoke of the past. He acknowledged that Hassan had treated him and his son badly when they had set out on their pilgrimage to Mecca five years earlier. The bey had shown no compassion toward the tribes during periods of drought. He extorted as much as fifty percent of their harvest. He was widely hated. Yet, despite this bill of complaints against Hassan, Muhi al-Din was a man of the Book. The Book counseled forgiveness over revenge. It was better to return evil with good. Providing hospitality to those in distress was a sacred obligation of the faith. Hassan was a fellow Muslim as well. To grant Hassan protection might also enhance the prestige of the Hachem. This would demonstrate the tribe's devotion to the duty of hospitality. Furthermore, the bey would be humiliating himself by coming to the Hachem asking the favor of their protection. Not to help him, on the other hand, would be a stain on their reputation.

Each man had his say in quiet tones. Out of respect for their master, and knowing well the Koran's injunctions, the group finally agreed with Muhi al-Din. Abd el-Kader had been listening attentively, and as usual had remained silent. This time, he felt compelled to speak. He asked for their forgiveness, and especially for his father's, but he did not agree with their thinking.

"What will happen if we cannot protect him?" Abd el-Kader asked, reminding the men of the anarchic state of the beylik and of the widespread hatred of the bey. "He will risk being attacked or insulted. His presence among us could even provoke a popular outbreak of violence. Who will extinguish those flames and at what cost? This will only bring dishonor on those who have promised his protection and show themselves incapable of doing so." Abd el-Kader continued. "There is another reason for not welcoming the bey into our family. Such a gesture will be regarded as a tacit pardon by the Arabs who have been badly treated by him. In other words, we will make ourselves the enemies of all the tribes in the beylik."

Muhi al-Din listened impassively. A long silence followed. The father then acknowledged the wisdom of his son's arguments. Other members of the council agreed. A message was sent to Hassan telling him that his request could not be granted. Two months later another French officer was dispatched to occupy Oran. In December 1830, Hassan surrendered the keys of the city, and more than likely some of his wealth, in return for free passage to Alexandria.

CHAPTER FIVE

The Obedient Son

"ONCE THE TURKISH GOVERNMENT was destroyed with no substitute to replace it, the country fell into appalling anarchy," Alexis de Tocqueville wrote seven years after French troops had occupied Algiers. "People sometimes submit to humiliation, to tyranny, to conquest, but never endure anarchy for long. No people are so barbarous as to escape this general law of humanity."

In a bid to win a seat in the Chamber of Deputies, the acclaimed young author of *Democracy in America* turned his observant eye to France's colonial adventure in North Africa, where the chaos and frenetic energy of the settlers reminded him of America. So too, the war of civilizations he saw taking place with the indigenous peoples; however, in Algeria, the natives far outnumbered the Europeans.* His observations were expressed in open letters to the public, but designed to get the attention of his constituents.

"The Arabs began to instinctively rebuild what we had destroyed," de Tocqueville wrote. "The most rapid and certain effect of our conquest was to bring back the political influence the marabouts had lost under the Turk." The Turks had prohibited the Arab religious aristocracy from carrying arms or directing public affairs, but once the Turks were gone, the marabouts became warriors and governors again.

De Tocqueville understood that religion was an essential part of the fabric of Arab life. France, he argued, had to rule in partnership with, not in opposition to the Arabs, and allow them time to see the benefits of France's superior civilization. He also believed religion was only a secondary cause for the struggle that had been going on since 1830. "We were attacked much more as strangers and invaders than as Christians. Experience has shown that religion does not prevent the Arabs from

---

* Some officers in the French army advocated extermination, also known as "the American strategy." In 1837, there were only about 20,000 colonists in Algeria; many were political malcontents deported from France, versus some two to three million Arabs and Berbers. By 1954, the number of colonists had grown to only one million compared to nine million indigenes, as the French called their Indians.

being our most zealous auxiliaries if they are treated respectfully and when patriotism and ambition do not turn against us."

France had allowed the religious aristocracy to be reborn. "Despite their impoverished appearance," he continued, "the marabouts should be considered the most influential members of Arab society." It was up to the French, de Tocqueville argued, to make good use of them. As an example, he mentioned a family of celebrated marabouts near the Moroccan empire whose leader was a saintly, elderly man named Muhi al-Din. He explained, "When the tribes began to feel the unendurable malaise that the absence of power causes in men, they asked him to be their leader. Unsuited for warfare and too old, he begged the tribes to transfer leadership to his son, who had already distinguished himself in battle. This puny young man, who was at the time only twenty-five years old, was called Abd el-Kader. Such was the origin of this remarkable leader. Anarchy gave birth to his power and anarchy constantly developed him."

∾

Muhi al-Din, de Tocqueville's "saintly, elderly man," had been asked by some of the tribes to lead the resistance after Bey Hassan fled Oran. But fighting was not in the old man's blood. Instead, he urged them to petition Sultan Abderrahman of Morocco to lead the resistance. The beylik of Oran, though ruled by the Turks, was under the spiritual influence of the Moroccan sultan and Muhi al-Din was always conscious of the correct order for doing things.

The sultan's response to the call to jihad from his fellow believers was to send his hapless fifteen-year-old son, Moulay Ali, to Tlemcen. Ali, with a contingent of 5,000 cavalry, soon alienated the Kougoulis and their powerful makhzan with his brutality and greed, imprisoning some and pillaging others, before being recalled to Morocco. Sultan Abderrahman was more inclined to see the Turks as the enemy than the French; thus, by default, Muhi al-Din became the reluctant, unofficial leader of jihad against the *franci*.

Hostility against France was needlessly sharpened by the harsh methods of General Pierre Boyer, the new commander in Oran. Boyer had fought guerilla warfare during Napoleon's ill-considered Spanish campaign. "To bring civilization, sometimes it is necessary to use uncivilized methods" was his rationalization for the harsh reprisals that won him his sobriquet, "Pierre the Cruel."

He practised collective punishment of tribes suspected of cooperating with the blockade of Oran that Muhi al-Din had ordered. The tribes in the area were not to sell food or forage to the French garrison, otherwise dependent on irregular supplies from France. Acting on bad information, Boyer often attacked the wrong villages, and then paraded heads on poles to intimidate the natives in their own grisly manner. But the Frenchman's aggressive sorties outside of Oran were temper tantrums that had no lasting effect.

In November 1832, the leaders of the tribes asked Muhi al-Din to officially be their sultan and to unify the struggle against the invader. But he had other ideas. When the chiefs of the seven tribes living around the plain of Ghriss came to Muhi al-Din with their petition, he slyly agreed.

"You know, I am a man of peace. I have given my life to God. The task you are asking of me requires bloodletting and brutal force. But if you insist, I accept to be your sultan. My first decision is to abdicate in favor of my son, Abd el-Kader.

"He is young, intelligent, just, and capable of continuing the struggle. He will do it better than me. I am too old and not suited for this job. Help him, so that he may be a father to the youngest of you, a son to the older, and a brother to his equals."

Muhi al-Din's decision was greeted with shouts of approval. Abd el-Kader had proven his courage and stamina many times over during the past two years. He had also become a trusted advisor to his father. Abd el-Kader had distinguished himself during the spring and summer when his father launched attacks on French forts around Oran. The young marabout had attracted attention when the Arab infantry fighting in ditches below the walls of Fort St. Philippe ran out of ammunition. While other cavalrymen hung back and watched, afraid of French cannon fire, Abd el-Kader raced back and forth on his black mare across open fields of fire, using his burnoose as a huge basket to carry fresh cartridges to the trapped men. At other times, he dismounted and led infantry armed only with old flintlock rifles, knives and slingshots. His bravery inspired the timid into action. Abd el-Kader lost a horse and an earlobe during those days, yet he gained an aura of future leadership and a reputation for his miraculous ability to avoid getting hit by the "black couscous."

The delegation dispersed to spread the news of Muhi al-Din's abdication.

∾

On November 21, Abd el-Kader was escorted into Mascara by a sea of men in black burnooses. They followed him through the Bab Ali gate to an elegant Moorish villa that had been the seat of the beylik when Oran was still in Spanish hands. In the courtyard of the villa, surrounded by sensuously sculpted white columns, Abd el-Kader accepted his father's abdication in the presence of dozens of tribal chiefs. "It is my duty to obey my father," he modestly declared.

Abd el-Kader then exchanged his black burnoose worn by the Hachems for the crimson burnoose of leadership. The assembled sheiks and caids showed their submission by kissing the hand of their new leader seated in the divan of the old beylicat. After the sheiks, leaders of the Jewish community in Mascara — rabbis and businessmen — came to pay their respects to the new sultan, as did leaders from the Christian and Mozabite minorities.* After receiving homage from the local Mascarans, the new sultan went to a nearby mosque, as custom required, to demonstrate his spiritual and inspirational credentials.

Before an overflowing crowd at the Ain Beida mosque, Abd el-Kader recounted the pitiful conditions afflicting their land: the mistakes, the crimes, the injustices, the immorality, and the horrors they had suffered — first from the Turks, then from themselves, and finally, from the foreign invaders. He painted a picture of their beylik ravaged by infidels who had destroyed villages, violated women and homes, and profaned their mosques by turning them into stables and warehouses. He described how the impious would suffer in the next world, a place

---

* The Christians would have been ex-slaves, men of commerce and the odd priest; the Mozabites would likely have been businessmen. Mozabites are Mzab Berbers who belong to a morally strict Kharajite Islamic sect known for producing honest, enterprising businessmen and merchants. Their communities are located in the Sahara around Laghaout, Quargla and Gardaia. The Jewish community in Mascara at the time has been estimated in the several thousands. (see chapter notes)

whose residents were condemned to quench their thirst with boiling water and putrid blood.

The time Abd el-Kader spent in Oran at Ben Khodja's zawiya practicing speech and rhetoric was repaid that day. His listeners stood for hours, transfixed by their new leader who spoke with the confidence of long-practiced authority. He moved them skillfully through emotions of shame, contrition and remorse for their own misdeeds. He then lifted them up, transforming them and inspiring them to imitate the martyrs of the past who had died for the faith and whose souls had found their reward in eternity. With passion and gesticulation, sweat and tears, Abd el-Kader worked his audience into a lather. By the end of his sermon it was shouting enthusiastically: jihad! jihad!

The next day, an enormous, early morning gathering took place on the Plain of Ghriss. Ten thousand horsemen from the seven largest tribes in the region — the Beni Amer, the Beni Abbas, the Beni Yacoub, the Hachem Gharabas, Abd el-Kader's own Beni Hachem and others — emerged out of the predawn darkness to affirm Muhi al-Din's abdication in favor of his youngest son. The men formed a huge crescent around a lone black tent pitched near the dedara tree, a venerable old ash, in a copse where tribal chieftains traditionally held important councils.

Flutes, drums and tambourines were competing with the fireworks of rifles when the royal escort approached the tent as the sun was rising over the Jebel Nusmut. As soon as Abd el-Kader rode forward on his favorite black charger, the noise stopped. He and his father dismounted and entered the tent. Minutes later the two men emerged with Muhi al-Din holding his son's hand.

"Here is your sultan announced by the prophecies!" proclaimed Muhi al-Din. "Here is the son of Zohra! Obey him as you would obey me. May God protect the sultan. Our lives, our property, everything we own is dedicated to serve him," he shouted. "We will follow no other law than that of our sultan, Abd el-Kader."

"There is no power and no strength except in God," replied Abd el-Kader. "I will recognize no other law than the Koran. There is no liberty except through defending the faith. Paradise is found in the shadow of the sword." He sprang nimbly into his saddle and galloped off to review the assembled cavalry. From time to time, he pulled up on his reins to stir the blood of his new army, crying out: jihad! jihad!

At his new headquarters in Mascara, Abd el-Kader dictated an official proclamation of his authority to lead the jihad.

> Praise be to God alone and blessings from on high to the Prophet Mohammed after whom there is no other prophet.
>
> To the tribes and to their sheiks, notables, and ulemas, may God enlighten you, guide and direct your counsels and give success to your deeds and actions.
>
> The citizens of the districts of Mascara, the Eastern and Western Plain of Ghriss, and their neighbors and allies, the Beni Chokran, the El Bordjas, the Beni Abbas, the Yacubies, the Beni Amer, the Beni Medjaher, and others have elected me unanimously and appointed me to govern their country. They pledged themselves to obey me in success and in distress, in prosperity and adversity, and to consecrate themselves and their sons and their properties to the great and holy cause of defending our faith and our soil.
>
> We have, therefore, assumed this heavy responsibility, hoping it may be the means for uniting the Muslim community and of preventing dissensions among them and of affording general security to all the inhabitants of the land, of putting an end to lawlessness, and of driving back the enemy who has invaded our country in order to subjugate us.
>
> As a condition of our acceptance, we have imposed on those who have delegated to us the supreme governing power the duty to conform all their actions to the precepts and teachings of the book of God and of administering justice in their various spheres according to the law of the Prophet, to wit: loyally and impartially to the strong and to the weak, to the nobles and the poor. This condition has been accepted by them.
>
> We hereby invite you to partake in this pledge, or compact, between ourselves and these tribes. Hasten, therefore, to show your allegiance and obedience, and may God help you to prosper in this world and the next. My great goal is to reform and to do good to the extent that good lies within me. My trust is in God, and from Him and Him only do I expect reward and success.

By the order of the Defender of our Religion, our sovereign and Commander of the Faithful, Abd el-Kader ibn Muhi al-Din. May God grant him victory. Amen."

Mascara, November 22, 1832

Abd el-Kader refused the title of sultan the tribes had offered his father. *Adab* had schooled him in the right order of things and to submission before higher authority. He needed whatever support he could get from the neighboring Moroccans. Abd el-Kader insisted that if his name were mentioned in the mosques, it always follow that of Sultan Abderrahman. He wanted at first to be called simply, emir, or commander. Later, he became *Emir al-Muminin*, Commander of the Faithful.

ෆ

A twenty-five-year-old marabout claiming authority to lead a jihad against France and inviting others to join in submission to him was laughable to many and insulting to others. Yes, he was the son of the wise and beloved marabout, Muhi al-Din. That counted for something, but not enough for Ahmed Ben Tahar, the learned cadi of Arzew and the emir's tutor who had first opened his mind to the great Greek and Arab thinkers.

Ben Tahar was a respected member of the Smela tribe. They were nobility of the sword. As makhzans, they had served as the enforcers for the Turks, and like most of their class, the Smelas had little respect for the fighting abilities of marabout tribes like the Hachem. The Smelas liked commerce as well as fighting. Why war with the French when they could trade with them? The French needed supplies for their troops and animals. Arzew was only a few miles down the coast and the Smela could easily circumvent the emir's blockade by sea. Why not live in peace and serve as enforcers for the new masters as they had their former ones?

Thus, it was painful for Abd el-Kader to learn that his former master was trading with the enemy. Selling food and forage to the French garrison was bad enough, but Ben Tahar had been selling horses. He had ignored three warning letters from his former student, mixtures of pleas to renounce his collaboration and threats to make an example of him. Finally, in the spring of 1833, Muhi al-Din raided Arzew and arrested Ben Tahar. Unfortunately for the emir's former teacher, he had in his possession a compromising letter from General Boyer. When Ben Tahar was brought in chains to Mascara, Abd el-Kader gave orders that no judgment be passed until he returned from an urgent mission.

Unrepentant, Ben Tahar wouldn't reveal what he had done with the money he had received from Boyer, nor would he renounce his activities. Muhi al-Din ordered the ulema of the Smela tribe to judge his old friend. The penalty for treason was a slow and gruesome death.* If not applied, other members of the Smela would also ignore the blockade and Abd el-Kader's claims to authority would melt away like the summer snow on the Atlas Mountains.

"Why such cruelty? Why did you do this when I was not here?" Abd el-Kader demanded of his father later. Inside the old Turkish palace of justice, the ulema had made their decision: Ben Tahar had to die, first by having his eyes gouged out and then his feet and hands cut off. Abd el-Kader had wanted to spare his old master's life and was willing to allow his tribe to pay a heavy ransom of five thousand francs to get him back.

"My son, you have to realize that from now on you must be our guide in war, as you are already in the faith. I cannot allow treason to enter your tent. Hard lessons must be taught in war. This in not a matter of inhumanity — these are tests. The sheiks are taking your measure. For you to lead them in war, the tribes must be like the fingers of your hand. With them, you have to be able to make a fist or cut off a finger."

Abd el-Kader was not simply the head of a tribe, his father reminded him. A nomadic war machine was an alliance of families and kinsmen who shared a certain esprit de corps, an *élan* based on blood which the Arabs called *asibiyya*. Nevertheless, these alliances were fragile. Each tribe, like mini-nations, valued its independence and freedom to make the best arrangement for itself — to balance the rewards of collaboration with the fear of punishment.

---

* The Koran doesn't specifically mention treason, but sura 5:34 presumably includes it under the language ... "Those that make war against God and his Apostle and spread disorder in the land shall be put to death or crucified or have their hands and feet cut off on opposite sides, or banished..."

"You will have many difficult tests. Beware of the tribal sheiks. You must bend them to your will, but be careful and distrustful of what they say. Remember the old Arab expression, 'The hand I cannot cut off, I will kiss until I can.' Even members of your own family are skeptical. I will be the advisor to you that you were to me when I was the leader."

Ben Tahar's gruesome execution provided the French with a convenient atrocity to lay at the feet of this upstart emir. They were not interested in making distinctions between father, son or ulema as to the actual responsibility for torturing to death their trading partner and ally. The savage killing of Abd el-Kader's former schoolteacher made good copy for the French propaganda machine, one that was transforming the emir into a monster.

☙

A treacherous road lay ahead. After drafting his proclamation, one of the emir's first acts had been to create a consultative council, just as the Prophet had done. No ruler was wise enough to govern without the advice of others. But the emir also broke tradition. His council of ten had only two family members: a cousin and his brother-in law, Mustafa Ben Thami. His council had included his old teacher as well, Ahmed Ben Tahar.

To unify the resistance, the emir had to make the tribes think differently. They needed to think of themselves as part of a greater Muslim community, as a nation of Muslims, rather than as small independent nations bound by blood. Abd el-Kader had to teach the tribes to sacrifice for the general good, in peace as well as in war. To succeed, he had to make the tribes understand that their vow of obedience to the authority vested in him was absolute. The Koran was his constitution. The deeds and sayings of the Prophet were his case law. Religion was the common denominator of unity. The sword was his enforcer.

In 1833, the emir's authority didn't extend beyond a radius of thirty miles from Mascara. Seven tribes had pledged allegiance to him, but his core of reliable supporters were only three: the Hachem, which was his own tribe, the Hachem Gharabas and Beni Amer. To attract more followers, Abd el-Kader had to show that he could dominate with the sword as well as with the Book. His capture of Arzew and the execution of Ben Tahar had made the powerful Smela think again about ignoring

54

the emir's proclamation. They soon became reluctant enforcers of the blockade.

Soon after Ben Tahar's execution, Arzew was retaken by French troops. Boyer had been replaced by General Louis-Alexis Desmichels, a former cavalryman in Napoleon's army who immediately began aggressive skirmishing with the tribes enforcing the emir's blockade. Abd el-Kader now began a pattern that would mark his greatness in the eyes of friends and enemies alike — his ability to rebound from setbacks, redouble his efforts to unify the tribes and emerge stronger. The French capture of Arzew required him to gain a victory to win over more tribes and to keep the confidence of those already with him.

The ancient holy city of Tlemcen, whose allegiance to the emir was slipping away, offered a good opportunity for Abd el-Kader to reassert his authority. Surrounded by rich plains covered with cherry, peach and almond orchards, Tlemcen was known as a center of learning and an entrepot for goods moving between Fez and Oran. Not only did an active intellectual life vibrate through the city's medersas and zawiyas, there was the hustle and bustle of Tuareg caravans from the Sahara loaded with dates, wool, ostrich feathers and ivory. From Morocco came fabricated goods: silk, knives, swords, leather slippers, rifles and English drapes, and a large colony of wealthy merchants. One of them, a certain Ben Nouna, had been recently made the caid, but his authority was disputed by the Arabs who had only contempt for sedentary merchants.

Tlemcen was a learned, but also a divided city. Moroccan merchants controlled most of the commerce, but vied for influence with Jews, Arabs, Kougoulis and Berbers. The Turks controlled the city from its heavily fortified citadel with only a hundred janissaries and four thousand Kougoulis. In the past, the Turks had acted as mediators among the competing groups, but in the summer of 1833, they were concerned above all else for their heads and their property.

When Abd el-Kader appeared with his army, the Jews were allied with the Kougoulis, the Turks were at loggerheads with the Moroccans, the Arabs, as usual, were full of contempt for the Moors, and the Berbers didn't like submitting to anyone. Ben Nouna was unimpressed by the troops gathered under the emir's standard announcing, "Victory comes from God and it is near" embroidered in gold on a white flag with an open red hand in the middle. Ben Nouna refused the emir's demand to submit to his authority. He recognized only the authority of the Sultan of Morocco.

The Commander of the Faithful easily defeated Ben Nouna, thanks to the Turks in the citadel who fired on the Moroccan's militia from behind. The emir treated the inhabitants graciously, but replaced Ben Nouna with his own caid. Bou Hamidi was an old friend from the zawiya in Guetna who shared Abd el-Kader's love of horses, books and the hunt. He was both a religious scholar, a courageous fighter and chief of the Oulhassas, a Berber tribe that dominated the coastal region around Tlemcen. By making him his caid, Abd el-Kader hoped to win the support of a tribe that had shown little enthusiasm for fighting the Christians, unless it felt directly threatened. The emir picked well — Bou Hamidi became one of the emir's most loyal lieutenants.

Abd el-Kader didn't have siege equipment or cannons to bombard the eighteen-foot-thick walls of the citadel. Yet, neither did he view the Turks as his real enemies. He simply left them alone, demonstrating a quality that would repeat itself in the years ahead: he preferred sugar to vinegar when dealing with adversaries. The emir departed Tlemcen with the symbolic gifts of submission he needed from the rest of the population: a beautiful chestnut warhorse and a gold-embroidered parasol, used to protect sultans from the relentless sun.

The emir had only a short time to enjoy his success in Tlemcen when he received an unexpected blow. He learned that his father had died suddenly, though history does not tell us the cause. There were whispers of skullduggery. Ben Nouna, it was said, had hired an agent to poison Muhi al-Din. The rumor was plausible. Ben Nouna was known to want to destroy the authority of Abd el-Kader, whose authority, he believed, was merely the reflected light from the father. Kill the father and the emir's authority would die. If the rumor was true, Ben Nouna had miscalculated.

Abd el-Kader had absorbed his father's conviction that he had been born with a divine destiny to fulfill. His life had to be an example for others. The five daily prayers, sermons and frequent homilies he preached at marabout shrines offered occasions to teach his compatriots respect for the laws of their religion and to set themselves apart from the Christians by holding to higher moral standards. With knowledge and exemplary behavior, he could achieve moral leadership — a necessary, but not sufficient condition to lead. The Commander of the Faithful also needed to show the tribes his political cleverness, courage in battle and skill in dealing with the French. Islam is like a tree: it points its believers heavenward, but is also rooted in the earth.

The "puny Arab" that de Tocqueville recognized as a remarkable leader was, in fact, physically small. Not much over five feet tall, Abd el-Kader was wiry, exceptionally strong for his size and had an iron constitution. He could ride for weeks surviving on a sack of the same barley they fed their horses. Precooked, the barley could be molded by hand when mixed with water into a doughy ball of *rouina* — the fast food staple of Arab horsemen. His pale skin, prominent forehead and aquiline nose were framed by a thin black beard. His dark gray eyes seemed to change color according to the light, which may explain why Abd el-Kader has been described as having, alternatively, blue, black, green and hazel colored eyes.

Like the changing color of his eyes, Abd el-Kader's capacity to adapt his personality to his different roles impressed those who spent time with him: dutiful son, holy man, scholar, orator, resourceful warrior, diplomat, scourge of the tribes, administrator and judge. Above all, he was a spiritual leader. The true colors this ascetic young Muslim monk marched under were the colors of obedience, an obedient servant of God.

De Tocqueville called him "a Muslim Cromwell."

CHAPTER SIX

France's New Ally, 1834

BOYER'S SUCCESSOR IN ORAN had a problem. General Louis-Alexis Desmichels had twenty-five hundred men and four hundred horses to feed. Dysentery, malaria, typhoid and undernourishment were depleting his ranks faster than were Arab bullets. Desmichels was also an officer who belonged to the optimist camp within the army and government. The optimists believed France had a future in Algeria. To some, its future was a "restrained occupation" limited to coastal enclaves. To others, it was outright colonization. With the right pacification policies toward the natives, France could establish an effective rule and enhance her influence in the Mediterranean and Europe. This, of course, was premised on her getting colonists to come and tackle this "Wild West" and work the soil. That meant assuring a decent measure of security, which required much more money than the Chamber of Deputies was willing to spend in 1833.

The pessimists believed there was no future in Algeria for France. They included leftist republicans, Bonapartists, and many in the army who saw this as another Spanish disaster in the making.* The struggle, they argued, was a tremendous waste of money, hardly worth the cost to France, divided as it was by an adventure that had been launched by a government that no longer existed. In the pessimists' view, the lack of knowledge of Africa and of a real plan to deal with people it didn't understand argued in favor of leaving before French prestige suffered.

Abd el-Kader was kept informed of these political divisions by his agents, who also served the French as intermediaries. These were Jewish merchants, known to both sides because of their commercial activities: Mordecai Amar who supplied the French with meat, Michael Bushnach of Bushnach and Bacri grain traders, and the gifted linguist and middleman, Judas Ben Duran. They, and others, became known as the emir's Jewish court, his unofficial diplomatic corps of skillful and often self-serving masters of playing both sides.

---

* Napoleon's intervention in Spain in 1808 became known as his "Spanish ulcer."

Desmichels understood that pacification of his province was impossible with the small force under his command. He knew that the only way to obtain peace was to follow the Turkish example and make an alliance with a strong Arab leader. Abd el-Kader also wanted peace, but for different reasons. He needed peace to build his Islamic state, and a treaty could act as a lever to unify the tribes whose proud chieftains were prone to deluding themselves that they could negotiate as equals with the French. However, a peace treaty would enhance the emir's prestige with the tribes only if it was France who appeared to be the suitor. For reasons of French prestige, Desmichels also could not appear to be the one seeking peace. Yet, he had to do something because his force was evaporating before his eyes.

A minor incident gave him an opening. The emir's tribal allies had taken four French soldiers hostage escorting a local chieftain who been violating the emir's commercial embargo of Oran; an inconsequential event in itself, it provided Desmichels an excuse to write to Abd el-Kader.

> I do not hesitate to take the first step. My position, strictly speaking, does not allow me to do so, but my humanity compels me. I ask for the liberty of those soldiers who were ambushed while protecting an Arab. I cannot imagine you will impose conditions on their release. When, by the hazards of war, some Smelas and Gharabas fell into my hands, did I not return them safely to their tribes without any conditions? If you hope to be considered a great man, I hope your generosity of spirit will match mine and you will immediately release the prisoners in your charge.

Desmichels had mistakenly thought he was negotiating from strength. Two months earlier, he had raided the powerful Smelas. The loss of their livestock and imprisonment of their women and children had brought the Smelas, led by Mustafa Ben Ismail, to conclude a temporary truce with Desmichels.

The emir's reply to Desmichels was nothing short of rude.

> Haj Abd el-Kader Ben Muhidin, prince of the faithful and defender of believers to General Desmichels, governor of Oran:

I received your letter in which you express the desire to obtain the liberty of the four prisoners who fell into my hands. I understood its contents and wish to respond.

I had not considered the idea of ransoming your prisoners. You say you have taken the first steps in this affair. This is your duty according to the rules of war. Between enemies each side has his day. One day, chance favors you, another day, me; the mill turns for both of us, but always there are new victims. When you took prisoners I never bothered you with demands for their liberation. As a man I regretted their unhappy fate, but as a Muslim, I looked upon their death (if it occurred) as a new life, and to engage in purchasing their freedom as shameful. You say that your soldiers were protecting an Arab. That carries no weight with me. Protectors and protected alike are my enemies. All Arabs in the province found with you are bad believers and ignorant of their duty.

You boast that you returned without conditions some Smela and Gharaba prisoners. True, but you surprised these people who were living under your protection and supplying your markets in opposition to my orders. Yet, your army pillaged them of all they possessed. When you march two days beyond your walls, we will meet and then we will know which of us should be master of the province. It is time to settle this because if you stay the sufferings of our poor population will be extended indefinitely.

Desmichels responded to the emir's challenge with more raids on the Smelas and Douairs, the two most powerful douad tribes in the province, but divided in their loyalty to the emir. On December 2, Abd el-Kader was visiting the Beni Amer tribe when he learned of an attack on the Smelas. He quickly came to their aid immediately. In four hours his horsemen covered sixty miles to fall upon Desmichels' astonished soldiers. For the tribes still unsure of this upstart leader, the emir had shown his alacrity in coming to the rescue of an ally, even one whose loyalty was uncertain.

As a distinguished cavalryman himself, Desmichels had been amazed by the emir's ubiquity and ferocity in battle. He also knew that his own dwindling resources would force him to evacuate if an arrangement with the emir could not be reached. He sent a second letter.

"…If you would agree to grant me an interview, I would readily consent in the hope that, with a solemn and sacred treaty in hand, we can stop the bloodshed between two peoples destined by Providence to live under one dominion."

Abd el-Kader sensed that the Frenchman was ready to build him his throne. The letter was that of a supplicant. The emir didn't respond. Instead, he let his agent in Oran, Mordecai Amar, know that he was willing to entertain more explicit proposals should the general express unhappiness at the deafening silence.

A month later a third letter arrived from Desmichels. This time he wrote what Abd el-Kader needed — words to give the tribes that proved it was the French who were humbly suing for peace. "…Not having received a response to my last letter, I prefer to think it never reached you than to believe that you judged it unworthy of your attention…If you desire to preserve the dominant situation where circumstances have favored you, you cannot do better than to accept my request for a meeting, so that the tribes might devote themselves to the land and enjoy the fruits and blessings of peace in the shade of treaties which would firmly bind us to one another."

The emir now had a document showing that the enemy was the first to seek peace. The Koran was clear on two points Abd el-Kader would revisit often in his dealings with both tribes and the French: if attacked, a Muslim must fight to his last breath to defend the faith, yet peace is permitted if the invader sues for peace. This time, Abd el-Kader accepted the general's proposal. His reply to Desmichels' letter was gracious and ended with his promise. "…You can be certain that I have never betrayed my word, once given. With God's help, these negotiations will be to the advantage of both sides."

On February 4, 1834, the emir's representative, Miloud Ben Arrach, met with Desmichels' intermediary. Ben Arrach had become a trusted councilor to Abd el-Kader, and become his de facto foreign minister. Ben Arrach combined administrative experience, intelligence and powerful tribal connections, powerful enough that the former Bey Hassan had made him his agha for the eastern part of the beylik. Ben Arrach had also maintained good relations with the Jewish merchants who served as the emir's secret agents. Thus, it was Ben Arrach who proposed to Desmichels that he use Mordecai Amar as his intermediary.

The use of Jewish intermediaries was practical. They were excellent linguists, more cosmopolitan than the Arabs and practiced in working with Europeans. Accustomed to commerce, they knew both sides had to benefit for an agreement to occur. And they understood the ways of the Arabs. Mordecai Amar was an Oranais merchant who was well known to Abd el-Kader. He sold their wheat and procured weapons for them through commercial channels in Britain and Spain. He also moved in high circles in Oran as well as in Algiers and in Paris, and kept the emir informed about French thinking.

Ben Arrach returned to the emir with unsigned draft peace proposals from Desmichels. After consulting with his council, Abd el-Kader sent Ben Arrach back to Oran on February 25th with his seal stamped on the proposals of Desmichels and a new document with his own proposals. Ben Arrach was instructed not to give back the general's proposals until he had first put his seal on the additional proposals of Abd el-Kader.

Desmichels' terms had contained six points: 1) immediate cessation of hostilities; 2) assuring respect for the religion and customs of Muslims; 3) return of prisoners held by the emir; 4) open markets for commerce; 5) return of French deserters by the Arabs, and 6) Christians traveling within the province must have a passport bearing the seal of the emir's consul in Oran and of the French general in command of Oran.

Abd el-Kader presented four additional conditions that either expanded or limited those of Desmichels: 1) Arabs were free to buy and sell gunpowder, guns and all other necessities of waging war; 2) commerce in Arzew is under the jurisdiction of the Commander of the Faithful; the shipping and receiving of all merchandise for Oran, Mostaganem and Arzew must go through Arzew; 3) the general must return deserters and not harbor criminals, and 4) no Muslim residing in the French-controlled towns will be prevented from leaving if he so wishes.

As instructed, Ben Arrach handed back Desmichels' conditions bearing the emir's seal only after Desmichels had attached his seal to the emir's terms. This gave rise to a peace agreement in two parts. The next day, Desmichels proposed consolidating the two documents into one agreement. The result was a document mined with misunderstanding.

The six-paragraph document that became officially the Desmichels Treaty was set out in two columns, one in French and the other in Arabic. The consolidated agreement made no reference to the emir's demand for a trade monopoly funneled through the port of Arzew, a demand inspired by Mehmet Ali during Abd el-Kader's visit to Egypt with his father. Having come so far, Abd el-Kader was also anxious for peace. He signed the second consolidated treaty despite the absence of this important condition because he had a separate document with the general's seal on it. The emir did not consider the possibility that the second agreement abrogated the first.

Desmichels' independent decisionmaking was to get him into trouble. Not only had he signed two agreements with the emir that were not in complete accord with each other, he had signed the consolidated treaty without the approval of his government. He had informed the war ministry of his negotiations, but the slowness of the mail and the urgency, in the general's mind, of seizing the moment had led him to execute the agreement before Paris could respond with its requirements.

Had Desmichels not been such an effective advocate for his own cause, and not had friends in high places, Paris might well have disowned his treaty. Desmichels presented it as a great diplomatic triumph. He wrote that he had achieved "the submission of the province of Oran, the largest and most belligerent of the whole Regency." This he attributed to the "advantages gained by the efforts of my troops." To disown the treaty, he was implying, would be to disown France's own brave soldiers who had suffered and fought so valiently.

General Desmichels' views could not be lightly dismissed. He had a brilliant career in Napoleon's army as a cavalry officer. As a lieutenant, he won fame when his platoon of thirty cuirassiers captured 500 soldiers of the Austrian Imperial Guard and several cannons on the eve of the battle of Austerlitz. Desmichels explained to Paris that only Abd el-Kader could guarantee a durable peace in the province. "The splendid intelligence of Abd el-Kader, his energy, the great influence he exercises among the Arabs thanks to his marabout birth, and the respect attached to his father — all that serves my plans," he wrote the ministry. And by serving the interests of a French general, Abd el-Kader was serving France. King Louis-Philippe approved the agreement.

Abd el-Kader was equally quick to declare his great success to the tribes. He had forced the French to beg for peace. He had won the terms he wanted and paid no tribute to France. The French had recognized his autonomy by recognizing the right to exchange consuls; the French could receive goods only through a single port and would have to pay tariffs. The treaty served Abd el-Kader's need to consolidate his authority by having, in effect, a French guarantee of support without formally recognizing French sovereignty.

Desmichels understood the importance of the marabout who was now an ally of France. Without Abd el-Kader, pacification of Oran province was all but impossible. He boasted that he would make the emir all-powerful from Tunisia to Morocco. With pitifully few resources, and vacillation and uncertainty in Paris, he had done through goodwill what Boyer's harsh methods had failed to accomplish. The general organized several days of balls and gala dinner events to amuse and impress the representatives of the emir with the advantages of European civilization.

"They showed neither the slightest attraction for all the refined luxury displayed on these occasions nor envy for any of our products," wrote Adolph Dinesen, a Danish officer who served in the French army as an artilleryman. "The only things that interested them were the military maneuvers which Desmichels organized for their benefit."

Miloud Ben Arrach presented four horses to General Desmichels — a gift from the emir, from one cavalryman to another. They returned to the emir's camp at the River Sig accompanied by several French cavalry officers, led by Colonel de Torigny, who only a month earlier had fought a bloody battle with the emir's men. Now he brought 100 muskets and fifty quintals of gunpowder as a gift for their new ally. Afterward, de Torigny reported his impressions to Desmichels.

"I was surprised by the perfectly organized war camp and the mass of men who obediently opened their ranks to welcome a French soldier. I admired their strong faces, their large, muscular bodies — the fruit of a free and unfettered life. I admired their horses which responded to the slightest movement and, at the first sign, are ready to fly like an arrow as we have so often experienced in battle.

"When we arrived at the emir's tent, he had us sit after shaking our hands. His two officers whom we had accompanied then threw themselves at his feet and kissed his hand. 'I am happy you had a good trip,' the emir said to us. 'I have written a letter to your general and thanked him for his generous presents. I hope with all my heart that the alliance we have now sealed will endure for a long time. Tomorrow, I am leaving for Mascara and ask you to accompany me. There, I will tell you of my plans and hopes. Now your tent is ready for you to rest after your long journey.'

"At sunrise the Arab camp was raised. In very short time the tents were taken down and loaded on mules and camels. Within a half hour the emir was ready to leave. Three Negroes brought him his horse. He mounted it with casual indifference, but once in the saddle, he showed us that he was indeed an accomplished horseman like other Arab chiefs. An officer held a gold-colored parasol over his head to protect the emir from the sun as he led his small army of three thousand men. The gaiety of the event was marked by rifle fire and military music which played non-stop until we reached Mascara.

"The emir asked many questions during our last meeting," de Torigny wrote. "He wanted to know about the state of France, how its armies were organized and about the role of religion in the life of the country. A marabout present with the emir asked if priests were ever consulted in matters relating to war and peace. Abd el-Kader smiled at our soldiers' embarrassment when they admitted the absence of priestly counsel in such decisions."

They spoke of the disinformation that was circulating already, spoors of ill will already being spread by opponents of the peace. The emir had heard rumors that the general was marching against him, that he had been duped by Desmichels.

"I have been to Mecca. I have seen the Prophet's tomb and my word is sacred. I also have faith in the word of your general. I did not believe the rumors."

Misunderstandings and crimes were possible, nevertheless. It was too soon for him to guarantee order in his province. Abd el-Kader thought it was dangerous that French soldiers were hunting far from Oran, even near Lake Sebha, in Douair territory.

"I cannot respond to isolated cases of ill-will by Arabs, and even the severest punishment would not compensate for any harm done. The embarrassment would be great for me," he explained to de Torigny.

Abd el-Kader told him to ask the general to forbid hunting excursions distant from Oran.

The emir wanted to punish the Arabs who had stolen livestock from French farmers in the Mitidja Plain near Algiers. He already had ideas of being France's ally for maintaining order throughout Algeria. The emir also knew from his agents in Oran that his ambitions fitted with those of General Desmichels.

"You will soon appreciate the power I will exercise. Those same hostile tribes that have camped around your walls to starve you will become responsible for the good behavior of others and for the supplying of your markets."

Before the Frenchmen returned to Oran, they gave one more gift to the emir: a magnificent double-covered tent fifty feet long, twenty feet wide, and fifteen feet high supported by three poles. The outer cloth was finely woven of hard, twisted yarns; the inner lining had panels of red, green, blue and yellow oversewn with crescents, arabesques and silver-spangled teardrops. Abd el-Kader, in turn, presented each officer with a horse, and to de Torigny, a letter for Desmichels as well. It explained to the general that he had already sent two cavalrymen to Algiers with news of their treaty and copies of his letters.

And so it was that General Theophile Voirol, the nominal superior of Desmichels, first learned that his colleague in Oran had signed a peace treaty with Abd el-Kader.

A Sufi Zawiya
Lithograph, Rigo Frères. Source; Zaki Bouzid

Algiers circa 1830
Lithograph by unknown artist. Source; B. Etienne

View of Mascara, 1835
Etching, unknown artist. Source; Zaki Bouzid

The Battle of Machta
Hocine Ziani, Source; Ziani Atelier

Arab Cavalry in Battle
Eugene Delacroix, 1832. Location; Fabré Museum, Montpellier

Arab Chiefs in Council
Horace Vernet,1834. Location; Condé Museum, Chantilly

Twin
pistol holster
Location; Djihad Museum, Algier
Source: Zaki Bouzid

Prayer rug
Location; Army Museum, Algiers
Source: Zaki Bouzid

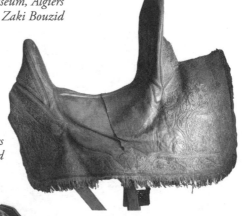

Saddle
Location; Army Museum, Algiers
Source: Zaki Bouzid

Octagonal field Koran
Location; Army Museum, Algiers
Source: Zaki Bouzid

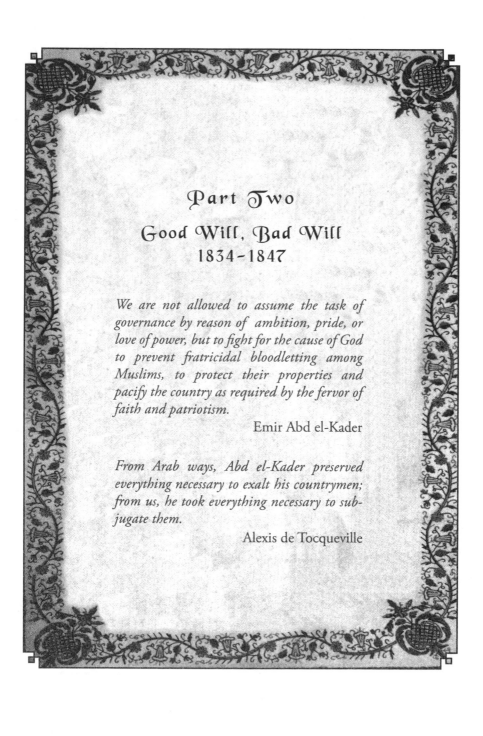

Part Two

Good Will, Bad Will
1834–1847

We are not allowed to assume the task of governance by reason of ambition, pride, or love of power, but to fight for the cause of God to prevent fratricidal bloodletting among Muslims, to protect their properties and pacify the country as required by the fervor of faith and patriotism.

Emir Abd el-Kader

From Arab ways, Abd el-Kader preserved everything necessary to exalt his countrymen; from us, he took everything necessary to subjugate them.

Alexis de Tocqueville

CHAPTER SEVEN

Building an Islamic Nation

MIGHT A WRY SMILE have crossed General Desmichels' lips? The emir was clever. Without formally recognizing French sovereignty, Abd el-Kader's letter asked for the general's support in his struggle to dominate the tribes. He went so far as to ask Desmichels to write General Voirol, requesting he cease hostilities against the tribes in the central province of Tittery in order to allow him, the Commander of The Faithful, to keep the peace. Abd el-Kader also wanted King Louis-Philippe to put his seal to the treaty to give it still further weight, unaware that the general had signed the treaty without his government's approval.

The French generals could also behave like independent tribal chieftains. Abd el-Kader soon learned that the *franci* were not one big tribe headed by a powerful sultan, but rather many smaller tribes fighting among themselves, even if they did wear the same uniform. Slow communications, personal rivalries and different approaches to the conflict frequently led generals in Oran to act independently of the generals in Algiers, or, in Desmichels' case, even of the king's council of ministers. "Desmichels was willing to take responsibility for acting independently," Pellissier de Reynaud noted dryly in his memoirs, "a vital quality in a commander operating far from Paris." It was also a quality that got him into trouble.

The treaty immediately caused unhappiness in Paris. By authorizing an exchange of consuls and issuance of visas, it implied that the emir was the head of a nation state — a sovereign, equal to the king of France. Indeed, a unitary state with a permanent administration, a system of justice and finance, enforced by a regular army was precisely what Abd el-Kader set out to create. It hadn't existed among the desert Arabs since the time of the Prophet. The tribes valued their independence above all.

To unify the Arabs, the emir had to reform them. To reform them, he had to set a personal example of rectitude and incorruptibility, as well as reeducate and remind them of that which was the ultimate source of their strength: Islam. The Koran emphasized one overriding virtue required of governors of an Islamic nation: equity. Justice, in turn, could only be achieved through knowledge and an intelligent application of the divine law. *The sultan is God's shadow on earth whose rule will not last if he is unfaithful or unjust.*

Abd el-Kader first had to repair the damage caused by years of overbearing Turkish rule. Justice under the Turks had become cruel and capricious, while his year in Oran had opened his eyes to the low state of public morals. Moral turpitude and injustice had the same cause — neglect of the Law. The once admired Turkish rulers had strayed from the straight path.

Nevertheless, the emir used the Turkish system of delegation and tax collection already familiar to the Arabs to overcome these debilitating legacies, but with one notable exception: even the tax collectors had to pay taxes. The Turkish beyliks became Arab caliphates, each governed by a caliph who acted on behalf of the Prophet, and therefore of God. When choosing his caliphs, Abd el-Kader sought men with reputations for moral integrity who were religious scholars as well as fighters.

The caliphs were responsible for raising taxes from the tribes, providing good governance and security for the inhabitants. In the fall and spring, they made the rounds of their caliphate to assure the payment of taxes, usually in the form of levies on livestock and harvests. The caliphates were subdivided into aghaliks, each headed by an agha to whom the tribal chiefs, or caids, were accountable.

The caids collected the *zakat*, the Koranically obligatory alms to feed the poor and students. They also had the important job of hiding a portion of the grain levy in underground silos to be used in times of war or drought. With his caliphs, aghas and caids loyal to him, the emir was creating a "national" administration to replace a flimsy checkerboard of tribal allies whose loyalties waxed and waned according to the interplay of French treatment of the Arabs and Abd el-Kader's fortunes on the battlefield.

There could only be one authority who could decide on war and peace, and that was the emir. Abd el-Kader could not allow the hardships of the tribes to become excuses for abandoning jihad. If so, he was building his house on sand. The fervor that gave him his strength of purpose and resilience — his sense of divine mission — was also the justification for being severe when punishing sluggards, backsliders and traitors. He would have to become more feared than loved. His own punishment was to be called a deluded and blasphemous tyrant by his tribal enemies.

"The tribes were like children. They only thought about the present," Abd el-Kader explained years later to his biographer, Charles Henry Churchill. "Their loyalty was often circumstantial. They needed stern, but just fathers to make them think about the future of the resistance and to punish them for backsliding on their commitments." For this the emir needed both cadis and a regular paid army.

The cadis were the justices of the peace. They were to be found everywhere, even with his army when it was on the march. "The Turks killed people capriciously and cruelly," the emir told Churchill. "I wanted to be certain that no person was sentenced to death unless it conformed to the law of God for whom I acted as lieutenant. Certainly, I had many people put to death, but never without a trial. All those who were killed had either committed capital crimes or had betrayed their religion by secretly collaborating with the French."

The caliphs, aghas, caids and cadis also had to be paid. The state treasury was located in Abd el-Kader's tent — large chests covered by rugs. The emir was also a realist. He knew that he could not prohibit tribal leaders from squeezing the tribes during lean times, which would be often. "For this reason, and to protect my servants, I had my caliphs and aghas make a vow on the holy book of al-Bukhari* to never commit injustices toward their people. I myself vowed to act as overseer of their actions. Despite my efforts, I could not prevent some evil deeds. My reforms were too radical to get immediate results. At times, there was no money to pay all my administrators," the emir admitted to Churchill.

Abd el-Kader, like the medieval kings of Europe, was creating something new by building a national consciousness. His task required solving three problems simultaneously: creating a central administration, financing the administration and enforcing the payment of taxes, while living with the constant threat of rebellion from the tribes and uncer-

---

* Al-Bukhari was a 9th-century, saintly religious scholar from Bukhara who authenticated 7,000 hadiths out of many tens of thousands attributed to the Prophet, though not claiming those omitted were unauthentic. This monumental and meticulous work of devotion required verifying chains of witnesses and their reliability.

tainty about French intentions A regular army was needed to complement the traditional system of tribal irregulars accustomed to coming and going at will.

Yet, a regular army needed to be paid. And taxes could not be raised without the enforcement powers of troops loyal to the emir. "His genius," observed the Danish Captain Dinesen, "lay in his profound knowledge of the ideas, needs, and prejudices of his people and in his capacity to take them into account when calculating the consequences of his actions." To improve the conditions of the Arabs, Abd el-Kader listened to the advice of many people, but none more than his mother's. Lalla Zohra liked to say, "borrowed customs can't be rewarmed like food." Abd el-Kader took to heart another of her dictums: "To maintain family relationships, friendship has to be built into them, and afterward, friendship supersedes blood." Abd el-Kader's brand of diplomacy strived to build or rebuild friendships, and he took risks doing so. The "deluded tyrant" wore a coat of many colors.

Outside of the military-technical arts, little or nothing the emir did to raise the moral, political and educational levels of the Arabs was borrowed. His reform book was already at hand: the Koran, the Sunna, Hadith, the different legal traditions, the wisdom of the prophets. But these needed continual illumination, interpretation and reinforcement. Re-vitalized Islam and knowledge were to be the twin pillars of his efforts. His "national" administration and "national" consciousness would be built on an Islamic foundation. Abd el-Kader was to be the chief educator.

The difficulties were enormous. Some sheiks were jealous of his success in achieving peace. Some were envious of this twenty-seven-year-old marabout's prestige. There were those who saw no need to go to war at all and were willing to accommodate the French, while others accused the emir of betrayal and of being a bad Muslim. His sin was that of making peace with the Christians.

"Where now is the head of our jihad?" asked the voices of dissent after the treaty was signed. "What has happened to the imperious voice that cried only for struggle and defiance, and preferred death to submission?" Was he not different from the corrupt Turkish beys who needed money to support their harems and luxurious, decadent life-style? "Why, O emir do you oppress us, you who live so simply and need so little?" they demanded.

&

General Desmichels stood by the emir during his first test. It came unexpectedly from one of Abd el-Kader's most zealous supporters on that November morning in 1832 on the Plain of Ghriss.

The Beni Amer had pledged their lives and property to serve Abd el-Kader. They had begged him to create a government that could inspire confidence in honest men and fear in wrongdoers. Now they were the first to balk at paying taxes. In the Beni Amer's eyes, a special war tax was only justified in time of war, and now there was peace. The emir responded by ordering Mustafa Ben Ismail to punish them. But two days later, Beni Amer chieftains attending the Friday sermon at the Ain Beida mosque in Mascara were reconciled by the emir's persuasive oratory and arguments. Abd el-Kader countermanded the earlier order for Ben Ismail to punish them.

But the proud Ben Ismail could not be easily manipulated like the fingers of the emir's hand, as Muhi al-Din had warned was necessary to rule the tribes. He loved plunder too much and respected Abd el-Kader too little. The sixty-year-old warrior had served the Turks for thirty years and considered Abd el-Kader a callow, untested youth — "a child of the rosary" who had once slighted him by not rising to his feet as proper etiquette required. Adding insult to injury, the emir hadn't entrusted him with a high position in his new government. For his past service to the Turkish beys, Ben Ismail had acquired considerable wealth in pasturelands near Oran. He owned tens of thousands of sheep, cattle and goats that he could profitably trade with the French. He ignored the emir's order to stop plundering the repentant Beni Amer. The emir immediately had to teach the old warrior a lesson in obedience.

The confrontation left Abd el-Kader humiliated by the wily old *makhzen* who nearly captured him during a night raid on his camp. News of the young emir's thrashing at Ben Ismail's hands circulated throughout the region. Other tribes defected, unhappy with the peace and the war tax. Seeing an opportunity, Ben Ismail wrote to Desmichels. He offered himself to the Frenchman as an alternative for keeping order in the province and holding in check the emir's ambition.

Desmichels never responded. Instead, he reaffirmed his loyalty to Abd el-Kader and assured him continued support. The general knew he had to strengthen, not weaken, the man he expected to pacify the tribes for France and in whose character he had placed his trust. Desmichels sent his ally new percussion muskets, gunpowder and military expertise. He ordered his consul in Mascara, a former Mameluke officer in Napoleon's army, to help train the emir's new standing army. Abd el-Kader was impressed by the machinelike discipline and maneuvering precision of the French infantry. His cavalry wouldn't accept training from Europeans, believing they had no peers when it came to their specialty: harassing, hit-and-run tactics. Abd el-Kader knew his infantry needed training, however, especially as fighting on foot was looked down upon by Arabs.

The emir announced that his regulars, or *askars*, would be paid a salary of five boudjous (nine francs) per month, and provided with a daily food allotment. Each received a half-kilo of hardtack in the morning, and in the evening, a full kilo of *chichah*, a kind of crushed wheat that was boiled in a huge cauldron to feed thirty-three men at a time, lubricated with a kilo of butter and other ingredients, depending on the location of the camp. Thursdays, each company received five sheep to slaughter.

Foot soldiers received their first uniform gratis, a French- or British-made rifle, and for cavalrymen, a horse. All his regular units had medical teams trained in the best traditions of herbal medicine developed over the centuries in Andalusia. *It is written in the sacred books that any sultan who doesn't teach the healing arts in his empire is acting contrary to God.** In addition to a surprisingly high level of medical knowledge at the disposal of his troops, there were always cadis attached to army units to address matters of military justice. Each cadi was supplied with two "assessors," or judicial assistants, for investigating the facts of a case. Recruits flocked to Mascara.

---

* French military doctors who had been prisoners of the emir observed that the Arab dressings used for treating wounds resulted in far fewer infections and faster healing than normally found among the French. They also developed a special clamping device (*djebira*) designed to push out bullets lodged in joints (see chapter notes; Bernadette Paillet-Flitti, unpublished paper).

The emir eventually built up a regular force that fluctuated between 1,000 to 2,000 cavalry and 5,000 to 8,000 infantry. From these, each caliph received a contingent of 1,000 infantry, 250 regular cavalry divided into five squadrons and an artillery company of 24 men to operate two artillery pieces. On the right sleeve of every officer were embroidered the words, "Patience and perseverance are the keys to victory," and on the left, "There is no God but God, and Mohammed is his Prophet." The epaulettes of his aghas carried other exhortations: "Piety and Courage" was on the right shoulder, and on the left, "Nothing is more harmful than dissension and indiscipline."

Building and training his infantry would take time and continued help from the French, often deserters from the Foreign Legion. More important than the training was the material assistance — weapons and gunpowder to discipline the tribes or resist the French, according to the state of affairs between the emir and France. Nor did he depend only on France. Soon his agents were procuring weapons through commercial channels in Spain, and especially in England where the press was making the emir into a folk hero for tweaking the French nose.

The tribal rebellions reinvigorated and toughened Abd el-Kader's fighting spirit. The Hachem, Gharabas, Beni Abbas and Mejahers held firm. The members of the Beni Amer confirmed the pledge made by their sheiks in Mascara following the emir's impassioned sermon at the mosque. With these tribes committed to him, the emir fielded 15,000 cavalry to go about setting things right.

Using measured combinations of punishment and forgiveness, within four months Abd el-Kader had rebounded from an image of a whipped child at the hands of the wily Ben Ismail, to being the dominant Arab authority in what was formerly the beylik of the Oran, now the caliphates of Mascara and Tlemcen. In July, the admiring Desmichels requested an interview with the emir.

Abd el-Kader appreciated Desmichels's loyalty and material aid as well as his realism about the balance of forces, one that did not favor the French at the time. Yet, in the subtle dance of perceptions each had to appear to his own side to have the upper hand. Abd el-Kader, as Commander of the Faithful, could not afford to meet Desmichels without putting the general at risk of appearing in a subordinate role, an embarrassment he wanted to avoid. As Commander of the

Faithful, the emir could only meet he Frenchman if he appeared as his equal. The orientalist in Desmichels understood this game, but the Frenchman in him made him understand that his other obligation was to assert France's sovereignty and obtain Abd el-Kader's symbolic acknowledgment of his dependence on French power. A meeting never took place.

ℰℛ

The tribes were a greater problem for the emir than the French. Abd el-Kader's carefully choreographed treaty had divided even his own family. Unhappy with the treaty, his brother, Mustafa, dismissed his pretensions of leadership and joined the rebellious Sidi el-Aribi. Even his father-in-law, uncle Abu Taleb, was a doubter. The emir would be denounced as a traitor to Islam by more fanatical spirits.

Haj Musa was one. This erratic, young dervish of Egyptian origin who had acquired the aura of a holy man and miracle worker was popularly known as Bou Hamar, the Father of the Donkey. His donkey was said to be some kind of sacred gift and was always kept tethered to his tent as a good luck talisman. In the spring of 1835, Haj Musa was stirring up the troublesome Derkaouis, a Sufi brotherhood given the name "the independents" by the Turks because of their unpredictablity.

His calling that summer was jihad; his enemies were Christians and their apostate allies, and in particular, the so-called Commander of the Faithful, Emir Abd el-Kader. Leading thousands of Saharan Arabs, Haj Musa had ridden into the Atlas and ravaged the area around Medea south of Algiers, supposedly under French protection. He denounced the Desmichels Treaty and summoned Abd el-Kader to join him in his fight against the infidels. The emir had no reason to break the treaty to appease a mercurial fanatic.

The intrusion of this whirling dervish from the Sahara into the Medea area provided Abd el-Kader with the excuse he needed to establish himself as an Arab guardian for the French in the central beylik of Tittery, in addition to Oran. The emir's ambition was to have no shot fired in anger from Tlemcen to Algiers without his permission. He told Haj Musa not to enter the Mitidja Plain south of Algiers where small shoots of French colonization were sprouting that, as France's ally, he wanted to protect.

The emir had only half as many troops as Haj Musa, but his four cannons made the difference. On the eve of the battle, Haj Musa foolishly prophesied to his men that the emir's cannons wouldn't fire when the time came to fight. A confident emir sent back a message saying he would submit if the cannons failed.

His cannons fired, the emir's opponents scattered and Haj Musa was heard from no more. Abd el-Kader trusted that his diplomatic representative in Algiers could explain to the governor-general that he was acting in both their interests by crossing into Tittery province to defeat a common enemy. Abd el-Kader named two new caliphs for Medea and Miliana in Tittery province.* However, the new governor-general, Drouet d'Erlon, was placed in a difficult position.

૯ఌ

Since his arrival in Algiers a year earlier, in July 1834, Comte Drouet d'Erlon had been the object of an intense lobbying campaign from pro- and anti-Desmichels advocates. The seventy-year-old veteran of the Napoleonic wars had come out of retirement to be the first governor-general of Algiers, a position created in July 1834 that combined military and civil authority. He came to the post knowing little and with few preconceptions about France's new North African possession. He was neither a pessimist nor an optimist about the colonization project, but a friend of the war minister and looking forward to an exotic, yet not overly demanding colonial post to end his career.

Before returning to France, his predecessor, General Voirol, had responded to Abd el-Kader's offer to help him enforce law and order among the Arabs in Tittery. He said, in essence, "No thank you." Calm had been established in his province and, he reminded the emir, the treaty signed by General Desmichels applied only to Oran province whose eastern limit was the Chlef River. By restoring order in Medea and naming caliphs for areas beyond Oran province, the emir had provocatively overstepped the limits set out by Voirol.

Many of the governor-general's officers believed Desmichels' strategy was dangerous for France. They saw Abd el-Kader using France as

---

* El-Berkani, the new caliph of Medea replaced the emir's rebellious brother, Mustafa.

an instrument for serving his own ambitions and that he was far from being a docile subject serving France's interests. As the emir began to enforce his monopoly of trade through the port of Arzew, French merchants also began to howl. But the emir had deployed his secret weapon in the struggle for a sympathetic response from Drouet d'Erlon to his incursion into Tittery.

Judas Ben Duran was a man of fortune and genius, descended from a family of rabbis who had emigrated with the last of the Muslims driven out of Spain. He had served as an interpreter for Dey Hussein and for the French after the sack of Algiers. In addition to Hebrew, he spoke fluently Arabic, French, Spanish, English and Turkish. He was charming, diplomatic and practiced skillfully his belief that God had given man the power of language so he could hide his thoughts. As a young man he had studied in France, and his wide-ranging business interests had accustomed him to dealing with Europeans. No person was better equipped to serve as the emir's diplomatic representative in Algiers.

A man known to speak and dress simply, Ben Duran's charm, cunning, facility with language and apparent candor quickly turned him into a valued confidant of the governor-general. He was seen regularly dining at Drouet d'Erlon's table and riding about Algiers with him in his carriage. "The emir's Jew," as the Arabs called him, was admitted to the governor's palace at all hours and had access to as much information as almost any of his own staff officers.

In December 1834, Ben Duran had also to counter the effects of the humiliating recall of their French ally, General Desmichels. Drouet d'Erlon had insisted that Desmichels be replaced by his own chief of staff, General Trézel, after he learned from Ben Duran of the existence of other documents that Desmichels had approved, but had kept secret from his superiors. Ben Duran revealed them only after the governor-general was informed that a commercial shipment of 1,000 guns, 1,000 quintals of powder and 1,000 bolts of Egyptian tent cloth were being shipped from Marseille to the Arzew for the emir in exchange for deliveries of wheat, barley and a large sum of money. D'Erlon was on the verge of blocking the transaction when Ben Duran explained that Desmichels' own seal had approved such trade and gave him a hand-copied duplicate of the agreement.

Desmichels denied to d'Erlon the existence of any such secret agreement. It was, he said, a fake that had been devised by enemies of the agreement. Regardless, the governor-general insisted that Desmichels' benevolent attitude toward the emir and implicit mixing into political matters were incompatible with his own views. In February 1835, General Trézel relieved Desmichels of command. During Trézel's interrogation of the general, Desmichels continued to deny he had a hand in any secret agreement. All doubts were removed, however, when the original Arabic version was produced for Trézel. It had the emir's seal at the top and that of general Desmichels at the bottom in Arabic: *A Slave of the One and Almighty God, General Desmichels.* The general's handwritten signature, however, was not on the document, as it was on the official French version. This omission left Desmichels room to continue denying its authenticity.

Despite French opposition to the Desmichels Treaty, Ben Duran's charm and quiet diplomacy had persuaded d'Erlon in the summer of 1835 that the emir could be trusted and that he was truly a man of peace. The emir, Ben Duran explained, made no secret that he would like to unite the Arabs under the banner of a purified and reinvigorated Islam, the Islam of peace, justice, charity and brotherhood that he learned from his father and saw practiced daily as a youth. He wanted to make the faith a living reality in the hearts of Muslims. Such an ally, he argued, would simplify French rule. If France followed the Turkish example of laissez-faire governance, France could accomplish its goals at very little cost.

Comte d'Erlon had little room to maneuver. The Scientific Commission created in Paris the previous year to study the situation in Algeria had recommended to the parliament a permanent, but "restrained occupation" of the coastal towns of Algiers, Oran, Bone, Bougie and peripheral areas. The commission recommended reducing the total number of troops in Algeria to 21,000. Even this modest plan of colonization had been hotly debated. "I would trade all Algeria for a shack on the Rhine," opined the deputy responsible for the war ministry's budget, Hippolyte Passy. Much of the debate was about cost. Others ridiculed cost as an argument, saying if cost was really the issue then many departments of France should be abandoned, as well as her colonies in North America. French honor and economic interest jousted with absurdity, uncertainty and wasted blood and money.

A restrained budget that reflected the strength of the political opposition was not the only problem the governor-general faced while considering ways to counter the emir's pretensions. In the course of a year, the ministers of war changed six times. Paris liked to control its generals, yet there was no guiding hand. D'Erlon's orders were to maintain the status quo and to not provoke a confrontation. The steady drip of Ben Duran's persuasiveness, combined with the practical realities facing the governor-general, led to a virtually inevitable conclusion. D'Erlon decided it was wiser to concede that which he didn't have the means to withhold — Abd el-Kader's de facto protectorate of Tittery.

೧

General Trézel did not share his superior's taste for temporizing. This feisty staff officer, whom Drouet d'Erlon had appointed to replace Desmichels for acting too independently, would quickly become a thorn in d'Erlon's side for being too belligerent in protecting France's honor.

Camille Alphonse Trézel was an unlikely looking warrior. His badger-like spirit was disguised in a small, delicate-looking frame with a high falsetto voice. He wore a misleadingly benign facial expression despite having lived for two years with a bullet lodged in his head until, by a miracle of physiological rejection, it worked its way down his respiratory duct to exit from the roof of his mouth. The wound had cost him an eye while fighting with Napoleon at Ligny. Two years earlier, during a battle in the eastern province of Constantine, Trézel's thigh had been opened up by an Arab saber.

Drouet d'Erlon's orders to Trézel were to approach the emir in the spirit of renegotiation, "without setting off alarms that would lead him to believe we are considering the disavowal of the Desmichels Treaty, and cause him to initiate hostilities." But the response of this French terrier to Abd el-Kader's promenade through Tittery was to propose marching on Mascara to punish the emir who, he believed, was dangerous and making a fool of France. This did not jibe with d'Erlon's strict adherence to his orders from the ministry of war, which emphasized maintaining the status quo. He ordered Trézel to stay put.

Drouet d'Erlon, assisted by Ben Duran's skillful diplomacy, continued to believe in the possibility of finding common ground with the emir. As a good-will gesture, the governor-general had offered to replace the rifles lost and the gunpowder consumed during Abd el-Kader's campaign against the Derkaouis.

Heady with a renewed sense of dominion over his territory, and the signs of support from d'Erlon, Abd el-Kader decided to stamp out the seeds of future rebellion that were still germinating in Tlemcen where his now implacable enemy, Mustafa Ben Ismail, had taken refuge with the Kougoulis in their citadel. In the spirit of his "alliance" with France, the emir asked Trézel for two mortars to subdue the citadel. Trézel refused. Abd el-Kader responded angrily by imposing a blockade of Oran.

He ordered the Smelas, Douairs and Gharabas to stop trading with the French in Oran. The Gharabas remained loyal to the emir, despite having to deny themselves lucrative business. But the Smelas and Douairs, ever interested in commerce, reacted to the emir's demands by asking Trézel for protection. When informed of this precarious situation in Oran, d'Erlon decided to visit his former chief of staff.

Their relationship had become strained. Trézel was obsessed with forcing Abd el-Kader to acknowledge his submission to France and limiting his ambitions. He also believed that the emir was much more dangerous than his superior appreciated. Drouet d'Erlon wanted to follow his orders from Paris, and was prepared to see Abd el-Kader more as an ally than enemy.

On June 6, 1835, D'Erlon came to Oran for the first time. The governor-general was armed with practical questions that showed a realistic appreciation of the situation his subordinate was facing. How could Trézel be sure the tribes were not being represented by a minority of malcontents? What guarantee did he have that they would actually be reliable allies? How would Trézel assure the tribes' protection when Abd el-Kader decided to punish them for their disloyalty, especially as the garrison in Oran was likely to be reduced in size? The governor-general still believed he might reach a new agreement with the emir if only he would make just a token sign of submission to France. Trézel's actions would compromise this thin hope. Drouet d'Erlon told him to decline the offer of submission by the Douairs and Smelas.

The predictable occurred immediately. Informed of their treasonous activity, Abd el-Kader ordered the two tribes to evacuate their tribal lands south and west of Oran, around the saline Lake Sebka. When they refused, he ordered the arrest of the pro-French tribal leaders and forcible removal of the rest of the families to the interior. The emir wanted to depopulate the area around Oran to create "a desert of eight leagues," Trézel wrote to d'Erlon. Abd el-Kader boasted that under his rule "no bird would fly into Oran without his permission."

On June 13, only days after the departure of the governor-general, leaders of the Smelas and Douairs again asked Trézel for protection. They pleaded with him, saying that they would not be able to live in the new territories assigned to them by the emir. Convinced that France's honor and whole colonial enterprise in Algeria hung in the balance, Trézel ignored his superior's order to withhold protection of the rebellious tribes. His disobedience would be overlooked if he succeeded in bringing the Gharabas, as well as the Smelas and Douairs, into the French orbit. Oran would then be surrounded by tribes allied to France and the emir's power in the province would be broken. So reasoned Trézel, convinced that his French soldiers would make quick work of Abd el-Kader's army if a confrontation were to occur.

Three days later, in an olive grove near Lake Sebka, Trézel signed an agreement with the unhappy Smela and Douair chieftains. They not only recognized French sovereignty but agreed to serve in the French army and to obey Muslim officers assigned to them by the French. The Gharabas were approached by Trézel, who insisted that he was not waging war against the tribes, but rather protecting them. Their caid rebuffed his invitation to ally with France: "We are under the orders of the sultan."

Mustafa Ben Ismail came from Tlemcen to offer his services to the general. Trézel was ecstatic. "The emir will finally have to do what he has constantly refused, to formally recognize the king of France as his sovereign, pay tribute and take orders," he wrote optimistically to the governor-general.

Trézel informed the emir of his actions, writing that he would be negligent in his duty if he did not allow the tribes the "free use of their natural rights, the freedom to remain on their ancestral lands and to cultivate them in peace." Trézel asserted that his actions were in conformity with the Desmichels Treaty, which only required return-ing "deserters," whom he defined as individuals, not whole tribes. Abd el-Kader ignored Trézel's letter and wrote instead to Drouet d'Erlon, whom he addressed as a friend and ally.

"Today, I ask you to write me a letter in which you say I have al-ways kept my word, that my house is free of deceptive and treasonous behavior, wanting to preserve with good faith and intelligence what exists between good neighbors. All the trouble is coming from General Trézel; it would be helpful if you replaced him by someone capable of maintaining the good relations that exist between us. Because of my friendship with you I will not mete out punishment to the tribes…"

Like Drouet d'Erlon, Abd el-Kader also needed to gain time to so-lidify his grip on the tribes. To avoid a provocation, he issued strict orders that no Arab fire upon a Frenchman except in self defense. Yet, the emir knew that if Trézel were allowed to assert French sovereignty over the Douairs and Smelas, the house of Islamic unity he was trying to build would soon collapse. Abd el-Kader wrote to Trézel insisting that the Smelas and Douairs were his subjects. As his subjects under Islamic law, he reminded the general, they had committed an act of betrayal, deserving punishment.

"You know the conditions that General Desmichels and I agreed to before your arrival and which you have promised to respect. Accordingly, any Arab who commits a crime, be it one or several persons, and who seeks refuge or protection from you, is to be returned. Is not then my claim even stronger if a whole tribe commits the crime of desertion? If you withdraw your protection and leave them as before under my authority, all will be well. If you persist in breaking your commitments, then withdraw your consul from Mascara. Even if the Douairs and Smelas take refuge behind your walls, my hand will not let go of them until they have repented their error and made compensation. You de-cide, otherwise the God of war will do it for us."

The emir waited for two days in the hope of receiving an encour-aging response from d'Erlon before sending the letter. None came. Trézel received Abd el-Kader's letter on June 21, then wrote to d'Erlon: "Despite the determined attitude of the emir, I doubt he will fight in order to keep, or rather, destroy the Smelas and Douairs."

Trézel was wrong. The emir had to draw the line on "deserters" in order to maintain tribal discipline. The next day, skirmishes with Arabs occurred throughout the region. On June 26, Trézel marched toward Mascara at the head of a column of 2,500 infantry, a regiment of light cavalry and four pieces of artillery. Three days later, what had been an army returned to Arzew, a stunned mass of terrified fugitives.

CHAPTER EIGHT

The Wheel Turns

TRÉZEL HAD SUFFERED A HUMILIATING DEFEAT: 362 dead and 308 wounded, 150 horses killed, along with the loss of his field artillery, rifles, ammunition and food supplies. The horrors of the battle along the Machta River had left the survivors with "death in their souls," Trézel wrote afterward. "In this deadly struggle, I saw the hopes I considered reasonable evaporate. I needed victory for them to be realized. Obviously, I overestimated our own forces and underestimated those of the Arabs."

News of tattered and terrified French soldiers staggering back to Arzew had an enormous impact on the Arabs, magnified by fanciful embellishments. Rumors circulated that the French lost 1,500 soldiers and 600 wounded; General Trézel himself had been taken prisoner and was sweeping the emir's stables; Oran, even, had surrendered. The tribes again flocked to the emir's banner. But "victory" was expensive. Abd el-Kader lost over a thousand men in the fighting that led up to Machta.

What had happened? Knowing the difficulty of moving the heavy transport wagons used by the French, Abd el-Kader had anticipated Trézel's movements through the Forest of Moulay-Ishmael, where he concealed his infantry in the rocky, pine tree-covered landscape. When his troops were ambushed, Trézel prevented a near rout with his personal bravery by forming his panicked men into squares of disciplined firepower that decimated the Arabs.

The bruising encounter didn't weaken Trézel's obsession with forcing the emir to recognize French sovereignty. The next day, Trézel sent Abd el-Kader a message proposing to end hostilities if the emir would pay an annual tribute to the king of France and take orders from the king's representative, the governor-general of Algiers. Abd el-Kader didn't deign to respond.

Trézel waited a day for a reply. Then, on the 28th, he decided to take his wounded to Arzew before continuing his march on Mascara. He chose a route along the Habra River that offered easier terrain for his medical wagons than returning directly through the mountains to

Oran. It was also a more risky path which required passing through the Habra Narrows where the Habra emerged renamed as the Machta River. Abd el-Kader immediately understood Trézel's plan when he learned about the Frenchman's new direction. He selected a thousand of his best cavalrymen and told them to gallop ahead, each carrying a foot soldier to hide in the wooded heights overlooking the marshy Machta delta.

When Trézel discovered the emir's riflemen concealed on the hill-sides, and confident of his men's ability to run off undisciplined Arab infantry, he ordered only two companies from the Italian battalion of the newly formed Foreign Legion to clear the slopes. But the Arab infantry had not been dislodged so easily when the rest of the emir's cavalry descended en masse at the rear of the French column, already exhausted from days of marching in the summer heat. In a panic to rush forward, wagon drivers and artillerymen cut their horses free of their harnesses and rode off, wagons were abandoned and units merged in a chaotic effort to close ranks. Caught between the Arab riflemen and the soggy delta, some tried to escape to the east, but became mired in mud bogs to be hacked or trampled by the emir's cavalry.

Abd el-Kader arrived on the battlefield that night to find his men celebrating around a horrifying monument they were constructing. "Heads, more heads," they chanted as Abd el-Kader passed by, silently revolted by the huge pyramid his men were building with their bloody trophies. It was a practice he would change, but this was not the time.

❧

Drouet d'Erlon first learned of Trézel's insubordination only after the general had received a bloody nose in the Forest of Moulay-Ishmael en route to Mascara. The governor-general had tried to protect the fragile peace from Trézel's aggressiveness by sending Captain Lamoricière to help him negotiate with the emir. He arrived too late.

Lamoricière had already distinguished himself by his energy and seriousness in understanding the complexities of native culture. While serving in Algiers, Lamoricière had thrown himself into the study of Arabic and the Koran. He was known for frequenting coffeehouses and markets where he could talk with Arabs to practice his Arabic, but also to learn about the customs of the Berbers, the Moors, the Arabs and their different tribes and important families. By the end of

1831, Lamoricière had become competent to negotiate in Arabic with the tribal leaders without an interpreter. His ability to speak Arabic and willingness to travel lightly armed and with small escorts won him respect. Talking directly with the caids and sheiks enabled him to help create an embryonic intelligence service, known as the Arab Bureau.

Lamoricière had shown the Arabs that a Frenchman could deal with them by means other than a "rifle butt or a bagette." Instead of trying to outdo the Arabs at committing atrocities or seducing them with bread crumbs as if they were pigeons, Lamoricière worked on building good human relations, and through those relations, trust, and its ultimate fruit — intelligence and lasting allies. The rules he developed were rooted in experience: don't take a village unless you can protect it indefinitely; there are no lasting allies unless you can protect and support them effectively. In the eastern provinces, the tribes were calling Lamoricière, "the agha of the Arabs."

Trézel had already been humiliated by Abd el-Kader when Lamoricière arrived in Arzew. Realizing that his mission no longer made any sense, Lamoricière returned to Algiers. How the future might have turned out had Lamoricière and Trézel met before the ill-fated expedition to Mascara is a tantalizing question.

℣

Machta didn't go to the emir's head. He knew it was an insignificant victory against the greatest power in Europe. But it did give him renewed moral authority to continue the difficult job of building unity among the tribes and a respite to work on his priority — building up his capability to manufacture weapons. Mascara's sole atelier could make only two rifles a day, and of doubtful quality. Without weapons and a well-trained regular army, he could not build a lasting organization capable of suppressing the tribes' natural tendencies toward independence and insurrection.

Diplomacy was his most potent weapon against the French. This had been demonstrated by his manipulation of Drouet d'Erlon, aided by his close attention to Parisian politics reported in the press and translated by members of his "Jewish court." Abd el-Kader was careful, after Machta, almost apologetic, in his communications to d'Erlon with whom he wanted to maintain friendly relations.

The emir wrote to the governor-general explaining that it was Trézel who had marched out of Oran with his column into his territory. For the sake of his friendship with the governor, he had overlooked this infraction of the treaty. Trézel had advanced to Figuier, then to Tlelat and finally to Sig where he began to destroy the harvest. Only then did Abd el-Kader decide to attack. "You know I am true to my word and I do nothing to trouble the peace. Make your own inquiries and you will find that I am telling you the truth," the emir concluded.

Trézel's offer of resignation had been accepted in Paris. Soon after, d'Erlon was also recalled, viewed by the imperialist camp as too old and conciliatory. The blood of Machta energized the French government. Adolphe Thiers, then minister of the interior, was an outspoken opponent of the policy of "restrained" occupation. During an impassioned speech before the Parliament, he expostulated: "This is not colonization, this is not small scale occupation, it is not large scale occupation, it is not peace, this is not war; this is war badly waged!"

To rid France of this troublesome bandit and restore its honor, Thiers successfully advocated the nomination of General Bertrand Clauzel for the post of governor-general. Clauzel's strong belief in France's civilizing mission matched that of Thiers. His pro-colonization stance made him a favorite with the Europeans in Algeria and the imperialists in Paris. He would set things right. Pompous declarations and blind optimism, however, were Clauzel's strongest suits.

On August 10, 1835, General Clauzel was warmly received by the Europeans in Algiers. The four intervening years of French "civilization" had transformed the face of the city. The waterfront had been turned into a plaza where European-style shops displayed frumpy, outdated fashions. Mosques had disappeared or been turned into churches. Buildings had acquired number plates and streets given names: rue Annibal, rue du Chat, rue Sidney Smith, rue du Lotophages, rue Sophonisba, not to mention rue Belisaire. The city boasted a circus, four *Grands Hotels* — "all execrable," according to the report of a British military observer, Major Grenville Temple, as well as eleven *Grands Cafés* frequented by "piquante" French ladies to amuse the troops. The veneer of civilization was thin indeed, noted Temple, who was informed weekly by *Le Moniteur Algérien* of the misbehavior of French soldiery. Its pages reported on the punishments regularly meted out for murder, robbery and desertion. Execution, imprisonment and forced labor were the lot of men one officer described as "robbers, pilferers and drunkards." The Parisian revolutionary rabble did not make for good soldiers.

If Algiers had changed during Clauzel's four-year absence, the general had not. As before, he arrived overconfident and unsobered by his mistakes in 1830, when he had optimistically expected the interior to collapse as quickly as had Algiers. In his first public declaration, Clauzel grandly announced his ambitions.

> Inhabitants of the Regency, my appointment to govern the French possessions in North Africa reflects the serious intentions of the king of France. However complicated the problems are at this moment, I will overcome them with the assistance of the administration and support of the inhabitants to reestablish peace after punishing the rebels wherever they may be and to promote all commercial and agricultural activities throughout the extent of the county... We will create through perseverance, a new people who will grow more rapidly than the one that began on the other side of the Atlantic over a century ago.

The general, however, was out of phase with the war ministry that was giving instructions to maintain a "restrained" occupation, to not provoke confrontation. Clauzel was speaking as an unrepentant imperialist in favor of total occupation — a goal that required massive emigration of European colonists to work the land in a climate of security. Unfortunately, neither colonists nor security, existed.

His arrival in Algiers coincided with another unwelcome visitor — cholera. For two months the disease ravaged the city, delaying the execution of his mission "to wash away the humiliation of Machta." Of the twenty-five thousand soldiers who were in Algeria at that time, four thousand were in hospitals and as many as sixteen hundred died.

Clauzel distributed a new map of the Regency to raise the spirits of the colonists, still demoralized by Machta. It was divided, in Turkish fashion, into new beyliks. Each was shown to be governed by a newly appointed pro-French bey. However, each of the beys was either hounded from office, had his life threatened or refused to even take up his duties. Clauzel's reality existed only on paper.

જી

"The wheel turns," Abd el-Kader had written Desmichels back in 1833, "crushing its victims; now one, now the other." The wheel was about to turn again.

The cholera epidemic had subsided, but had left the ranks of France's army weak and demoralized. The ministry of war was still cautious about resuming hostilities with the emir, but an outraged public was clamoring to avenge France's honor. The government bowed to this new political force — public opinion — and ordered a punitive response to the debacle at Machta. Clauzel received reinforcements and was told to demolish Mascara. The Duke of Orleans, King Louis-Philippe's oldest son, was sent to witness France's retribution. Paris assumed that the destruction of the emir's capital would rid France once and for all of the upstart Arab.

On November 21, 1835, five months after Machta, Clauzel set sail for Oran to lead an army of 11,000 men. The poetically-minded Duke of Orleans noted in his diary that the marching column of soldiers resembled "a long, glittering serpent surrounded by a halo of dust lit by the setting sun." The crown prince would soon be writing of horrors he had never imagined.

Abd el-Kader again discovered the limits of his newly trained regular army. His artillerymen alerted the advancing French by firing prematurely and were quickly silenced by more accurate return fire. His infantry lacked the discipline of the French to hold ground and concentrate their fire. French artillery fire sowed confusion and chaos among the emir's troops. His cavalry fled back to their tribes and his infantry vanished into the woods as disorganized bands of fugitives. It was Machta in reverse.

The tribes neighboring Mascara descended on the town and pillaged it in the name of removing everything of value for the French occupiers. When news of the looting reached the French army, its own native irregulars — Douairs and Smelas — broke away, carrying bags and baskets to join in the fun. Powerless to stop the sacking of his capital, Abd el-Kader withdrew to his family estates at Cacherou among the Hachem, six miles from Masacra on the Plain of Ghriss.

There, too, he found an unpleasant surprise. The emir learned that he and his family had been turned upon. Kheira's earrings had been snatched off her ears and the magnificent tent he had received as a peace gift from General Desmichels cut to shreds. His golden parasol had been stolen and behind his back some called him "Sultan of the bushes" and "Sultan of straw."

Dejected, the emir revealed to his family and remaining followers doubts about his divine mission. How could he unify a people who would not unite and who disappeared at the first rumor of defeat? How could there be a future with such unreliable material? That same day, Abd el-Kader received curious news: the French had abandoned Mascara after only three days' occupation.

The next day, December 4th, a lone rider on a black horse appeared before the Bab Ali gate wearing a tattered black burnoose, indifferent to the cold drizzle. He gazed at the remnants of the town he had hoped to make a center of Arab unity. As people recognized the rider, word spread through town. Gradually, skulking and shamefaced former supporters and allies approached him. One was the agha of the Hachem who had taken the golden parasol. He wanted to give it back to the emir. "Keep it, you may be sultan one day."

Other chiefs sheepishly came to him. Maybe they had misjudged the French, who had now abandoned the capital. Perhaps they had deserted their emir too hastily. They asked him what orders he had to give.

"Orders? Ah, yes, my orders are that you relieve me of this burden you have placed on my shoulders and which only the dictates of my religion have enabled me to bear. I order that the tribes choose a successor. I am leaving with my family for Morocco."

The chiefs gathered around the emir suddenly threw themselves at his feet. They kissed his burnoose. They kissed his hands and his feet. They begged for forgiveness and promised renewed fidelity. He was their father. He was their sultan appointed by God to direct the jihad. If he abandoned them, they would be forced to live under the infidels.

As if yanked by a leash, these last words reminded the emir of his divine duty and of his promise to his father. Abd el-Kader relented. "May God's will be done, but mark well, I swear I will never return to Mascara except to enter the mosque, until the day when you have avenged your shameful defeat."

Overnight, the fighting spirit of the emir's followers was rekindled. Once again, their leader had shown his mettle. He was devoted to doing God's will. He could persevere in the darkest of hours. He could pardon and he could punish. Abd el-Kader understood as few leaders when to be soft, when to be hard and when to be both.

Abd el-Kader kept three secretaries busy that night dictating orders for the tribes to assemble in the Plain of Ghriss to renew the struggle. The next day, by the dedara tree where he first had been proclaimed emir, a reinvigorated Abd el-Kader met the first few hundred followers to respond to his call. Their ranks swelled as the word spread that the emir was again in his saddle and the golden parasol was over his head. Like rivulets feeding a stream after a rainstorm, the horsemen came.

❧

Why did the French abandon Mascara after only three days? The sudden departure had damaged their credibility in the eyes of tribes who switched sides according to the vagaries of the battlefield. Clauzel himself admitted later to the parliament that it had been a mistake not to have left a garrison. Clauzel had justified leaving Mascara by saying it had no strategic significance — the expedition had been purely punitive. He may, however, have been protecting the reputation of the crown. The twenty-five-year-old crown prince quite possibly had become ill, as well as shaken by his baptism of fire.

The Duke of Orleans recalled with sickening clarity the Smela tribesman who had galloped through a hail of bullets to proudly show off his prize. "A few paces before he reached me, he drew his horse up and produced from under his burnoose a head dripping with blood. He held it by the mouth, its clenched teeth biting his fingers... the head of a rather handsome man, but the expression of the face defied description...Abdallah stared at me with wild eyes and threw the head at my feet. It bounced several times before it came to rest. I offered him a few pieces of gold, but he refused: 'I am a soldier. I don't fight for money.'"

Inside the walls of Mascara, the crown prince was shaken by the grim desolation and destruction. "In the square, which must once have been beautiful, pools of rose oil lay smothered with heaps of tobacco, which someone had tried to burn and which looters had mixed with all kinds of filth to make unusable...Hundreds of snarling dogs were nosing about in the refuse…A thousand Jews, all who were left from the population of ten thousand souls, threw themselves at our feet sobbing and kissed our stirrups." Some of the Jews were given the job of cleaning the emir's palace to turn it into the headquarters for the general staff.

The troops were shocked to learn they were abandoning the city. Before leaving, the small-arms atelier, the stores of sulfur, the law courts, the mint and the emir's palace were torched. The Douairs and Smelas who owned property in Mascara burned down their houses rather than let them fall into the emir's hands. At the head of the army as it trudged back to Oran in the cold rain were Mustafa Ben Ismail's men. Hungry for the wages of war, they had humbled themselves to walk like mere foot soldiers to allow their horses to carry the booty they had gleaned. Behind the Smelas and Douairs were those Jews who had not abandoned Mascara before the arrival of the French. Their pathetic condition had moved Clauzel to allow them to flee the city with his army. During their incomprehensible retreat, the duke proudly noted the chivalry of the French soldiers, many of whom were suffering from dysentery and exhaustion:

"These wretched Mascara Jews, feet bare, clothes tattered and covered with mud, staggered under the weight of the children they carried wrapped in their shawls. I saw women in almost biblical costume, and still good looking, collapse in the mud, who would have perished if our soldiers hadn't dragged them out…I saw a blind man hanging on to the tail of a donkey singing a psalm to keep up his courage…I saw camels crash down and remain stuck in the clay, a shapeless, colorless mass… sobbing mothers pick out the weakest of their children, near death, and leave them along the way, in order to save the others…During those awful days most of the cavalrymen carried a child under their cloaks. One I saw had two children so young he could feed them only by chewing pieces of biscuit which he gave them to swallow."

Overnight, the hundreds of Arab cavalry that had gathered in the Plain of Ghriss became thousands of reenergized Muslim warriors anxious to remove the stain of their cowardice and desertion. Pursuing the French was easy. The Arabs had only to follow their wagon tracks and the carcasses of their animals lying in the mud, dead or dying from exhaustion. By the time they caught up with the struggling convoys, the emir had six thousand men biting and nibbling at the cold, exhausted stragglers. The French victory at Mascara had acquired the look of a Napoleonic retreat from Moscow.

ɕʒ

Clauzel's next objective was Tlemcen. The isolated Kougouli garrison had remained in the citadel since the city had submitted to Abd el-Kader, but it was now under the command of France's ally, Mustafa Ben Ismail. Knowing the cumbersome preparations required of the French army and the slow pace imposed by their heavy convoy wagons, the emir decided to strike first. Abd el-Kader resorted to a ruse to draw out the Turks from their citadel, as he lacked both equipment and time to mount a siege.

A letter pretending to be from the traitorous Beni Angad tribe, allied with the French, was delivered to the Kougoulis. It proposed a rendezvous outside the city to deliver food for the garrison. Abd el-Kader pretended to withdraw toward Oran, but actually prepared an ambush at the agreed location. When 300 Turkish troops came out to get the provisions, they were slaughtered.

Abd el-Kader had barely a chance to enjoy this small victory when Clauzel's column approached. The emir made a tactical withdrawal across the Moroccan frontier, but took with him most of the Arab population of Tlemcen. This provided Clauzel with the opportunity to make another serious error.

The general entered Tlemcen on January 13, 1836. He was greeted enthusiastically by the city's remnant — Kougoulis and Jews professing their sincerest gratitude and devotion to France. Clauzel was not moved by words. He needed proof of their sincerity. A collective contribution to the French cause of 100,000 francs would show genuine devotion to their new masters.

The sum was impossible. They were not rich merchants. Clauzel turned a deaf ear to their outcries and applied more brutal methods of persuasion to get the earnest money. Threats, beatings and torture were used to extract money, diamonds and precious stones from the pathetic households that had put themselves at his mercy.

The emir did not lose time to spread the news, whose tag line was always the same: "If this is how France treats its friends, imagine what awaits its enemies." It was bruited about that the French used the Jews to choke money out of the Muslim Kougoulis. True or not, the news enraged the surrounding Arabs. The Beni Angad, France's newest allies, wanted to renegotiate their relationship with the emir after witnessing Clauzel's stupidity and brutality. The Kougoulis, in turn, sent secret messages to the emir saying they wanted to turn over to him the citadel as soon as the French departed. This time, Clauzel left behind a small garrison in the hope of establishing a line of communication between Tlemcen and the coast, at a point near the mouth of the Tafna River that could serve as a resupply post.

The self-assured Clauzel returned to Algiers after two more months of campaigning to cheerfully declare: "The war is over! Abd el-Kader has fled to the Sahara to lick his wounds."

CHAPTER NINE
He Looked Like Jesus Christ

NOVEMBER 1836, CLAUZEL WAS RECALLED to Paris. He left behind an Algeria that was virtually no different than it was after Machta.

In October, he had lost 3,000 men during a disastrous attempt to capture Constantine, ruled by France's archenemy in the east, Bey Ahmed. Clauzel's sole and dubious accomplishment after the sack of Mascara was the capture of Tlemcen, whose garrison of 500 men was isolated, starving and powerless outside the city walls. Its commander was paying forty francs a head for the privilege of eating cat meat. Supplies were intercepted, couriers were beheaded and the men were dying of disease, hunger and suicidal depression.

The emir controlled the countryside. Nothing moved without friendly eyes reporting to him. The French were trapped in their static strategy against a liquid enemy that could ebb and flow like the tides, whose leader was a perpetual motion machine that was recharged by the struggle itself. Abd el-Kader continuously circulated among the tribes. His finely tooled, high-cantaled saddle was his throne. The emir ate and slept in it, punished and harangued the tribes from it and gave orders to his retinue of mounted administrators, secretaries and servants — one of whom always held the golden parasol of authority, another led three spare horses, bridled at all times. He could ride for thirty-six hours, dismounting only to pray.

In the countryside, the emir's eloquence served him more than his sword. More important than his victories in the field were his words and his religious knowledge that he used for explaining, teaching, soothing and punishing. He understood that the tribes were fragile and vulnerable — battered by the retributions from each side, the lack of food, the divided loyalties and, for the women, the long absence of their husbands.

The emir recalled for the tribes his father's words: man is made of silk and iron. If he gets accustomed to luxury, soft living and good food, silk will dominate and soon he will be good for nothing. But if a man shows self-restraint and resists the little pleasures of life, the iron will dominate and he will be fit to carry out the hardest tasks. The Bedouin life was hard already, and to resist the *franci* it would be even harder.

Abd el-Kader went without seeing his family for months. He had hardly seen his young son, Mohammed, or his wife, Kheira. After he became emir, Abd el-Kader offered to release her from her vows, since at age fifteen, she clearly hadn't anticipated that she was marrying a holy warrior who would be more often absent from her tent than present. Kheira declined Abd el-Kader's offer of freedom, choosing to suffer with the other wives whose husbands also were never there.

But the warrior monk was also a poet monk. Lurid poetry gave release to his own suffering: *"You are in my thoughts, my beloved, when the wings of fate throw me into battle, when hands severed by the sword fly into the air… The memory of your love fills my soul and my chest is about to burst…"*

The leitmotif of Abd el-Kader's message was always the same for a people who were naturally anarchic: the importance of unity. Muslims must fight as one. The words of the Prophet were often on the emir's lips. *The Muslims are like a body. If an eye suffers, the whole body suffers with it…*

೧

Clauzel's recall deprived the imperialists of their strongest advocate in the army for a policy of total subjugation. Ironically, the new champion of complete colonization to emerge had been a skeptic of the whole French enterprise in North Africa.

Thomas Bugeaud had learned about guerilla warfare as an infantryman in Napoleon's ill-conceived Spanish campaign. He knew it was dirty, savage kind of warfare and difficult to win against a hostile population. Bugeaud had retired after the Napoleonic wars to his native Dordogne where he managed his estates and represented his district as a deputy in Parliament. After the July Revolution of 1830 that had unseated Charles X, the army had reactivated Bugeaud as a brigadier general. His simple peasant constituents found it hard to grasp how France's adventure in Algeria was benefiting them. Bugeaud had wondered as well.

A peasant at heart, the son of an Irish mother and a Perigord blacksmith, a lover of the soil and the hunt, Bugeaud respected the common sense of the toiling classes and was suspicious of intellectuals, especially utopian socialists and political troublemakers. One day, he would light-heartedly propose to King Louis-Philippe that such people be sent to Algeria so he could be sure they were killed.

Bugeaud was also a plainspoken soldier who gave his all once assigned a task. "I am convinced that the country can be subjugated, at least for a certain period of time, and with great effort and cost, but I don't believe at all that France will ever be compensated for the money and blood spent," Thomas Bugeaud wrote to his government after his great victory at Sikkak.

Sikkak. The word sounded good to French ears still suffering from the humiliation of Machta. Back in June 1836, the war minister had sent Bugeaud with 4,500 fresh troops to save from starvation the garrison Clauzel had left behind at Tlemcen. Bugeaud landed a punishing blow against the emir who had to learn once again to never fight a frontal battle with the French. Abd el-Kader lost over 1,200 men and 700 hundred rifles. One hundred and thirty of his men were taken prisoner. His favorite black charger, Zain, was shot from under him. His infantry was virtually destroyed, though he had launched his attack as the French were crossing the Sikkak River. Bugeaud's losses were miniscule: thirty-two dead and seventy wounded. The battle made him a hero to his soldiers, won him the confidence of the king and his ministers, and a promotion to lieutenant general.

France entered its seventh year of occupation as 1837 slunk onto the calendars of gloomy officers in the war ministry. Clauzel's defeat at Constantine the previous year had caused many tribes in Kabylia to join the emir. Abd el-Kader dominated the countryside in the west and continued to doctor the vacillating tribes by instilling now love, now fear. Paris had moved from a debate over whether to colonize to how to colonize. What the government lacked was the commitment to do the thing properly.

On January 19, the hero of Sikkak stood before the Chamber of Deputies to give his assessment of the occupation. At fifty-two, Bugeaud presented a tall, solid, uncommonly strong-looking figure. He was known to endure fatigue and hardship better than men half his age. His face was plump with muscle, florid and slightly pitted from smallpox. A few silvery spikes of hair rose above his broad, powerful forehead. He spoke with the authority that went with years of experience, a habit of command and a certain disdain for politicians.

"After six years it is time to achieve some real results. A halfway war will accomplish nothing. We must have either war or peace." The reversal at Constantine, Bugeaud explained, resulted from the absence of any overall strategy and from the failure to realize that the army had to be strong throughout the colony. For this, Bugeaud proposed that France mobilize a force of no less than 45,000 men, doubling its troops on the ground. Colonization, especially agriculture, required peace and security, and a restrained colonization would not work. He proposed that the interior be occupied as well. "If France really wants this conquest, and is serious about it, it can have it. It is capable, but it is necessary to want it very badly. France cannot want it half-way, because half-way measures lose everything."

The government heard the general, but still didn't want conquest badly enough. In March, the council of ministers chose peace. But who better to negotiate peace than the iron general himself? Bugeaud was conservative to his bones, a supporter of the monarchy and enjoyed the confidence of the government and of King Louis-Philippe personally. He was thought capable of outsmarting the emir, flexible enough to adapt to circumstances without violating his orders and aggressive enough to cut short delaying maneuvers, and if necessary, impose his will by force on the emir. After all, Bugeaud was the only French general who had given Abd el-Kader a sound thumping.

౿

Bugeaud arrived in Oran April 7, 1837. His orders were to negotiate within the framework of four conditions set from Paris: obtaining Abd el-Kader's recognition of French sovereignty; limiting the emir's power over the tribes to the beylik of Oran as far as the Chlef River to the east; payment of tribute to France; getting hostages to guarantee Abd el-Kader's execution of the treaty.

The agile Ben Duran had persuaded the emir to end the blockade and to resume trade with Oran. Ben Duran knew Abd el-Kader wanted peace to build up a line of strong points where critical materials could be manufactured and stored. Tagdempt, his new capital, as well as Saida, Taza and Boghar were far enough inland to make them difficult for the heavily laden French to attack, reliant as they were on slow-moving wheeled convoys. From these strong points, he could more safely build up his armament-manufacturing capacities. But to do this he needed iron, sulfur, steel and experts to instruct his men. Oran needed food.

Ben Duran persuaded the emir that it was in everyone's interest, not the least being his own, to open up trade with the new French commander in Oran, General Brossard. The tribes could again sell their products, the French would have meat and grain, and Abd el-Kader would receive materials needed to make weapons. All this would be organized through the services of Ben Duran, who would receive commissions on each transaction, yet insulate the emir from the criticism of dealing with the infidel, after having so long enforced a blockade. The emir's fingerprints would not be present, Duran argued. However, Abd el-Kader demanded a price that would put him in good standing with the tribes. The 130 prisoners taken by Bugeaud at Sikkak would have to be released in return. Brossard agreed.

Unsurprisingly, Ben Duran was among the first to pay a visit to Bugeaud. He told the general that Abd el-Kader was inclined to negotiate a new treaty. Despite Bugeaud's instructions to let the enemy take the first step, he used Ben Duran's information about the emir's state of mind to initiate contact. He sent a letter to Abd el-Kader, repeating the psychological duel Desmichels had had with the emir three years earlier.

Bugeaud's opening gambit was to assign responsibility for future hostilities to the emir by making him choose peace now or war very soon. "…Before entering into the cruel arena of combat, my sense of humanity toward Arabs and my own soldiers demands that I offer you peace. Politics demands the same because if you reject the peace I will offer you, then the responsibility for the horrors of war will be on your head."

The emir was not impressed by the Frenchman's imperious tone. "Are we under your orders that you send me such a letter? …You talk of your strength. We too have ours. We have courageous men who are not afraid to die and prefer to die as Muslims."

With Ben Duran as the intermediary, negotiations between the emir and Bugeaud began. Both men wanted an agreement. Bugeaud's orders were to get a peace agreement signed. France needed to buy time in the west in order to deal decisively with Bey Ahmed in the east. The general told his minister that he had only twenty days to negotiate, during which time he could threaten the Arabs in the only place they were vulnerable — the destruction of their spring harvests. Afterward, he would have little leverage. Abd el-Kader also needed time to consolidate his position with the tribes. He had to strengthen his own war fighting capability, not only to fight the French for the day when they would likely resume hostilities, but to subdue the tribes who refused to submit to his authority — that is, would not pay the special war tax. Ben Duran wanted peace in order to advance his far-flung commercial interests.

The emir's response to Bugeaud's overture was to refer him to Desmichels. He could not sign any agreement that put him in a position inferior to the Desmichels Treaty. Nor did his religion permit him to allow Muslims to live under Christian rule except by their own consent. Furthermore, he had entered Tittery in response to calls for protection from its inhabitants. Neither his honor nor his religion allowed him to abandon those who had put themselves under his protection. After Clauzel's failure to take Constantine in 1836, many of the tribes to the east of Algiers had placed themselves under the emir. Wasn't France's true purpose to gain commercial advantages by occupying coastal ports and not to try to extend their empire over populations that were hostile? Abd el-Kader asked.

The emir was well aware of the divided French command and rivalry between Bugeaud and General Denys de Damremont, Clauzel's replacement in Algiers. His Jewish merchants kept him informed of the debates in Paris where the liberal opposition was denouncing the occupation as a fatal legacy of the old Bourbon monarchy that would cost France dearly if not abandoned. Abd el-Kader would except no delimitation of his territory west of Algiers and threatened to negotiate separately with Damremont over Tittery.

Bugeaud faced the same dilemma as Desmichels before him: to recommence hostilities or make new concessions to achieve peace, even if a provisional one. Renewed warfare, however, required resources the government was not prepared to commit. He demanded plenipotentiary power from the war ministry to negotiate without having to obtain Damremont's agreement. While confidently waiting for a positive response from the ministry, Bugeaud offered more concessions.

He justified his concessions to the minister of war with arguments that echoed Desmichels. Abd el-Kader was the only Arab chieftain with the stature to guarantee peace. He was the only person who could lead and reform the Arabs towards progress and a higher level of civilization. To Comte Molé, the president of the council of ministers, Bugeaud explained why he had exceeded his instructions, anticipating, in particular, the objections of those who doubted the emir's good faith. "The knowledge I have acquired of the emir about his religious character, sincerity and of his influence over the Arabs, has given me the conviction that all the conditions will be perfectly respected. I offer myself as guarantor for the emir. This is proof of the faith I have in his word and of the great responsibility I have taken upon myself." To his rival in Algiers, Damremont, he offered only the limp excuse of being hoodwinked by a Jew. "I was deceived by Ben Duran who played a double game to extract concessions from both sides. Mainly, he works for his own fortune."

Bugeaud, nevertheless, would honor Ben Duran's contribution to achieving peace. When a complete breakdown seemed to be at hand over the issue of submission to French sovereignty, Ben Duran counseled prudence to the emir. "I see that the French don't understand your obligations under the sharia, but you don't understand the importance of national honor to the French." Ben Duran submitted a final draft to Bugeaud consisting of ten points, later revised several times to become twelve. Their seals were affixed to the agreement on May 30, 1837. Abd el-Kader agreed to Bugeaud's request for a personal interview two days later to confirm their understanding.

❧

Punctually, at nine o'clock in the morning on June 1, Bugeaud arrived with six battalions of infantry, field artillery and cavalry at a location overlooking the junction of the Tafna and Isser rivers, surrounded by the open, rolling green hills of the Trara Mountains. A clutch of officers surrounded the general, who, like him, were eager to finally meet the elusive emir.

Four hours later, there was still no sign of Abd el-Kader. Some of the officers began to think that their general was being snubbed. Another hour passed. Bugeaud himself began to show his impatience. His men were formed up, inappropriately dressed in their nine button, woolen blue field coats and red pants sweating profusely in the spring heat and beset by flies. Was a French general, the victor of Sikkak, being humiliated? Around two o'clock, the first of several Arab emissaries galloped up to their lines, each bringing conflicting messages. The sultan had been taken ill…he would like to delay the meeting until tomorrow… he was late getting started… he is on his way.

At five o'clock, another messenger galloped up to Bugeaud. He urged the general to advance. The sultan was not far away, but Bugeaud wanted his men to return that same night to camp. With an escort of only twenty officers, Bugeaud rode ahead, led by the emir's messenger. They rode for half an hour over rolling hills until Bugeaud's troops were completely out of sight. They entered a narrow gorge and exited to see the emir's advance guard. His caliph of Tlemcen, Bou Hamidi, rode up to Bugeaud to announce that the emir was just over the next hill.

Noticing a concerned look on the faces of some of the French officers, Bou Hamidi reassured them. "Don't worry. There is nothing to fear."

"I am not at all afraid," the general answered, "but I do find it rude that your chief made me wait so long and then to have to come so far."

"He is just over there. You will see presently." Bugeaud would not know until much later that the delay was orchestrated to allow time for tribes from the area to come and see the French general, victor of Sikkak, pay homage to the emir.

Bugeaud's escort rode another quarter of an hour. Suddenly, the emir appeared with an entourage of 150 of his chiefs, some in white, others in crimson burnooses, carrying weapons encrusted with silver, mother of pearl, coral and other precious stones. Abd el-Kader introduced himself with an effortless display of horsemanship, accompanied by sound of drums and flutes. His charger danced on its hind legs, boxed with its forelegs and kicked out all fours — difficult maneuvers the French had learned at cavalry school as the capriole, pesade and levade.

"Abd el-Kader, his chieftains gathered around him in a semi circle, his cavalry numbering in the thousands spread along the crest of the hills…the sight made us breathless," an officer in Bugeaud's escort wrote later. "Our lives were in his hands. It would have been folly to have tried to defend ourselves…the emir did not abuse his position and his behavior was as noble as his conversation. He treated the general as an equal, if not of lesser rank…"

There had been anxious moments among the officers left behind when Bugeaud had not reappeared after half an hour. Should they go see what happened to their leader? The Arab-wise Colonel Laidet showed cool presence of mind when he restrained fellow officers who wanted to gallop to Bugeaud's rescue. He knew that the Arabs valued courage, whereas the sudden appearance of a horde of French chasseurs could endanger the general's life. The trust shown by Bugeaud in the emir's good faith would serve both sides.

Anxious to get down to business, Bugeaud rode forward, interrupting the emir's solo performance. The emir shook the general's hand twice before they agreed to dismount and sit on the grass. He asked for the emir to silence the screeching of oboes, flutes and pounding drums that made it difficult for him to hear the translator.

"His clothes were no different than the most common Arab," Bugeaud reported to Comte Molé afterward. "He is pale and resembles portraits one sees of Jesus Christ. His eyes are dark, his forehead prominent, and has a large mouth with crooked, white teeth. His entire physiognomy is that of a monk. Except at first greeting, he keeps his eyes lowered. His clothes are dirty and worn. It is clear he affects a rigorous simplicity."

The general began by making a virtue of his independence. "There aren't many generals who would have agreed to the treaty I have concluded with you because it is contrary to my instructions from the king. People in France think you are powerful enough without going beyond the boundaries of Oran province. I have not been afraid to increase your power because I have confidence that you will use it to improve the condition of the Arab nation and to maintain peace and commercial relations with France."

"I thank you for your good intentions toward me. If God wills, I will help make the Arabs prosper, and if the peace is broken it will not be my fault."

"On this point, I am your guarantor to the king of the French."

"You risk nothing. We have a religion that obliges us to keep our word. I have never broken mine."

"I am counting on this. And it is with this conviction that I offer you my personal friendship."

For some forty minutes, they touched upon the reestablishment of commercial relations, the emir's reoccupation of Tlemcen, the relocation of the troublesome Douairs and Smelas and their leaders, the time needed for the King to ratify the treaty and other matters.

Bugeaud finally rose to leave, but saw that the emir remained seated, pretending to talk with his interpreters.

"When a French general gets up in front of you, you must rise as well." Before the interpreter could translate the sentence, Bugeaud had taken the emir by the hand, and smiling, pulled him off the ground. Abd el-Kader bowed his head slightly to appear to thank the general for a courtesy, though he had intended a subtle snub.

They shook hands one last time before the emir sprang into his saddle. The two departed in opposite directions, accompanied by the rousing beat of Arab martial music and cries of "Long live our Sultan Abd el-Kader."

☙

Bugeaud had won the competition. Abd el-Kader had acquired a mythical status among French generals and Bugeaud wanted to be the one to collect the laurels for signing a new peace. His ultimatum to the ministry to grant him sole authority to negotiate or to recall him had produced the desired result: his authorization to negotiate with a free hand arrived, a week after he had signed the agreement known as the Treaty of Tafna.

Many French generals had tried to meet this unusual adversary who had put their military talents to the test. Only Bugeaud was given the honor during all the years of fighting. It was an encounter of great delicacy. By making an exception, the emir paid honor to Bugeaud yet, in its manner of orchestration, he had increased his prestige among the Arabs. The French general had also paid homage to the emir by putting himself at his mercy, by sealing the treaty man to man. They were now friends and equals.

Bugeaud also had been out-maneuvered on every requirement set in Paris two months earlier.

CHAPTER TEN

An Uneasy Peace

KING LOUIS-PHILIPPE RATIFIED THE TREATY and the minister of war sent an aide to Oran to congratulate the general. Raison d'état had prevailed.

"We need peace to establish a solid base on our territory. We need time to familiarize the Arabs with our customs and our way of doing business in order to really make something of our colonization effort," Bugeaud explained to skeptical members of parliament. "After five or six years of peace, if war breaks out again, we will be in a much stronger position than we are today." The Chamber of Deputies, reflecting the feelings of the general population, had received news of the treaty's terms with indignation.

Many of Bugeaud's military colleagues shared the popular view. The treaty was a sellout. Governor-general Damremont, his rival in Algiers whom he had finessed out of the negotiation, spoke for many in uniform when he wrote Molé disavowing the agreement. "It makes the emir more powerful than he could ever have achieved by a victory on the battlefield, and places us in a precarious position confined within disadvantageous boundaries. It is not honorable because our claim to sovereignty rests on nothing and we have sold out our allies..." Old Mustafa Ben Ismail also understood the treaty's implications. "Now, I have nothing more to do than go to Mecca and do penance at the Kaaba for having trusted in France," he announced bitterly to officers in Oran.

The Tafna Treaty was Desmichels replayed, dividing supporters and opponents along similar lines — bow to reality and buy time, or stand on assertions of national honor without the resources to back them up. Bugeaud knew that France was preparing another campaign to take Constantine in order to consolidate its control of the east. This required peace in the western provinces dominated by Abd el-Kader. The treaty simply granted the emir what he already possessed in reality.

The army needed revamping, as well — its equipment, tactics and recruits. This, too, required time. Bugeaud had seen the ineffectiveness of slow, plodding European style warfare against a fluid power, one he described as having "no fixed location and whose vitality was in all the members of its organization."

The emir had reason to be pleased. The Tafna Treaty had effectively made him master of two-thirds of Algeria. Bugeaud had agreed to withdraw from Tlemcen, where Clauzel had established an inland base. The emir's de facto authority extended from Morocco to the Kadara River east of Algiers, blocking the army's ability to communicate overland with its eastern outposts at Bougie, Stora and Bone. The emir could freely engage in trade, so long as it was conducted through the ports controlled by France: Oran, Arzew, Mazagran and Mostaganem. Abd el-Kader could buy arms, gunpowder and war materiel from France, or elsewhere. He also agreed not to cede any ports to foreign powers without the agreement of France.

The touchy question of French sovereignty was finessed, thanks to adroit variations in the French and Arab versions. For France, only the French translation was considered the authoritative text, and for the Arabs, the Arab text was authoritative. Abd el-Kader had put his seal only to the Arab version.

The all-important Article 1 stated in the French version that the emir "recognized the sovereignty of France." The Arab version read that the emir "recognized that the Sultan was great," not even specifying who was the sultan. "Sovereignty" in the European sense was a difficult word to translate into Arabic. Ben Duran, who surely understood its meaning, knew that acknowledging French sovereignty was unacceptable to the emir. Bugeaud's Syrian translator knew too little French to appreciate the different nuances. With the help of Ben Duran's influence on the emir, the symbolism of submission, represented by the requirement of annual tribute to the French sultan, had been reduced to a one time "gift" of 30,000 measures of wheat and barley, and the delivery of 5,000 head of cattle. To Bugeaud's critics, France's position was no different than under Desmichels. Her occupation was limited to the same coastal towns and their buffer zones. Only now, the emir's position among the Arabs appeared vastly stronger.

જ

The treaty called for an exchange of consuls to smooth over problems and misunderstandings that would inevitably arise during its implementation. Bugeaud, an avowed monarchist, wanted his own man as "royal commissioner" to the emir's court in Mascara. Without consulting General Damremont, his nominal superior in Algiers, he selected for this important post a battalion commander, Colonel Menonville. Menonville was a veteran of past campaigns who had distinguished himself by his spirit of rectitude and conciliation, qualities Bugeaud thought would be desirable for the representative of a Christian power at an Arab court.

However, Menonville would only accept the assignment if his friend, Dr. Warnier, was his second. Warnier was a medical doctor who knew the countryside and the people well. He spoke Arabic and had many friends among the Arabs he had treated. He was also known to be a prudent, solid character knowledgeable of the mores and prejudices of the Arabs. By Warnier's later account, this first diplomatic mission to the emir under the Tafna Treaty was mined with duplicity, dishonor and suspicion on the French side that made for an embarrassing diplomatic debut.

Bowing to a minimum of politesse towards the governor-general, Bugeaud agreed to add to his delegation an interpreter recommended by Damremont, a certain Zaccar, a Syrian who had once wanted to be a priest. He was known to be cunning, overtly ambitious and servile at the same time. The head of the Arab Bureau had recommended him to act as the governor-general's eyes and ears.

The emir's representatives had arrived in Oran and Mostaganem as agreed in the treaty, but Menonville had still not left for Mascara. He was waiting for the "specific instructions" from Bugeaud that his general orders from Paris indicated he should receive before leaving for his new post. Warnier, impatient over their continued delay, finally told Menonville he would depart early the next morning. Bugeaud then told Menonville he would give him his specific orders the day of Warnier's departure. Warnier left early, agreeing to rendezvous later.

When Menonville finally caught up with him, Warnier noticed a change in his commander's demeanor. He seemed somber and depressed. Asked about the instructions, Menonville said only that he would talk about them later. Warnier assumed they were of a delicate nature and Menonville did not want to be overheard by their escorts. As they approached Mascara, they sent a rider ahead to announce the arrival of the king's royal commissioner. No one came out to receive the delegation. When they entered Mascara, no caid or notable welcomed them. The town was deserted. The delegation's arrival had been delayed so long, the emir had left the city, but without giving the local authorities any instructions.

Thus, the king's own men spent their first night at the emir's court in a barn that had been converted into an ammunition depot whose only other occupants were large rats. The next day was hardly better. They were transferred to a house near the emir's place, which was to be their consulate. However, it lacked European-style windows, chimneys, armoires and other conveniences, requiring Menonville to request military engineers from Oran to remodel their new home.

Menonville's mood continued to get worse. When pressed by Warnier, he would mumble some words of regret at having accepted the position. One day, Menonville exploded, blurting out to Warnier the dark secret that had so depressed him. Bugeaud had made additional agreements, secret ones, that Menonville found dishonorable for a French general. And he was to be an instrument of their execution.

Bugeaud had consented in writing to send into exile Mustafa Ben Ismail and other chieftains of the Smelas and Douairs the emir considered as troublemakers who would try to undermine the peace. There was also agreement that the emir would be supplied with rifles and gunpowder. For these goodwill gestures, the emir would give the general a gift of 100,000 francs. To the upright, good soldier Menonville, Bugeaud had shamefully sold out their brave allies to appease a vengeful emir. And the arms that Bugeaud was also willing to supply the emir, Menonville believed, would surely be used one day against French soldiers.

Three times, Menonville wrote Bugeaud asking to be relieved of his assignment. Three times Bugeaud denied his request. The worsening mental state of Menonville was aggravated by the irritating presence of the Syrian interpreter. It soon became apparent to Menonville that Zaccar was acting as a spy for his bosses in Algiers and did not consider himself in any way under his authority. Menonville began to nurse a deep dislike for Zaccar who hardly attempted to mask his true role, one that became overt the day he refused to sign a register acknowledging as his copies of an Arab translation he made of a letter to the emir written by Menonville. The only conceivable reason for not doing so would be that he had altered the original French content.

The alchemy of Menonville's silent hatred of Zaccar and the humiliating falseness he felt about his own position, led to his mental unraveling. Curiously, this happened as a result of Dr. Warnier's efforts to minister to Abd el-Kader's infant son, Abdallah.

Warnier knew the risks when the emir's wife sent an emissary begging for his immediate help. Yet, he left unhesitatingly, cantering the nine miles across the Plain of Ghriss to her family encampment in Cacherou where he found a two-year-old boy suffering from severe peritonitis.

The doctor's position was delicate. If he saved the boy's life, he would be a hero and give a boost to French prestige. If the boy died, he ran the risk of being accused of medical skullduggery. To avoid the latter, Warnier took precautions. He used only externally applied substances that had been provided by the family members themselves. Abd el-Kader's majordomo and family members were invited to witness his ministrations. The next day, Abdallah was no longer at death's door. Three days later, the boy was up and about. Everyone congratulated Warnier for his success. But no sooner had he returned to Mascara, than another messenger arrived with bad news. The convalescent had a relapse.

Again, Warnier galloped back to the family tent, armed with an enema bag flung over his shoulder. He learned that Kheira had violated one of his most important proscriptions. She had allowed Abdallah to eat an apple, a fruit that was uncommon in the desert, but much desired by the Arabs. Warnier told her what he needed to do to prevent his death. She refused. The Arabs considered an enema a form of medical sodomy. Kheira was afraid Abdallah would be mocked for receiving such a treatment once word got out beyond the tent. Twelve hours, later she changed her mind. It was too late. Warnier took it upon himself to tell the young mother the terrible news.

"God has taken your son."

"God wanted him. May His will be done." Kheira took his hand and kissed it affectionately. She thanked him for all his care and effort.

The next day, Warnier and Menonville attended the burial ceremony along with several thousand Arabs. No traces of illwill were shown toward the Frenchmen. The gratitude shown the doctor by the emir's family was enough to reassure the other Arabs of the commendable behavior of the French *tabib*, as the Arabs called Warnier.

Nevertheless, Zaccar used the episode to needle Menonville. He took a perverse delight in irritating Menonville with jibes, saying the Arabs would believe the boy had been poisoned by the doctor, though plainly this was not the case, and that there would be a violent massacre of the French delegation. The already emotionally overwrought Menonville persuaded himself that Zaccar was plotting with Arabs to deliver them his head and that the consulate would at any moment be invaded by a bloodthirsty horde. Menonville was soon carrying two loaded pistols with him at all times. Warnier tried vainly to calm his superior who, he believed, might easily shoot the first Arab to enter the building. Fearing an incident, and not wanting the outside world to know of the pitiful state of his commander, Warnier would not allow anyone to enter or leave the building. As for Zaccar, Menonville treated him as a prisoner and kept him in his sight at all times.

At dinner one evening, a heated argument broke out between Zaccar and Menonville. The commander attacked the interpreter with a knife. Warnier attempted to intervene but could not calm down his chief, realizing he had truly become a madman capable of shooting anyone who got in his way. Menonville was convinced Zaccar was going to give the Arabs a secret signal to attack that night. He ordered Zaccar to lie on the floor and ordered the servants, Warnier as well, to sit against the walls of the dining room. He then sat down in the middle of the room next to Zaccar armed with his pistols, ready for the imminent assault.

Sometime after midnight, Warnier heard two explosions. He looked up and saw his commander lying on top of Zaccar. Both lay motionless, covered in blood. From the positions of their bodies, locked in a grotesque, inverted death hug, Warnier concluded that Menonville had knelt in front of the supine interpreter and placed the barrel of one pistol on Zaccar's eye and the other on his own forehead and pulled the triggers simultaneously.

The Arab authorities would not believe that this was the act of a demented French officer, unaware that he had become unhinged by a devious interpreter and his sense of shame over the dishonorable orders he had received from Bugeaud. Their first thought was that this double murder had been the work of dissident Arabs who were against the peace and had created an incident to stir up hostilities. The local caid was terrified that the emir would hold him responsible for allowing this crime to take place and that his own head might fall. Thousands of Hachem cavalry arrived outside the walls of the city as the news of the assassination spread.

Rumors were flying. The French would arrive within twenty-four hours and destroy the town in retaliation and the Hachem had come to protect the inhabitants of Mascara. Others believed they had come to massacre the population for allowing the crime to occur. Calmer heads were saying the emir wanted peace, and if the emir wanted to re-ignite hostilities, this was not how he would have done it.

Warnier defused the situation by getting the Arabs to examine carefully the room where the deaths had occurred and to look at every tiny piece of evidence. He finally convinced them that their initial conclusion was a mistake.

&

Bugeaud's secret terms leaked out, as had Desmichels'. The general had agreed to deport a dozen of the Douair and Smela caids and aghas hostile to peace. He had also agreed to allow the emir to purchase 3,000 military rifles as well as iron and sulfur for gunpowder. The emir would, in turn, make a gift to Bugeaud of 180,000 francs or 100,000 boudjoux. Like Desmichels, the general later denied any such agreement.

The emir had insisted the Smelas and Douairs be relocated further west, beyond the Rio Saldo, away from Oran. He gave Bugeaud the names of ten chiefs he wanted deported. When Bugeaud proposed to the minister of war to remove troublemakers hostile to the treaty, he added that certain of them, including the old man, Mustafa Ben Ismail, had expressed a desire to go to Mecca. "I told them that was possible and the government might pay them a nice pension to stay there." In fact, Bugeaud had already tried in vain to get Ben Ismail to go to Mecca for the good of his soul, but the old *makhzen* was not that concerned about his soul.

Bugeaud argued that Ben Ismail was a demanding and rapacious intriguer who thought only of his own interests. He kept for himself one-third of the money France paid his troops, protected thieves and assassins and could not be trusted, Bugeaud told the minister. (The same reasons the emir never appointed Ben Ismail to a high position in his government.) The war minister required that any such "removal" be at their request, that it be in writing and be publicly known. There could be no indication that such actions were in response to demands of the emir.

This condition alone would have made it impossible for Bugeaud to carry out the secret agreement. Then he learned that Mustafa Ben Ismail was going to be named brigade commander for native troops by King Louis-Philippe. This not only made the old *makhzen* the first Algerian general in the history of the French army, but also untouchable. Indignation was rampant in the army when word spread of Bugeaud's secret agreements. "France has climbed a bit too low in consenting to treat with a miserable little marabout...Bugeaud has been woefully befooled," wrote an officer for the local army newspaper, *Le Moniteur*. Bugeaud instructed Warnier to destroy his letters to the emir in which he agreed to relocate the tribes and to deport certain of the chiefs. His attempt to get the Douair and Smela chiefs to take a holy vacation to Mecca failed abysmally.

As for the money from the emir, when the scandal later became public, Bugeaud forthrightly explained that the money was not for him. Eighty thousand was going to be distributed to some of his officers and one hundred thousand was for repairing roads in his district in the Dordogne. Before a military tribunal that investigated the scandal, he admitted with his customary candor, "I declare to all my officers that I committed an act unworthy of a member of the nobility and the dignity of my command."

When the minister asked Bugeaud to explain why he hadn't been informed of these supplementary demands, the general replied in his offhand way. "There are things which I haven't told you because it would require volumes. I have smoothed over many difficulties which I have not bothered you with, and finally, because one can't and shouldn't talk about everything." Furthermore, Bugeaud explained, the gunpowder and lead that he agreed to supply the emir were things that could be purchased through Morocco, and even in peacetime the Arabs use huge amounts of gunpowder. "Besides the powder consumed for hunting, there is hardly a celebration, a reception of a chief, a marriage or other event when they don't burn a lot of powder," he added.

At Bugeaud's request, Warnier told the emir that the gift of 180,000 francs could be forgotten. What Menonville had not known was that the Ministry of War had made liberal use of money to lubricate the peace process.

Negotiations had bogged down in early May as a result of Abd el-Kader's stubbornness. He insisted on maintaining the prerogatives of the Desmichels Treaty, but also demanded the French abandonment of Tlemcen and Rachgoun Island, while politely offering to bear the cost of moving all the garrisons' baggage to Oran. An exasperated Bugeaud was ready to use force, yet he realized his supply capabilities were inadequate and his men not ready for campaigning in the summer heat. His one clear requirement was to get a treaty signed so French forces would have a free hand to besiege Constantine again in the fall.

The useful Ben Duran had been authorized by the war ministry to dispense up to 300,000 francs, as "gifts" to help bridge gaps between the French and the Arabs. Of that, 100 thousand francs had been promised Miloud Ben Arrach, the emir's foreign minister and 60,000 for the emir's influential majordomo, Haj el-Jilali. These men and others around the emir may well have tipped the balance in favor of the treaty when it was discussed on May 27, at a gathering of influential tribal leaders and marabouts from all over the province held by the banks of Habra River.

There were important leaders strongly opposing peace with France — genuine fanatics who opposed any compromise with the invader; those who thought the emir was becoming too ambitious; others who preferred their independence to the discipline of the emir's authority, but would use the argument of faith to support their opposition. Abd el-Kader wanted the decision on the treaty terms to be seen as a national one, even if justified on religious grounds. The argument for peace ultimately hung on a distinction: a peace imposed by the enemy and a peace that was solicited by the enemy. Nowhere does the Koran recommend the useless shedding of blood. If the infidel is willing to sheath his saber and accept terms dictated by Muslims, then peace is acceptable. And the emir, his supporters argued, had dictated terms accepted by the enemy.

Once the treaty was signed, the war ministry opened another account to pay "gratuities" to several individuals in the emir's court who had helped turn the negotiations around. One hundred and twenty thousand francs were authorized for Menonville to distribute — half to Ben Duran for his role as interlocuter to the Arabs and the rest to selected Arab chieftains who had argued for peace. But Menonville, suffering from acute paranoia, killed himself before he could carry out this assignment.

Ben Duran was less interested in money than in security for his family and his status. For his services, he asked the ministry for an annual pension of 5000 francs in the name of his children, and for himself, he wanted French nationality and the Legion of Honor. Bugeaud wrote to the war minister that Ben Duran "had worked zealously for peace," and a reward was justified. Yet, Bugeaud did not approve of giving him French citizenship. "It would be a mistake to give cunning and intriguing Jews French citizenship which they would then use to fleece us."

Bugeaud also wanted something: to return to France in time for the parliamentary elections scheduled for November fourth. He would be coming home triumphantly as the man who brought peace for his overtaxed constituents uninterested in glory. His job was done, he wrote the ministry. The minister of war thought differently. General Bernard told Bugeaud that he could return to France after three conditions were satisfied: when Constantine was retaken, the emir paid tribute to France and the matter of the eastern boundaries was settled.

In early October 1837, four months after Tafna, General Damremont besieged Constantine — this time successfully. France's honor was restored, but victory cost the governor-general his life. The emir did make a partial delivery of cattle to Oran, which he interpreted as a "gift" and the French as "tribute," but the third condition was not mentioned when, in November, Bugeaud reiterated to the minister that he was not needed anymore. In December, the minister authorized Bugeaud's return to his estates in the Dordogne.

A new governor-general had been appointed to wrestle with the poisonous ambiguity of the Tafna Treaty. An artillerist of renown, Marshal Sylvain-Charles Valée was the opposite of the independent-minded Bugeaud. Cold, dignified and of solid character, he was considered controllable even if his personality left something to be desired. "Silent as a tomb, mulish as a Breton, capricious as a pretty woman, as attractive as a prison door and as polite as a bear," a junior officer described him years later. Like the Comte d'Erlon after the Desmichels treaty, his instructions were to sort out the boundary issues in France's favor without re-igniting war with the emir.

෬෨

In reality, peace was more harmful to the emir than war, an irony most of the imperialists obsessed with lines on the map and formal declarations of submission overlooked. This simple truth was missed by all but the most astute Frenchmen. A prolonged peace would have resulted in the internal collapse of the emir's so-called empire had the French not succumbed to their own *amour propre*, for there was a deeper truth at work than that reflected in the flimsy pieces of paper to which France attached so much significance.

This contradiction soon became clear to Warnier and the observant Captain Daumas, the new consul in Mascara. In reality, Abd el-Kader's nation-in-the-making was no more than a fragile federation held together by personal charisma, his wise use of fear and forgiveness to punish and motivate, and Muslims' inherent respect for religious law.

Yet, the law was also the emir's problem. His title was Commander of the Faithful. But if he was now an ally and friend of France, what legitimacy did he have to coerce tribes to pay onerous taxes? And how could he be flexible with the French if the law forbade Muslims to live under non-Muslim rule unless by consent? And how could he allow tribes to choose French protection without his goal of unification disintegrating like a house of sand? Such questions were at the heart of the Habra debates over ratification of the treaty.

Internal divisions among the tribes would eat away at the emir's power in peace more quickly and at a much lower cost to France than by trying to break the emir by force of arms, which only strengthened his cause. Warnier passed these observations on to his new commander in Algiers and to his friends in Paris. But, to fight by not fighting was neither in the DNA of the military, nor conducive to career advancement. Not surprisingly, this wise counsel from France's representatives in Mascara was ignored by the ministry, yet its accuracy was demonstrated the following year.

CHAPTER ELEVEN

The Emir's Frenchman

G ROW OR DIE. Add or subtract. Despite his sense of divine duty, the emir knew his position was inherently unstable. If he were not perceived as getting stronger, the tribes would perceive him as getting weaker. The French obsession with having their sovereignty acknowledged by the emir differed little from the emir's need to obtain submission from all the tribes over which he claimed sovereignty. Abd el-Kader's lofty ambitions to reform and unite the tribes made him vulnerable to the petty ambitions and jealousies of lesser men.

Sidi Mohammed el-Tidjani was a respected marabout among tribes throughout the Sahara and beyond, but especially in the south. His influential Tidjani Brotherhood was centered in a fortified oasis called Ain Mahdi, near Laghouat, on the edge of the Sahara. Tidjani's submission would establish the emir's authority over other tribes in the Sahara — tribes generally more enamored with hunting, trading, fighting and poetry than with their religious rectitude.

Troublemakers spread rumors that sheik Tidjani wanted to check the power of the emir and was plotting against him. Others whispered to Tidjani that the emir had eyes on his fabled treasury, a useful reserve for fighting the French or hostile tribes. Still other marabouts wanted the emir to believe that there was widespread unhappiness with Tidjani. A certain Haj Issa (or Haj Jesus), a local marabout in Laghouat, detested Tidjani and offered horses to the emir as a sign of submission, assuring him that he had thousands of men ready to join the emir were he to come south to demand Tidjani's submission. The emir made Haj Issa his caliph of Laghouat, unaware that Haj Issa was using him to bolster his position in a power struggle against factions sympathetic to Tidjani.

Late spring, 1838, the emir set off from his new capital of Tagdempt in the blazing June heat to aid the dissidents in Laghouat, 180 miles to the south. Haj Issa had led him to believe that his small force of 400 regular cavalry, 2,000 regular infantry and 400 Kougoulis would be augmented by local Arabs unhappy with Tidjani. Fifteen hundred camels carried food and water, cannonballs, disassembled artillery pieces, wives, tents and personal baggage. The women rode in their *âatatiches* — small tents shaped like chestnut pods mounted on their camels that protected them from the sun as they undulated along on their "ships of the desert," while grinding corn or sieving flour.

Marching 3000 soldiers for eight days through barren high plateaus into a waterless desert would prove to the tribes that no one who defied the emir's claim to sovereignty would escape punishment. Neither distance, hunger, heat, thirst nor fatigue was an obstacle to his army, one that had come prepared only for a quick one-month campaign. As he neared Ain Mahdi, Abd el-Kader sent an emissary to sheik Tidjani, demanding his submission.

"Tell your master," Tidjani replied, "I am neither an enemy nor a rebel. I am ready to recognize and have my inhabitants recognize the authority of the sultan, but that as the head of a religious brotherhood. I do not occupy myself with the things of this world and wish to avoid all contact with princes invested with temporal power. My ancestors have suffered too much from them. My intentions are peaceful, but if the sultan wants to see me, he must knock down my walls and run swords through the chest of my brothers."

Tidjani had, indeed, bad memories of temporal power. His brother had been imprisoned by Bey Hassan of Oran and an uncle put to death thirty years earlier when he had led a revolt against Turkish misrule.

The emir knew nothing about siege warfare, a form of fighting contrary to the Bedouin style of hit and run. He asked Leon Roches, the newest member of his staff of foreign advisors,* whether a siege of Ain Mahdi could be successful. Roches was not expert in these matters. He needed to get inside the walls before he could recommend anything. Roches offered to go on a peace mission to negotiate a settlement with Tidjani that would also allow him to assess the defenses of the city.

"That will mean almost certain death," the emir warned.

"Have you not told me that the hour of death is written in the book and man cannot advance or retard it?"

---

* His foreign advisors generally were prisoners who defected to the emir's cause, often from the Foreign Legion, which explains the presence of Italian and Polish soldiers in his entourage.

The emir continued to protest, but he finally gave in to Roches' fearless insistence. "Omar," as he was known to the Arabs, would ride one of the emir's own horses and be guided by one of his most loyal men. As Roches prepared to leave that evening, the emir emerged from his tent. In a loud voice, for all to hear, Abd el-Kader implored God to cover "Omar" with the mantle of His protection.

♥

Who was this "Omar" so dear to the Commander of the Faithful? Six months after Tafna, this twenty-eight-year-old Frenchman had entered the emir's camp professing to be a convert to Islam. In fact, he was a quixotic, adventurer in pursuit of an imagined true love.

Leon Roches had experimented with the law and commerce in France when, in 1832, he decided instead to seek adventure. He joined his father, who had purchased a farm near Algiers. But Roches soon became bored and depressed, and sensed that the farm was failing. His father offered him the distractions of the local social circuit, but the banality and parochialism of "Algiers society" depressed Roches even more. That is, until one day he was invited to the house of a former minister of Dey Hussein where he met a shy and beautiful fourteen-year-old girl. He was instantly smitten by the young Khadijah, as was she by the swarthy, handsome Frenchman who was the first Christian she had ever met.

Roches couldn't get her out of his mind. He sought her out at social gatherings, yet they never found an opportune moment to speak openly of their emotions. Roches convinced himself that he had fallen hopelessly in love, a love undoubtedly inflamed by Khadijah's inaccessibility. Then, Roches fell seriously ill. One is tempted to conjecture lovesickness, but it seems to have been malaria, common among the colonists. He recovered only to learn that Khadijah was no longer circulating in society circles. From a chance conversation at a dinner party, he discovered she had married unwillingly an older man, but she was rumored to be in love with a young Frenchman.

Encouraged by this scanty report, Roches began to study Arabic. He tracked down Khadijah's former nanny, a Negress named Messaouda who, with the help of a few francs, became Roches's intermediary for carrying on a clandestine relationship. Khadijah's suspicious husband, however, moved her to Miliana, the capital of one of the emir's caliphates in Tittery. The Frenchman's quest was temporarily stymied.

Roches's love-inflamed interest in Arabic got him employment as an interpreter in the French army. When the Tafna Treaty was signed, our Gallic young Werther acquired new hope of obtaining the object of his desires. He resigned from the army to put into play a wild scheme to win his true love.

By the fall of 1837, Roches had become fluent in Arabic, had studied the Koran and knew enough about Islamic rituals to pass for a Muslim. The peace would now make it possible, he believed, to present himself as a convert to Islam. He could offer to help the emir build his new Islamic state. Once he gained the emir's confidence, he would ask him to use his influence to arrange a divorce for his true love, Khadijah.

Armed with his fanciful plan, Roches set off to find the emir, said to be camped near Miliana, along the Chlef River. Along the way, he told the local chieftains he had converted to Islam and wanted to meet the emir.

"He was alone at the end of his tent," Roches wrote later of their first meeting. "I approached slowly, keeping my eyes lowered, knelt before him and took his hand to kiss as was the custom. It was the first time I made an act of submission to a Muslim and it was repugnant."

"You are welcome here," the emir greeted him, "for every good Muslim must rejoice when he sees the numbers of true believers grow. Our holy Prophet has said, 'It will be more profitable to you at the great Judgment Day to boast of one Christian won for Islam than of one thousand slain in battle.' God has sent you to us and we must keep you, teach you and love you more than our other brothers."

Roches, who had adopted the name Omar, offered to the emir gifts of a new Lepage rifled musket and a French-Arabic dictionary.

"We should give presents to you, not you to us, but I appreciate your kindness and accept them. I never accept presents except from those I mean to like."

Roches approached the emir, but the emir withdrew and kissed the Frenchman on the shoulder, an honor reserved for persons of distinction.

Abd el-Kader's first concern was furthering the Frenchman's religious education. "It is not enough to say, 'I am a Muslim,'" the emir told him after a few days. "You must understand what that means. Do not follow the example of most of the Arabs in my camp. God had chosen me to regenerate them and to rekindle the flame in their stony hearts. They have been governed for centuries by ignorant soldiers who were Muslims in name only, and are used to cringing before cruel and unjust tyrants. But God in his mercy has driven out the tyrants whom our law forbids us to rise against, and has given us these Christians whom our ancestors attacked even in their own lands. God has now brought them here and forced us to make war to defend our homes, our women and children, and above all, our religion…"

The emir had a low opinion of the French. He thought they would be like the crusaders of yesteryear whom he admired — believers known for their bravery, generosity, and strict observance of their religious customs. He had been told that some of the French who had conquered Algiers didn't believe in God and that they built no churches, did not respect their ministers, didn't pray, broke their word and betrayed their own allies. "God will abandon them because they have abandoned Him."

After a few months with the emir, Roches wrote to a friend his impressions:

> His physiognomy is fluid and, despite his famous self-control, his face reflects the emotions that are stirring within. When he prays he is an ascetic; when he commands, he is a sovereign; when he talks of war, he is a soldier. When he talks with his friends about matters other than statecraft or religion, he is good humored and open, with an inclination toward self-deprecation. When he talks of his father, it is never without tears in his beautiful eyes.

Roches, now "Omar" to the Arabs, had become a confident of the emir, sharing privileges enjoyed only by Abd el-Kader's most-trusted servants. Roches often ate with the emir and had the honor of sleeping under his tent in the area provided for his Negro bodyguards — muscular former slaves, well-trained in the martial arts. Abd el-Kader frequently invited Roches to pray with him and used these occasions to further instruct him in the faith.

Roches had been in camp for a short time when the emir set out to do what certain tribes feared when the proposed treaty had been hotly debated at Habra: consolidate his power over the new territory he claimed for his rule. This required showing what was in store for a tribe that had collaborated with the French. The Zouatna were Kougoulis, Turkish half-breeds who had been living in the Djurdjura mountains of Kabylia for 300 hundred years. They had sided with the invader by accepting the caid appointed by the former governor-general, Clauzel. Their mixed origins would allow Abd el-Kader to attack them with less risk of stirring up a fraternal hornet's nest among other native Berbers in Kabylia.

At first, the caid of the Zouatna offered gifts as a sign of submission, but Abd el-Kader demanded more than gifts for the atonement of their sins. The emir imposed a war tax that exceeded the tribe's ability to pay, providing the justification he needed to attack.

"The time for leniency is past," the emir declared to his questioning troops as they prepared to kill fellow Muslims. "The Zouatna allied themselves with the Christians when Arabs were shedding blood in jihad," he explained to his men. "They refused to pay the taxes prescribed by the Koran." The day of punishment had come.

Roches later witnessed the fate of eighteen prisoners. Abd el-Kader sat on the ground, eyes down as he rapidly worked his beads, silently pronouncing God's ninety-nine names. The only sound was the chattering teeth of a shivering old man.

"You have revolted against God's law," the emir announced in a leaden voice. "You were taken prisoner with arms in your hands; God's law condemns you to die."

"Do not profane the name of God," cried out one of the prisoners. "You did not consult God's law when you despoiled and imprisoned our brothers in the west. You did not consult God's law when, having given yesterday your aman to a handful of Muslims, you today hurl thousands of soldiers against them… Order your executioners to strike. Death is a hundred times preferable to having submitted to you. We shall be awaiting you on that great day when God shall judge the victim and the executioner."

Some of the emir's sheiks tried to silence the man. Momentarily, he dominated the assembly with his loud brave voice, erect bearing and fierce eyes. The man berating Abd el-Kader was the French appointed caid of the Zouatna.

The emir looked up at the insolent prisoner with stony, angry eyes. The sheiks led the caid two steps forward and made him kneel. His head fell as his lips were reciting the act of faith. Abd el-Kader's hand sliced sideways a second and third time. The shivering old man's turn came. The executioner was about to strike the kneeling figure, when several children broke into the tent. They threw themselves at the emir's feet. A pretty little girl grabbed Abd el-Kader's hands and started kissing them.

"In the name of your mother, of your father's memory, of your children, in the name of God, please forgive my father," she cried out, clasping his neck.

The pall of horror that hung in the air a moment before, was instantly transformed. Eyes welled with tears that seconds earlier had been filled with bloodlust. The emir's expression became gentle. He kissed the girl's forehead and made a sign for the other prisoners to be taken away and to remove the grisly evidence of the executions.

A shaken Roches found out the next day that the rescue of the old man had been organized by the emir's personal attendant, Ben Fakha, a former slave. He was in charge of the emir's tent, and been his trusted servant for years. He had given Abd el-Kader some of his first riding lessons as a boy, accompanied him on all his expeditions and was treated as a confidant. Ben Fakha was known to have a rough sense of humor, but a heart of gold. On more than one occasion he had tempered the emir's strict sense of justice with mercy.

For two years, "Omar" would be both a friend and secretary to the emir, enjoying a relationship shared by no other European in Abd el-Kader's entourage.

❧

As Roches and his guide approached the north gate on the morning of June 2, 1838, only the jutting towers and high terraces of Ain Mahdi were visible through the lush gardens and palm trees that ringed its thirty-foot-high walls. Inside were 2,000 inhabitants, including deserters from the French army, three Jewish families, various Arab refugees and students attending the zawiya.

A guard hailed him from the rampart. What was his business? He had a letter from his sultan for their marabout. It would be given to their master. Strangers were not permitted within the walls. No, it had to be personally delivered. Roches turned to leave when a voice called out in French.

"Wait, sir. I will get the marabout to let you enter."

A rope was dropped from the wall. Roches pulled himself up to come face-to-face with a French military engineer who had deserted the emir's camp. He supposed that the Frenchman had persuaded his new masters that, like himself, Roches had been recruited by Tidjani's spies and abandoned the emir.

Roches found himself inside a small courtyard surrounded by ribbed, gothic-style arches supporting tiled walls punctuated with small windows protected by intricately wrought iron grills. He could make out the shapes of women behind them, but before he had time to think about their lot, a young boy appeared with a gentle expression.

"Are you Omar, the son of Roches," he asked.

"Yes, but who are you? Why do you know my name?"

"That doesn't matter, but listen. The people of the town want my father to take your head. He will find it hard to refuse them, for they think you are a spy. The Negress, Messaouda, recognized you from the window and sent me to save your life. Here, take this rosary. It belongs to my father. He gives it to those to whom he wants to give his aman. May God be with you."

When the boy disappeared, a dozen Negro guards arrived and roughly grabbed Roches and hustled him to their master's ornate receiving hall. Roches found a huge man of bronze complexion who looked to be in his forties, seated on a platform covered with cushions. He had a thin beard and was obese, though his smooth face was "not without dignity or distinction." Sidi Mohammed el-Tidjani looked at Roches with an expression of curiosity and benevolence before turning severe.

"You serve an ungrateful master and a poor servant of God who knows you are devoted enough to go on a death mission for him. You have come to look at the town and examine its walls, but you know the fate of spies. Prepare to die, unless you are willing to leave your master to serve me. In that case, I will reward you with great riches."

"Matters of life and death are in God's hands. Neither your threats nor your promises tempt me. You don't know my lineage if you think me capable of betraying my master. Go ahead and have your men slit the throat of a person who came to you in a spirit of trust and who has in his hands a sign of your aman," Roches replied, as he raised Tidjani's rosary above his head for all to see.

"Who gave that to you?"

"I asked your son for it. The poor boy didn't dare refuse me."

"God wanted you to have it. You are also a faithful servant. Go tell your master what you have seen here and maybe your report will cause him to reconsider this aggression against me. It has no justification and is bound to fail. Tell him I bear no ill will toward him and I desire only peace and tranquility between God's creatures."

Tidjani summoned his chief of the guards to show Roches whatever he wanted to see. He saw twelve-foot-thick and thirty-foot-high walls, ample supplies of food, firewood, ammunition and the five wells that would supply the inhabitants with water. The defenders were few, 800 he estimated, but they seemed tough and determined. After the tour, Tidjani asked the Frenchman if he still believed Abd el-Kader could take his town.

"He will, if it takes him ten years. His will is unshakeable, no matter how great the obstacles. I beg you to surrender and avoid the useless shedding of blood." Roches started to hand back the rosary. Tidjani told him to keep it.

ᘒ

Roches was touched by the emir's look of relief when he returned to camp. The rumor had been circulating that "Omar" was dead. Abd el-Kader listened to the Frenchman's frank assessment of the difficulty of taking the town, then wrote messages to all his caliphs ordering them to send artillery and more supplies. He also sent Sheik Tidjani another ultimatum. But this time, Tidjani's reply was laced with contempt. "I was a chief when you were still a child. I don't understand what you seek to accomplish here. Perhaps you are used to dealing with women, but I will show you true lions. You will never set foot in my town."

Before launching his first attack on the outer wall, Roches heard Abd el-Kader explain to his uncertain, questioning soldiers why they were fighting a fellow Muslim and venerable marabout.

"Every Muslim who revolts against the authority invested in me, who does not accept my stature as sultan in order to repel the invaders from the land of the faithful, by the fact of his rebellion, provides assistance to our enemies, and thus should be considered an enemy of Islam. You who may die fighting those inside these walls will receive the same eternal compensation reserved for dying in combat against infidels."

Roches was put in charge of mining the walls after two failed attempts to breach them. Abd el-Kader told him to draft the services of a Polish deserter from the Foreign Legion — an artilleryman who went by the name of Hassan. Hassan spoke no French and little Arabic, but Roches discovered they could communicate with the help of their common classical education: Latin. So they tunneled together by speaking the language of Cicero. Roches soon discovered that the townsmen had built counter-mines that became arenas of grim hand-to-hand combat in the Stygian darkness. Informants for Tidjani had revealed the location of the tunnels.

In October more siege equipment arrived. From Morocco came four cannons and from Valée in Algiers, a goodwill gesture of four hundred artillery shells and special fuses, a compass and a theodolite. Ain Mahdi was bombarded for three days without effect. Many of the shells didn't explode and the defenders, with mock courtesy, threw them back over the walls.

Bad food and exhaustion took its toll on Roches, who had undertaken new, camouflaged mining activity that he had kept secret even from the emir. In late October, Roches stumbled into the emir's tent with a raging fever and suffering from dysentery. He pleaded for help; otherwise, he was ready to die.

Abd el-Kader first calmed him with *schieh*, a desert version of absinthe derived from the mugwart family of plants. Roches lay with his head resting against the emir's knees. He removed "Omar's" turban and gently massaged his head until he feel asleep. Roches woke up later that night feeling refreshed, only to witness a scene he would never forget.

"The smoking wick of a lamp dimly lit the emir's tent. Barely three paces from me, the emir was standing with his arms raised over his head. He was gazing upwards. His lips were slightly parted, he seemed to be uttering a prayer, yet they didn't move. He had reached a state of ecstasy. His spirit was so intent upon reaching heaven that he seemed to be levitating. I had observed his prayers and his mystical élan before, but that night he presented an extraordinarily gripping image of faith. Thus so, must the great saints of Christianity also have prayed."

Roches wondered afterwards whether he owed his recovery to the magnetic powers of Abd el-Kader's hands, or to the emir's prayers. One thing was certain. Throughout the camp, all the Arabs believed Omar's life was saved thanks to the emir's intercession with the powers above.

૭૩

The siege dragged on into November 1938. Valée's cannonballs had bounced off the thick city walls. Abd el-Kader's new caliph, Haj Issa, turned out to be a duplicitous nobody. The thousands of horsemen he promised would join the emir's jihad never materialized, nor did they even protect the supply caravans that came down from Mascara and Oran with much needed supplies.

Roches continued his secret mining project. They dug at a depth of fifteen feet, in order to pass below a moat and to place explosives under Tidjani's palace. The tunneling had just been completed when a supply caravan arrived at the emir's camp.

The caravan brought two mediators — the emir's respected older brother, Mohammed Said, and Mustafa Ben Thami, his stern but scholarly brother-in-law. Both men were disturbed by this battle of marabouts. Abd el-Kader's prolonged absence was causing trouble at home. His tribal allies were restless and Tidjani's stubborn resistance was turning him into a hero. The two men had come to counsel the emir in moderation and prudence. Roches requested a meeting with Mohammed Said. He didn't want to blow up the town either and risk harming his beloved Khadijah, if she were indeed there. The two agreed to work in concert. Roches asked him to be present when he briefed the emir on the progress of the siege.

The next day, Roches told the emir he had important details to explain to him alone. When Abd el-Kader dismissed the functionaries in his tent, leaving only his brother, Roches pretended to hesitate, and looked skeptically at Sidi Mohammed.

"Speak, Omar. My dear older brother represents for me Muhi al-Din, our beloved father. I have nothing to hide from him. He is my master." Roches explained how his construction of a counter siege rampart for attacking the city was in reality a ruse to divert attention from a new tunnel that was being dug at night in a disguised location amid the earthworks. He talked of the effect it would produce and his plan of assault. The emir's eyes seemed to light up. "Tomorrow," he said in his jerky, staccato voice that signaled excitement, "I will order you to set off the charges. The day of victory is near."

"Remember our father," Mohammed Said injected gently, "and how he was known for his gentleness and mercy. It is God who sent me to you, to have you listen to the words that our father would say if he were alive. Think, as Muhi al-Din might have: Sidi Mohammed el-Tidjani has been a victim of Turkish tyranny and cruelty; the demons of discord have made him distrustful, and yet perhaps his motives are pure. Think of the blood that will flow if you attack the city. Think about the women and children and old people who will be massacred by your soldiers who will be overcome by their desire for revenge for the deaths of their comrades. And, Omar," Mohammed Said looked at him intently, "are you really certain of success? And you, my brother, remember that the desert tribes in the south detest your theocratic rectitude and are waiting for the moment to attack your army."

Sidi Mohammed asked Abd el-Kader to give him several hours to meet with Tidjani to find a solution that would avoid further bloodshed and yet safeguard the dignity of the sultan. "This is my prerogative as head of our ancestor's zawiya. This is my obligation as a Muslim, for God is with the merciful."

The next day, accompanied by Roches, Sidi Mohammed met Tidjani and his counselors. The two marabouts embraced each other and had a long discussion alone. Mohammed Said then signaled to Roches to come over and confirm to Tidjani the information that a huge explosive charge had been buried beneath his palace and the city walls.

"And you know," Roches added after describing the device, "Omar, never lies, even to save his life."

"What he did not tell you," Sidi Mohammed added, "was that before setting off the mines, he pleaded with the sultan for a chance to find a peaceful solution." Tidjani's face dissolved into a mixture consternation and scepticism as he looked hard at the Frenchman before joining his counselors in another room. After a lengthy discussion, one of Tidjani's servants invited them in. Sidi Mohammed sat next to Tidjani. Roches, left standing, was asked to repeat what he had said earlier. He ended his description of the devices and the damage they would cause, vowing in a loud voice, "I swear before God that I am telling the truth and that my most sincere desire is for peace between my master and yours!"

The council voted unanimously to authorize Tidjani to negotiate a peaceful solution. Several days of discussions with Sidi Mohammed Said and Ben Thami produced a six-point agreement: Tidjani would pay a sum that would compensate for the cost of the siege; Tidjani would evacuate the city within forty days; he was free to take all his personal wealth and belongings without exception; the inhabitants were free to leave with all their weapons and belongings; Abd el-Kader would raise the siege and withdraw twenty-four miles during the forty day period; as guarantee for executing the terms, Tidjani would hand over his son to the emir. After the city had been abandoned, it would be destroyed.

On December 3, 1838, Abd el-Kader reviewed his army and praised his men for their courage and endurance. Omar received the most distinguished decoration of all — the *richa*, a headdress of seven ostrich plumes first used by the Prophet Mohammed to reward his fighters. But decorations were not uppermost on Roches's mind.

Three families from Algiers living in Ain Mahdi had asked for safe conduct to Algiers. This was easily obtained with the help of Sidi Mohammed's influence over the emir. One of the names on the list was Messaouda, Khadijah's nanny and former co-conspirator with Roches. Suspended between fear and joy, Roches arranged a meeting with her. When Messaouda was escorted into his tent, she fell to her knees sobbing. "She is dead. She is dead!"

Khadijah had been with her husband in Ain Mahdi, where her health had been deteriorating. When she recognized Roches in the courtyard that first day, she had aroused the sympathy of other women in the harem for the Frenchman she was sure would be killed. The mother of Tidjani had sent her grandson to bring Roches the rosary that saved his life. But the shock of joy mixed with the stress of the siege had aggravated her sickness. She died, Messaouda explained, asking that God bestow his forgiveness and blessings upon her beloved "Lioune." Khadijah's husband also died at Ain Mahdi. He was the only person during the six-month siege to get hit by a cannonball.

CHAPTER TWELVE
Jihad

THE DELIVERY OF 400 CANNONBALLS to Ain Mahdi didn't have the effect Marshall Valée had intended — not on the siege and not on the emir. It had been a poisoned gift. Their arrival had temporarily raised the morale of the emir's troops demoralized by the tenacity of Tidjani's defenders. It had also tarnished the image of the emir in the eyes of tribes that disapproved of his alliance with the infidels. Nor did the gesture soften, as Valée had hoped, the emir's opposition to the French interpretation of the boundary clause of the treaty.

The ink on the Tafna Treaty was barely dry when the translation of the Arab word *fauk* in Article 2, defining boundaries, became for France the overriding issue to be renegotiated. The question of the eastern boundary that Bugeaud had avoided before returning home in December of 1837 had landed now on Valée's desk. His orders were to get the boundary issue settled in France's favor without starting a war.

It was hard for the French to deny that Abd el-Kader was right about the correct translation of fauk. The word meant "above," not "beyond." The emir had proposed to Valée to settle the matter by having twenty Arabs randomly selected who would be asked to define fauk. If the replies supported the French interpretation, the emir was willing to concede the disputed territory. Valée wisely declined the offer. The Arab versions of the treaty posted around Algiers were removed. Article 2 defined areas reserved for France in the province of Algiers as "Algiers, the Sahal and the Mitidja Plain to the Kadara River in the east."

But the river changed names as it flowed north, hence "above" referred to the Kadara and its alternate names. The Kadara and *au dela*, or "beyond," as the French translation of the treaty read, would be meaningless. To say that the limit was the Kadara "and beyond" would mean there was no boundary. Abd el-Kader refused to accept this nonsensical interpretation.

Valée argued that the matter of boundaries was the only question that threatened a lasting peace. The emir was evasive, conciliatory and yet adamant that the treaty read "and above," not "and beyond." His ultimate argument was always the same: he could not abandon tribes that had declared loyalty to him.

Nevertheless, Abd el-Kader had been anxious to keep the peace in order to consolidate his emerging Arab nation and to prepare for the likelihood of new hostilities with France. Back in March 1838, three months before embarking on the Ain Madhi adventure, Abd el-Kader had sent Miloud Ben Arrach to Paris. With him were Judas Ben Duran and several other members of his "Jewish court," armed with bales of much sought after ostrich feathers, six magnificent Arab horses, Berber rugs, jewel encrusted yatagans and other objects prized by Europeans. Officially, the purpose of the delegation was to offer these gifts to the royal family as a sign of their new friendship and desire for peace between the two peoples. In reality, the goal of the delegation was to inveigle itself into the court's good graces to plead the emir's case directly with the king.

Alerted by Valée of the likely attempt by the emir to circumvent Algiers and play on French political divisions, officials refused to allow themselves to be drawn into any discussions about the treaty. The position was firmly maintained that the Arabs' visit was a courtesy call by the emir's representatives, not an occasion for renegotiating Tafna. All discussions about the treaty were to be held with the governor-general in Algiers.

After three months of polite evasions and being feted by the French as a salon celebrity, Miloud Ben Arrach realized that their plan to outmaneuver Valée had failed. He returned to Algiers to discuss modifications with the governor-general who, it had become clear, possessed the sole authority to resolve the issue of boundaries for the French government.

On July 4, 1838, Ben Arrach, freshly impressed by the power and wealth of France, reached an understanding with Valée on modifying the treaty — the July annex as it became known. When Ben Arrach had protested that it still needed ratification by the emir, Valée exploded. "Then why are you wasting my time? You are supposed to have full powers to act on the emir's behalf." Valée insisted that Ben Arrach put his own seal on their agreement. Its ratification, he argued, would make the peace endure. Valée also knew that whatever the treaty might say, however foolish Bugeaud had been, raison d'état required the army have overland access to Constantine once it had fallen under French control.

Not until January 1839, did the emir finally meet with Ben Arrach for the first time since his dispatch to Paris in March of the previous year. "Never! Never!" he shouted at Ben Arrach, outraged by his audacity to have put his seal to the annex. "I will never ratify an agreement that will give the French a land route between Algiers and Constantine and make me lose the advantages gained from their carelessness."

ⴰ

Both sides knew war was inevitable, though neither side wanted it — yet. Valée was frustrated by his orders to get the eastern boundary renegotiated without provoking a war with the emir. So, he used petty irritants to punish the emir. Valée refused to approve the emir's choice for consul in Algiers, the Italian merchant, Carlo Garavini, who also represented the United States. The Frenchman rightly feared that Abd el-Kader might use this connection to get the Americans to support his cause. He invented excuses to throw the emir's commercial agents in jail or expel them from the city, though they were permitted under the terms of the treaty. Muslims who wanted to leave Algiers and live in the emir's territory were mistreated.

These measures added to the illwill caused by Bugeaud's inability to fulfill the secret terms and the bad translations of the treaty, becoming, like a marriage going sour, an irreversible tide of bickering and mutual recrimination. The new governor-general may have had his orders but he inherited a treaty that had left Algiers out of the negotiations. Valée had little goodwill to offer, and even less of a stake in its success.

With "Omar" translating for him, Abd el-Kader had appealed directly to King Louis-Philippe in February.

"Great King of the French! God has appointed each of us to govern some of his creatures. You are in a position far superior to mine by the number, power and riches of your subjects; but on both of us He has imposed an obligation to make our people happy. Let us look together at our positions, and you will agree that on you alone depends the happiness of both our nations. 'Sign,' you say, 'and if you refuse there will be war.' Well, I will not sign, yet I want peace and only peace...

"If war breaks out again there will be no more trade, no more security for your colonists, prices will go up and production down, the blood of your soldiers will be shed in vain and it will be partisan war to the death. I am not so foolish as to believe I can oppose your troops head on, but I can harass them ceaselessly. I shall lose ground, no doubt, but I will have on my side knowledge of the country, the frugality and toughness of my troops, and more, the arm of God who supports the oppressed.

"If, however, you wish for peace, our two countries will be as one. The least of your subjects will enjoy the most perfect security among the tribes. The two peoples will intermix more and more and you will have the glory of having introduced into our lands that civilization of which the Christians are the apostles."

Was the emir cynically trying to buy more time or was he sincere in his expressions of amity? Most likely he was sincere and trying to buy time. He had Roches at his elbow urging him to make peace and telling him not to be misled by the divisions reported in the French press. France, Roches insisted, was in Algeria to stay.

Valée sent his son-in-law, Commander de Salles, on a mission to persuade the emir to approve the treaty modifications obtained from Ben Arrach. In advance of de Salles' arrival, Abd el-Kader had summoned a conclave of legal scholars to discuss the modifications presented by Ben Arrach. The emir emerged with a sad look on his face, surrounded by his scholars with tears in their eyes. They could not give de Salles the response he wanted. Their religion, they explained, was an insurmountable obstacle to accepting the modifications. Islam forbade the emir to abandon tribes that had sworn allegiance to him. And, if he were to move them into his territory, there would not be sufficient space for asylum. De Salles later described the display as "theatrics."

De Salles learned here for the first time of Bugeaud's secret terms. As proof of French bad faith, the emir pulled out the general's written promises he had kept: the delivery of 3000 rifles, relocation of Douairs and Smelas and exile of troublesome chiefs, including Ben Ismail. The emir still wanted to appear persuadable, not simply stubborn or capricious. So de Salles was invited to present Valée's terms to an assembly of seventy tribal chiefs. After hearing out the French officer, they discussed for three hours whether to ratify Ben Arrach's July 4 annex to Tafna. The ubiquitous Ben Duran had distributed French money to influence the voices of some of Abd el-Kader's chiefs, but this time to no effect. The decision of the chiefs was unanimous — rejection.

Frustrated by the failure of his son-in-law's meeting with the emir, Valée proposed that his government treat the annex as if it had officially settled the question of the disputed territories. Ben Arrach was, after all, the emir's foreign minister and the document bore his seal. Valée then offered his government three different responses to the stalemate: 1) to adopt an attitude of an injured party by protesting the assertions of the emir and hope with time and continued negotiation to convince him to give up his claims, 2) to simply declare renewed warfare, or 3) to occupy the disputed territory militarily while at the same time informing the emir that this was not to be viewed as a hostile act, but a temporary occupation until the matter was settled definitively. In time, the government would choose Valée's third proposal, believing that the emir might protest, but not dare to do anything.

☙

May 1839. With Roches translating, the emir appealed again to the king, this time using a mixture of flattery, politesse, naiveté and re-crimination. But was his naiveté feigned or genuine, like the Russian peasants who always wanted to believe in the essential benevolence of their Tsar, whose good intentions were twisted by the self-serving functionaries around him? Reminding the king that he had already sent three letters that, the emir assumed, must have been intercepted, he wrote, "You are too kind and courteous to refuse me the satisfaction of knowing your true feelings. May my last effort to communicate be successful."

"…Yes, your soldiers dream only of new fighting and fresh conquest. I am certain this is not your idea. You have not landed on the shores of Africa to exterminate the inhabitants or to drive them into the desert. You have not come to turn them into a nation of slaves but rather to implant in them a spirit of liberty which is your nation's most powerful lever, one which it has also granted to other countries.* Is it by force of arms and by bad faith that your representatives are going to achieve this

---

* Declaration of Human Rights, Napoleonic Code adopted in 1804 and spread throughout Europe.

end? If the Arabs end up believing that you have come to attack their religion and conquer their country, their hatred will become stronger than ever. They will escape my control and my authority, and our common hopes of fraternal cohabitation, will disappear forever..."

To General Gérard, the new Minister of War, he wrote: "... I thought that as one who has nothing to add to his military glory, you would never see in the French occupation of Africa an occasion for gaining some additional military glory. You, who know how to make war, surely must know how to make peace and appreciate its benefits.

"Why is peace threatened? For a few miles of territory and an overland route whose natural barriers make impractical. Doesn't France have enough glory, enough space, or must it acquire still more at the expense of my influence over the Arabs whom I am trying to keep under my control?

"...I pray to God that you use your influence on the king to affirm my peaceful intentions; and that you and the king's noble son might come and visit this country and meet the man whom you wrongly regard as you enemy. Once you recognize my sincerity and desire to do good, your genius and clarity of mind, will help me to calm — be it through civilizing or through arms — the fanaticism of populations which are only just beginning to value the advantages of peace and industry.

"May God give your armies victory so long as they fight for a just cause."

The emir's appeals were in vain. He was writing to a government that was paralyzed by the unspoken realization that it had put itself in an embarrassing situation, and was ready to do anything to escape it. The French government had misled the Parliament by declaring that the difficulties surrounding the Tafna Treaty had been smoothed over to France's advantage — meaning they had treated Ben Arrach's signature as authoritative on behalf of the emir.

&

In Abd el-Kader's mind, European "industry" meant armaments. Developing his own weapons-manufacturing capacity was the primary goal of the emir's modernization campaign in 1839. To keep the tribes under control, he needed a disciplined, standing army. For it to be effective, he needed the best weaponry of the day. He had surrounded himself with foreign experts and, while some were military deserters, others were professionals under contract from France and elsewhere.

In July, Roches had been sent by the emir to inspect the manufacturing facilities in various locations. When he arrived in Taza, Roches was shocked to learn that two days earlier a fateful decision had been taken during a gathering of chieftains. They had decided to declare jihad the next time France violated the treaty.

Prior to the meeting at Taza, the emir had asked for guidance from the most-respected legal scholars in Morocco, including the cadis Ali al-Tasuli and Abd al-Hadi al-Alawi. He had sent them a long list of written questions related to war and peace, to his assertion of authority over the tribes, and justifications for imposing taxes in time of peace, punishing rebellious tribes and for declaring a just war. On all these questions, the emir wanted reassurance that he was acting in accordance with religious law.* The emir's agents had brought back their lengthy responses, which affirmed the emir's authority to act as he was doing. These scholarly affirmations were backed by the gift of Sultan Abderrahman's caftan, a gift that officially vested the emir with the mantle of his authority. Roches protested, but saw that it was futile. He knew what he had feared most would now occur — that he would have to fight his own countrymen.

The emir, however, had other things on his mind. Abd el-Kader had frequently told Roches he should marry. Every Muslim knew a man was not complete without a family.

He had proposed giving him for a wife a member of his own family. Roches knew these suggestions from the emir were really commands that he had only deferred. One day the emir called Roches into his tent.

"Because war is imminent, I shall live in Tagdempt. You too will live there. I have ordered a house to be prepared for you and on your arrival you will marry the daughter of the former hakem of Medea." Roches began to protest, but the emir cut him short. "The matter is fixed. She knows the town. Her ways are more like your own than the girl from

---

* Algeria didn't have any recognized centers of religious scholarship on a level equal to those in Fez or Tunis. Because of proximity and a longer history of learning, Moroccan religious jurisprudence was considered authoritative for Muslims in Oran.

my own family that I originally intended. It has been decided by the council. You must obey." Three weeks later Roches found himself a reluctant married man.

Summer turned to fall. In late October, the emir and Omar were inspecting the factories at Tagdempt when two exhausted couriers galloped up to them. They had just ridden 180 miles in twenty-four hours to blurt out the news. The French had violated the treaty by marching through the Iron Gates — a narrow defile through the Biban Mountains that would give them their desired overland link from Algiers to the province of Constantine.

Speechless at first, Abd el-Kader began speaking rapidly to the messengers in short jerky phrases as he often did when he was emotional. Afterward, he became calm and said quietly to Roches, "God be praised. The infidel has broken the peace. We will show them we are not afraid of war." Immediately, the emir dictated letters to Roches for his caliphs.

When the emir had finished, Roches started to return to his tent. But the emir asked him to stay.

"Why are you sad, Omar," he asked sharply. "You ought to rejoice that God has now given you an opportunity to prove your faith."

"Have I not often told you that I dreaded war because it will bring disaster to you and your people. Cannot you understand that my heart is torn at the thought of fighting the country that bore me and which shelters my father?"

"Those are blasphemous words. Have you forgotten that the day you embraced Islam, our holy religion, you broke the bonds that tied you to the infidels? You speak like a Christian, Omar. Remember, you are a Muslim."

Flushed, Roches looked the emir in the eyes and blurted out his secret. "I am not a Muslim."

The emir was stupefied. He turned pale and his lips quivered. He raised his hands and eyes toward the sky. He went to the front of his tent and opened the flap in case anyone might have overheard. Abd el-Kader came back and said more gently, "You must have misheard me, Omar. Those words deserve death. Your mouth spoke, but not your heart. Drive out the devil in you and repeat with me the shahada."

"No! Let us make an end of the lies. I am not a Muslim. Take my life. It is yours," Roches answered trembling.

La'ib bi al-Din, the emir repeated, horrified at what he had just heard. A trifler of religion. A trifler of religion. The emir then stood up and said coldly, "Go! I leave God to punish your soul. Take your body out of my sight. Go, and never repeat before a Muslim the blasphemy I have heard, or I shall no longer be answerable for your life."

Roches bowed his head and withdrew. Dazed, he somehow managed to reach his tent where he collapsed in the grip of fever. A few days later he escaped to the French lines. "I have always believed," he wrote later, "that Abd el-Kader feigned not to notice my escape. I owe him an immense debt of gratitude."

℃

The emir left Tagdempt with a small escort for Medea, where he issued orders to his caliphs to prepare for jihad. He also sent to Valée a letter warning him of his intentions.

"...The son of the king set out with an army corps from Constantine to Algiers. This was done without the least warning to me, not even a few words to explain such a violation. You have now proclaimed all the territory between Algiers and Constantine to be no longer under my authority. So, the rupture comes from you. Nevertheless, so you do not accuse me of treachery, I am warning you that I am about to launch an attack. Warn all travelers, your garrisons, your farmers to take whatever precautions you deem necessary."

The governor-general had expected the emir to protest. But he had wrongly assumed he could mollify Abd el-Kader with soothing assurances. Valée, believing the letter was nothing more than the expected huffing and puffing, chose not to alarm the colonists in the Mitidja. Instead, he asked Ben Duran to take his reply to the emir. Ben Duran dutifully rode up to Medea, where he read Valée's letter out loud to the emir's war council.

Couched in soothing phrases, Valée asked him to have patience while he was awaiting orders from Paris. Things would be arranged in due time. Ben Duran, the consummate middleman, had been charged by the governor-general to dissuade the emir. "Reconsider your decision," he advised the council. "France is strong and its army is courageous and well-disciplined in the arts of war. You will be defeated." Ben

Duran continued disingenuously, "You are wrong to be offended by a minor event such as this. The French had no intention to deceive you. This was merely a distraction, a pleasure trip for the king's son."

The council adjourned to reconsider Ben Duran's words. That night, Ben Duran spoke privately with Abd el-Kader about the dangers of starting a war. He warned the emir that his resources were limited and his troops were not ready. "I know all that," the emir replied, "but my caliphs want war and some consider me an infidel because I have wanted to keep the peace."

On November 18, 1839, the council reconvened. Again, the caliphs and caids unanimously proclaimed jihad. But before dispersing, Abd el-Kader addressed the council one last time to express his own reserve.

"If jihad is what you want, I will agree, but on one condition. You will suffer losses, great trials and tribulations. Swear on the book of Sidi el-Bukhari that you will never abandon me as long as I am holding the banner of jihad." The emir had not forgotten the aftermath of Clauzel's sack of Mascara, when defeat had sent his allies flying away.

With one voice, a vow of loyalty to the emir was declared. Ben Duran was sent back to Algiers with a letter for Valée from the emir — an apology and a justification in one. Everyone wanted war, he explained. He didn't want it, but the majority did and he had to submit to the law. His heart was pure. He had warned him in advance. His cause was just.

The emir announced the unpopular special war tax, or *maaouna*. Abd el-Kader made the first extraordinary contribution to the state treasury by selling his family's jewelry. The emir's three caliphs surrounding Algiers were ordered to lead the attacks: Sidi Embarek Ben Allal of Miliana, El-Berkhani of Medea and Ben Salem, his Kabyle from Djurdjura. The emir reminded them of the tactics they were to use: No frontal assaults. Harass, and then harass more. Cut their lines of supply and communication. Exhaust their soldiers. Let the sun and heat do their work.

CHAPTER THIRTEEN
Total War

THE AMBITIOUS, SELF-ASSURED DEPUTY from the Dordogne was frequently consulted by the Parliament. The politicians were in a quandary. What to do about the situation in Algeria? How to deal with the devilish Emir Abd el-Kader? How to go about colonization? While General Valée was grappling with the Arab onslaught, Robert-Thomas Bugeaud propounded with conviction and clarity what needed to be done.

"A restrained occupation is a fantasy, and a dangerous one," Bugeaud proclaimed, "yet this was the idea behind Tafna. Recent events have shown it to be really a fantasy."

There was only one solution — domination of the whole country and the destruction of Abd el-Kader's power. Bugeaud had hard-to-digest views about how this should be done. If he were appointed commander in chief, he would not chase Arabs. Quite useless. No, he would make their lives utterly miserable by preventing them from growing crops or from harvesting them or from pasturing their livestock. Threaten those who supported the emir with starvation. Scorched earth. To those in the Chamber who protested that such tactics were barbarous and unworthy of France, Bugeaud offered no consolation.

"Gentlemen, one doesn't make war with charity. Whoever wants it to end, must also want the means to end it. We must fight ferociously and tenaciously, yet to succeed we need greater numbers of soldiers and great perseverance. We need a leader who will be implacable and wage unlimited war."

It was clear to everyone who he was proposing for the job.

❦

February 22, 1841. An anxious crowd was waiting for General Bugeaud at the quay as his boat steamed into Algiers. The colonists wanted to hear what their new governor-general had to tell them as soon as he stepped ashore. He had made enemies in Algeria with his high handedness, suspect anticolonialism and his hated Tafna Treaty. Yet, for all that, he was the only general who had really thrashed the emir in battle.

And his gruff, blunt competence and irreverent humor appealed to the troops. He now had 80,000 men at his disposal and virtual carte blanche from the king and his war minister, Marshal Soult.

"Our country is committed," Bugeaud told the hopeful faces. "The Arabs must be conquered and the flag of France the only one on African soil. But war is not the goal. The conquest will be sterile without colonization. I will be an ardent colonizer and you must understand that I attach less prestige to military victory than I do to doing something useful and lasting for France."

A month later, Bugeaud had issued three decrees to signal to colonists and Arabs alike that the days of lazy half measures were over. Any tribe that refused peace terms offered by France would be prohibited from engaging in any form of commerce with France. Secondly, no more freelance defections to the French side by tribal leaders. They would have to bring the whole tribe with them. And, thirdly, all Arabs circulating inside the French controlled areas would be required to wear a hexagonal* metal medallion with the words, "Submitted Arab," inscribed in French and Arabic. The decrees reassured the army and the colonists that a new and determined Bugeaud had set foot on African soil. The governor-general immediately began planning a spring campaign, a time when the Arabs were most vulnerable.

"No impedimenta" was the catchword for the new African army. Gone were slow, clumsy wheeled convoys. Gone was the heavy field artillery. Camels had proven too difficult to handle. Mules became the unsung heroes of the French army and the veteran porters of howitzers, ammunition, water, the sick and wounded. Field packs were lightened up, shakos and stiff collars were replaced with kepis and soft collars. The infantry carried only four days of rations for twenty-day campaigns. The rest, they had to get from raiding enemy camps or from finding the underground silos that concealed the Arabs' food supplies. The infantry had to form search lines that snaked across the hills and valleys as far as the eye could see, like a sideways marching centipede, stabbing the landscape with their bayonets hoping to strike the telltale capstones that sealed the enemy's strategic treasure — underground stores of cracked barley, oats and wheat.

---

* Mainland France is shaped like a hexagon.

If the men didn't live so well, at least they could march faster and comfort themselves by beating Arabs. "It is the legs of our soldiers that will win us the country, not our rifles," Bugeaud told his men. "A bullet can travel only 300 meters, legs can go forty leagues." His infantry was expected to endure forced marches of 120 miles in thirty-six hours. His officers had to be tough enough to endure a merciless sun, a waterless landscape and still motivate their men.

ʚɞ

Clouds of smoke smudged the skies of Tittery and Oran provinces during the spring of 1841. Tribes that supported the emir could expect to have their harvests torched, orchards chopped down, livestock seized, tents and *douars* burned, men decapitated, women and children left destitute or imprisoned. "Papa" Bugeaud was true to his word — to support the emir would mean to know hell.

To fight the emir was also hell for all but the most hardened French veterans. Achille de Saint-Arnaud was one of Bugeaud's devoted young officers — a spendthrift, classically educated, royalist aristocrat turned soldier-adventurer. He not only fought with ruthless passion, he also wrote voluminously about his African years. Even for him, the pillage, the killing and the cruelty of nature took its toll.

"Not for a general's epaulettes would I live those ten hours again," Saint-Arnaud wrote of his march on Mascara in the July heat. Commanding the rear guard that was being tracked at a safe distance by harassing Arab horsemen, Saint-Arnaud recalled, "The wretched Light Infantry Battalion was having its first taste of African warfare and was in complete chaos. Stragglers were dropping out by the scores. It had formed the van and was nearly two leagues ahead of me, but I picked up its men in the rear guard. I saw the most hideous scenes of weakness and demoralization — soldiers who had thrown away their weapons and lay down awaiting death, overcome by sweltering heat, fatigue, fever and dysentery. To avoid me, they threw themselves into the thickets and ravines. I followed them and took their rifles and packs and made my Zouaves drag them along...many begged me to kill them so as not to die at the hands of the Arabs... I saw some clasp the barrels of their rifles in a voluptuous frenzy as they placed them in their mouths... That day I shall never forget. Afterward, I understood Machta and the other disasters."

Nor was he pleased with the new, systematic ruthlessness and its cumulative effect on Frenchmen. "We lay waste, we plunder, we destroy crops and trees. The enemy flees before us, taking his flocks. We have burnt everything, destroyed everything. As for engagements, few or none; just a hundred or two wretched Arabs who fire on the rear guard…" But killing and devastation either drives soldiers mad or hardens their souls, and Saint-Arnaud was no exception. Two years later, he wrote almost gleefully, "I shall leave not a single tree standing in their orchards, not a head on the shoulders of these wretched Arabs…Those are the orders I have received from General Changarnier and they will be punctually executed. I shall burn everything, kill everyone." Four years later, Saint-Arnaud would be vigorously defended by Bugeaud for sufocating hundreds of men, women and children who had hidden in caves and refused to surrender.

To wage his total war, Bugeaud demanded experienced senior officers who had built their careers committed to achieving success in Africa — men who knew the land, the traditions, the customs, and preferably, the language of the Arabs. Lamoricière, Changarnier, Bedeau, Cavaignac, Saint-Arnaud had all shown undisputed bravery and leadership in battle.* Of the five, Lamoricière was the most dangerous rival. He had been instrumental in creating the Arab Bureau and, during the second campaign to take Constantine, was the first to break through its walls at the head of his hardy Zouaves. Not only was he a brave and a proven leader, he spoke Arabic and had a knack with the tribes.

Lamoricière became known as a man who could make careers for younger officers, and many aligned themselves with him rather than the Old Man in the twilight of his career. He had his own constellation of young stars and was viscerally incompatible with Bugeaud whose brusque, imperious manner and crude speech offended the politically smooth Lamoricière. Bugeaud valued Lamoricière's bravery and capacity for work, yet also considered him an ambitious intriguer

---

* Alexis deTocqueville noted a big difference between those officers who made a career serving in Algeria and those who were there temporarily. The former were "ardent, ambitious, full of energy; they love the country and are passionate about its conquest." The latter were "sad, mournful, sickly and disheartened and speak and think only about France. The first wage war, the second endure it."

who talked too much and tried too hard to please those in power — a "courtesan."

Bugeaud, however, possessed the admirable ability to not allow his assessment of an officer's defects blind him to the man's strengths. Changarnier, he considered disagreable and bad tempered, but a "fine soldier, the strongest of all my generals." Bugeaud thought Cavaignac vain and touchy and disliked his republican leanings, but had the confidence to give him the most difficult and thankless tasks. Bedeau, it seemed, had hardly a flaw. He was modest and avoided intrigue as well as the limelight. He didn't spare his men, but neither did he spare himself. He allowed neither himself nor his officers luxuries not shared by his men. Bugeaud called him "a man of duty and conscience, firm and unflinching under fire."

By the end of 1841, Bugeaud's "columns from hell" had much to be proud of: Tagdempt, Mascara, Boghar, Taza, Saida had fallen into French hands. The emir's interior line of strong points had been destroyed without a fight. All were abandoned, except for stray animals. Frustrated by finding no Arabs to kill in Tagdempt, French soldiers took out their bloodlust by shooting dogs.

❧

The emir possessed one weapon that left Bugeaud defenseless: his humanity. The bishop of Algiers, Antoine-Adolphe Dupuch, was the bearer of the inconvenient news of the emir's charity just as Bugeaud was inciting his troops to fight a merciless adversary who was said to be little better than a savage beast. Abd el-Kader had proposed a prisoner exchange.

It all began with a woman in distress. The desperate wife of an officer, one Massot, had come to the bishop's residence on a wet, stormy March night holding a little girl in her arms. She pleaded with the bishop to help: her husband, the poor child's father, was a prisoner in the hands of Abd el-Kader. The tenderhearted bishop was moved by the woman, but what could he do? Impulsively, he decided then to write a letter to the emir.

"You do not know me, but my calling is to serve God and to love all men as His children and as my brothers. If I knew how to ride a horse, I would fear neither the darkness nor the howling of the storm to come to you. I would come and present myself at your tent, and would tell you in a tone of voice which, if I am not mistaken about you , you would not resist. Return this unfortunate brother who has fallen into your worthy hands. But, I cannot come in person.

"Therefore, permit me to send to you one of my companions. May this letter which he will give you, written in haste, take the place of my prayers which God would bless because they come from the depths of my heart.

"I have neither money nor gold and can offer in return only the prayers of a sincere soul and the most profound gratitude of the family in whose name I write you. Fortunate are the merciful for they will receive mercy themselves."

The emir gave his response to the bishop's intermediaries on the spot.

"I have received your letter and I understand. It does not surprise me based on what I have heard about you. However, permit me to note that in your double role as servant of God and of men, you should have asked me not for the freedom of only one, but of all the Christians who are imprisoned.

"Further, would you not have been twice as worthy of your mission, had you not only asked for the liberation of two or three hundred Christians, but offered to extend the same favor to an equal number of Muslims who languish in your prisons? It is written: do unto others as you would have them do unto you."

With the happy news of the emir's response, Dupuch asked General Bugeaud for permission to proceed with negotiations to exchange French prisoners for an equal number of Arabs held in Algiers. This offered a way to show the alliance of sword and cross. France's civilizing mission would be advanced, Dupuch told Bugeaud. For the Arabs to become civilized they must become French, and to become French, they must first become Christians — not by forced conversion, to be sure, but through charity and example.

Permission was not withheld, but neither was the idea enthusiastically endorsed. Some of Bugeaud's senior officers strenuously opposed it on the grounds that the bishop was overstepping his bounds. He was supposed to restrict himself to providing chaplains for the army and ministering to the spiritual needs of the colonists, not mix into military affairs. The bishop was on his own.

e/ɔ

A curious fellow, this curé from Bordeaux who had expended his personal inheritance to provide for orphans and shipwrecked souls of all kinds back in his native parish. To the nonbelievers and anticlericals in the French army, the first bishop appointed to France's new colony had a strange addiction. He couldn't resist helping those in need. Dupuch had even been so imprudent as to go into debt to care for Arabs as well as Christians. "I don't look at the poor with my eyes, but with my heart," the bishop told people mystified by his wanton charity.

Dupuch first wanted to improve the appearance of the 130 Arab prisoners: 43 men, 48 women and 39 children had been captured during a razzia by French soldiers. Their clothes were rags. Stress and malnutrition had dried up the breasts of nursing mothers. Invoking the spirit of Christian charity, the bishop appealed to his parishioners for money to buy clean clothes, goat's milk for the children and to pay for the cost of renting the carriages that would be needed to take the Arabs back to their territory.

On May 17, 1841, a small convoy of carriages filled with women and children set out from Algiers accompanied by Dupuch's vicar general, Abbé Jacques Suchet. Trailing behind were the men who were denied the luxury of riding in rented carriages. The bishop's representatives were to meet the emir's caliph of Miliana, Mohammed Ben Allal, at a place called the Mouzazia farm on western edge of the Mitidja Plain. As Suchet approached with their Arab prisoners, French soldiers launched an attack on the farm. Treachery, chance or incompetence? Niether Dupuch's nor Ben Allal's men knew. They knew only that the exchange had been compromised.

Ben Allal's cavalry had to flee with their own prisoners, forcing Suchet and his companions to gallop behind them for two hours until finally catching up with them. An angry and suspicious Ben Allal was mollified only when the Suchet showed him his good will offering — a liberated prisoner he had brought along, a man known to be valued by the emir. The confidence was reciprocated by Ben Allal who turned over Massot, the officer whose wife had launched the drama.

A new location near Boufarik was negotiated with Ben Allal. Suchet and his companions gave themselves as hostages until the trade was completed. The caliph spent several hours in Dupuch's carriage, where the two discussed final details of the exchange. The bishop ended their talks by giving him a clock and two candelabras to mark the occasion. Ben Allal took the gifts out of politeness, adding as the emir might have, "the presents that I like best at this moment are to see your face and know your heart."

On May 31, a herd of forty goats and nursing ewes appeared at Dupuch's doorstep. The emir had been touched by the prisoners' reports of the bishop's charity. With the goats came a letter which began with an effusive salutation, typical of the emir's missives: "Praise and honor to God alone; prayers to Jesus Christ, the spirit and soul of God! To Sidi Mohammed Ben Allal, may God protect him! To the servant of God, servant of Jesus Christ, Bishop Antoine, our beloved, may God preserve and bless him..."

The emir described the anguish of the friends and families who came to meet the prisoners only to learn that their loved ones were not among the liberated. The disappointed families came to the emir's tent every day begging him to ask the Christian marabout to release more prisoners. Abd el-Kader asked Dupuch to return the remaining prisoners held in Algiers. As a gesture of good faith, the emir had freed four more Christian prisoners, including a woman and her little daughter. Dupuch's representative, the emir added, would be given safe conduct to meet with him. The emir recommended he come through Hadjout territory.

The bishop had become a minor celebrity as a result of his success. He suspected there were still more French prisoners in Arab hands. Dupuch was interested in the emir's proposal. His suspicions were confirmed after Lamoricière's troops took Mascara. Their victory bulletin announced they had found fifty-six names etched into the wall of a building, above which was written : *"Nous ne savons pas où nous allons... à la garde de Dieu"*. They didn't know where they were being taken, but they were still alive, under God's protection.

Dupuch decided to try to free the prisoners. His stalwart Abbé Suchet volunteered for the mission. The bishop's vicar had proven his mettle in tracking down Ben Allal after the aborted exchange at the Mouzazia farm. But this time, he would have to go further into enemy territory, unsure of the emir's whereabouts and armed only with Abd el-Kader's aman.

The day of his departure, Suchet said his prayers more fervently than usual and prostrated himself before the Virgin Mary, the beloved Lalla Miriam, as she was known to Muslims who also asked for her interventions.

☙

With Bugeaud's half-hearted blessing, the vicar set off in search of the emir. He and a small band of eight freed Arabs, an interpreter and two mule drivers disappeared down the rue de Chartres to the applause of well-wishers lining the dusty road. At the frontier post of Boufarik in the Mitidja Plain, Suchet obtained more medical supplies from the military doctor before he entered hostile territory. He knew that the best form of charity was to treat the sick. The Arabs had come to look upon the Christian fathers, or *Babas-Roumi,* as skilled healers and Suchet didn't want to disappoint.

"I am going into enemy territory," Suchet warned the officers with an ironic grin. "So don't kill me if I fall into your hands." He told the soldiers that he was expected by the caid of the Hadjouts who would take over his prisoners and then guide him to the emir.

The full-bearded Suchet rode into the *bled* wearing all the trappings of his holy office — long black cassock and cravate-like rabat, a large wooden crucifix hanging from his neck and a broad, stiff-brimmed "colonial" on his head, an ecclesiastic version of a pith helmet. Not only was he proud of his divine uniform, it gave him additional protection among the God-fearing Arabs. Shortly, he was met by a detachment of Hadjout cavalry. They relieved him of his prisoners and led him to the camp of their caid, the brother-in-law of Ben Allal. The caid greeted the vicar as a distinguished guest and ordered a beautiful tent raised for him. "It was furnished with superb rugs. An honor guard stood watch over my tent and his personal servants eagerly attended to my needs," Suchet recalled.

The next morning, he discovered that the caid's camp was near the famous "Tomb of the Christian." Arabs throughout the region venerated this enormous circular stone monument to an unknown Christian of saintly reputation.* The validity of the man's reputation seemed to be confirmed by oral tradition that anyone who desecrated the monument in the past had come to a bad end. The caid brought Suchet to this holy site overlooking the Mediterranean Sea before sending him on his way with a fresh guide and cavalry escort to bring him to Ben Allal. But only a few leagues into the *bled*, his escort told him it was better to turn back. They didn't think he would be able to reach Ben Allal, much less Abd el-Kader. Both men were too busy fighting the French to receive him and, anyway, two French columns were invading their territory.

Suchet was not one to be deflected by vague and uncertain dangers. He insisted they carry on. He had letters from his bishop and would only stop when they were in the emir's hands. In the face of his escort's stubborn refusal to go on, Suchet proposed sending his guide back to the caid to get his consent to continue. Three hours later, the guide returned with the caid's verdict: The Christian marabout should be allowed to continue. That evening, Suchet arrived at Ben Allal's camp in the Chlef Valley, guarded by eight or nine hundred regular cavalry wearing their distinctive crimson burnooses.

The twenty-five-year-old caliph greeted the vicar warmly, remembering their earlier exchange at Boufarik. The two talked for several hours under a magnificent carob tree. The Christian's courage and determination impressed Ben Allal, who was known for the same qualities in battle. Ben Allal had once been regarded as a debauch. He still looked the part with his sensuous lips, one dead eye and plump physique, yet he was also the great grandson of a famous marabout, Sidi-Embarek. The Hadjouts were fierce fighters, yet their influence over the years was built on their reputation as conciliators and peace-makers among the tribes in the Tittery beylik and as fair-minded interlocutors for the Turks. His own father, like Abd el-Kader's, had resisted the French after a two year peace agreement broke down in 1833. Ben Allal offered his services a year later to the emir to become one of his most loyal and feared caliphs.

---

* Close to Tipaza, this tomb measures 180 feet in diameter and 90 feet to the apex of the cupola. It is thought to date from the first-century AD, but as Christianity had not yet spread to North Africa, and the Arabic word for Roman and Christian is the same, the mausoleum is more likely the Tomb of the Roman.

Ben Allal didn't try to discourage Suchet from continuing, but warned him that he might have to ride as far as Tlemcen. In any case, Ben Allal didn't know where the emir was. For more than a week, Suchet followed his young Arab guide who seemed to assume the vicar's endurance was the same as his own. They rested infrequently and ate only one meal a day — always the same couscous, washed down with muddy water. "Living themselves from ground wheat mixed with olive oil, or eating, like their horses, a little cracked barley, he no doubt considered that I was being treated royally," Suchet recalled. When the vicar pleaded mercy for himself and his horse, his guide would only make a joke. Though the heat and fatigue nearly killed the forty-six-year-old priest from Villefranche, he didn't fail to notice the misery around him.

Suchet frequently encountered refugees with their animals and meager belongings. They had been told by the emir to abandon their *douars*, to leave nothing but a desert for the French. Surprisingly, he found himself an object of great curiosity and respect. "They wanted to touch everything and to know its name and significance — my cassock, my belt and especially my crucifix which hung on my chest. They are like big children." They wished him well and wanted the Frenchman to tell Abd el-Kader to make peace.

When Suchet came to the camp of the Ouled Abbas, their marabouts eagerly kissed his hand and spoke of their desire for peace. This tribe was home for Abd el-Kader's foreign minister, Miloud Ben Arrach, who received Suchet with full honors; like the others he had met along the way, he seemed tired of jihad. While staying with the Ouled Abbas, Suchet learned that Ben Arrach recently had refused to send cavalry to the emir. Unfortunately, he didn't know where the emir was either.

They headed to the emir's old capital of Tagdempt. They were told Abd el-Kader could be in Tlemcen or in the Sahara. Suchet's discouraged guide urged they go home.

"You should never have come along. You're not up to the job," the Frenchman goaded.

"But I don't know where to take you."

"Let's go toward Mascara. Our troops are there and your master should not be far from his enemies."

❧

Suchet's persistence was rewarded when they got closer to Mascara. Two white-haired old men told him the emir was camped on the western edge of the Plain of Ghriss. They galloped together until one of the old men pointed to a grove of fig trees. "He is over there," he whispered in the guide's ear, as if they had entered a sanctuary. Negro guards materialized out of the grove to take their horses, and then some more men silently greeted Suchet before gesturing toward a figure sitting under a fig tree.

Like others before him, Suchet was surprised by the appearance of the much-feared Arab chieftain. He had none of the look of a warrior. He wore only a simple white burnoose. No knife, no pistols stuck in his belt, no courtiers hovering around him. A secretary invited Suchet to sit beside the emir. After an exchange of pleasantries, a translator read out loud the bishop's letters.

"I admire the charity of your *baba el-kebir* (bishop)," the emir responded.

"We also admire him for his good works."

"I know what he did for our prisoners. I have great admiration for him."

Suchet spoke of the bishop's joy at seeing the prisoners freed, but added that his joy would be complete if all the French prisoners were released. There were still fifty-six men held by the emir. The vicar read the names taken from the wall in Mascara. His purpose in coming so far, he explained, was to obtain their release for the bishop.

After a moment's hesitation, Abd el-Kader said that he couldn't grant the bishop's wishes unless the French side released all the prisoners they held. Suchet reminded the emir that the agreement with his caliph, Ben Allal, was without conditions. The bishop simply promised to try to obtain the release of all prisoners that the French government judged appropriate to free. He would do whatever he could, but would not question the reasoning of the authorities. Underlining the good faith of the bishop, Suchet told the emir of the eight additional prisoners he had already turned over to Ben Allal, including a secretary important to Ben Salem, the emir's caliph for Kabylia.

Suchet pressed the emir to uphold the commitments of his caliph.

"Do you promise that your lord and master will make new efforts on behalf of the four Arabs who are especially important to me, and for my agha who is now doing hard labor in France?"

"My bishop has already made an appeal to the king about the latter. As to the others, it is out of my bishop's hands."

After a long silence, he replied solemnly. "Your prisoners will be released."

"When?"

"Tomorrow. I will order one of my sheiks to take them to Oran. They are only a twelve-hour march from the city."

Their business finished, the emir was anxious to talk to Suchet about his favorite subject.

"Is that Jesus Christ?" the emir asked, pointing at the crucifix hanging on Suchet's chest.

"Yes, that is Jesus Christ, our God."

"What does that mean? He was a man."

"He is the Word of God — the Word became flesh to save the world. Our God is the father of Muslims as well as Christians."

"But what is the ministry of the catholic priests?"

"You should know, since there has been a bishop now in Algiers for three years. Their ministry is to treat all men as brothers, whatever their religion."

"If your religion is so beautiful and benevolent, why don't all Frenchmen observe it?"

"You can answer that yourself. To you, Islam is a good religion. Why don't all Muslims observe it?"

Abd el-Kader raised his eyes and hands toward the sky despairingly. After a moment of silence, the emir began to ask more questions about Christianity, but the interpreter interrupted, saying he lacked the vocabulary to translate properly. And so ended the emir's first theological discussion with a catholic priest.

Suchet finally offered presents from Dupuch. "I will take them, but only because they come from your bishop. I would not accept them from anyone else."

There was one last question from the bishop. Would the emir allow the bishop to send priests to live among future French prisoners to console them in their hour of need? He could. Would he also allow the bishop to send to the priests food, medication or clothing for prisoners, and allow them to write letters to family members so long as they were first shown to the emir's translator? The emir agreed. The priest would be treated with the dignity his position deserved as man of God and representative of the bishop, but on one condition: the representative must solemnly swear, once and for all cases, to not disclose any information about the emir's location or troop movements.

"Would you write a letter to the bishop in your own hand confirming your agreement, knowing you will fill his heart with the greatest joy?"

The emir agreed.

"We willingly accept your blessed proposition and will receive with pleasure whomever you might send to minister to your prisoners," Abd el-Kader wrote Dupuch, "We have complete confidence in you and count on your promises to free those Arabs who remain …"

The bishop had only promised to try his best, and try he did, but to no avail. The generals had no weapons with which to fight an enemy with a generous spirit, nor could they afford to have news of such a thing spread among the troops. Bugeaud squashed any further communication with the emir. Military chaplains were not allowed to comfort French prisoners. Dupuch was ordered to stop this dangerous humanitarian game.

∽

Men may apply religious injunctions selectively because their knowledge is limited or they are partial to some verses over others. Others may have wide knowledge but allow insincerity, prejudice or political convenience to decide their ethics. Abd el-Kader was a puritan by taste, manipulative as required by the necessities of war, but sincere in his desire to be rightly guided by the Law. Rejuvenating his Arabs would require attentiveness to all the rules of good Islamic behavior.

He had banned gambling, drinking, smoking and prostitution. Banditry had been reduced to a minimum. Islamic ethics also had things to say about the treatment of prisoners. The mountain of heads the emir saw piled up that night along the Machta River made him resolve to tame a monstrous custom that was not Islam.

For millennia, the ethics of desert warfare had been to give no quarter and to count the enemy dead by the number of heads carried home.

A mudjahid's compensation required evidence of his good work. Heads and booty were the currency of desert warfare. Convincing his Arabs to stop the time-honored tradition of chopping off the heads of everyone found on the battlefield was fiercely resisted.

Under the emir's new rules, scything heads in battle was legitimate, quite different from decapitating men who had surrendered. No matter that in the desert prisoners were unwanted baggage that needed feeding and watering. Live prisoners would now bring a reward of eight douros for a man, six for a woman. Heads, however, unless taken in battle, would bring a reward of twenty-five strokes with a rod on the soles a warrior's feet. Prisoners were questioned by the emir to assure that they had been treated well.

Abd el-Kader's religious knowledge had persuaded a special council of 300 chiefs to adhere to the reformed morality under the pain of severe punishment for maltreatment. After all, he was only implementing the admonitions of the Prophet himself. The emir knew the hadiths by heart. Mohammed once scolded his brother-in-law, Ali, for massacring 500 infidels after they had surrendered their weapons.

Once the new edict had been distributed throughout his caliphates, Abd el-Kader was merciless when interrogating his first offender, as witnessed by Suchet during his journey to find the emir.

Was the prisoner dead or alive when beheaded?

Dead.

Twenty-five strokes to teach the lesson that a dead person is no one's enemy and that it is forbidden to mutilate a corpse.

The man started to leave, thinking his punishment was over. Wait. Another question.

Where was your rifle when you were cutting off the man's head?

On the ground.

Twenty-five more strokes for putting your rifle down in a battle zone.

Barely conscious after the second round of beatings, the crippled offender crawled away. Not so fast.

How did you carry the head away afterward?

With the head in one hand and my rifle in the other.

So you were carrying your rifle in a way that made it impossible to use. Twenty-five strokes.

The emir had to administer such savage punishment only once. Justice had to be severe to instruct and tame the baser instincts of the Arabs whose nature he knew so well. French prisoners, had they known, would have had little to fear in Arab hands.

Abd el-Kader particularly disliked seeing women as prisoners. All female captives were placed under his mother's protection, who kept them in a tent close to her own. Two Negros guarded it at all times and no one could enter without Lalla Zohra's permission. Each morning, she brought them butter, olive oil, some meat and other things to improve their lot; the sick she nursed personally with tea and sugar, as well as maternal attention and sympathy.

Religious authority and brutal example were needed to expunge old ways and drive home the importance of the emir's new morality. His caliphs Ben Allal, Ben Salem and Bou Hamidi were his most faithful representatives in applying his edict. Among other Arabs, the best assurance of good treatment was the emir's presence. In later years, when the wheel of fate had turned against the emir, former French prisoners would be his most ardent champions.

Arguing in the name of humanity and of Christian charity, Abd el-Kader bombarded Bugeaud and his generals with requests to continue prisoner exchanges. His efforts were met with silence. Bugeaud could not afford to weaken the fighting spirit of troops who believed that to be captured by the Arabs meant a certain and gruesome death.

ॐ

Toward the end of 1841, Bugeaud summarized the military situation for his minister. He was not shy about offering his ideas about colonization, the resources needed and the realities of taming an Arab population.

Europe was not Africa, he explained, responding to the criticism from generals schooled in continental warfare. There, it was possible for good generals to do great things with small armies. One or two decisive battles could bring down a government. A well-led, battle-hardened force of 60,000 could defeat an enemy twice that size. But in Africa, the enemy is diffuse and everywhere, and a European-style army was "like a bull being attacked by wasps." There were no such things as decisive battles in Africa, only perseverance.

Only perseverance and domination would achieve lasting success, but once submission was achieved it had to be maintained. A strong army that dominated the country, Bugeaud argued, would eventually pay for itself by creating the conditions for growing revenue. An army that was too small would always be a drain on the French treasury.

"History shows us the Arabs are quick to revolt. Their antipathy toward us and our religion will last for centuries. An army that is big enough to administer the country, keep it pacified, and promote commerce will be able to collect from the tribes the taxes necessary to cover the costs of occupation. An army that is too small to govern will not be able to collect taxes except from those neighboring tribes easily accessible to our punishments." The weaker the force, the harder to collect taxes. Bugeaud presented to his minister the implications for maintaining peace that were rooted in the same problems Abd el-Kader faced.

Just as the emir's support from the tribes waxed and waned with his fortunes, neither did Bugeaud have illusions about Arab fidelity to France. To spare the treasury in Paris, it would be possible over time to substitute native troops for French, especially their cavalry. But, he warned "even the most devoted tribes will leave us if we are not in a position to punish them for their disloyalty. The basis for our power is our sturdy infantry." He imagined the infantry performing double duty as worker-colonists.*

Once the natives were docile, the troops would be put to productive uses such as building roads and bridges. No other mass of workers, Bugeaud insisted, could be organized to get things done as fast or as well. Each battalion could also be given the job of building a village and clearing land for settlers. Soldiers to be discharged within a year would be offered an allocation of land as compensation for their services, then told to go back to France and return with a wife.

"In all respects," Bugeaud concluded, "it will be wise to maintain a force and system of occupation in Algeria that will no longer pose questions of cost, but rather of recruitment." A secure peace would lower costs, and provide an atmosphere of security that would attract colonists. This would only be possible if leaders don't follow their natural political instincts. "Rather than weaken the army when its warriors

---

* In 1840 there were only about 25,000 Europeans living in Algeria, of which 11,000 were French. The rest were mostly Spanish, Maltese and Italian immigrants.

are crowned with success, we must instead send new reinforcements. This show of determination will have a powerful effect on the Arabs by making clear the wheel of fortune will not turn again."

Abd el-Kader was far from ready to quit despite seven months of Bugeaud's relentless scorched-earth tactics that was grinding down Arab resistance. Instead, the emir was issuing warnings to Bugeaud that dripped with scorn and bravado, even as his own Arab confederation was crumbling around him.

"What is this greed that drives France, a country that considers itself a powerful and peaceful nation? Why does it make war on us? Does it not have enough land? Do you think the land you have taken is important when compared to what we have left? France advances, we retreat. But its turn will come to retreat and we will return.

"And what harm do you, who are the governor-general, think you do to us? You lose as many men as we do fighting and your men are decimated by sickness. What are you offering your King in return? A bit of land. Stones from Mascara!

"You burn and pillage our harvests and silos. Do you think the loss of the Plain of Ghriss means anything when we possess so much more? The land you possess is a drop in the sea. We will attack you whenever it suits us. We know it is madness to attack head-on the forces you drag around. But we will harass them, wear them down, and chop them up piecemeal. The heat and sun will do the rest. Does a bird flying over the water make the waves rise? That is what your are in Africa!"

There was a horrible reality to the emir's brave words. To fight like the Arabs was a new kind of boot camp for the French, one that took years to produce desert-hardened soldiers. The marching and counter-marching, harassing attacks, malnutrition, 130 degree heat in summer, vermin and disease — most commonly malaria, dysentery, cholera, scurvy and infected wounds took a horrible toll during Bugeaud's inaugural year as army commander and governor-general. Sixty thousand men were under his command at the beginning of the 1841. Twelve months later, only 4,000 men were still fit enough to fight.

ᘓᓕ

Bugeaud needed political as well as military measures to win. Who better to deploy than the versatile Roches, now that he had become a trusted aide? But winning trust from his French compatriots had been a struggle ever since Roches presented himself to the commanding officer on duty at an outpost near Oran back in October of 1839.

At first, his story seemed so improbable that Roches was considered a deserter and put in jail until Col. Daumas, the French consul in Mascara, vouched for his loyalty. After being released from prison, Roches immediately got a divorce, arranged by the French-appointed cadi of Oran. He then sent a letter to Abd el-Kader explaining the reasons for his desertion.

Roches also wrote a long memorandum about the emir and his relations with the various tribes and their chiefs. Its value was immediately recognized in government circles, which led to him making a personal report at the war ministry. For two months afterward, Roches was lionized in Paris and legends about him invented. His newfound fame brought him a promotion to the grade of translator first class and was assigned to the staff of the king's son, the Duke of Orleans, who was leaving for Algiers.

In Algiers, Roches was still widely regarded with suspicion, and by General Valée in particular, who told the prince that he was an untrustworthy renegade. As a result, Roches saw little action during the difficult year of 1840, nor was his advice ever sought. Bugeaud, however, had quickly recognized the value of Roches' unique knowledge when he became governor-general in 1841, and trusted him even though the army as a whole continued to view him sceptically. Yet, the continued mistrust among his rank-and-file compatriots depressed him and made him think about ways to redeem himself. What better than a dangerous mission?

Roches proposed to Bugeaud a plan that was simple and bold. He had become convinced that many tribes did not submit to France because they believed that the Koran threatened eternal damnation to Muslims who would do so, an interpretation Abd el-Kader found useful in enforcing his authority. Roches was aware that certain commentators disagreed. They held that when further resistance was hopeless and caused pointless suffering, submission was permitted, so long as Muslims were allowed to practice their faith.

He found a willing ally in his old friend from Ain Mahdi, Sheik Mohammed el-Tidjani, who had become an implacable enemy of Abd el-Kader. To have any chance of a legitimate fatwa being issued condoning peace with France, Roches needed Tidjani's influence to gather together the doctors of the law in Tunis. With a letter of safe conduct from Tidjani in hand, Bugeaud's financial support and wearing Arab dress, Roches slipped undetected by the emir's spies into Tunis, where he met with the ulema of the prestigious Kairouan Center of Islamic Learning. On August 19, 1841, the subject of jihad was discussed at length in light of the Koran's teachings and those of its greatest commentators.

A long and contentious debate finally produced a fatwa. It declared: "When Muslims whose territory has been invaded by infidels have fought so long as there was hope of driving them out of the country, and when it is certain that continued struggle will only lead to the ruin of Muslims without any chance of defeating the conquerors, and while preserving the hope of their yoke being removed with the help of God, they may live under the domination of infidels on the condition that they are allowed to freely exercise their religion, and their women and daughters will be respected."

Abd el-Kader did not attach much significance to the fatwa because Tidjani's hand was present in the Kairouan fatwa, as was French money. Yet, the emir would to come to a similar conclusion five years later.

CHAPTER FOURTEEN

Trail of Tears, 1843

T HE TRIBES HAD TO DECIDE who was stronger, who could best protect them from punishment by the other. Bugeaud's "columns from hell" were in constant pursuit, yet the emir still could evade, elude, strike back when and where he wanted.

"We want to protect our allies, but the great distances make protection very difficult against an enemy that has better horses, is lighter and more mobile and can cover twenty leagues at night to fall upon their prey," Saint-Arnaud wrote. "By the time we are warned something will happen, they have already come and gone; the harm is done and very difficult to mend. The victims want only one thing: security. ' Protect us. They took our wives, our children, our animals.' The ghost of Abd el-Kader is always there, whispering, 'I have your women, your children and your livestock; abandon the French, return to me and I will forgive and give back everything.' Each side gets more fanatical and the war becomes a war of extermination."

Saint-Arnaud was not quite right. Abd el-Kader continued to discriminate between deliberate treason and exhaustion. If a tribe had actively colluded and connived with the French, heads fell. The Koran was clear about the treatment of traitors to the faith. However, the emir was more lenient with tribes like the Beni Ouragh, which simply couldn't bear the pain anymore. Their caid, Mohammed Ben Haj, had lost six of eight sons fighting fo. Abd el-Kader. "I served the emir with all my strength," he told Bugeaud at the end of 1842, "but he can't protect us any longer. If you are humane, I will serve you loyally until I die. The word of a Beni Ouragh is sacred." Hardly had Mohammed Ben Haj submitted to France when Abd el-Kader returned to punish him for his weakness. Unlike those the emir considered traitors, the war-weary caid was merely arrested.

℘

Abd el-Kader no longer had any fixed bases. Tagdempt, Saida, Boghar, Taza were all abandoned. The emir was again a pure Bedouin, a child of the wind. His crumbling federation had become a migratory city of goat and camel skins: the smala.

Necessity was its mother. The families of his loyal followers, refugees who had abandoned their douars to the French or been pillaged by them, prisoners, hostages of the tribes he had punished, tribal factions unwilling to submit to French sovereignty, merchants and artisans as well as deserters from the French army — they all needed a secure place to go. Abd el-Kader needed a center from which to govern. The emir's troops sent to the smala their families and their livestock. Sixty, perhaps seventy thousand souls, inhabited this enormous tent city by the beginning of 1843, each in their douar, according to their tribe.

The smala was a place of internal exile. It was also an umbilical cord for keeping tribes attached to his cause — having the flesh and blood of their families under his guard dampened the temptation of troops in the field to defect. The shear massiveness of the smala with its schools, bazaars and workshops was also a reminder to tribes whose loyalty was wobbling of the emir's continued power.

Abd el-Kader was rarely at the smala, yet he thought often about his responsibility, and when he did, he thought about moving the whole agglomeration to Mecca. What a spectacle it would be! Tens of thousands of Arabs, remnants of those who had conquered North Africa eight centuries earlier, returning to the cradle of their faith because they were unwilling to live under Christians. When he raised the idea, his chiefs and marabouts were not opposed.

But the time had not yet come. He had his divinely ordained duty to persevere in the struggle. The smell of defeat was in the air, yet Abd el-Kader had known adversity before and recovered. He would outlast the infidels. There was still money in the treasury to buy grain, money that was dispensed by the emir's mother, Lalla Zohra and guarded by 400 regular infantry commanded by Mustafa Ben Thami. And the emir's Jews were providing money to help the destitute.

Women and children, servants, old people, adventurers, deserters, renegades, prisoners, cadis, tolbas, marabouts, saddlers, farriers, tailors, musicians and artisans of all kinds mixed with groaning, bleating, neighing herds of goats, sheep, horses, camels and mules numbering in the tens of thousands. This sprawling mass of organized life had to be capable of folding up and moving quickly, then replanting itself in the identical order elsewhere. A hidden geometry provided order amid seeming chaos.

⨍

Four concentric circles formed the smala. In the first were the emir's most important lieutenants and their families, among whom was his principal secretary, Sidi el-Haj Mohammed el-Kharroubi; his brother-in-law, the former caliph of Mascara, Ben Thami; his foreign minister, Miloud Ben Arrach and Bou Klika, ex-caid of the Zdama tribe. In the center of this first circle was the emir's douar. It contained the tents of his mother, his three wives,* four children, his money boxes and, most valuable of all, his intellectual treasure: the manuscripts covering law, medicine, astronomy, mathematics, philosophy and sacred writings he had painstakenly acquired over the years for the library that he had once imagined building in his capital of Tagdempt.

The second circle included the douars of Ben Allal, Ben Yahia, agha of the cavalry known to his opponents as "the Devil", and his former consul of Oran, Haj el-Habib. The third ring was formed by the douars of the emir's own Hachem tribe, charged with protecting the smala as a whole. The fourth circle was reserved for the rest, many of them douars belonging to nomadic tribes from the south and refugees of all stripes, including chiefs who had submitted to France and later changed their minds. Between the second and third circles were the camps of the regular infantry, the hostages and the military orderlies, or camp police.

"Complete order prevailed," Abd el-Kader told his friend Daumas years later. "The cadis administered justice, exactly as in the towns. Markets were held. There was no stealing or immorality. When we set camp, the education of our children continued. Prayers were observed five times a day. Families carried their own provisions depending on their capabilities. The poorest had enough for at least two weeks, the wealthy for two or three months."

---

* Aicha was the seductive daughter of Ben Salem, an important caliph in Kabylia. Kheira was also a political wife, though true love was evidently present. Embaraka or Baraka may have been a negro servant (*zinijate*), though it is unclear whether they were ever married.

Each of its three hundred and fifty plus douars was composed of fifteen to twenty tents arranged in still smaller circles, like beads on bracelets, along the circumferences of the four big circles, positioned according to the importance and trustworthiness of the inhabitants. The douars were autonomous. Each was responsible for its own property, livestock, provisions and family members, who, if separated in this sea of ordered chaos, could be lost for days.

Even Arabs allied with the French came to the smala to sell products in its markets. But this huge mass of humanity that covered hillsides and valleys also needed pasture and water. Wherever they camped, wells and springs dried up. Special police were needed to prevent water from being wasted or polluted by animals, yet with all these precautions, people died of thirst.

By the spring of 1843, the smala couldn't leisurely remain in one place even when water was plentiful. The burial stones that marked the smala's movements bore witness to the toll taken on the old and the sick, pregnant women and small children.

℥

Bugeaud's columns were moving farther south as he pushed new bases into the high plateaus from where he deployed his newly trained lighter, faster columns to track down the emir. He had created three large bases — at Tiaret in the Ouarensis, Boghar on the edge of the high plateaus and Miliana in the Chlef. From these outposts, his mobile columns radiated continuously, returning to recuperate as new columns were sent out to replace them at three-week intervals.

But where was the smala? Since February, the French had been obsessed with finding the emir's mobile capital. They assumed it would be moving farther south, but in which direction? The distances were great and the water scarce. Information from the tribes, even their allies, was unreliable. However, many eyes followed the French army for the emir. Particularly useful were the marabouts from French allied tribes who had refused to submit for religious reasons and joined the smala. These men still maintained contacts with their former tribesmen and kept the emir informed of French movements.

Among the tribes whose loyalties were divided was Abd el-Kader's own Hachem. Nevertheless, the emir's personal magnetism and aura of saintly authority was still strong — strong enough that his mere presence could rally the sheiks and caids back to his cause. In April, after being pursued for weeks along the Moroccan border, Abd el-Kader returned unexpectedly to Lamoricière's base of operations at Mascara. Crisscrossing the Plain of Ghriss, wavering Hachem tribesmen were shamed by his oratory into returning with him to his smala.

The smala moved from Goudjilah south toward Ain Taguin on the edge of the Djebel Amour. A report came to the emir that two French columns were setting out to destroy his roving capital — one led by Lamoricière and another by the king's young twenty-one-year-old son, the Duke of Aumale. The general was coming from Tiaret, while the duke was heading south from Boghar with a force of 1500 infantry and 600 cavalry.

In the emir's mind, Lamoricière was the more dangerous threat. Once he had delivered the repentant Hachem to his smala, the emir rode back to Tiaret with 250 men to keep an eye on the Frenchman's movements from a well-hidden campsite. Bugeaud, however, had detached from Lamoricière's division the experienced Colonel Yusuf to advise the duke.

Colonel Yusuf had become a legend in his own time. Born Guiseppi Vantini on Corsica in 1808, the same year as Abd el-Kader, Yusuf was one of the French army's most remarkable soldiers. Like the emir, he was a learned scholar and outstanding cavalryman, although his career began not in a zawiya, but as a slave.

Captured at sea by Barbary pirates, he was sold to the bey of Tunis, who took a liking to the quick-witted young man. Vantini ended up serving in the bey's Mameluke corps, converted to Islam, changed his name to Yusuf and became a respected scholar of Islamic law. Bold in love as well as war, Vantini had to flee Tunis when the bey learned of his romantic escapades with his own daughter. With the help of the French consul, Ferdinand de Lesseps, Yusuf escaped from the palace by stowing away on a French warship that took him to Sidi Ferruch in 1830, just as Bourmont was invading Africa. Yusuf's natural intelligence, resourcefulness and knowledge of French, Italian, Arabic and Turkish won him a career in the French army — first as an interpreter, later as a much-decorated cavalryman and commander of the spahis, where we find him in May of 1843 hunting down Abd el-Kader with the crown prince. Yusuf's famed boldness would augment the knowledge of Ameur Ben Ferhat, the agha of the Beni Ayads, auxilaries who were acting as local scouts to the French.

Bugeaud had a fatherly concern for the fourth and youngest son of King Louis-Philippe. The handsome blond was a neophyte with a peach-fuzz, spade mustache who had performed only two short tours of duty in the colony. He and the Duke of Orleans had been the king's only sons to show an interest in the military life, but his older brother had died a year earlier in a carriage mishap. Eager to learn, yet also aggressive and insistent that he be treated no differently than other officers, the Duke of Aumale had gained enough respect to be given command of a column to hunt for the smala.

The inhabitants of Goudjilah agreed that the smala was moving toward the Djebel Amour. The prince divided his force: his cavalry and a battalion of fast marching Zouaves, unburdened of their gear, would march at a forced pace to catch the smala, while a second column of two infantry battalions would stay behind to protect the supply train.

After twenty-nine hours of marching, the prince was worried. His men were near exhaustion and needed to stop. Yet, the trail they were following was freshly tramped down. From the breadth and variety of the animal tracks, Yusuf knew they were following an immense migration of men and animals, not simply a band of cavalry.

"We must continue," Colonel Yusuf objected. "We may never get another chance. The exhausted Negroes we found along the way all agreed the smala was headed for the Djebel Amour."

"We have marched all night. Human beings have a limit. I have already pushed them about as far as they can go. The men and horses are dying of thirst. I don't want a disaster," the duke protested.

"Ben Ferhat says there is water nearby, at Ain Taguin. "

"In that case, take us to Taguin, but send some guides back to the infantry to help them find our new course."

In the early twilight, two cavalry squadrons scouted ahead, led by Yusuf. Suddenly, his scouts were galloping back, shouting, "the smala, the smala." They had seen it, or part of it, on the other side of a rise.

The duke wanted to be sure his exhausted men's bodies were not playing tricks with their imaginations. Two officers of the Arab Bureau went back with Ameur Ferhat and Yusuf to look. They returned to confirm the news, but the duke was still skeptical. He sent his personal aide to verify the presence of the smala with his own eyes. The aide returned to report that he saw only a "few wretched tents" pitched on the other side of the hill. He even doubted whether they were Arabs. Some of the tents were white and could belong to a French encampment.

"You didn't look properly, or you can't see," Yusuf angrily interrupted. "I assure you, it is the smala. I will even go look once more myself." Lieutenant Barail, who described the scene later, accompanied Yusuf. "They were setting up camp. Women, children, regular askars in their brown uniforms, muleteers, animals of every kind mingled together. We could hear in this immense mass the yelling of the women, the bleating of the sheep...There were a few white tents for the wives of the emir. The place was like a beehive. Everyone was working at something. Thousands of camels and mules waiting to be unloaded, while those that had been relieved of their burdens were drinking dry the small sinews of water flowing through this chaos..."

Yusuf estimated some 18,000 people camped on the other side. Perhaps 3000 were armed. More were coming.

Faced with Yusuf's certainty, the prince gathered his officers. If they waited for the Zouaves still two hours away, they would likely be discovered. Surprise was their only chance. If they retreated, they would be without water and the men were already near the end of their endurance.

"We can't retreat. It is too late," Yusuf insisted.

"My ancestors never retreated, and I will not be the first," the duke retorted. "We will attack now."

❧

May 19, 1843. Still with his eyes on Lamoricière, Abd el-Kader was inside his tent when the flap was opened to a grim-faced messenger. He came forward silently and fell on his knees to grasp the emir's outstretched hands.

"They have attacked your smala," the man finally blurted out. "The king's son has taken your douar."

The emir was speechless for a moment, then recovered enough to issue orders summoning his regular cavalry. He then withdrew to his private corner at the back of the tent. An hour later, he reemerged to speak to his anxious men.

"Praise be to God!" he said quietly. "All those things which I prized so much and were dear to me only impeded my movements and distracted me. Now I shall be able to fight the infidel free and unencumbered." Seeing some of his men with tears in their eyes, the emir added: "Why should we mourn? Are not the ones we have lost in paradise?"

Abd el-Kader rode south to rescue those who had fled during the attack on the smala three days earlier, news of which had been delayed by the difficulty the messenger had finding his camp. Following the tracks of the French who had already returned to Tiaret with their booty, the emir saw thousands of pages from his precious manuscripts fluttering about the barren, flinty landscape like wounded butterflies. From refugees, the emir learned that his family had escaped capture thanks to the heroic efforts of Ben Fakha. They were somewhere in the Djebel Amour. At Taguin, he found the remnants of his library. Heaps of ashes. The French had burned everything they couldn't take away.

The emir stared disbelievingly. The destruction of his books was a sacreligous act. What is more valuable than knowledge? How could this be the act of a higher civilization, as the franci claimed to be? The pain of his loss was offset, in part, by the discovery of his family. His mother, wives and children were safe among other refugees from whom he learned details of what had happened.

In the early morning light, people in the smala had mistaken the spahis galloping over the dunes in their red burnooses for Abd el-Kader's returning regulars. The women shouted out their shrill *yous yous* of joy that became screams of terror when the first shots were fired. In the chaos and hysteria, there was no organized defense. Panicked animals got snarled in tent ropes, pulling tents down on whole families trying to escape. Several hundred Hachem sacrificed themselves defending the emir's douar, allowing his family to escape on mules with Ben Fakha amid the madness.

Within two hours, the French had seized the emir's tent given him by Desmichels, his standards and even his richly embroidered caftan that the Moroccan sultan had sent him to ratify his authority as commander of the faithful. Gone too was his treasury worth millions of francs. The French rounded up 3000 prisoners and tens of thousands of sheep and other livestock.

An officer wrote afterward: "To do as the prince did, to attack such a huge mass of people with only five hundred men, one must be twenty-one years old, not know what danger is, or have the devil in him. The women alone could have defeated us if each had simply drawn a tent cord across the path of our horses as they charged through the camp and then knocked us on the head with their slippers."

"When we saw the small numbers of the victors, our faces were red with shame. If every man in the smala had fought, even with a stick, they would have been beaten. But the decree of God had been fulfilled," a refugee declared.

൚

Another decree had also been fulfilled, but it gave the emir no consolation. A few days later, some members of the Flitta tribe brought a gift for the emir. They knelt before him and unwrapped an object covered in a red cloth.

Abd el-Kader looked at it in horror, then closed his eyes. In front of him was the familiar white-haired, hawk-nosed face of Mustafa Ben Ismail, as well as his scarred right hand. But Abd el-Kader didn't see a haughty, devious enemy, but a fearless warrior who had respected his father and saved Muhi al-Din's life from Bey Hussan's paranoia. "Why didn't you listen to the voice of God and our holy Prophet? Why didn't you fight with me to serve a just cause?" the emir murmured.

As the grisly remains of the seventy-eight-year-old *makhzen* were respectfully buried, Abd el-Kader declared: "With the death of Mustafa Ben Ismail a great fighting spirit has departed, but also a terrifying spirit of personal hatred."

Arrogance, lust and greed had each played its part in the death of this remarkable septuagarian. When Lamoricière had received the news of the prince's great coup at Taguin, he headed southeast to intercept remnants of the Hachem fleeing west. Riding with him was Ben Ismail and several hundred of his Douairs and Smelas happy to have been given the job of killing and plundering the remaining members of the Hachem loyal to the emir.

The Hachem were hated not only because they were the emir's tribal family, but because they were effete marabouts who needed to be taught a lesson once and for all — men of the book were not true fighters. Ben Ismail's cavalry headed back to Tiaret loaded with the wages of war. Their booty was so immense, he asked Lamoricière for permission to continue on to Oran, where his men could divide up the hundreds of camels and sheep, personal belongings and provisions they had captured from the demoralized Hachem.

Lamoricière advised the old *makhzen* to go north through the Mina Valley, a longer but safer route. The more direct path to Oran would take him through Flitta territory. Though they had formally submitted, the Flittas were known to be still sympathetic to the emir, whose very presence could unravel French alliances with the tribes. Lamoricière offered Ben Ismail a battalion of infantry as an escort, but the proud warrior would have none of it. He had other things on his mind.

Ben Ismail was obsessed. A young girl was waiting for him in Oran, a new flower to be added to an already rich bouquet of concubines. Infantry would only slow his return. Nor did the Flittas worry him. He had 600 battle-hardened horsemen with him, though now their swift horses were sagging under the weight of plunder.

The returning Douairs and Smelas were attacked in Flitta territory, just as Lamoricière had feared. Ben Ismail was shot in the chest as he rode back to help his men in the rear. His men were not so brave. When they saw that their leader had fallen, they panicked and abandoned their chief's body in favor of saving their plunder. So ashamed were they afterward by their cowardice, that the survivors did not approach their wives for forty days. The truth of an old Arab proverb had been demonstrated: "Fear enters the heart of a lion through the door of greed."

The French had to buy the remains of their *makhzen* from the Flittas. Ben Ismail's mutilated corpse was buried in Oran with full honors due an ally who had already been awarded the Legion of Honor, been made a brigadier general of native spahis and again, in 1842, made a commander of the Legion of Honor. Few Muslims came to his funeral, however. Ben Ismail's nephew forbade his tribesmen to be present. They didn't deserve the honor.

"So ended the life of this man whose base jealousy of Abd el-Kader threw him into our ranks," wrote Pellissier de Reynaud. "He showed astonishing bravery in battle, but his character was hard and greedy." Pellissier knew something about Ben Ismail. He had succeeded Lamoricière as head of the Arab Bureau.

ↈↈ

Six months later, the emir suffered another blow. Abd el-Kader had regrouped along the Moroccan frontier after the capture of his smala and left Mohammed Ben Allal in command of the remnants of his regular army. In November, the emir learned that Ben Allal's head had been on display throughout much of Oran and Tittery.

His caliph of Miliana had lost his whole family on May 16. He too had been absent when his mother, his wives, children and brothers were taken prisoner; yet, their capture had only made him more determined to fight. The chief of the Arab Bureau, and thirty native troops composed of guides, translators and informers tracked him down west of Tlemcen, near the Rio Salado, where he and the last of his men died fighting. The French ordered their native troops to deliver the famous caliph's head to General Lamoricière. This was a great victory for France.

Ben Allal's aggressive tactics, influence among the tribes in central Algeria and fierce loyalty to the emir's cause had won the admiration of French officers. Only a year earlier, Bugeaud had tried to pry him away from the emir with massives bribes: a down payment of 500,000 francs, restitution of his family's ancestral lands and annuity of 50,000 francs in return for submitting to French authority. His contemptuous response was recorded in Gen. Changarnier's *Memoirs*:

> "From Djebel Dakhla to the River Fodda, I command, I fight,
> I forgive. In exchange for this power that I exercise for the glory
> of God and the service of my sultan, Abd el-Kader, what do
> you propose? My lands, which my guns will get back in the
> same way they were taken, money, and the title of traitor."

When rumors and disinformation are the currency of the realm, indisputable facts become gold doubloons. Lamoricière had Ben Allal's head salted, sacked and taken to Algiers. The famous one-eyed head was shown along the route to the locals as irrefutable proof that the emir's much-feared lieutenant really was dead. The grisly displays contained a simple message: further resistance was futile. Miliana, once the seat of his caliphate, was honored with a three-day exhibition of Ben Allal's remains. Bugeaud then ordered that the twenty-seven-year-old warrior be given a burial worthy of a respected senior officer.

To Bugeaud, it seemed now the war was virtually over. At a banquet in Algiers at the end of November, the general congratulated himself.

"After the spring campaign, I might have proclaimed that Algeria was conquered and subdued. I preferred to state less than the truth. Today, after the splendid victory of November 11, when the remnants of the emir's infantry were annihilated and his first and most distinguished caliph killed, I will boldly declare that all serious fighting is over. With a handful of cavalry that remains to him, he might execute a coup de main against former tribes who have submitted to us, but he can do nothing on a large scale. He has lost all power of raising taxes and recruiting men. The country is organized by us and for us. Everywhere taxes are paid to France and our orders obeyed."

There was an ominous calm as the year 1843 drew to its close.

♋

When despair seeped into his camp, the emir often spread false rumors: France was at war with England and was going to withdraw most of its troops; Bugeaud had been dismissed; Paris was seeking peace once again.

Like all good rumors, these had a kernal of truth attached to them. Criticism of Bugeaud was real. The liberal press in France despised him. Impatience with Bugeaud's inability to capture the emir was growing in Paris. The British popular press was very anti-French and its government was concerned about French designs on Morocco. Tribal loyalty to France had been weakened by the "Tafna effect," or fear that the French would leave them in the lurch. Word had to be put out that there would be no more negotiations with the emir. France wasn't leaving Algeria.

CHAPTER FIFTEEN

Mischief Makers, 1844-1847

"WHY DON'T YOU WRITE? The sight of your seal alone will revive our hopes." Ben Salem's couriers had ridden for weeks to deliver his desperate plea to the emir, who had taken asylum in Morocco with his much shrunken smala. "The French are saying you are dead and that your mother writes in your name...They are threatening to march on me and I don't know what to tell my Kabyles...Please respond in your own hand."

"I received your letter telling me of the news of my death," Abd el-Kader replied to his loyal caliph in the east. "...My time has not yet come and I will never regret serving a cause for which you have given everything...Be patient in adversity," Abd el-Kader counseled, "for patience is the mark of superior spirits. Encourage your subordinates — help them, tolerate their errors of judgment. Be charitable in your assessment of their capabilities...I hope to be with you soon so we can come to an agreement about the best path to follow. In the meantime, please accept this horse. It is a gift I received from Sultan Moulay Abderrahman. Maybe it will bring you good fortune..."

The Moroccan sultan's position as leader of the faithful required at least a pro forma support for the emir, though Moulay Abderrahman also saw him as a dangerous rival for his people's affections. Abd el-Kader also had politics on his mind — international politics was his last hope. If he could draw the French into Moroccan territory, he might provoke an intervention by Great Britain, whose foreign minister, Lord Palmerston, was known to be watchful of France's actions in the Mediterranean.

Abd el-Kader succeeded all too well at getting Bugeaud to violate Moroccan sovereignty. When the Sultan didn't respond to Bugeaud's ultimatums to hand over the emir, Papa Bugeaud occupied Oujda with 6,500 men, dismissing fears of the diplomatic fallout expressed by some of his more cautious officers. He would teach Abderrahman a lesson. "They may have 100,000 men, but it is a mob. We have an army," Bugeaud bluffly told his vastly outnumbered troops the night before the engagement. The general's instincts were right. Following his crushing victory at Oued Isly in September of 1844, no British intervention occurred.

Bugeaud's rout of the Sultan's army at Isly made him the man of the hour in Paris. For a short while, the general the French press called "the ogre" and "the monster," was undeniably a hero. King Louis-Philippe honored his victory by conferring upon the general the title Duke of Isly, and Marshal of France. Not since Napoleon had a French general been so celebrated.

An admiring Saint-Arnaud was pleased that his chief had been finally recognized properly: "The Marshal is quite indescribable," he noted in his journal. "He is interested in everything and talks about everything in a lively, cleverly sensible way. Yet, he is quite illiterate, not able to translate a word of Latin, but capable of everything, and carved out of a block of granite."

The Treaty of Tangier imposed by France was not vindictive and reassured a skeptical Lord Palmerston that France's aims were not territorial. France wanted only to end its "war without end" in Algeria by forcing the Sultan to deny Abd el-Kader asylum. The Sultan agreed to declare the emir an outlaw and to prevent him from getting aid — conditions difficult to enforce when frontiers were vague and tribes independent-minded.

In January 1845, the "block of granite" defended his Algerian strategy before the Chamber of Deputies. The framework of Abd el-Kader's federation, Bugeaud explained, had been dismantled piece by piece. One by one the tribes that had been loyal to the emir had submitted to France. The emir had been forced to hide in Morocco where he was now *persona non grata*.

"This does not mean he will not come back. However, he will no longer be dangerous though he will make mischief. That is why we must remain strong and on our guard… We are in a position to make the Arabs repent of any insurrection, but they must be made to feel the use of force as little as possible. It is by means of a government that is strong, paternal and just that we can obtain the submission of the Arabs. Not absolute submission; there will be occasional uprisings, but they will be rare."

Every Arab, he went on, was a fighting man. Warfare between tribes was the normal state of affairs. From childhood, they were taught to ride and use weapons. Stealing from one's enemies was a form of virtue as it accustomed them to danger. Though civil colonization might work in the towns, military colonization was essential in the interior. "Our colonists must never let their muskets rust, and be always ready to grab them. They must be disciplined, for discipline alone can give strength to the few. I strongly insist on this idea of military colonization…it seems to me fundamental."

But Bugeaud would not conceal his admiration for the emir, in particular his method of organizing the country. "He is a genius," said the Marshal, "and we did not think we could in any way improve upon his system of administration. We have changed the men but left the system untouched."

Bugeaud forgot to mention some important differences. Under Abd el-Kader, taxes, even when paid under duress, were for the benefit of a common cause. And Abd el-Kader was known to take nothing for himself or his family. Under the French, tax money went overwhelmingly to benefit the conquerors. Further, their supercilious attitude and contemptuous display of superiority infuriated the Arabs.

⌘

Bugeaud was more foresighted than he may have imagined. Not only was Abd el-Kader capable of causing "mischief," so were others. In September 1845, Bugeaud had returned to France to do some politicking in the Dordogne, to promote his ideas for military colonization and explain to Paris why 80,000 troops still could not capture the emir. A month later, the "mischief-makers" had forced the Marshal to rush back from France to put out brush fires that threatened to become a conflagration. He was given another 26,000 troops to stamp out the flames, bringing the total to 106,000 men, one-third of the French army.

What had happened during the nine months since his January speech? At first, the phenomenon was not taken seriously. In the Dahra, a mountainous region honeycombed with caves between the Chlef River and the Mediterranean, lived a young man who went by the name Mohammed Ben Abdallah. He shared his rare meals with his pet goat and, it was said, received prophetic inspiration from it. He was also young, handsome, pious, wore ragged clothes typical of a holy man and lived with a wealthy elderly widow who had been seduced by his saintly aura.

The twenty-year-old spoke of Abd el-Kader dismissively. A Muslim legend foretold that a man named Mohammed Ben Abdallah would come from God in the hour of need and drive Christians into the sea. One evening at dinner, Ben Abdallah suddenly announced to the widow that he was the one foretold by the prophecies, the Destined One who would appear at the hour of deliverance. He promised she would hear more of him.

Before long, Mohammed Ben Abdallah was being hailed as Bou Maza, Father of the Goat. His claim to have been called by God to exterminate the French and to create a new monarchy based on Islam had aroused followers. Many of the Arabs who had half-heartedly submitted to the French joined his movement after Bou Maza executed two pro-French caids.

In the summer and autumn of 1845, the French were facing a Bou Maza hydra. Dozens of imitators were cropping up in the Chlef Valley, calling themselves Mohammed Ben Abdallah. Many also adopted the name Bou Maza, causing enormous confusion before they were caught. Another Mohammed Ben Abdallah rose up in Tittery where he also decapitated two "French" caids and unleashed new rebellions around Algiers. A force of 3000 men was needed to hunt him down. There was Mohammed Ben Abdallah of the Beni Menacer, but he was quickly abandoned by his own tribe as an ineffectual imposter and handed over to the French. Another Mohammed Ben Abdallah El-Fadel claimed he was the resurrected Jesus. He invited his followers to go unarmed into battle, assuring them he would strike down the enemy by supernatural means. To General Cavaignac, El-Fadel wrote, "Cease to do injustice and wrong. God loves it not...I am the likeness of him who issued from the breath of God. I am the likeness of our Lord Jesus. I am Jesus restored to life, as all know who believe in God and His Prophet..."

Then there was Bou Maza of the Beni Zaqzooq who claimed to be the brother of the original Bou Maza. An officer of the Arab Bureau remembered parts of the interrogation following his capture.

"What do you accuse the French of? Theft, exaction, injustice? Don't be afraid to speak the truth."

"None of that. The Arabs hate you because you are foreigners, you are not of their faith, and now you come to take their country. Tomorrow you will want their virgins."

"Despite what you say, a great many Arabs like us and are loyal to our cause."

"I will be frank with you. Every day you will meet Arabs who say they love you and are your faithful servants. Do not believe them; they lie to you out of fear or self-interest. But whenever a leader arises who they think can conquer you, they will follow him."

"How can Arabs hope to conquer us when they are led by chiefs who have no army, no cannon, and no money?"

"Victory comes from God. When He chooses, He makes the weak to triumph and casts down the strong."

℘

The dream of every French officer was to be the one who captured Abd el-Kader. In September 1845, when Bugeaud had left for Paris to promote his ideas of military colonization, the champion of all mischief-makers profited from the difficulties Bou Maza was creating in the Chlef valley. Abd el-Kader, with 6000 horsemen, reentered Algerian territory to unite the brushfires burning in the Dahra region. In the emir's path was a small garrison at the port of Djemaa Ghazaouet, a sliver of sand surrounded by cliffs. This boring supply depot for troops in the Tlemcen area, renamed Nemours, had an overly energetic and ambitious commander.

Lieutenant Colonel Montagnac was born to fight. He first made a name for himself in 1832, when he refused a Legion of Honor cross from King Louis-Philippe for his display of bravery while crushing bloody street riots in Paris. His principles, he explained, would not allow him to take a medal for killing Frenchmen. In Algeria, under the command of Lamoricière, he had found happiness and scope for his ambition. "My blood is up, I have a well tempered body, two horses and a love of warfare — that is all I need to gallop boldly into the future," he wrote his brother.

Since coming to Africa in 1837, Montagnac had impressed his superiors with his intelligence, hard work and desire to understand the native cultures. He advocated using the Arab system of justice, not sentimental French mores. He had only contempt for General Cavaignac who had put him in the brig for four days, merely because he had summarily executed a Kabyle who had assassinated a fellow officer, and following Arab custom, planted the culprit's head on a stake as a message to others. "If they know you will use the saber when needed, they become as supple as gloves on your hand. Strike them justly, and they never complain, but hit them hard and promptly."

His thin, powerful physique was always in training to hit hard. Few officers were his equal in fencing, horsemanship and shooting. He had a remarkable talent for drawing and painting as well. "He could have earned his living with his paint brush," his commanding officer noted, adding: "He was adored and feared by his subordinates, always solicitous of his men but known also for dispensing severe discipline and being unforgiving when his code of honor was violated — the art of war was a cult for him."

Which was why he was bored that September. Montagnac had been ordered not to leave Djemaa Ghazaouet. "I love this austere life," he wrote his uncle. "I eat twice a day. Three eggs and coffee is my breakfast. In the evening I have rice or potatoes, a glass of water and a cup of coffee. That is my diet and I feel healthy and vigorous." Montagnac was overflowing with energy, but inactivity was killing him. "I feel like a bullock pulling a plow. My plodding life is putting me to sleep."

Montagnac learned that Abd el-Kader was in the area, possibly trying to link up with Bou Maza in the Chlef Valley. Tribes recently submitted to the French were in danger of being punished by him. Crazy for action and a chance to measure himself against the emir, Montagnac threw caution to the wind on the night of September 21. Ignoring his orders to stay put, he led a force of 425 light cavalry of the recently arrived Chasseurs d' Orléans to hunt the emir.

The impetuous Montagnac foolishly allowed his small force to be drawn into an ambush. Trapped in a ravine and attacked on all sides, he died as he wished — on the battlefield, sword in hand and a bullet in his chest. The remaining chasseurs scrambled to a nearby marabout named Sidi Brahim, and took cover behind its white, stubby walls while the Arabs were rifling through the belongings of the dead Frenchmen. Some figs, a few rolls of bread, a couple of handfuls of potatoes and a bottle of absinthe was all the eighty-two soldiers had to survive a siege.

In his rush for glory, Montagnac had not even seen that his men had brought extra water.

Abd el-Kader had qualms about attacking a marabout, qualms that were sharpened by the prospect of losing many men in a frontal assault. Four times Abd el-Kader tried to get the trapped soldiers to surrender. The first message was honey coated. If the men surrendered, they would be honorably treated; if not, they would all die. The second reminded them that the emir held eighty of their comrades. If they did not surrender, the prisoners would be executed. "They are in the hands of God. We have plenty of food and ammunition," the chasseurs bravely shouted back.

Abd el-Kader's third message was written in French by one of his prisoners, threatening to starve them to death.

"Shit on Abd el-Kader!" was all the chasseurs had to say.

Finally, the emir ordered a captured officer to go out and reason with his compatriots. If he failed, he was told he would be killed. Instead, he shouted: "Hold out against these butchers. Fight to the death." The captain was immediately shot in the back.

The emir withdrew his main force, leaving behind Bou Hamidi's men to watch the trapped soldiers, who were soon reduced to drinking their urine and sucking moisture from the grass. When the chasseurs finally understood that they weren't going to be rescued, they decided it was better to die fighting than "to be cooked in a pan." Shortly before dawn on the third night the men slipped over the walls of the marabout to get back to Ghazaouet.

Bou Hamidi's cavalry followed the pitifully formed defensive square at a respectful distance as the chasseurs gamely dragged themselves the twelve miles back to their base, while singing the "Marseillaise." One thousand meters from the gates of their fort, the delirious men saw a small creek. At the sight of water, the demons of thirst overwhelmed the last shreds of discipline holding together the ragged little force. That was when the Arabs descended.

The chasseurs were still fighting when three shots from the fort's cannons scattered Bou Hamidi's men. But that day, Arab fear of cannon fire was matched by a Frenchman's fear of treachery. So convinced was the fort's commander of the reliability of a report he had received, indicating that Montagnac's detachment had been completely annihilated, he wouldn't open the gates to send out a rescue party. Until the men were virtually at the threshold, he had imagined the pitiful figures in front of him were Arabs wearing the uniforms of the dead soldiers.

Seventeen soldiers of the original four hundred and twenty-five who left Nemours made it back alive to the fort, four of whom died of exhaustion soon after. Ninety-seven prisoners had been taken. The rest were dead.

⁂

A few days later, another disaster landed on the French. Bou Hamidi's men surprised a convoy loaded with food, ammunition and convalescents. The outnumbered guards assigned to protect it had simply fled. Two hundred more prisoners fell into the emir's hands.

The two events had a predictable effect. Paris was in a tizzy. Lamoricière wrote a somber report about the situation, worried that the emir would join forces with Bou Maza farther east and that recently submitted tribes would have a change of heart. Bugeaud cut short his politicking to hurry back to deal with the crisis. Abd el-Kader was again the man of destiny. A tremor of hope fluttered through tribal councils.

The emir continued to weave and evade his way east to consult with his loyal caliph of the Kabyles, Ben Salem. Abd el-Kader knew that confronting French forces directly was folly, but he clung to the hope that by his mere presence he could rekindle enthusiasm for jihad and get submitted tribes to defect. From the fall of 1845 through the spring of 1846, the emir seemed to be everywhere, miraculously avoiding capture by the eighteen columns Bugeaud had set in motion to find him. In England, where Bugeaud was known to the public as "The Butcher of the Bedouins," the press wallowed gleefully in the reports of his difficulties. *Punch Magazine* mockingly suggested that no such person as Abd el-Kader actually existed.

He was seen near Tiaret in December, but had vanished to the south by the time more troops arrived. Then he was north in the Ouarsenis Massif after evading Lamoricière; Saint-Arnaud was looking for him in the south. In February, the emir suddenly appeared in Kabylia while Bugeaud was hunting him in the Chlef. In Kabylia, Abd el-Kader joined forces with Ben Salem. Algiers was in a state of panic. French military prisoners were taken out of jails and formed into two battalions of militia to defend the city.

Three generals died of exhaustion that winter, along with thousands of horses that simply dropped dead. Two hundred and thirty French soldiers froze to death near Setif. "What a war," wrote Saint-Arnaud. "Four days ago it was 20 degrees, today it is three degrees frost. There is no wood, no fodder, not a shack. Everything has to be brought. The Arab carries nothing but his rifle, his cartridges and a knife to cut off your head…They flee and they attack with equal speed and fury. We are always at a disadvantage. We wage a war that brings us no glory."

In early March 1846, Abd el-Kader held a meeting with leaders of tribes who had come from all over the mountainous Kabylia. He employed all his oratorical talent to convince them to unite and fight harder. Some of the chiefs were ready to reenlist in the struggle. Others were hesitant.

When word came that Bugeaud was advancing into the region, the voices of doubt prevailed. The imbalance of forces was all too apparent.

Abd el-Kader returned to Morocco in July. He had narrow escapes, been continuously hunted, yet saved many times by the support of a population that kept him informed of French whereabouts. If people wouldn't fight for him, they were sympathetic and admired his tenacity. But even in the Sahara, the French had made their presence felt. Among his most reliable supporters — the Ouled Sidi Sheikh, the Beni Nail, the Beni Hassan — he found only weariness and discouragement. "You are like a fly that torments a bull," the chiefs told the emir. "After you have angered it, you disappear, and we are the ones who are gored." He had covered 2,100 miles. It had been a Herculean effort to rekindle the dwindling fires of rebellion. The emir began to think that God must have another plan for him.

༄

The emir would face a different crisis when he returned to camp. A moral one.

The prisoners captured during the fighting at Sidi Brahim the previous September had been taken to Morocco. The wounded were put on mules that did double duty carrying baskets full of heads coated with honey whose antibacterial properties, the Arabs had learned, preserved

180

the grisly evidence of their laurels won in battle. Able-bodied prisoners walked for three days on empty stomachs until dusk when they received some biscuits and, if they were near a village, could trade the buttons on their uniforms for some figs.

The once impressive smala had become a mere camp, a deira in Arab parlance, whose inhabitants of mostly women and children were spread along the Moulouya River. In the center of the deira were the green and white banners that marked the tents of the emir's mother, Lalla Zohra, and his wives. His alter ego, Ben Fakha, received the prisoners, made coffee for the officers and bound up the wounds of one whose life had been saved by Bou Hamidi. The enlisted men, however, were marched around the camp to satisfy the curiosity of the women.

Bedouin notions of natural aristocracy, evident in horses and men, could also save lives. Worthy opponents should be treated respectfully in defeat. And officers were more worthy than ordinary soldiers. One officer who benefited from these chivalrous notions was Cpt. Courby de Cognord, a chasseur who fought courageously while wounded in the head. Bou Hamidi had noticed his officer's epaulettes and had checked the hand of an Arab who was about to cut the Frenchmen's throat.

After Sidi Brahim, the emir continued east toward Algiers and beyond, leaving Bou Hamidi in command of the deira. His old friend and schoolmate from the zawiya had scrupulously followed the emir's instructions for treating prisoners from October through April 1846. As commander, de Cognord had been allowed to write letters to Algiers on behalf of all the prisoners. Money, medicines and linens had, indeed, been sent and received — money to buy things from the Moroccan tradesmen peddling their wares at the deira, and linens to mummify themselves at night from scorpions, tarantulas and snakes.

The treatment of the prisoners had been consistently humane, even if they were paraded around the camp during certain religious celebrations. One day, Bou Hamidi rebuked his Arabs who taunted them, telling them, "you insult these Frenchmen because they are few and unarmed. If they had weapons, they would show you how to deal with a couple hundred men like you."

The prisoners suffered, though not alone. The heat by day, the cold by night and the vermin did not discriminate between Frenchman and Arab. Neither did hunger, as the prisoners received the same rations as the Arabs. Moroccan merchants would no longer accept the emir's currency, even those willing to defy the Sultan. The capture of the convoy the preceding October had added 200 more prisoners to the ninety-seven from Sidi Brahim. Feeding them became a heavy burden for the Arabs.

On April 6, 1846, Mustafa Ben Thami arrived at the deira with the sick and wounded from the emir's long campaign. He had been with the emir since the previous September, and had been ordered to take command of the deira. Bou Hamidi was to rejoin the emir with any troops not essential for guarding the prisoners. But few tribal contingents wanted to fight anymore. Only 500 regulars were available, but they were needed to guard the prisoners and the camp.

Ben Thami and Bou Hamidi spent their nights discussing the problems caused by having so many French prisoners. French and Moroccan troops were constantly searching for them, as Bugeaud had refused to consider a prisoner exchange. The prisoners required a heavy guard. There wasn't enough food for their own people, much less the Frenchmen. Morale was low and their tribal allies were melting away. However, the two men were opposite spirits and couldn't agree on a solution.

Ben Thami had just experienced a long hard campaign with the emir. He was known to be severe in dealing with the Christians and Muslims alike. Ben Thami could conceive of only one solution — to kill them and gain a double benefit. They would not have to feed the Frenchmen anymore and their blood would make tribes considering defection think again about the kind of welcome they would receive from the French side. Bou Hamidi thought that murdering them would go against everything the emir believed. He argued for taking the prisoners near some French post and simply releasing them, as the emir had done after the visit of Abbé Suchet five years earlier. However, Ben Thami was officially in command of the camp, and he disagreed.

By April, the prisoners were being held at a separate location, twelve miles away from the deira. On April 23rd, a courier brought a message from the emir to warn Ben Thami of possible razzias by the French and Moroccans. It urged him to do everything possible to save the prisoners' lives. Only if they were in imminent danger of falling into the hands of either the Sultan or the French, they should be killed.

The next day, Ben Thami invited the officers to eat couscous with him in the deira that evening. Though suspicious, the officers were not allowed to decline the honor. The remaining prisoners were divided into groups of five and ordered to sleep in separate tents for the night. By morning, 170 prisoners had either been shot or had their throats cut. Two men had escaped during the madness. The night of the massacre, Abd el-Kader had been far away in the Sahara with the Beni Nail, who were explaining why they could no longer support his jihad.

෴

The government was angrily questioned by deputies outraged by news of the slaughter. Some wanted revenge. Other wanted to know why the emir's offers to exchange prisoners had been ignored. The president of the council of ministers, Guizot, explained that Marshal Bugeaud was against any further prisoner exchanges. The governor-general was convinced that any exchange would be exploited by the emir as evidence that France was seeking peace, which, in turn, he would use to discourage tribes from submitting to France.

The killing of the prisoners was a gift that Bugeaud immediately used to undermine the emir's moral authority. He spread far and wide news of the outrage. "Every Arab endowed with good sense and religion will know that this was an act of desperation which proves that the son of Muhi al-Din has been abandoned by both men and God," read the governor-general's announcement.

A year earlier, Bugeaud had been before the Chamber to face deputies apoplectic over atrocities two of his own commanders had organized, each condemned for "the cold-blooded murder of a defenseless enemy," and for "staining the honor of France." During the Bou Maza uprisings in the summer of 1845, Pellissier de Reynaud and Saint-Arnaud had each separately suffocated thousands of men, women and children who had taken refuge in caves and refused to surrender. Whereas Bugeaud stood by his offending officers, Abd el-Kader had no one to argue his case.

Bugeaud and others knew the truth, but it wasn't useful. After the massacre, the French consul in Fez had been informed by defectors from the emir's camp of what had occurred. Ben Thami had ordered the killing, of that there was no doubt, and he had misused the emir's instructions to do so. There had been no immediate danger of an attack

by Moroccan or French forces, but Ben Thami exploited the condi-
tional clause in the emir's instructions and exaggerated the threat to
justify the slaughter. But the French consul, de Chasteau, advised the
government that it was useful to hide the truth. "Our politics requires
us to maintain that the emir is the sole author of this crime because it
has done him great harm, even among his closest allies."

ço

The emir didn't learn all these details until July 18, the day he returned
to his deira, three months after the fact. Lalla Zohra was in mourning
and still had not spoken to Ben Thami. Abd el-Kader was furious with
his brother-in-law. His letters proposing to Lamoricière and Bugeaud an
exchange had gone unanswered. But what to do with the survivors?

De Cognord was allowed to send letters to Bugeaud, Cavaignac and
the French consul in Morocco, informing them that the emir was going to have eleven men taken to the Spanish port of Melilla. A private
transaction had been arranged, the details of which the emir chose to
remain ignorant.

Four of his chiefs had colluded with the prisoners to have them
formally appeal to the emir to be returned home via Spanish intermediaries, a request that the chiefs would support. But the same four men
had independently offered their help to the French consul to liberate
the prisoners in return for 6,000 piasters, about 33,000 francs. The
planned transaction was never acknowledged by the French command,
but on November 24, 1846, two Arabs presented themselves to the
authorities in Melilla to explain the procedures for consummating the
business. The next day, the eleven tired and happy men disembarked
at Djemaa Gazaouet where they were treated to raucous celebration by
the garrison.

Letters from the emir were forwarded by Captain de Cognord to
Louis-Philippe, War Minister Soult and Bugeaud. Out of loyalty, he
would not disavow his brother-in-law's action. He also couldn't leave
the impression that his authority was disregarded by his caliphs. The
Commander of the Faithful publicly would always take responsibility
for the crime. Yet, the emir wanted to shift the blame. "…Recently,
when we had a certain number of prisoners in our hands, we wrote
more than once to your representatives to propose an exchange," the
emir wrote to Louis-Philippe. "We never received a response and all

our couriers were thrown in prison. This was a violation of French customs, more so because a messenger between two hostile sides is always
considered as a neutral..." He ended by making an appeal to the king
to release certain prisoners captured at his smala. The letters were never
answered.

Before being ransomed, de Cognord was summoned to have coffee
with the emir. The two talked at length, and when the painful subject of
the killing came up, Abd el-Kader told the Frenchman: "If I had been
in my deira, your men would never have died. Moulay Abderrahman
would never have tried to rescue your men," Abd el-Kader told him,
defending his brother-in-law. "This war is a scourge."

On the eve of the prisoners' departure for Melilla, Abd el-Kader
expressed before all his chiefs his deep regret at what happened. On
November 23, 1846, fourteen months after being captured, Courby
de Cognord left the camp at Äin Zohra on a beautiful stallion the emir
had given him for his ride to the coast. When de Cognord reached
Melilla, he sent back the tainted gift to its owner.

Later, an indignant Bugeaud told an emissary from the emir: "Tell
your master that if you had returned the prisoners without ransom, I
would have freed three Arabs for each Frenchman; because he made us
pay for their liberty and had the others killed, I owe him nothing but
my indignation for his barbarity."

"You forget that the circumstances of life change," a wounded Abd
el-Kader wrote back. "We never step in the same river twice. I know
this better than you. From the birth of Adam until the human race dies
out, nothing can be durable on this earth."

CHAPTER SIXTEEN
Men of Honor

S ULTAN ABDERRAHMAN HAD TO DECIDE which he feared the most: French reprisals for not fulfilling his treaty commitments, or his subjects' bile for not supporting the emir's jihad. The sultan also worried that Abd el-Kader had designs on his throne, which made it easier for him to do France's bidding.

Abderrahman's imagination was not working unassisted. Many of the tribes were not happy with his capricious rule. Along the eastern frontier were thousands of Algerian émigrés whose sympathies for the emir could be unpredictably roused from the dormant to the active state by the slightest movement of Fortuna. Rumors were circulating in the *bled* that Abd el-Kader might replace the apostate sultan, who preferred compromise with the infidel French over support for jihad. Yet, Abd el-Kader was his father's son. And his father had practiced his belief that all authority, whether good or bad, is ordained by God. Bad authority was better than no authority. The sultan would have to abdicate first.

Abd el-Kader was also a hunted man who had to keep moving in the summer of 1847. Rif tribes were pressured not to trade with the emir's deira, his foraging parties were attacked and even a murder plot was hatched. The emir headed southeast, back toward the Moulouya River along Morocco's frontier with Algeria. The sultan ordered an attack at Ahlaf. When Abd el-Kader saw the huge Moroccan campsite, he struck first. The next night, he scattered the Moroccans by stampeding into their camp hundreds of panicked camels harnessed to bundles of fagots that had been set on fire.

Abd el-Kader made one last, desperate effort at reconciliation with the sultan. In early November, Bou Hamidi volunteered for a risky peace mission to Fez. He was to appeal to the sultan in writing and remind him of the sacred traditions of hospitality, of the bonds of friendship and religion and the deep respect the emir and his father had always shown to the sultan. With little hope and much sadness, Abd el-Kader said goodbye to Bou Hamidi, sensing that he might never again see his faithful caliph.

For six days, the sultan kept the ex-caliph of Tlemcen waiting as if he were the lowliest delivery boy. Once granted, the audience became stormy and Bou Hamidi was thrown in prison. A return message was sent to Abd el-Kader telling him to surrender to the sultan in person or return to the Algerian desert. If he refused, the sultan's army would march against him.

The emir's choices were few. The year 1847 had been marked by submissions. In February, his caliph Ben Salem had finally submitted. He had been convinced of the futility of continued fighting by his son, who had studied in France after he had submitted in 1843. In April, Bou Maza had surrendered to Saint-Arnaud. Abd el-Kader's brother, Mustafa, had taken refuge with the sultan.

Bugeaud had resigned that year as governor-general, but there was no relaxation of the pressure. Opposition to the general's ideas about colonization, fatigue and the unrelenting nipping at his heals by his many enemies in the press and outside, had driven him to ask to be relieved of command. In May, he had announced to the population of Algiers: "My health and the situation caused by opposition to my views make it impossible to take charge of your destinies. I have asked the king to send my successor." His replacement was the man he had recommended: the Duke of Aumale. Younger and gentler, he was no less dedicated than Bugeaud to total domination.

As the odor of despair in his deira became stronger, Abd el-Kader sought wisdom and understanding where he always found it. He spent much of his time in prayer or surrounded by his remaining devoted followers — a hard core of 200 battle-hardened infantry and 1,200 cavalry, who had lived through the same trials of mind, body and spirit as he. When not praying and exhorting his followers to endure, Abd el-Kader would remain alone in his tent. At night, the emir was heard frequently reciting the holy book he had learned by heart as a twelve-year-old.

℘

A violent winter rainstorm was pelting the emir's tent, where he gathered his council the evening of December 21. An important decision needed to be made.

To the west, a frightened and hostile sultan was marching with a new army to chase him back to Algeria. To the east, the tribes had all gone over to the French, seduced by the new governor-general's policy of generosity and reconciliation. No more uprisings in the Ouarsenis Massif, the Medea or Kabylia were possible. The intrepid Ben Allal was dead, his only caliph to die on the field of battle. Ben Salem and Bou Maza had submitted. To the north was Lamoricière. The only escape was south, into the Sahara, where they would get help from friendly factions of the Beni Snassen. Once through the Guerbous Pass, Abd el-Kader could make trouble indefinitely with 1400 men willing to fight to the bitter end.

But that day, Abd el-Kader's scouts had returned with surprising news: two squadrons of Lamoriciére's spahis already occupied the pass. They had exchanged their usual red burnooses for white ones to be less conspicuous to the all-seeing locals who would normally report enemy movements to the emir well in advance. Now the spahis would alert the general in case Abd el-Kader fled into the desert. Though Lamoricière had 3,000 cavalry, Abd el-Kader was informed they were twelve hours away.

His brother-in-law, Ben Thami, Bou Klika, the caid of Tagdempt and Kaddour Ben Allal, a cousin of the caliph, all wanted to attack. The few troops opposed to them could be easily overcome. Once through the pass, they would reach the friendly Beni Snassen. However, Abd el-Kader knew that the inhabitants of the deira would not get through. They were at the end of their strength. So too their horses and camels, which had been reduced to bags of bones. The sick and wounded, the women and children were weak and hungry. Their families would be taken prisoner. He and his men could still create trouble, but to what end? To continue the resistance, some chiefs argued, even if it meant sacrificing their families. To never give up.

Abd el-Kader reviewed the past with them. He reminded them of the vow taken eight years earlier after Tafna was violated — to struggle and endure no matter how great the danger and the suffering. It had been a mutual commitment. The caliphs nodded in agreement.

But the emir thought otherwise.

"I don't think any Muslim can accuse me of not doing everything possible to honor that vow. If there is anything more I can do, tell me." A long silence acknowledged he had done everything in his power.

"Believe me, the fight is over. We must lay down our guns. God is our witness that we have fought as long and as hard as we could — so long as there was hope of liberating our country. But most of the tribes have quit the struggle. My own brothers have submitted to Lamoricière. Now Muslims are killing Muslims. The sultan has imprisoned our brother in arms, Bou Hamidi, massacred the Beni Amer and sold their wives into slavery. The French kept their word after Ben Salem submitted. I would rather put my trust in those whom we have fought against than those who have betrayed us.

"If I thought there were still a possibility to defeat France, I would continue. Further resistance will only create vain suffering. We must accept the judgment of God who has not given us victory and who in his infinite wisdom now wants this land to belong to Christians. Are we going to oppose His will?"

❧

In the early hours of December 22 , a young officer of the spahis was straining to see into the wintery murk. Lieutenant Bou Khouia was proud that General Lamoricière had entrusted him to guard the pass that would be the emir's only escape route. Messengers had told him that the emir was following behind with three of his chieftains. He was going to ask for Lamoricière's aman.

As Bou Khouia and his detachment of spahis rode forward, they suddenly found themselves gazing at the famous emir as he emerged from behind two spots of light made by lanterns tied to the end of long poles. The emir had only one condition for his surrender: that he, his family and followers who chose exile with him, be given a free passage to a Muslim country. He would give his word to never return to Algeria.

Abd el-Kader pulled a piece of paper out from under his burnoose, but the downpour, howling wind and dervish dance of the lanterns made it impossible to write. Instead, he stamped the paper with his seal and told the lieutenant to report his terms to Lamoricière. Bou Khouia rode as fast as the darkness permitted to his general's advancing main column. Lamoricière could not write in the storm either, nor could he find his seal. So he gave the lieutenant his saber and the seal of a fellow officer to take back to the emir. Bou Khouia was to tell Abd el-Kader that the Frenchman's aman had been granted.

The rain had slacked off when Bou Khouia returned to the emir's camp. Abd el-Kader dictated his response to Ben Thami, asking that the general write in his own language "words that cannot be changed or diminished" guaranteeing passage either to Saint John of Acre or to Alexandria, and nowhere else. "… I am ready to sell my camels, mules, horses, and other things belonging to me or my family when others who wish to come with me are free to do so. Please take care to try to liberate Sidi Mohammed Bou Hamidi as soon as possible so that he might accompany me." Abd el-Kader returned the general's sword with his letter.

Bou Khouia galloped back to Lamoricière with the emir's response. This time, Lamoricière had his seal. The general sent word to the governor-general, expected to arrive at Djamaa Ghazaouet by sea, of the commitments he was making in his name. The general knew and respected the prince well enough to be confident that he would ratify them.

"I have the order of the son of the king of France, may God protect him, to grant you his aman and to grant you passage from Djemaa Ghazaouet to Alexandria or Acre. We will not take you anywhere else. Come when it is convenient, day or night. Do not doubt our word. Our sovereign will be generous towards you and your family…As for Bou Hamidi, I will send a boat to Tangier with a letter for the French consul requesting Sultan Moulay Abderrahman to free him…"

The morning of December 23, Abd el-Kader was getting reports telling him that his chiefs at the deira had gone to Lamoricière promising submission and asking protection. Spurred by knowledge of the emir's surrender, some tribes had pillaged his deira. Lamoricière sent a cavalry detachment to protect the remaining families.

ও

Abd el-Kader was anxious. He dreaded having a spectacle made of his surrender in front of the French army. Rather than go east toward Lamoricière, the emir headed north, where he believed his deira was located. Riding with him were Ben Thami, Bou Klika, agha Kara Mohammed and some sixty other chiefs. Abd el-Kader called a halt when they reached the ridge overlooking the valley where two years earlier Colonel Montagnac's cavalry had been slaughtered. Below them was a knoll where the French had formed a square to make their last stand, and where a wounded commander Courby de Cognord had had his life saved by Bou Hamidi. Further west across the valley was the white dome of Sidi Brahim where the Chasseurs d'Orléans had languished for two days without food and water. The snow-covered Trara Mountains could be seen to the East.

For an hour, the emir and his men waited, plunged in thought, gazing silently at the immense sky and open countryside. There was much to think about: their past struggles together, their families, the uncertain future that awaited them, to join or not the emir in permanent exile. Some would never see again the ocean of green, rolling hills speckled with olive orchards spread before them.

A column of cavalry came into view, moving at a steady trot. Abd el-Kader ordered two men to find out who they were and who their commander was, but only after waving their burnooses as a sign they wanted to talk.

The column was under the command of Colonel Cousin de Montauban, who had been guarding the emir's deira all night from pillagers. Montauban was a name familiar to the Arabs. He was one of the few French officers who spoke competent Arabic, and had been the officer chosen to escort the emir's brothers, Hussein and Said, to the French camp two days earlier. The emir sent back word that he wished to talk with him. Montauban agreed, proposing they meet on the knoll, each with an escort of fifteen men. After the customary greetings, Abd el-Kader asked abruptly if Lamoricière would keep his word. Montauban replied that it was not customary for French officers to break their promises. In any case, he was going to meet Lamoricière and could take the emir with him, speaking as if his decision to submit was a *fait accompli.*

Before leaving, Abd el-Kader asked the colonel if he could go down to the marabout and pray. The Frenchman agreed. As they approached the site, Montauban drew up his 500 chasseurs into two rows. With the colonel on his left, and Ben Thami and several other chiefs trailing behind, the chasseurs saluted as the emir rode by. "If I had men like these fine soldiers, I would now occupy Fez," the emir told Montauban.

The wall around the marabout tomb was scarred from the bullets of two years earlier. Abd el-Kader removed his sword before he entered, bending his head to go through the small door leading into the mausoleum of Sidi Brahim. An hour later, the emir stooped out into the light. His unsought-for career as a warrior and nation-builder was over.

While Abd el-Kader was praying, Montauban had been sending messages — one to Lamoricière informing him that the emir was now in his company, another to Djemaa Ghazaouet asking that tents be pitched nearby at Äin Safra for the emir's family. During their brief time together, the emir learned to appreciate the French officer's delicacy and good manners. Mountauban's Arabic was remarkably good, even for someone who had served in Africa for fifteen years. His eighteen-year-old son had lived with Arabs growing up and was widely known and respected among the tribes for his knowledge. Montauban's unplanned arrival on the scene proved to be a godsend for Lamoricière. A less-adroit officer could have spooked the emir, whose horses, even when tired, could always outrun the French.

The distant rumble of a cannon signaled the Duke of Aumale's arrival at port. A message from Lamoricière came telling Montauban to go immediately to Djemaa Ghazaouet. Abd el-Kader hesitated, became stubborn. He refused to go. A humiliating surrender in front of the whole army unnerved him. Montauban understood the emir's position and applied the emir's own principals to dislodge him. What would he have done to an officer who refused to obey him? the colonel asked. That was the position he was being placed in before his own commander if the emir didn't cooperate. But Montauban also understood the emir's pride. They would surely meet Lamoricière en route, he added, well before they arrived at Djemaa Ghazaouet. Relieved by Montauban's assurances, the emir mounted his black mare.

The emir and his chiefs were passing in front of the marabout when, unannounced, trumpets sounded and 500 chasseurs drew their sabers as one. A startled Abd el-Kader asked if they were going to all be killed. A tribute to the men who had died there, Montauban assured him. They had barely left Sidi Brahim when a cloud of dust announced the arrival of Lamoricière at the head of a small detachment.

Abd el-Kader dismounted when the general approached. Lamoricière did the same and walked forward to greet him in Arabic. At forty, he was the youngest general in Africa, one of the brightest stars in the French army, committed to serving God and France. The famous Bou Herawa, "The Father of the Stick" (the only weapon he carried when among the Arabs), was about the same height as the emir, though of stockier build. He cut a dashing figure in his red tarboosh, dark-blue field coat and red pants. His black eyes flashed an authority that had made him feared and respected by tribes throughout Oran. The emir handed Lamoricière his sword and ordered his men to lay down their guns at the general's feet. Visibly moved at the sight of these legendary warriors, their burnooses smudged with gunpowder and blood, submitting in dignified silence, Lamoricière told them to keep their weapons. "Use them to serve France. I will enroll you at once in our *makhzen*."

∞

Lamoricière escorted the emir to Djemaa Ghazaouet. Tremors of excitement and barely controlled glee were almost visible among the French officers trying to maintain a dignified solemnity as Abd el-Kader rode with an air of calm resignation in the chilly dusk. His life had been one of surrender to a Higher Power, and that Higher Power had now decided that France should rule Algeria.

Accompanied by Lamoricière, Cavaignac and Colonel Montauban, Abd el-Kader was led through a small garden to a candlelit cottage where the twenty-five-year-old prince waited expectantly. Abd el-Kader hesitated as he looked at the distinguished figure before him. The prince was the same age as he had been when he declared jihad fifteen years earlier only he had blond hair and a face as smooth and delicate as a girl's. "I would have liked to have done earlier that which I have done today," the emir offered after a moment's hesitation, "but I awaited the hour appointed by God. The general has given his word and I have put faith in it. I am not afraid it will be violated by the son of a great king."

"I affirm what the general has said to you — that you will not be kept captive and you will be taken to Saint John of Acre or Alexandria. And if it pleases God, so it will be; but this requires the affirmation of the king and his ministers. I will report what has been agreed and send you to France to await orders from the king."

The emir excused himself, saying he was tired and wanted to see his family whom he had not seen since they had crossed the Moulouya River. He was taken to nearby Äin Safra where he explained to the remnants of his deira the agreement he had concluded: that they would sail for the Middle East the next day, and those who wanted to accompany him could do so. All their personal belongings — tents, horses, mules, camels — would be bought by the French.

The next morning, the Duke of Aumale reviewed his troops as they paraded around the little pocket of land the Arabs had named a "gathering of pirates," or Djemaa Ghazaouet : Zouaves in white spats, cherry-red pantaloons and navy blue vests; Legionnaires in red pants, gold-buttoned blue field coats; white-turbaned spahis in Fez-blue tunics under crimson vests and cloaks — maneuvered against a gleaming sea that seemed to dance in the early morning light. After the review, the young prince rode over to Abd el-Kader, who had been watching the demonstration of that admirable discipline that his own troops too often lacked. The emir sprang down from his black mare when the duke approached.

"I offer you this horse, my last to ride into battle. She is a great favorite of mine, but we must part now. This gift is a sign to my gratitude for your guarantee. I wish it will always carry you in safety and good health toward happiness."

"I accept it as homage offered France whose protection you will have henceforth and as a sign that the past will be forgotten."

Before leaving for Oran, where they would be transferred to larger boat, Abd el-Kader found himself a celebrity. Everyone wanted a souvenir — a belt, a knife, a piece of clothing or even an autograph. Colonel Montauban asked for a few lines stamped with the emir's seal,* attesting to his considerate treatment at the time of his surrender. Abd el-Kader addressed his words to the colonel's son, and praised his father's courtesy.

General Lamoricière accompanied the emir to the landing where he would board the Solon, a small frigate that had brought the prince to Djemaa Ghazaouet and would take them to Mers el-Kebir, Oran's natural port from where he would continue his voyage. Before parting, Lamoricière handed the emir a heavy purse. It was full of gold pieces

---

* His seal was composed of two triangles, one inverted over the other to form a sixpointed star, surrounded by a circle. The upward pointing triangle represented the spiritual power, the downward pointing one, the earthly power. The circle represented divine compassion.

worth 6000 francs, a paltry value for the emir's personal belongings. Abd el-Kader thanked the general; then, as a final gesture of submission, gave him his sword. To Abd el-Kader, the gesture was a voluntary act in accordance with Divine Will. To France, it was surrender.

The prince wrote to the minister of war that night: "A great event has just taken place. Abd el-Kader is in our camp. This is a matter of immense importance. It is something most of us dared not believe could happen. It is impossible to describe the tremendous effect this has had on the tribes in the region, which will spill over into all Algeria," adding, "I have the firm hope that the government will ratify it."

Composition and installation of the Smala d'Abd el-Kader (plan).
Location; Musée Condé, Chantilly, France
Photo Credit : Réunion des Musées Nationaux / Art Resource, NY

Panoramic view of the capture of the Smala of Abd el-Kader by the Duke of
Aumale at Taguin, May 16, 1843.

By Jean Antoine Simeon Fort, 1847
Location; Chateaux de Versailles et de Trianon, Versailles, France
Photo Credit : Réunion des Musées Nationaux / Art Resource, NY

Return of the Duke of Aumale from the Mitidja Plain after the capture of the Smala of Abd el-Kader in May 1843.

Engraving, Location: Chateaux de Versailles et de Trianon, Versailles, France
Photo Credit: Réunion des Musées Nationaux / Art Resource, NY

General Bugeaud
*Carle Vernet. Location; Musée de l'Armée, Paris,
Photo Credit: Musée de l'Armée/Dist. Réunion
des Musées Nationaux / Art Resource, NY*

General Lamoriciere
*Location; Chateau de Chillon,
Switzerland*

Armistice Ceremony at Ghazaouet, December 23, 1847
Augustine Regis, Location; Musée Condé, Chantilly

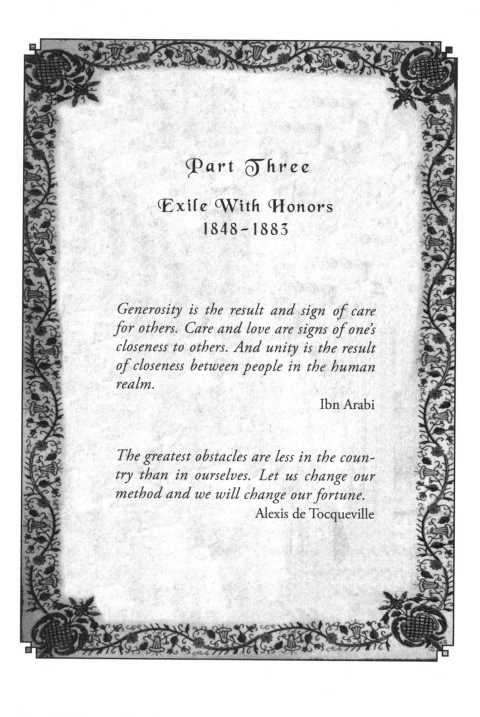

Part Three

Exile With Honors
1848–1883

Generosity is the result and sign of care for others. Care and love are signs of one's closeness to others. And unity is the result of closeness between people in the human realm.

Ibn Arabi

The greatest obstacles are less in the country than in ourselves. Let us change our method and we will change our fortune.

Alexis de Tocqueville

CHAPTER SEVENTEEN

Betrayal

CHRISTMAS MORNING, A SOMBER CROWD of Arabs milled around on the white, crescent-shaped beach of Mers el-Kebir. Some came to show their last respects to the emir; others would be going with him into exile. Those close enough snatched a piece of his black woolen burnoose to kiss. Men's eyes glistened and women cried out their haunting *you yous*. To his great astonishment, Abd el-Kader saw Abbé Suchet coming through the crowd, looking like an Arab in his long black cassock and bushy black beard, now flecked with gray. He had been sent via packet boat by Bishop Dupuch to convey his gratitude for the emir's decision to end the suffering on both sides.

It had been six years since Abd el-Kader first met this intrepid man of God who had braved hostile tribes, bandits, thirst and hunger to find him in the *bled*. The two embraced and exchanged some words. Abd el-Kader took off his turban and gave it to Suchet, who clutched it as he watched the emir and his entourage move slowly toward the rowboats that would take them shipboard and away from their homeland forever.

As the Arabs were filing past officers checking the list of those who had chosen exile with the emir, a young colonel noticed several white women among them. If those were Europeans, they could go free, the colonel announced. There were twenty-one Europeans, but none wished to leave the group, except for an elderly Spanish lady. They had married Arabs, had children to care for and said they had been well treated. The surprised officer let the women pass.

Over 100 men and women had cast their lots with the emir: relatives and servants and their children, and those of his former chieftains. Among the forty-five members of Abd el-Kader's immediate family were his seventy-four-year-old mother, Zohra; his three wives — Kheira, Embaraka and Aicha; his sister, Khadijah; his two daughters, Zohra and Yamina, thirteen and five; and his four sons: Abdallah, twelve, Mohammed Said, nine, and Muhi al-Din, six, who were under the charge of their tutor, Si Mohktar. His year-old infant, Ibrahim was being cared for by Mohra, his Negro domestic who had also suckled him.

Rocked by a rough sea, Abd el-Kader stood at the porthole of his cabin looking for the last time at the distant mountains of his native land as the steamer, Asmodée, headed northeast, past the Balearic Islands toward the port of Toulon before undertaking the much longer trip to the Middle East. The crew tried to share their seasonal cheer with their nervous Arab passengers, who knew only the great sand seas of the Sahara and could not swim. They provided them with their familiar couscous and dried fruit and the doctors on board looked after the sick and wounded. The Arabs were also objects of endless curiosity, exotic animals in a French Noah's ark. Most of them became seasick and preferred to stay below rather than publicly display their infirmities. Abd el-Kader never left his cabin, where he devoted himself to prayer, reading and reflection.

After two days of dampness, noise, the unfamiliar oily smell of the engines and the roiling sea, the Arabs were relieved when they were told they would soon be arriving at Toulon. Fresh supplies had to be brought on board, and negotiations with Mehemet Ali of Egypt and the Turkish Sultan were taking place. The emir readily agreed to the delay. But when the Asmodée arrived at Toulon, there was no evidence of preparations to resupply their ship.

✧

The breathtaking speed of events took Paris by surprise. The emir had become a figure of almost mythical proportions. He was like a ghost who seemed to be everywhere and nowhere at once. Abd el-Kader had confounded French generals since 1832, when he was elected to lead the jihad, and suddenly, amazingly, he was now in the government's hands. Abd el-Kader's old foe, General Trézel, was the minister of war. Like many a French officer, he had not only seen his career advanced by years of constant struggle with the emir, but had come to respect the emir's powers of resistance and recuperation. On January 1, Trézel wrote to the Duke of Aumale acknowledging the promises made to the emir, saying that the king wanted to honor them.

However, there was hesitation and uncertainty clouding the royal will. Abd el-Kader did not know that the "French Sultan" was politically weak. King Louis-Philippe was facing growing discontent among the middle classes for reneging on his promises of electoral reform. The popular press in Paris and Algiers was outraged by the news of what it called "the dangerous and irresponsible commitment" made to the emir by the Duke of Aumale. And, most damaging, there was dissent within the royal family.

The Duke of Nemours, the king's oldest son and heir apparent, was pressing his younger brother to retract his word. The prince refused, reminding his family in a long letter that Marshal Bugeaud had once offered a similar exchange to Abd el-Kader and had even allowed one of the emir's most loyal caliphs, Ben Salem, to go into exile. The marshal, he pointed out, knew what a difficult enemy France faced. Bugeaud's chasseurs had lost 4,000 horses from exhaustion in one winter, chasing the elusive emir. Furthermore, the prince argued, "no person who had actually fought the emir disagreed with Lamoricière's transaction." The duke was convinced that if the government took a clear and firm position that was favorable, public opinion would follow. "We also gave our word as soldiers," he concluded with his ultimate argument.

The president of the royal council, Francois Guizot, a history professor who had made a career of politics, was not one to take a strong stand in favor of the commitment. He was weighing the honor of France with raison d'état: "No general, no chief of staff, not even a prince has the right to commit the king's government, without examination or recourse to such an agreement," he declared to the Chamber of Deputies in early January. The new era of public opinion and the popular press had created forces that were rattling the monarchy's tentative steps toward greater democracy and making difficult the rendering of justice to the emir.

With the authority of ignorance, public opinion was certain that the emir was more dangerous in the Middle East than in the Sahara. The influential journal *La Revue des Deux Mondes* opined: "It seems to us unwise to send him to Acre or Cairo as he wishes. The public has expressed itself, and president Guizot would be ill advised to ignore it. If his tent is planted in the Middle East near the pilgrimage routes to Mecca and our African possessions, the emir can sow conspiracy and rebellion among those expecting his return."

The public did not know the emir, just as the emir did not know what forces were acting on the honorable men in whom he had placed his trust. Instead of obtaining new supplies in Toulon and continuing on with their journey, the emir and his companions landed at a quarantine station on a barren peninsula south of the port. The unprepared local prefect had hurriedly delivered to the hospital a herd of live sheep, assorted fowl and, knowing little of Muslim customs, flagons of wine. The prince's aide, Colonel Beaufort, who had accompanied the Arabs on the steamer, came to say goodbye to the emir after telling the local officers he was to be treated as a guest, not a prisoner.

Ten days later, rowboats were sent to the peninsula to take the emir to a more secure location. At the quay in Toulon, the Arabs were met by a convoy of carriages, omnibuses and wagons. Again there was disappointment. Abd el-Kader learned that his entourage would be divided into two groups. When he protested, he was told it would only be temporary. The emir's immediate family and servants were to go straight up to Fort Lamalgue, just above the landing; the others would be taken elsewhere. So determined to stay in the emir's company was Kara Mohammed, an intensely loyal former agha of the cavalry, that he claimed to be one of Abd el-Kader's personal servants, which meant being a family member. From that day on, he acted as the emir's steward.

In the gray winter dusk, a convoy of wagons and carriages clacked their way up the cobblestone road that led into Fort Lamalgue, which once held British prisoners captured at sea during the American Revolution. The emir and his family were met by Colonel Lheureux and the fort's translator, Captain Rousseau, who showed them to their dank, lugubrious accommodations. When the emir asked about their departure for the Orient, Lheureux, knowing little himself, could only awkwardly apologize and give evasive answers. The inevitable correspondence with the Sublime Porte and the Egyptian Viceroy…these things took time, he explained.

"I am not anxious. I have confidence in France," the emir replied stoically. "Furthermore, the eyes of the world are watching. It will judge if I am treated as I should."

The authorities were obsessed by the fear that the wily emir would somehow escape, perhaps with the help of the treacherous English, who were not averse to creating problems for France. In his report to war minister Trézel, Colonel Lheureux emphasized the tight security he had established. "The emir does not know a single word of French, and in accord with your intentions, we will take all necessary measures to be certain that he doesn't learn a word. I give you my assurance that I will not leave my post for a single minute until the end of my mission here and that he will be closely guarded night and day."

The Arab men occupied the second floor, above the officers of the garrison, in a diamond-shaped bastion of an eastern corner of the fort known as Cavalier. The English officers who had been kept here in an earlier era were allowed to promenade during the daytime in the streets of Toulon, giving as bond their word of honor that they would return before sundown. No such freedom was allowed the Arabs, who would have spurned the opportunity anyway. They were in mourning, and an Arab in mourning doesn't leave his tent. Abd el-Kader's tent was the middle one of five glacially cold apartments, about fifteen feet square, which he shared with Abd er Rahman and his oldest son, Abdallah — mute and sullen witnesses of the emir's conversations with the many visitors who wanted to meet him. The women were placed on the north side of the fort under the authority of Lalla Zohra. They kept their shutters closed day and night and were never seen to come out of their rooms. Arab men would be seen during the day squatting on the embrasures once occupied by cannons, staring for hours at the sea and their lost homeland.

In mid-January, the emir expressed to Lheureux his concern for his companions who had been taken elsewhere. He insisted they be brought to Lamalgue and they remain together. It would be even more crowded, the colonel pointed out, and unhealthy. "Don't worry, bring them to me," the emir countered. "If necessary, I will pile them on top of each other like grains of wheat in a silo. We are one family. It is better than being separated." Two days later, Lheureux acquiesced, and an emotional reunion took place on the steps leading to the emir's quarters.

Life for the "guests" at the fort soon became a routine that would have impressed a Trappist monk. Lamalgue became the emir's monastery. The clammy foreign walls were unwelcome, but God can be praised anywhere and soon they echoed with remembrance of the All Powerful One in whose hands they were entrusted. To the annoyance of off-duty soldiers trying to sleep, the fort was transformed into a mosque, resonating five times a day with the cries of the muezzin calling the faithful to prayer. The zawiya of the emir's youth had been burned to the ground by Bugeaud. Now, in Toulon, Abd el-Kader created his zawiya anew, this one guarded by a hundred French soldiers as he organized his followers' lives around study and prayer, as reported to Paris by Colonel Lheureux:

> The prayer of first light, when a dark thread can be discerned with the naked eye, the emir is doing his ablutions...after which, a brief visit to his mother and the rest of his family...he returns to his room to rest for an hour or so, followed by quizzing his three oldest children about the lessons they had been taught by their tutors the previous day. Eight to eleven o'clock he devotes to reading and writing, and visiting with the commandant and Rousseau, before taking his first meal of bread, butter, and dried fruit. At noon, midday prayers, after which he retires to his room and reads or writes and receives visits from his companions or from the outside until three o'clock, when he prepares for afternoon prayer. All the males gather in the courtyard for the prayer of *el asr*, including servants and boys. Readings from sacred books and discussion with his whole family follow until 5:00 PM. Another hour is devoted to visiting his mother, different wives and other family members. After the prayer of sunset, *el maghreb*, around six o'clock, the respected Abd er Rahman, Ben Thami, the tutors and Kara Mohammed join the emir in learned conversation, usually a discussion around a point of law or the meaning of verses in a sacred text that continues until the fifth prayer of the last light at eight o'clock. The emir takes his evening meal of couscous and conversation with intimates lasting until about ten o'clock.

Such were the diurnal rhythms that kept the minds and bodies of the emir's extended family knitted together to face the trials ahead.

☙

France's word was also being tested. In order to preserve France's honor yet satisfy its security interests, real or imaginary, Trézel had selected Lieutenant General Eugene Daumas for a delicate mission.

The government was on the horns of a dilemma. If the solemn word, given in good faith, of a crown prince and a French general was disavowed by the government, that could bring dishonor and shame on France. Honor was not an obsolete concept to a government and army still heavily populated with members of the old nobility. And there were the English to reckon with, who surely would use France's betrayal to undermine its credibility in Europe. But public opinion, that new devil unleashed by the Revolution, was demanding that the savage Abd el-Kader be kept a prisoner. If Abd el-Kader could be persuaded to adopt France as his new country, and thereby release the government of commitments made in its name, then France would no longer be open to the accusation abroad of behaving treacherously, while still appeasing popular opinion at home.

Daumas was a wise choice. He was urbane, fluent in Arabic and was knowledgeable of Arab ways. More importantly, Daumas had been France's consul in Mascara for two years during the period of the Treaty of Tafna. He had frequently spoken to fellow officers of his good relations with the emir. These qualities made him well suited for the conflicting roles he would be asked to play — negotiator, informant to the ministry, as well as advocate, companion and confidant to the emir. Now a commander of a regiment of native spahis in Algeria, Daumas happened to be in Paris on leave just when the war minister needed someone with his abilities. More from his soldier's sense of duty than from conviction, Daumas took up the first task assigned to him: to persuade the emir to allow the French government to renounce the promises made in its name.

Abd el-Kader had just returned to his room after visiting his mother when Daumas appeared at his door, unannounced. Speechless at first, the emir embraced warmly the now balder and thicker Daumas like an old friend, which he had been during the Tafna peace. Daumas was amiable but reserved, not yet ready to reveal his assignment. He wanted to read the emir's mood, to determine his strategy. Abd el-Kader clearly was pleased to see him and to be able to talk about the last days before his surrender. He continued to express his simple trust in France's word and seemed to want to justify to Daumas his past actions.

"The fight had become too unequal and it only would have heaped more misery upon the considerable sufferings of my people. I preferred to place my trust in the hands of those I had fought so long and so tenaciously. The only real glory is to treat well an honorable enemy. We Arabs have a saying: 'The hand loves to heal the wounds it has made.' The Beni Snassen tribe didn't want me to stop fighting. But I regret nothing. I believe in the written promise of General Lamoricière, agreed to by the son of the king of France, that I would be transferred to Acre or Alexandria from where I could reach Mecca."

"You did not say anything about Mecca in your negotiation with Lamoricière," interjected Daumas.

"When I designated Alexandria for exile," the emir replied hotly, "of course I was only thinking about Mecca. I did not expect France to deliver me directly to the city of the Prophet. What else could anyone offer me in place of Mecca? Honors? Money? You know, Daumas, that I despise these things. You saw me when I was powerful and surrounded by flatterers who have long since betrayed me. A tent for shelter, simple food and clothes, my horse and weapons…that was all that I wanted in this world. I repeat, I have no other desire than to go to Mecca, read holy books, worship God and be buried in Mecca after visiting the tomb of the Prophet in Medina. My role on stage is over. I have given you my word. I wouldn't even fight France if all your men in Algiers were dead and the city was occupied only by women. Believe me, my friend, I may look alive, but I am dead."

Daumas left believing he had gained insight into the emir, who seemed naive and almost desperate. He surmised that taking away his hope of going to the Land of Islam could break his spirit and lead him to agree to the betrayal. Before leaving the fort, Daumas decided to have Rousseau tell Abd el-Kader the true purpose of his visit: the government of France refused to ratify the promise of General Lamoricière.

❧

"Yes, it is true," Daumas reluctantly admitted the next morning.

"I can't believe it!" The emir was stunned. "The government will not honor the promise of General Lamoricière and the son of the king? Marshal Bugeaud himself had made a similar offer to me. You tell me now they don't consider themselves bound?"

"They are afraid of public opinion," Daumas ventured. "There are those who don't trust you and think you are more dangerous in the Middle East. The massacre of the prisoners is still placed at your feet."

Abd el-Kader jumped angrily out of his chair. "Very well, let them put me back in the position I was in when the promise was given. They will see whether it is easy to capture me." Pausing a moment, he went on, speaking as a virtual supplicant to Daumas. "Are we to remain in France? We do not speak your language. Our customs, our laws and religion are not yours. Our clothes, everything about us, are made a subject of mockery. Do you understand this is a death sentence?" Sitting down, he continued with an air of resignation, "Why so many words? I am in your hands. You are the knife and I am the flesh. Cut it as you please."

Daumas said nothing for several moments before replying with a verse from the Koran. *Work, O my servant, and I will help you.*

"What can I do?" cried Abd el-Kader. "I do not know your ways. I have no one to guide me on the dark sea that surrounds me." After a pensive silence, Daumas suggested that he should write directly to the king. "Put your fate in his hands. He is kind and generous. At the proper time, he will grant your request."

Abd el-Kader was puzzled. Should he do as Daumas suggested? Why should he appeal to the king's generosity for what was due as simple justice? Keeping one's word was a sacred obligation. The emir took up a pen, believing Daumas' sympathy to be sincere. After several drafts, he succeeded in producing a letter that Daumas and Rousseau together translated, maintaining the purity of Abd el-Kader's sincere, if grandiloquent, epistolary style. After his cries for mercy and justice, and a plea for a personal interview with the king, the emir ended his letter with a phrase that Daumas had hoped for: "The Almighty has ordained that I put myself as a child in your hands."

Hours later, Abd el-Kader was having second thoughts. His brother-in-law Mustafa Ben Thami had questioned the wisdom of such an abject appeal, which he thought undignified and implied acceptance of whatever the king decided. The emir asked to have the letter back. "It has already been sent," Daumas lied.

Trézel ordered Daumas to take up residence at the fort.

Daumas kept a diary of his conversations with the emir. He realized that he was capturing an historic voice as well as valuable intelligence — all part of his job of keeping his minister informed of the emir's morale. Sometimes they would revisit the African campaigns. What was his opinion of French soldiers, Daumas asked? They were brave and well disciplined, the emir thought, but he couldn't really judge since his resources were so unequal to the French. Only another opponent equally equipped and trained could properly judge. Other times, they talked about matters of religion, philosophy or politics. Sometimes they talked about mathematics, its relevance to war. They talked often about horses. Daumas was particularly interested in how the Arabs raised and trained their horses to make them so tough and fast, and valuable for war. Throughout, Abd el-Kader revealed his enormous knowledge of Algeria, its different peoples and their customs. Daumas also took the opportunity of his growing intimacy with Abd el-Kader to ask advice about how best to govern Algeria. The emir answered simply: "Govern as I did, with only the Law in your hand, then you will succeed."

His daily talks with Abd el-Kader soon convinced Daumas that his assignment to get the emir to release France from its word was doomed to failure. Not admitting in his official reports the private anguish that Abd el-Kader sometimes shared with him, Daumas wrote to the ministry, "Abd el-Kader is indifferent to his own needs. He is calm and resigned and controls the situation. I am convinced he not only regrets having written the king, but, furthermore, that we will never get him voluntarily to release France from its promises. Not withstanding our power and wealth, there is nothing in France to tempt him. He is not interested in worldly things."

A private bitterness alternated with the emir's public politeness and resignation to the mysterious Divine Will. Sometimes it seeped out in Abd el-Kader's conversations with Daumas, who was himself becoming less the false friend and more the overt admirer. "The best way to slay an honorable enemy is to pardon him. Then he becomes your slave," he told Daumas one day. The comment reminded the colonel of Napoleon's variation on the emir's words: "One should never fear doing justice to an enemy; it is always honorable and sometimes wise."

Daumas gradually fell under Abd el-Kader's spell. The emir, in turn, became increasingly dependent on this sophisticated Frenchman with whom he could display his true feelings. "He is both warrior and saint," he wrote the minister. "War failed him and now he seeks consolation in religion." But Daumas was wrong. Religion was not a consolation, nor was war a métier in which the emir sought satisfaction. Religion permeated his whole being and gave him strength, whether in war or peace.

As a sign of their growing intimacy, Daumas invited the emir to have dinner with him and his wife, who happened to be the niece of Marshal Bugeaud. Out of respect for Abd el-Kader's religious sensibilities, Daumas asked if he would mind if his wife joined them dressed in the European style, her face uncovered. It was not the laws of their religion, Abd el-Kader explained, but rather custom that required Arab women to veil their faces.

The emir was charmed by the intelligence and gentle elegance of Madame Daumas, whose face he discreetly scanned for resemblances to the great marshal. He noticed that her dress fit closely around her throat and its sleeves covered her arms to the wrists. A billowing skirt extended to the carpet covering even her feet. But for the narrowness of the dress at the waist, she was no less modest in her dress than an Arab woman, he told Daumas later.

While the emir was noticing in Toulon similarities in the coverage of properly dressed Christian and Muslim women, in Paris important figures were pleading his case based on their shared values of honor and trust. Before the Chamber of Peers, the Prince of Moscow, son of the illustrious Marshal Ney, who had covered Bonaparte's disastrous retreat from Moscow, declared: "The government cannot hesitate to ratify the agreement. The danger the emir might pose in the Middle East is secondary to what is of prime importance: the word of France. You must choose. Do you consider Abd el-Kader a brigand, a sort of pirate, or, as the general of a vanquished enemy? In the first case, make him a prisoner. In the second, treat him in accordance with the Rights of Man promulgated by our own revolution." Then General Fabvier rose to speak and urged supporting the commitments of its generals: "The interests of France and its honor are completely united in the immediate ratification of the accord. The reason is simple: the interests of France can not be separated from its good reputation..."

☙

Louis-Philippe never responded directly to Abd el-Kader's painstakingly crafted letter, written at Daumas's behest. Daumas was instructed to let the emir know the king would not be inviting him to come to Paris and Trézel stubbornly continued to believe that Abd el-Kader could be seduced by worldly promises. Daumas was given a new task to test the emir's resolve.

He was to offer the emir a choice: reside in France under conditions that would be nothing short of luxurious, or go to Alexandria and be under a virtual house arrest. There, he would be allowed to take with him only blood relations and indispensable servants, who would be spied on night and day by French and Egyptian agents. Should the emir choose to remain in France, reasoned the government, that would be the equivalent of releasing France from its word by demonstrating that he preferred France over a Muslim country. It would be a moral victory for French civilization.

Daumas knew he was playing the role of Satan before a Muslim Jesus. He sketched in glowing terms the vast realm that would be at the emir's disposal free of prying eyes: a fine chateau in the countryside, a specially constructed private mosque, separate bathhouses for men and women, and a stable full of horses to ride and hunt across rolling plains and deer-filled forests. It took Abd el-Kader mere seconds to give his answer, "I have no hesitation in choosing Alexandria, even under the conditions you impose. I shall find there doctors of our Law, people of our own religion, wearing the same clothes and having the same customs and manners. You should know me better, Daumas. If you placed in my burnoose all the diamonds and treasure of the world, I would throw it without hesitation into the sea in front of us."

Daumas reported his failure to Trézel. Yet, despite the emir's disinterest in material things, Daumas took it upon himself to improve the physical conditions of the Arabs. He urged the ministry to procure for them more of their customary clothing and to provide better beds and furniture for their damp, stone quarters. He did this without consulting Abd el-Kader, who would have only expressed his indifference toward such things. His companions, following the emir's example, had also refused to demand anything of their captors.

But as February progressed, cold and despair became the Arabs' greatest enemies. The emir's main concern was for the welfare of his companions. Daumas found the Arabs morose during the Feast of Mouloud, normally a time of exuberant celebration of the birth of the Prophet. The accidental death of one of their companions had deepened their gloom. The agha of the infantry, Haj Said, had died of asphyxiation from burning charcoal at night for warmth.

However, word of negotiations with Cairo and the news of General Lamoricière's testimony in Parliament kindled some hope. On the fifth of February, the adversary in whom Abd el-Kader had placed his trust stood before the Chamber of Deputies to defend his actions. Lamoricière spoke honestly about the difficulty of capturing the emir. He acknowledged that his written agreement with Abd el-Kader had been confirmed by the Duke of Aumale, who had supported the conditions. The deputies were divided over the question of honoring their generals' word or treating the emir as a savage killer unworthy of France's honor.

Bending to those voices favorable to the emir, the war minister allowed the Arabs some relief from their confinement. A tour of the naval arsenal in Toulon was organized in mid-February for the emir and a dozen of his companions. The ubiquitous Daumas noted that everywhere he went the emir was received with great consideration and respect. "Throughout, he maintained his reserve, never showing great emotion or curiosity." As the prayer of sunset approached, Abd el-Kader thanked his various hosts for the visits, indicating he wanted to return to the fort.

"No more excursions," the emir told Daumas on their way back. He would not leave the fort again unless it was to go to Alexandria. He and his companions didn't appreciate being gaped at by passersby. He also didn't want to give the government reason to draw false conclusions about his taste for honors and things of this world that might tempt it to hold him longer.

The emir knew Daumas was working to make their lives less miserable. To thank him, he penned some poetic lines in honor of Toulon, and to plead his cause — a rose with a thorn:

May Prosperity be yours, O Port of Toulon
She is resplendent with the glory of your warlike pageant
And the cavalcade of your learning
With your yellow-bodied ships
Whose sighs are a consuming flame
Your castles inspire wonder,
The thunderbolts hurled by your cannon

Your ramparts and your vast army too.
Complete now the roster of your praise!
Give the guest who has entered your harbor
And received your hospitality
Leave to continue his journey to the Holy City

There were a few bright spots in the general gloom that enveloped the emir. One day, a Captain Morisot came to visit. Morisot wanted to personally thank the emir for the treatment he had received while a prisoner back in 1840. After his conversation with the emir, Morisot wrote him a letter of appreciation that passed through Daumas's hands. "I have taken the opportunity to write Colonel Daumas in order to address a few lines to you, as I want to show you that, whether I am near or far away, you are always in my thoughts. Could I ever forget a man so good and generous, who surrounded me with medical care when I was wounded and with kindly attention when I was suffering? Did I not say to you when we met last Friday that it was one among the most wonderful days of my life? And you certainly know that such days are rare in this world."

The emir never saw the letter. Knowing the government's desire to dissuade the emir from leaving France and of gaining a cultural victory, Daumas thought the letter too favorable to the emir. He might use it to prove to the skeptics that he wasn't responsible for massacring the French prisoners after Sidi Brahim, as this was still the public perception and the main cause of their distrust. Daumas still had his masters to serve.

Religion, more than any other, was Abd el-Kader's favorite topic of conversation. Though it was obvious that the emir's knowledge of the Muslim world was extraordinary, Daumas thought his knowledge of Christians and Christianity was deficient. He arranged a meeting with Father Cordoran, a local curé, to help the emir get better acquainted with Christians. The emir's past correspondence with Bishop Dupuch had left him with a pleasant sense of anticipation about meeting another Christian marabout. Abd el-Kader felt an instant affinity with the curé whose simple black cassock resembled his own black burnoose. The two men spent many hours together discussing their faiths.

The emir wondered: If God had a son, did that mean God had a father too? If Christianity could reinterpret the teachings of Moses, why couldn't Islam reinterpret Christ? He explained to the curé his own view of the great prophets: Abraham is the beloved of God; Moses, His interpreter; Jesus Christ is the goodness of God; Mohammed is His Prophet, sent to emphasize the unity of God. God is God. There is no God but God. He has no associates, partners or children.

They talked about reason as a divine attribute and found themselves in agreement. Reason is necessary for knowledge, and knowledge is good, but also it is more suited for terrestrial knowledge, which is knowledge of the husk that surrounds the deeper knowledge that belongs to the heart, not the head. Knowledge of external things is like rainwater. It comes and goes, but inner knowledge is like a fountain that never dries up…and so they talked for hours.

On a particularly cold day in late February, Daumas found the emir in his room wrapped in his burnoose shivering in front of a cold fireplace, his supply of wood exhausted.

"Why don't you get some wood from your companions?" Daumas asked.

"Instead of asking for theirs, I would give them mine, if it were in my power."

"You are not like other Arab chieftains."

"Had I been like them," the emir answered softly, "do you think the Arabs would have continued to fight as long as they did, and sacrificed their fortunes, their flocks, their lives to follow me? Throughout the fifteen years I never kept anything for myself. I could only lead by sharing in their sacrifices. Now, I have to continue to be disciplined."

Tantalizing rumors were reaching the Arabs. The great master, Horace Vernet, had been selected to paint a portrait of Abd el-Kader. The king had given him a message to deliver secretly. "Tell the emir that I will honor the promise of my son," he told Vernet. "My ministers are cowards. They are afraid of the Chambers. I am not afraid in the least of Abd el-Kader." Colonel Beaufort also paid a visit to the emir to assure him that the king intended to honor the agreement.

☙

On February 28, the world changed. The emir learned that the king had abdicated in the face of a Parisian mob. A new provisional government had been established, headed by a committee of five. Louis-Philippe

213

fled to England traveling incognito as Mr. Smith, and took with him Abd el-Kader's best hope for freedom.

To those following French affairs closely, the fall of the monarchy was unsurprising. To the emir, its disappearance was unimaginable. Daumas soon learned the emir's opinion about the turn of events during his daily *tête à tête* with him. "Look, my friend, I have read in books of the Greeks about the republic, that it is supposed to be a good form of government, but see how my culture is more prudent than yours regarding the destiny of man? Am I not right to believe there is no other real force, no truth or reality but in the will of God? Believe me, this world is a carcass; only dogs fight over it. There was Louis-Philippe, a great and powerful sultan, who everywhere was esteemed, who had a large family to perpetuate his line, was renowned for his wisdom and experience, but in one day he was overthrown." (Louis Philippe was neither known for his wisdom, nor everywhere esteemed, yet he was the French "sultan" only a few eye blinks earlier, and now nobody.)

Republican government was a mystery to Abd el-Kader. A body without a head, he told Daumas. Five heads, Daumas explained. "I predict there will not be five but thirty-five million heads — and that is far too many," the emir replied. In March, a representative of the five-headed government, Citizen* Emile Ollivier, paid Abd el-Kader a visit. As the commissioner from the departement of the Var, he was selected by the fragile republic to assess the emir's state of mind.

Citizen Ollivier found him in his white burnoose, sitting cross-legged on his divan between two windows, wooden rosary in hand, with an expression of serene melancholy. Citizen Ollivier, Daumas explained, had come to inquire if the emir was satisfied with the arrangements, if he had any particular needs for himself or his family. "My body lacks nothing," he replied, "only my heart is empty."

"What are you missing?"

"My freedom. I should not be here. You know that I was not taken by force of arms. I voluntarily put myself in France's hands."

"Would you and your chiefs sign an oath sworn upon the Koran by which you solemnly declare never to return to Algeria or involve yourself, directly or indirectly, in its affairs?" Ollivier asked at the end of his

---

* Everyone was "citizen" during the Second Republic, evoking the egalitarian spirit of the First Republic.

interview. The question disturbed the emir. Why did the government need such guarantees when the agreement with General Lamoricière was already clear?

"I have no better proof of my firm intentions for the future than what I have already done," the emir answered. "I came to you voluntarily. Had I not wanted to lay down my arms, I would not be here. That act is worth more than all other guarantees. But yes, if my hand is not enough, I will even sign with my eyes."

The commissioner left Fort Lamalgue carrying a letter from the emir to the new government, translated by Daumas. Like all the others he had written before, the letter was a plea for justice, exquisitely tailored to the sensibilities of his new masters.

"Praise to One God, alone whose empire is eternal," he began his address to the provisional government. "...I rejoiced at the news of this new form of government because I have read in books that this republican government by its nature seeks to eliminate injustice and to prevent the strong from abusing the weak, considers all men brothers and avoids the errors that arise when a single person decides. You are generous men and desire the good of all people. Therefore, I consider you as my natural protectors.

"Remove the veil of suffering which has been thrown over me and my companions. I ask only justice from your hands..."Abd el-Kader reiterated the voluntary nature of his surrender and the trust he had placed in the Frenchmen whose word he had believed. He made no apologies for defending his country and his religion so tenaciously. However, he explained, "when it was clear that God for His own inscrutable reasons had withdrawn His support, I took the decision to withdraw from the world..." Repeating his words to Daumas, he ended saying, "consider me as among the dead. My only desire is to go to Mecca, to pray and worship God until He calls me."

Abd el-Kader then added his personal oath, written in his own Arabic hand with all the comprehensiveness of an Islamic lawyer.

Glory to God Alone!

I declare from henceforth to never provoke trouble for the French people, whether in person, or by letters, or by any other means. I make this oath before God, Mohammed — praise be to him — before Abraham, Moses, and Jesus Christ; by the Torah, the Gospels, and the Koran. I make this oath with my heart as well as with my hand and my tongue. This vow binds me and all my companions, more than one hundred, both those who sign this document as well those who don't because they cannot write.

Salutations, Abd el-Kader Ben Muhi al-Din

Ollivier returned to Paris a champion for the emir's release. He wrote to the Duke of Arago, the new minister of war and one of the five heads of the government. "To keep Abd el-Kader is to kill him, and it is our breach of faith that is killing him. Our honor, our most precious possession, is at stake. I am personally convinced of Abd el-Kader's sincerity. His oath will be known throughout the length and breadth of Algeria. That will make it impossible for him to attempt a coup as he would lose his reputation for integrity which is the basis of his strength. France is strong enough not to fear such an enemy."

The Ollivier's request for a pledge from the emir brought the Arabs renewed hope. But the only response to the emir's vow was a vague and pompous acknowledgment from Arago. "The republic is the government of the people. The people are generous and do not kick the vanquished. You, your family, your servants can count on the consideration which France accords its defeated enemies. May circumstances soon allow the Republic to show you its generous nature." Indeed, the Second Republic was no more capable than its predecessor of wrestling with its difficult inheritance from Algeria. It was as weak and fragile at birth as the monarchy had been in its death.

ᘓ

Opinions varied widely on what to do about France's interests in Algeria. Marshal Bugeaud had grown cynical from the constant, almost monthly changes of governors-general in Algiers. He expressed a change of heart before the Parliament. "We should get out of Algeria and let the native chieftains run it the way the Turks did and just retain the ports for commercial purposes." The great Victor Hugo saw the situation differently, believing his country was embarked on a noble mission: "We must keep Algeria because we are bringing it the benefits of our great civilization." And the skeptical Alexis de Tocqueville worried about the French becoming like hate-filled Americans in their conquest of the Indians: "Algeria will sooner or later become an armed camp where two peoples will fight each other without mercy until one or the other is wiped out."

The days dragged by without word from Paris, while a deepening despair took hold of the Arabs. Daumas begged the emir to have patience. Abd el-Kader lashed back angrily. "Is it really surprising that my patience flags before my misfortune? My people are losing faith in me. I keep telling them this is only a temporary delay, that France will honor its word. Now my mother and my wives cry day and night and no longer believe my words of hope. Even the men are weeping, not for themselves, but their families. My brother-in-law, Mustafa, came to me in tears to say that his wife, my own sister, was asking to leave him and return to Mascara. And I am the cause of all this misfortune. Is there no tribunal in France charged to hear the complaints of the oppressed? Summon all your doctors of the law and I will convince them of my rights."

On March 30, one of the emir's former opponents, General Changarnier, stopped at Toulon to see Abd el-Kader before taking up his post as governor-general of Algeria. Though sympathetic to him, Changarnier came to deliver the final blow. The political instability in France and the reduction of forces in Algeria, he informed the emir, meant it would be impossible for the new government to order his release. The republic considered itself bound by no obligation. Abd el-Kader was found a prisoner by the new government. He would remain one for the foreseeable future.

"I am betrayed," Abd el-Kader cried wildly, "and by those in whom I had placed my trust. This is unbelievable. And you would give me all the riches of France that I might purchase my own death."

Turning to Daumas, the emir exclaimed: "If you keep us here, many of us will take their lives."

"That is a deadly sin in your religion, as it is in mine," countered Daumas.

"True, but there is one circumstance which permits it; that is when a Muslim is forced to renounce his faith."

"No one is forcing you to renounce your faith."

"Today, no, but will it be the same tomorrow? The promise of French commanders has been broken." The emir turned to Changarnier, who looked silently at the floor not understanding the words but recognizing the expected emotions. "How can I be sure that sooner or later that which is most sacred to me will not be taken also?"

The next day, Daumas wrote an urgent letter to General Cavaignac, yet another minister of war whose career was advanced by fighting Abd el-Kader. In 1833, he had been reduced to eating cats when he was besieged by the emir in Tlemcen, and later, had been with Lamoricière during Abd el-Kader's surrender at Sidi Brahim. "Our humanity demands that something be done," Daumas pleaded. "Their quarters are cramped. These people are used to sunshine and outdoor life. Sooner or later they will all fall ill." Colonel Lheureux, ever security conscious, had also written his own report to the minister which reflected a different concern. "The emir never ceases to talk in the most energetic manner about his betrayal. If the provisional government is not going to make a decision, then it is advisable to find a different location than Fort Lamalgue, far from the sea to avoid the possibility of escape."

On April 5, the emir received another visitor from Paris. Charles Poncey, a poet with connections to the provisional government, came to personally deliver a letter from the committee of five giving assurances of justice and eventual release, but pleading the need for time to elect a new constitutional assembly. This body would be elected by all the people, that is to say, all male voters over twenty-one, toward the end of April and would draft a new, more democratic constitution.

Poncey then told Abd el-Kader that he would write articles and letters on his behalf to various journals and magazines. He promised to intercede with three of the members of the provisional government who were his friends. They talked about the political divisions in France that made taking action so difficult at that very moment.

France, Poncey explained, was having its own problems determining the role of God's will in its affairs. The French were divided over their revolutionary past. The conservative, Catholic legitimists argued that any authority, even tyranny, was better than the chaos and anarchy of republicanism. France had experienced the horrors of the mob, the guillotine, and democracy run amok during the Revolution. Government power was absolute and had to be considered infallible. This could only happen if its authority was rooted in divine law and had the sanction and moral authority of the Catholic church. Legitimists considered the loss of the monarchy as God's punishment for France's evil ways.

The radical republicans were equally absolute in their rejection of monarchy and the privileges of birth and property. Many were atheists who saw religion only as a prop for tyranny and a tool for brainwashing. The republicans had forced the abdication of the king, yet they were splintered into factions, running the gamut from rabid socialists to constitutional monarchists. It was a difficult time for making unpopular decisions, and popular opinion, especially among the outspoken French colonists in Algeria, considered the emir a savage, infidel butcher.

The next day, Poncey handed Daumas a letter for Abd el-Kader. "I was moved when we met and you remarked on my humble poet's clothing which you said was a sign of a sympathetic heart, of a French heart. Yes, I liked what you said, that the splendor of a person's clothing doesn't give any measure of his intelligence or virtue...As a poet, I admire your exploits, but as a Frenchman, I have to deplore them for they were directed against my mother, France. You were fighting fire with fire. And you did it inspired of a faith which I understand and respect. Today, all intelligent hearts admire you, and don't consider your courage in defense of the freedom of your country a crime. France is the last nation in the world which would find in your devotion something hateful, because there is not a single Frenchman that would not give his blood to chase away anyone mad enough to invade his land...The current government can't make a decision on something as important as this because it is only provisional. It needs to have the consent of the nation represented by the deputies who will soon be elected...Have confidence in us..."

After Poncey's visit, while no less unhappy, Abd el-Kader could better explain to his followers the complexity of the problems facing the new government. There was nothing to do but wait.

But more bad news came. In mid-April, Abd el-Kader's three brothers arrived with their families, believing that they would be joining him on his way to exile in the Middle East. From them he learned what he had feared — his devoted caliph, Bou Hamidi was dead, poisoned in the sultan's prison. In all, thirty-five more people came with Mohammed Said, Hussein and Mustafa.

When his brothers were brought to his quarters, Abd el-Kader turned to Daumas. "Only one calamity is missing. And now it has arrived. I am a prisoner in defiance of international law, and now my family, which was free, is lured into an insidious trap. I never would have believed that a nation such as yours could sink so low as to snare men the way children cruelly snare little birds. Why should they share my fate? You have heaped treachery upon treachery!"

Daumas stood wordless and ashamed. He knew that at that moment workmen were busy cementing iron bars into the windows of an ancient castle in Navarre.

CHAPTER EIGHTEEN

"The View Is Most Magnificent!"

A POET HAD SELECTED the emir's new residence, Alphonse de Lamartine, Poncey's friend in the provisional government. His literary fame and fiery oratory had won Lamartine a public following as an opposition deputy during Louis-Philippe's reign. After the February Revolution, he became one of the five heads of that provisional Hydra in which Abd el-Kader had so little confidence. Charged with the portfolio for foreign affairs, Lamartine had been given the assignment of recommending a more suitable location for emir.

He recommended a place, "with a salubrious atmosphere, a pleasant climate and royal setting that would make the emir feel at home," and urged his colleagues to treat Abd el-Kader as a temporary, but honored guest until the National Assembly decided his fate. Asked where such a place was, he described the chateau at Pau, in southwest France.

"The view of the Pyrenees is the most magnificent in France and will remind him of Algeria. The chateau is perched above the river Gave and is surrounded by lush semi-tropical vegetation," the sensitive Lamartine told his committee.

Nestled in the foothills of the mountains shared by France and Spain, the chateau was the of Henry of Navarre, who became Henry IV. This first Bourbon king was a determined unifier and a devout warrior king who erred on the side of magnanimity. Born to the Protestant confession, he converted to Catholicism in order to appease the Catholics. "Paris is worth a Mass," Henry announced upon his conversion in 1593, thus ending the religious warfare that was tearing apart France. Two hundred and fifty-five years later, a man of different lineage, but made of similar qualities, would be its last occupant.

Daumas told Abd el-Kader he would leave Fort Lamalgue on April 23, the very day a Constituent Assembly was being elected to draw up a new constitution. Pau would be more suitable for him and was only a temporary expedient, Daumas explained. But there was a catch. Limited space at the chateau required that only the emir's immediate family could accompany him. The others would be transferred to

Ste. Marguerite Island. Abd el-Kader was again thrown into a state of despair by the thought of being separated from his companions. "I will not leave except with all my people. You will not tear me from here except by force. Put ropes around our necks and drag us through the streets. I will give warning to all people everywhere that they may know what fate awaits those who trust the word of Frenchmen."

Daumas and Lheureux tried to convince him that this was merely a temporary measure. There simply wasn't enough space at Pau for 137 people. It was important, they argued, for him to avoid unfavorable publicity by not appearing to be an ingrate while his fate hung in the balance. His prison, after all, was a royal chateau and the residence of one of France's greatest princes. Undeterred, Abd el-Kader stubbornly negotiated with Daumas to enlarge the list of family and servants.

"Don't you understand, Daumas, they are all family. It is not the blood that is important; it is their loyalty, their friendship! These people have sacrificed everything to stay with me. I can't choose. What if I asked you to choose between your best friend and your brother?" Each caliph was like a brother. And each one had his family and servants from which he too could not be separated, and the servants also had families. The whole entourage was a single tissue.

The approved number of "immediate family" finally reached seventy-seven.

⁊

On Easter Sunday, April 23, Abd el-Kader's extended family, along with Daumas, boarded three packet boats that took the group west to the coastal town of Sète, at the mouth of an inland waterway. From there, they transferred to paddle-wheel barges that splashed up the Canal du Midi to the river Garonne and finally, to Toulouse. Waiting for the Arabs at Port St. Etienne the evening of April 26 was a large, curious crowd, as well as an infantry unit and mounted cavalry to escort the emir's retinue through the winding streets of the ancient red-brick city to the Hotel Bibent. "The eyes of the crowds were searching for the famous emir who was dressed like a Trappist monk in his simple white burnoose. His thin face had the firm, expressionless gaze of a man who was tormented, but not beaten," wrote Daumas to a friend.

After recuperating in Toulouse for a day, the emir and his entourage climbed into large four-in-hand diligences, forming a caravan that rolled south through the Midi toward the Pyrenees. From his coach, Abd el-Kader could see the rich French earth — its fields of grain, its vineyards and early blossoming orchards and, for the Arabs, unusual humped-back Charolais grazing in lush meadows. All day and night they traveled, stopping at local inns for fresh horses and food. Toward midnight of the second day their coaches pulled into the dark, cavernous courtyard of the chateau formed by crenellated three-story-high walls. The curious citizens who had lined the streets all afternoon to catch a glimpse of the new arrivals had long since gone home.

At first, the decision by the provisional government to send the emir to the chateau Pau had horrified the good burghers of the city. It was an insult, they said. The presence in the chateau of the cruel "monster of the desert," as the local press called Abd el-Kader, would be a desecration of the memory of the great Henry IV. The citizens immediately asked their mayor to urge the authorities to find another location for him.

"The municipal council has asked me to bring to your attention," the mayor wrote to the minister of the interior, "the fact that the chateau is Pau's only important monument, and has been recently restored at great expense. The entire city wishes that it be maintained in its current condition and not be degraded by guests whose customs and habits are such that they would have not the least idea of what conservation means...You would surely not want to have that which is held most dear by the citizens of Pau to be sacrificed for a purpose so unworthy as the detention of a horde of savages who would be happy to wreck it." The mayor proposed the chateau at Lourdes as a more suitable place.

Paris stood by its decision. It took two days for the emir's retinue to get settled into their new accommodations that, by a decision of the municipal council, had been stripped of all historic tapestries and antique furnishings. Abd el-Kader, his three wives and five children occupied the rooms on the third floor during the day. The windows facing south offered a panoramic view of the snowcapped Pyrenees that had so impressed Lamartine. Yet, as he looked around, the emir could only have heard the sound of a jail door slamming shut.

The windows with the beautiful view were covered with newly installed bars. Worse, Abd el-Kader was informed that, as an added security precaution, he would have to spend his nights in the dank tower dungeon of Gaston Phoebus on the north side of the courtyard. Soldiers were stationed on every stairwell floor and by each door. The fact of the emir's imprisonment was now incontestable. Any pretense that Pau was a temporary relocation was absurd.

Until now, Abd el-Kader had not revealed to his family and followers the contents of the letter from the minister of war, the Duke of Arago, which he had received during the last days in Toulon and which offered so little hope of freedom. Nor had he revealed fully his conversation with General Changarnier who, en route to Algeria, had bluntly told the emir that the new government considered him a prisoner. Rather than sharing fully his own disappointments, which he reserved only for Daumas, he had tried to keep their hopes alive. He had colored his family conversations with optimistic intimations of French goodwill, of progress toward resolving difficulties and of the need to endure what were surely only temporary setbacks caused by the passing political chaos. But it was now apparent there was nothing temporary about the new security arrangements. In spite of the grim facts, Abd el-Kader vowed to his companions to keep fighting for justice. He would do so by appealing to the noble side of the French character.

To make matters worse, Daumas would be leaving him. During the three months Daumas had spent with Abd el-Kader, a true friendship had grown between them. He had impressed the emir with his excellent Arabic, wide knowledge of Algeria and finely tuned sensibilities. Daumas was deeply touched by the sense of loss, even tender vulnerability, the emir expressed in a letter written to him on the eve of his departure.

"I learned that you are going to leave, but not abandon me. The pain I will feel by your separation will be without any doubt greater than what I have endured in the past. Who will console me when I am sad? Who will remove my tears with a smile? Who will be patient in my misfortune? The physicians heal the body with medications but you soothed my heart with your gentle words. The whole time I spent with you it seemed as if I never left my country…Once you leave me I will be a foreigner in a foreign country."

Daumas had changed, too. Assigned a distasteful job by his minister, he had done his duty for his country. But doing it, he had also developed an immense admiration for the emir, and in the same measure had grown to despise his role of giving him false assurances. He wrote a friend: "I am relieved to be returning to my regiment. I know that Colonel Daumas can never again be a jailor for a man like Abd el-Kader."

Before leaving, Daumas spent several days briefing his successor, the young Baron Estève de Boissonnet. He told him about the emir's mental and physical toughness, his sense of guilt over what had befallen his followers because of him and his need for someone to whom he could privately express his anguish. Daumas also sketched the important figures in the emir's entourage.

In first place was Abd el-Kader's mother, Lalla Zohra. She was the cornerstone of his family, known for her wisdom, strength and resilience. She was the person to whom he showed the utmost deference. Daumas told Boissonnet of the incident of the bed. When the emir moved into his new quarters at Pau and saw his ornate canopied daybed, he would not take it. It was better than his mother's and he insisted that she have it. The emir had told Daumas repeatedly that it was his mother's patience, courage and moral support that had maintained his will to carry on the fight. She stood by him throughout his crises, and she was the guardian of his treasury. Kheira was clearly his favorite wife. Like the emir, she was educated and wrote poetry.

Among the men in Abd el-Kader's entourage, Daumas mentioned the ever-present Mustafa Ben Thami, the emir's brother-in-law. He was a logician, learned in philosophy and theology, as well as a highly literate advisor and confidant who acted as the emir's personal secretary. The former caliph of Mascara was known for his intense loyalty, but not for bravery. The few horses he lost in battle had earned him the nickname "Fatma" by other Arabs. Tension remained within the family, as it was Ben Thami's desperate decision to kill the prisoners that fueled French mistrust of the emir. He was known to dislike the French intensely and Abd el-Kader rarely allowed him out in public.

Kara Mohammed was another stalwart. He was an agha of the cavalry who had commanded a thousand horsemen and embodied the fierce spirit of loyalty the emir inspired in his followers. Like most of the emir's commanders, he was learned in religious matters, though finding men who were both learned in religious law and inspiring leaders in battle was not easy. Compromises were often made, usually on the side of favoring savants of the Law, but Kara Mohammed represented no compromise. He was a regular participant in the theological discussions that were part of the Arabs' daily routine. Nor did he lack physical courage — he had lost twelve horses on the battlefield.

Like Daumas, Boissonnet was well chosen to play the double role of soul mate for the emir and informant to the war ministry. Boissonnet was an artillery captain, had served under the Duke of Aumale in Algeria and had been director of the Bureau of Arab Affairs for the region of Constantine in 1844. He had written several scholarly works in Arabic and was one of the first Frenchmen to work on deciphering the alphabet of the Touareg Berbers.

A nobleman, scholar and linguist, and known for his gentle personality, Boissonnet warmed Abd el-Kader's heart by his solicitude for the emir and his family after the loss of their fifteen-month-old son, Ibrahim, who had fallen ill en route from Toulon. When the emir's son succumbed to fever in the early morning of May first, it marked the second death within three days of the Arabs' arrival. The previous day, a two-month-old daughter of one of Abd el-Kader's servants also had died. Both were buried in a garden near the chateau.

Boissonnet intervened on the emir's behalf to delay the official reception ceremonies by the municipal authorities, who were torn between distaste for their guest and duty to follow protocol. On the third of May, Pau's outgoing mayor, local dignitaries and society women anxious to meet the "Noble Savage" visited him in his third floor suite directly above the room in which Henry of Narvarre came into the world. At one end was a large fireplace. The ceiling was decorated with delicately wooden inlaid tiles. From the south-facing windows, the emir could follow the sun each day as it traced its path over the mountains in the evening.

Abd el-Kader displayed his usual courtesy toward the mayor. He rose from his bed, greeted his guests in the traditional Arab manner. His hand over his heart, he made a slight bow as he asked his visitors to take a seat. They observed a man of forty with ink-black hair, whose body still had a lithe and vigorous quality that contrasted with his air of impassive melancholy.

Asked about his trip to Pau, Abd el-Kader replied by praising the French countryside. "You have a very rich and beautiful country. Trees are green everywhere, yet it seems that the green of your trees is brighter and more cheerful than ours." When one of the ladies in the mayor's company told the emir that a considerable crowd was outside pressing against the chateau gates to see him, Abd el-Kader asked if "the people" might be allowed into the courtyard. Then, like an Arab Pope, he stood at one of the windows looking down upon the multitude. Extending his arms, the palms of his hands turned heavenward in a gesture of submission, the emir said some words of appreciation that were translated by the still-present Daumas.

Much of the local population was outraged at the profaning of the residence of the great Henry of Navarre by Arab barbarians, yet others thought differently, influenced by a mixture of curiosity and admiration for the emir. Madame la Maréchale de Grouchy, the widow of the general whose troops had failed to arrive on the battlefield in time to save Napoleon from defeat at Waterloo, appeared at Pau two days later for her own inspection of the captives. She left posterity a telling report of her impressions and disappointments.

Today, I was presented to Abd el-Kader. I found the emir sitting on his bed, his bare feet on the floor. He had a white woolen garment covering his head; his face is handsome and features regular, his beard black. His voice has an unusual, sonorous quality. He sat with a pained but intelligent air about him. He took my hand in greeting and answered my questions in a spirited manner. When he learned who I was, he said many flattering things about the marshal and his military career. One understands how easily he impresses the people who visit him. General Daumas explained that it was thanks to the modesty of his clothes that he often escaped French soldiers who mistook him for a simple Arab. Sitting in his room in a big armchair was his old uncle, a marabout, who watched us attentively while saying his rosary and coughing.

He ordered a black servant to prepare coffee and introduced to us his children — who are sickly, dirty and ugly. From his chambers I went to visit his wives, expecting to find the typical Arab beauties depicted in the paintings of Horace Vernet. I was certainly disappointed. In the first room was his mother, who was old and had a menacing look…I had been warned not to wear jewelry so as not to evoke any feelings of envy, so I brought Zohra a present of bonbons but she ignored completely the pretty box they were in.

In a third room were the emir's wives. Kheira, his legitimate wife and mother of three of his children was squatting on a mattress on the floor enveloped in a white muslin gown with a design consisting of large squares. The cloth was very dirty and revealed nothing of the shape of her body. Her feet and arms were bare, her arms tattooed in blue ink and decorated with bracelets…All the women are ugly, though at first glance, their eyes look beautiful thanks to the black mascara they all wear. Their features are irregular — noses thick and short, mouths big and fat lips, their teeth crooked and broken. Abd el-Kader's fifteen-year-old daughter looks thirty. The women all talk at once with great animation. Their voices are guttural and harsh…Many have pock marks on their faces and all are disgustingly dirty. Young, hideous children squat on the floor, practically naked. The slaves carry on their backs the infants who have the look of little monkeys.

Like some of the emir's visitors, Madame la Maréchale came as a curiosity seeker and left confirmed in her unvarnished prejudices, prejudices not easily softened by the cramped, overcrowded living conditions and the sullenness of people kept in cold and unjust confinement.

To raise Abd el-Kader's spirits, Boissonnet offered to take him for a carriage ride in the countryside to enjoy the early spring sunshine and also show him around the historic chateau. Abd el-Kader politely declined. He would not leave his apartments. He did not want anyone to get the impression that he was enjoying his forced stay in France. If he was to be unjustly imprisoned, then he would live as a prisoner. "The sun comes in my windows and I can travel with my eyes," he told Boissonnet.

⌘

A great sympathy soon developed for the emir — a kind of conspiracy of benevolence — among Captain Zaragossa, the commander of the two-hundred-strong garrison, Captain Boissonnet and a growing lobby of admirers from near and far who were impressed by the emir's gracious stoicism and generosity of spirit. Conversation in the homes of Pau now turned around two subjects: the ever-changing political constellations in Paris and their celebrity prisoner whose activities and words were grist for the social gossip mill.

The emir was reading an Arabic translation of the Bible given him by Comte Albert de R__ and comparing the Koran with the Gospels... The emir's mother was suffering from severe arthrititis...The Arabs don't trust French medicine, preferring their amulets... He was writing his autobiography and a history of the Arabs...Abd el-Kader is studying algebra...The emir had served champagne in his quarters to local dignitaries who dined with him one night, pouring it himself...The rest of his followers, separated at Ste. Marguerite, had joined his family, they were sleeping in the stairwells, and befouling the chateau...The emir had been seen at the circus one night, or was that his brother in the red robe? And then there were reports of unexpected remarks, bons mots, observations and gracious replies to his visitors that circulated back to the local population.

When a colonel and veteran of the African wars had come with some junior officers to pay his respects, Abd el-Kader ended the interview with a note of irony. "I am touched by your visit. You fought me courageously and won. How I adore God's ways. Your visit shows me that you think I too did my duty — but you are the best judges. After all, many officers in the French army are indebted to me. Without me many of your colonels would still be captains and many generals would still be colonels."

He had a special way with women, and never failed to charm and flatter. "Why do you Arabs need to have four wives, and not one as in France?" asked a lady from Bordeaux. "We marry one for her eyes, another for her lips, still another for her body, and one for her good heart and spirit," replied the emir. "But if we found all those qualities united in one woman, like you, Madame, we would not need others." Abd el-Kader added that the Arab man merely does in the open what the European does in secret.

The demand by Frenchmen and women to see the emir became so great that he asked to have visits restricted to only two days a week so he would continue to have time to devote to study, meditation and writing. All petitioners were screened by Boissonnet. Toward the end of May, two of these petitioners succeeded in lifting the emir's spirits.

A local high school teacher whose father was a veteran of the Napoleonic wars was given permission to visit the emir. Abd el-Kader had learned much about Napoleon, with whom he was sometimes compared by French soldiers. There were obvious parallels. Both had tried to create a new order, both incited fierce loyalty from their troops and were known for the rapidity of their movements, and both had been betrayed, Napoleon by the British in whose hands he had also voluntarily placed himself after Waterloo. So when the professor presented Abd el-Kader with his father's ring in which was set a stone carved from a fragment of the emperor's tomb on St. Helena, the emir was hesitant to accept it. He was unworthy of it, he said. The professor pressed the emir, saying he would be honored for him to have it.

"What you offer me is more than a precious stone. It is something priceless. There is neither pearl nor diamond in the world which has the value of a stone from this tomb." The emir looked up at the professor as he put the ring on his finger. "Perhaps this will bring me good fortune."

"I too wish it for you, with all my heart," the professor replied.

A few days later, Abd el-Kader was informed of an unusual request. News of it circulated through the salons of Paris and Pau. A guard at the Tuileries had asked to be transferred to Pau. He wanted the honor of guarding the emir to repay the consideration with which he had been treated as a former prisoner. It was the legendary young trumpeter, Escoffier, who had distinguished himself by his gallantry in the bloody battle of Sidi Yussef. General Bugeaud had awarded him the Legion of Honor in absentia for giving his mount to his commanding officer, whose horse had been killed. Bugeaud had sent a letter to Abd el-Kader, along with the medal. The emir not only read the letter out loud before his own troops in a formal ceremony but personally pinned the medal on Escoffier's tattered uniform and praised him for his bravery.

A cult of sorts began to form around the personality of the emir. People streamed from all over France to visit him. Everyone who met Abd el-Kader left admiring his outward serenity, his erudition and his spirited, often playful conversation. Combined with his aura of sanctity, determined endurance and unrelenting tactfulness, he was viewed by his growing legion of admirers as representing the *bel ideal* of physical and moral greatness, combining feminine grace and masculine hardiness of mind and body.

One such admirer was none other than General Daumas himself, who remained in correspondence with Abd el-Kader and others who sought the emir's liberation. Upon learning that Monsignor Antoine-Adolphe Dupuch, the former bishop of Algiers, had returned to his native Bordeaux and intended to visit the emir, Daumas wrote him, describing the emir.

"So, you are going to see our illustrious prisoner in Pau. You will certainly not regret taking such a trip. You knew Abd el-Kader in prosperity, when practically all Algeria recognized his authority and now you will find him even greater in adversity than prosperity…

"He never complains for himself, though he is determined to hold France to its word. He forgives his enemies, even those who can still make him suffer and he will not allow anyone to speak ill of them in his presence. Whether they are Muslims or Christians who are the subject of his complaints, he has forgiven them. As to the former, he excuses their treachery by the force of circumstances. As to the latter, their conduct is explained by the flag under which they fought, for its safety and honor — though he considers nationalism yet another false idol. By going to comfort this noble character, you will be adding another charitable act to all the others that have already distinguished your life."

Dupuch's much-anticipated visit was delayed. Nevertheless, with Daumas's help, the bishop established a correspondence with the man who had inspired him to initiate the first wholesale exchange of French and Arab prisoners in the dark year of 1841.

❧

Hope once again sprang to life in the wake of new political turmoil in Paris. This time, the government came under attack from its own radicals. The Constituent Assembly that had been duly elected on April 4, the day of Abd el-Kader's departure for Pau, had the task of drawing up a new constitution within nine months. A slim majority of the 900 delegates were moderate and conservative republicans, followed by monarchists, many of whom wanted to abolish republicanism, and finally, a handful of eighty radical republicans who wanted far-reaching social reforms for the working class. Particularly important to the radicals was the continuation of the National Workshops, established two months earlier in the heady, fraternal days following the February Revolution that had sparked democratic revolutions all over Europe. The workshops were a controversial experiment in public works to provide employment for farmers and others suffering from the worsening agricultural crisis that had taken hold already in 1847.

The provisional government was replaced by an executive committee of the Constituent Assembly while a new constitution was being drawn up. Rather than seeking unity, the moderate republicans decided to root out the radicals who had been in the provisional government and banish their presence on the committee. Lamartine, a left-leaning republican, wanted to avoid an open breach between the radical and moderate republicans. He used his popularity among voters to insist that, if he was to serve as a member of the executive committee, a radical republican must also be represented. His demand was begrudgingly accepted by the assembly, yet Lamartine still could not prevent the hated National Workshops from being abolished. The breach Lamartine had hoped to avoid through political maneuvering became open warfare.

The men who were employed in the National Workshops had been told to enlist in the army or to go to the provinces to drain pestilent swamps. Instead, they erected barricades in the streets of Paris. For three days in June 1848, Paris was soaked in blood. Abd el-Kader's old adversary, General Cavaignac, had been charged with defending the city. He applied tactics learned in Algeria — letting the weakly armed rebels commit themselves and mass in strong positions, and then blasting them away with artillery. This method had been used effectively in Africa, but in Paris it was politically devastating. Some 3000 insurgents were killed in those three bloodiest days in the history of Paris. Another 12,000 were arrested, many of them were shipped off as colonists of compulsion to break Algeria's dry, hard earth.

The after effects of the June riots brought a deepening class hostility that inspired Victor Hugo's *Les Miserables*. General Cavaignac was made interim dictator of the Second Republic, replacing the fractious executive committee. Workers retreated into sullen opposition to the new republic, while the middle classes and aristocracy acquired a deep hostility toward the "reds," as the socialists were known. Out of this chaotic situation, hope emerged for Abd el-Kader in the form of Cavaignac's new minister of war — none other than the man in whose word he had placed his trust, General Leon Christophe Juchault de Lamoricière.

After Abd el-Kader's surrender, Lamoricière had returned to Paris and served briefly as minister of war before the fall of the monarchy. When the February Revolution broke out, he declared his republican sympathies. Two months later, in April, he was elected a delegate to the Constituent Assembly. The June Days, as the worker uprising came to be known, had brought Paris to a boil with intrigue and uncertainty as different forces jockeyed to influence the drafting of the new constitution. Public opinion still held the emir personally responsible for the massacre of the French prisoners in 1846. The French colonists in Algeria were stridently opposed to his liberation. But to Abd el-Kader, the complexity of Lamoricière's new position was immaterial. He saw things simply: Lamoricière had given his word as a French soldier. He was expected to honor it and he now had the power to do so.

On July 9, Abd el-Kader decided to write Lamoricière. "I have given thanks to God that after having triumphed over those who made trouble, it is you to whom the welfare of France has been entrusted. Many Frenchmen come to me and say that I should consider myself virtually free because my friend who gave his word is now in a powerful position. I have rejoiced at the news of your nomination to the ministry certain that this will result in my liberation..."

Abd el-Kader reviewed the solemn commitments made by Lamoricière and the Duke of Aumale and by himself to not incite any trouble..."I have in my hands your written words saying that France accepts all my conditions...You must rescue me from oblivion, for I am like a man thrown into the sea whom only you can save...The majority of Frenchmen don't understand what my position was and think that I was forced to surrender to you, yelping like a wounded dog. Tell them the truth; that if you had not made your promises, I would not have come to you. You must explain that you were far away when our emissaries met — a distance of at least ten-hours march separated us and that the negotiations took forty hours and that the south was open to me.

"Explain this affair to the French people whose honorableness is famous. It is not possible, that learning the whole truth, they will not grant me my freedom…If you do not honor your word, may shame fall upon you, and may no person have faith in your word and may no one, not even your wife, have respect for you."

After several weeks waiting vainly for a reply, the emir came to understand that raison d'état trumped all other considerations. "I had hoped the minister would keep the promises of the general," he dejectedly told Boissonnet when no response was forthcoming. Publicly, he kept a brave face, telling a visitor, "I know the situation in France now is like having your house on fire and the time is not opportune for me to insist too much on my liberty. I ask only that I not be forgotten for too long a time."

The emir's companions were less resigned after learning of the silence that followed the emir's letter to Lamoricière. Angry and desperate, they hatched a suicidal plot to attack the guards barehanded — not to escape, but to die. "We wanted our blood to become an eternal source of shame for France, to be massacred for demanding that the promises made be honored," they told Abd el-Kader when he learned of the conspiracy and intervened.

Lamoricière was also concerned. A scandal caused by the martyrdom of dozens of Arabs for their leader was not a welcome thought for the war minister, who was also concerned about the image of the new Second Republic among the skeptical European monarchies — above all, England. Abd el-Kader was a sensitive subject, but not central to Lamoricière's many other pressing worries. A decision, he thought, could be deferred. Security continued to haunt the war ministry. Spain was within view of the chateau and the British were considered quite capable of plotting to rescue the emir. Lamoricière ordered the transfer of the emir and his immediate family to chateau Amboise on the Loire but allowed his followers to return to Algeria.

The announcement was greeted joylessly by the Arabs. The emir's companions-in-arms rejected the offer of freedom. They told Boissonnet they were prepared to share their master's suffering, and would never leave him in his misfortune.

And his misfortune continued. In August, during Ramadan, Abd el-Kader's health deteriorated, but he insisted on fasting from sunup to sundown, saying to those who questioned the effect on his health, "when the body suffers, the spirit is strengthened." His mother, mother-in-law and other women became seriously ill, they refused to see French doctors. Only the intervention of nurses from the Sisters of Charity succeeded in getting the women to accept their medical attention. The sisters not only healed the bodies, but helped mend the spirits of the Arab women through gentle kindness and their shared embrace of the Almighty. The women's suffering was gradually alleviated, yet two more children died in August, adding to the emir's sense of guilt for being so naïve and trusting of the French. The eight-month-old son of one of his servants died of pneumonia and a six-year-old daughter of his oldest brother, Mohammed Said, died of convulsions.

Throughout their tribulations, the disciplined routines of the Arabs' collective lives never slackened. Like an iron lung, the daily rhythms of prayer, study, visits with family and companions sustained them in their fetid, overcrowded and unnatural confinement.

⁐

The emir's piety and outward patience continued to win him allies among influential persons. Bishop Dupuch was one. Strong willed and authoritarian, yet capable of immense generosity, his experience with the emir in Algeria had already convinced him of the genuineness of this "Muslim Jesus." In time, Dupuch would become a tireless advocate for the emir's release.

The two men had never met. Yet, they felt bound together by the good fruit born of their common humanitarian efforts back in 1841 and the goodwill they had developed for each other. The bishop's arrival on September third was announced just after the emir's midday prayers.

Dupuch had experienced a kind of exile of his own in Italy since his resignation as bishop of Algiers in 1845. The bishop's authoritarian manner, profligate generosity toward Arabs and understanding of the Muslims' inherent respect for all sincere believers had made him enemies among the French authorities. Civilian administrators feared he was proselytizing, or offending Muslim sensibilities by displaying crucifixes and holding Mass in the hospitals run by his Sisters of Charity.

The military authorities were continually draining away his meager budget for their own needs.

In the end, Dupuch's entrepreneurial zeal to do good works had been his downfall. He had, with little governmental support, succeeded in reproducing many of the accomplishments he had achieved in Bordeaux: setting up orphanages and halfway houses for juvenile delinquents and women in trouble, building and running hospitals for civilian and military personnel alike. All this was accomplished by raising money from his parishioners or by borrowing money to speculate in land he believed would appreciate as conditions became more peaceful and more colonists arrived. But that didn't happen, for the reasons Bugeaud had predicted. There was too little security.

Facing a growing flock of angry local creditors and constant opposition to his energetic charity from his own government, Dupuch had finally handed in his resignation in 1845. He landed in Toulon a year later to be met by still more creditors, one of whom threatened to throw him into jail if he did not pay 10,000 francs immediately. Dupuch fled to Turin where a friend, an Italian priest, gave him a post and refuge from his pursuers. But when the ripple effects of the February Revolution came to Turin, anticlerical democrats chased Dupuch and his patron out of town.

All this was unknown to the emir as he left his room and went down the wide, vaulted staircase, past the guards on each landing, to meet Dupuch in the great courtyard. The emir, followed by Boissonnet, moved forward swiftly as the bishop stepped out of his carriage. Abd el-Kader seized his hand the Arab way, interlacing his fingers with Dupuch's as a sign of undying friendship and pressing it against his heart. The bishop embraced the emir, and Abd el-Kader, putting his hand on Dupuch's shoulders, kissed him on his forehead.

"I hope the blessing of God will enter with you into this house."

"From the depths of my heart, I ask it of God," replied the bishop.

"I feel a great good will come from your visit and our knowing each other."

"Of what good do you speak? I have come with hands as empty as my heart is full."

"How much better than with full hands and an empty heart," Abd el-Kader replied, taking him by the hand upstairs to his reception room. He seated the bishop in a high-backed armchair near the window where they could look out at the still snowcapped Pyrenees. "Speak to me like a brother, or perhaps I should say a father," said the emir eagerly, as he pulled up a chair beside the bishop.

Dupuch stayed in Pau for three days. As a sign of respect not shown ordinary guests, Abd el-Kader put on socks before Dupuch entered his room. They talked about the Bible, which the emir had read in translation, and about Rome, the Christian Mecca that he wanted to visit. Abd el-Kader enjoyed speaking freely, knowing he was understood by another man of God. He summed up his reading of the Bible as many a Christian had in the past: "Parts of the Old Testament seem harsh, even terrible to me. But the religion of Christ is the very goodness, grace and mercy of God." The emir felt there was much about himself he needed to explain to Dupuch. "As you can see from our conversations, I was not born to be a soldier...It seems I should not have been one for a single day. By the mysterious designs of Providence, I was diverted from the path for which I was intended by birth, education, and natural inclination. I pray continuously to be allowed to return to it."

Several times during their conversation, Dupuch had observed the emir glancing at his bishop's ring. "The stone is shiny but not of great value," he explained.

"Yes, I noticed it because of its great luster, but I realized that a man of your faith would not wear on his finger the price of bread for so many of the poor."

The emir thanked Dupuch for arranging to have the Sisters of Charity visit the chateau to care for the Arab women and to heal them with their simple goodness. He told the bishop of the ministry's intention to move them to Amboise in November.

"The authorities are still afraid I will try to escape to Spain. How little they understand me."

"Yes, I know, and you will stop on the way in Bordeaux, which is my town where you will be honored. I will accompany you from there up to Amboise."

The Arabs were scheduled to depart on November second. The previous day, Abd el-Kader at last consented to Boissonnet's final offer of a tour of the chateau. Boissonnet showed him the fine tapestries that had been stored in other rooms of the residence, the goblets and silverware, the heavy Renaissance furniture and the huge tortoise shell that had served as a cradle for Henry of Navarre.

A large crowd pressed around the chateau gates wanting to see him off. Abd el-Kader asked Boissonnet if he could leave in an open caleche to go to the hippodrome from where he was to take his official leave of the city. Descending the stairs, the emir gave a member of his escort an envelope, asking that it be given to the local curé. "It is for the poor. Excuse the small sum but my resources are few," he explained. The emir caught sight of the handyman, Rullier, who had helped him almost daily with practical problems small and large. "I have no more money, but take this, it has pearl buttons," he said, giving him a simple cloth waistcoat. Rullier had made a treasured coffee filter for the emir and had built the coffins for those who had died at Pau.

The controversy over the emir's residence at the royal chateau had completely evaporated. Instead, he had become a heroic figure in his suffering. At the hippodrome, a convoy of heavy diligences was assembled to transfer the emir's entourage to Bordeaux. So too were the mayor, the prefect and a multitude of wellwishers to say goodbye. Abd el-Kader left as he came, with a few gracious words: "I leave Pau physically, but my heart remains. All the expressions of sympathy which I have received since being here make my departure sad and difficult. But there is consolation in knowing that I have so many friends among you."

⁂

The decision to move the emir to Amboise pleased those who were in a position to help him. Amboise was close to Paris, where decisions were made. At the same time, others preoccupied with security and with imagining every embarrassing possibility for his escape saw Amboise as a safer prison, buried in the interior of France. Nevertheless, Abd el-Kader's passage from Pau to Amboise had the marks of a royal progress.

Bishop Dupuch had organized a warm welcome in Bordeaux. The emir stayed at the famous Hôtel des Princes. There were banquets, a visit to the opera and countless meetings with local dignitaries. The morning of his departure for Nantes, the emir appeared on the balcony of the city hall before a large square full of an enthusiastic crowd of wellwishers. He was flanked by Dupuch and the chief prelate of

Bordeaux, Archbishop Donnet. Cheers went up from the people. Abd el-Kader wrongly assumed these signs of affection were for his clerical companions, to whom he remarked, "because of your vows, I know you cannot have a family, but the love you give to people who need your help and the devotion they give back to you must be a divine consolation."

Afterward, the archbishop offered his personal carriage to drive the emir's mother and his wives to the port and the waiting corvette, *Caiman*, which would take them up the coast to Paimboeuf. From there, they would transfer to a riverboat and enter the mouth of the Loire at Nantes. The emir was accompanied by the ever-solicitous Boissonnet and Dupuch, who stayed with him all the way to Amboise. The emir's arrival at Nantes was announced with a thirteen cannon military salute. The prefect of the department of Indre et Loire grasped Abd el-Kader's hand and asked sympathetically if he was not suffering from the cold. "Thank you," replied the emir with his customary graciousness, "I don't suffer as much as you think, for the warmth of your reception melts the glacial air of your autumn."

As the emir's flotilla of paddleboats and barges approached Amboise on the moonlit evening of November 8, fairyland towers seemed to grow like majestic, topiaried trees out of the dark rock cliffs overlooking the broad flowing Loire, swollen from the fall rains. Despite its impressive majesty, Amboise was still another prison.

CHAPTER NINETEEN

A Prison Fit for a King

FOR HUNDREDS OF YEARS, Amboise had provided security for its royal descendants of Europe's ax-swinging warlords. Like Abd el-Kader, these tribal chieftains of the northern climes wanted to unify warring, lesser tribes under the banner of greater mutual security, tranquility and Divine Will. Like the emir, a Christian monarch's rule was legitimized by God.

The chateau had played host to Leonardo da Vinci when it was the residence of the state-building King Francis I in the 16th century. Napoleon Bonaparte confiscated the chateau from the Bourbons to use as a prison for monarchist sympathizers. By 1848, it again belonged to the Orleans branch of the Bourbon line, the Duke of Aumale's family. The ancient residence had been restored by the duchess dowager of Orleans, who bequeathed it to her grandson and future king, Louis-Philippe. The emir's new prison was, indeed, royal.

A large crowd of eager and curious residents were on hand to greet the emir upon his arrival, despite the late hour. Two days later, a banquet was held in his honor by the mayor of Amboise. Glasses were raised and a toast given to the absent emir who chose, as in Pau, not to be seen as a merry prisoner of French treachery.

The warm welcome by the local population stood in a stark contrast to the new rules of confinement imposed by the war ministry. The emir was allowed no visits from the outside unless authorized by Lamoricière. He was prohibited from sending or receiving letters without permission. An unseemly large contingent of 200 soldiers, sixty more than originally budgeted, was assigned to protect the "Prince-Prisoner," as he was being called in the local newspapers. Interpreters were constantly being changed by the ministry to guard against their growing too sympathetic toward the Arabs and becoming potential accomplices in skullduggery. The available barracks could not hold more than 150 men. Citizens happily accepted troops quartered in their homes for the privilege of vicariously hosting their illustrious prisoner. They also supplemented the paltry war ministry budget for the prisoners of 1.3 francs per day with donations of clothing, food, linens and furniture.

The prisoners in the chateau may have belonged to the ministry, but the emir now belonged to the people of Amboise. The bridge between the two was Captain Boissonnet. He immediately set about trying to make them as comfortable as possible and to soften the severe rules imposed from Paris. Rugs were obtained to cover the cold stone floors, and straw mats for the Arabs to sleep on. Lalla Zohra slept in the only bed available. Boissonnet made sure the many fireplaces were kept well fueled with wood. He arranged with the shopkeepers of Amboise to find semolina and mutton for making couscous, as well as dates, fruit and other customary ingredients of the Arabs' diet.

In certain ways, life was better for the Arabs at Amboise. They were perched on top of a cliff and surrounded by openness and light, the chateau's unbarred windows a welcome contrast to the foreboding walls and confined atmosphere of Pau. An outdoor gallery off the great reception room facing the Loire and the open stairwell to the north tower landing gave their new prison the feeling of a large eagle's nest. They had several acres of private gardens stretching away from the river that were accessible only through the heavily guarded ascending tunnel cut through the cliff wall leading up to the chateau grounds. Under different conditions, it could have been a vacation paradise.

A month after Abd el-Kader's arrival at Amboise, his hopes were raised once more. But he had also learned how treacherous French political waters could be in this multiheaded new republic. A new constitution had been written, and a new unicameral Legislative Assembly and a new president of the Second Republic were voted into office on the tenth of December. The victor was a candidate considered by the cognoscenti least likely to succeed.

Louis-Napoleon Bonaparte had surprised all the politicians with his overwhelming margin of victory: 5,500,000 versus 1,500,000 for General Cavaignac and a mere 17,000 for the once popular Lamartine. Among the least-likely-to-succeed candidates in the election was none other than Abd el-Kader himself. The good impression he had made on the people of Bordeaux the previous month even produced a political result: his admirers obtained enough signatures to put his name on the presidential ballot. Soon after the emir's departure, the regional journal *Progrés d'Indre et Loire* had written: "We have learned that certain voters of Bordeaux were so impressed by the manners, the character and royal air of Abd el-Kader, they put his name on the ballot for president of the Republic. If this idea spreads it will hurt Louis-Napoleon. To be a good president one must have a reputation for courage, wisdom and talent. Of the two, would not Abd el-Kader better meet those conditions?" Though undoubtedly flattered upon learning of this symbolic gesture of support from some voters, the emir had other reasons for a mild case of optimism. He had learned that Louis-Napoleon was favorably disposed toward releasing the Arabs.

Boissonnet was filling the role Daumas had played for the emir of confidant, conversational partner, moral supporter and go-between. He was impressed by the emir's interest in learning more about Christianity, the new technical developments that were taking place in the world, and about the customs and history of the French people. Abd el-Kader had been particularly interested in the great sultan of France who had died in captivity after being betrayed by the British, who had promised Napoleon exile in England, then changed their mind. Now the emir wanted to know about the new prince-president and Bonaparte's nephew.

He learned that the man in whose hands his freedom rested was something of a romantic and idealist who had left France after the Bourbon Restoration in 1815. His mother, the wife of Napoleon's brother, Louis, took him to Switzerland to be educated. A visionary — some would say a harebrained dreamer — who believed in helping oppressed peoples fulfill their destinies, he became involved in Italian revolutionary politics before turning his attention to France. After several ill-considered coups against King Louis-Philippe, he was sentenced in 1840 to life imprisonment in the fortress of Ham, from where he wrote political pamphlets that revealed a socialist, populist bent. Six years later, the future president escaped disguised as a mason and fled to London, where he became a free-spending society figure and befriended influential Englishmen. Louis-Philippe's abdication in February brought Bonaparte back to France, where he became popular with the working classes. The toxic atmosphere left over from the June Days, in addition to Napoleon's famous name, made this much underestimated, seemingly incompetent "cretin," as professor Guizot called him, the people's choice.

On January 14, 1849, one month after his election, the new president called a meeting of his ministers to review the emir's case. Citizen Ollivier, from the former provisional government, had been working behind the scenes, enlisting supporters of the emir's cause. He knew also that Louis-Napoleon's own history of imprisonment made him sympathetic toward the emir. Generals Bugeaud and Changarnier were also invited to offer their opinions. The emir's former military adversaries all voiced support for his release.

However, the unyielding opposition of General Rulhière, Louis-Napoleon's new war minister, was not expected. He had replaced Lamoricière, whose anti-Bonapartist leanings were well known. The French military occupation in Algeria had been reduced to a mere 30,000 troops. Many colonists, tempted by exaggerated hopes of easy money and great estates, had returned home disappointed by the difficult conditions and backbreaking work. Even the remotest possibility that Abd el-Kader might return to create trouble was something Rulhière wanted to foreclose. The new legislature was still against freeing the man thought responsible for the slaughter of 130 unarmed French prisoners. Too insecure in his new position, Louis-Napoleon decided to wait for a more propitious moment.

The emir accepted the news of the president's position with his predictable stoicism. "Ambition often blinds men's hearts," Abd el-Kader told Boissonnet, "and prevents them from believing in the sincerity of others, sometimes causing injustice." The new disappointment pushed the emir more deeply within himself to meditate and reflect upon the meaning of his fate.

Abd el-Kader rediscovered Abraham, the father of three religions, "neither Jew nor Christian, but a true believer who submitted to God." He wrote of having a vision of Abraham, "this intimate friend, the Beloved of God...I saw Abraham and I am one of his children that most resemble him...I sense a share in his inheritance... " This "blessing of Abraham," as he called it, gave him a mission to fulfill — to be a sign of the oneness of God, the merciful, the patient and loving God for all people. That had been the message of Abd el-Kader al-Jilani, the saint of Baghdad and founder of the emir's Kadiriyya brotherhood.

He wanted to help a France that he saw becoming a power in the Muslim world, to better understand Islam, but also to guide the French people to understand their own spiritual needs. By "France," the emir meant the Occidental world as a whole, which he saw as strong in material things but weak in the realm of the spirit, where the most enduring knowledge resided. One day he told Boissonnet: "Your savants have an impressive spirit of practical application. But where is the spirit of metaphysical speculation which will allow them to go beyond the narrow confines of material reality to attain a knowledge which serves the needs of man's soul?"

∞

Many people wanted to meet the emir, but were turned away on orders from the war ministry. Abd el-Kader's once iron constitution began to fail in the winter of 1848-49. He refused to leave the chateau and avail himself of the opportunities to promenade in the gardens or in the town below. The doctors became alarmed at his deathly pallor. When they attempted to reason with him, he would only reply: "Prison has nothing to do with my health; what I need is the air of freedom."

Abd el-Kader wrote to Dupuch, with whom he felt he could bare his heart: "…The cold, damp climate here wears us down little by little. We will not be able to last much longer before we die. Even the French doctors believe this and are apprehensive about our well-being. They also wish for our prompt release…We hear it said that the French fear we will start trouble once we leave. On the contrary, we know how committed we are to keeping the peace. We want to be useful to all people without exception. Life, prosperity — we respect these and advise others to respect them as well… "

Permission was granted Dupuch to see the emir, though it was obtained with great difficulty, and thanks to efforts behind the scenes by Boissonnet and Daumas. His visit in the early spring would be a tonic for the emir's spirit, who kept on display a portrait of his beloved bishop that his admirers in Bordeaux had sent.

On the much awaited day, the Abd el-Kader brought Dupuch to view himself hanging in the royally furnished neo-Gothic salon in the north tower. There he sat, slightly askew in a finely carved, stiff-backed chair, wearing his black cassock, a large silver cross over his chest, the Bible in his left hand, and staring with benevolent eyes at something unseen. The Christian marabout's grey hair was short-cropped and his black, patriarchal beard grey-flecked, looking every bit the Abrahamic cousin. "All my people have your beloved image implanted in their hearts, and now we are delighted to have it before our eyes."

Dupuch was worried about Abd el-Kader's health and that of his family as they paced back and forth on the arcaded gallery that overlooked the Loire. In Pau, Dupuch had prevailed upon the emir to accept Christian medical care; this time it would come from the Dominican Sisters of neighboring Tours. The bishop told him about the booklet he was preparing, which would be dedicated to President Louis-Napoleon. It was to be a testimonial to the emir's character, buttressed by the opinion of many others, together with a long historical and personal argument for his release. Abd el-Kader showed Dupuch the many letters of sympathy he had received from his former French prisoners, now that he was himself a prisoner. Dupuch left with promises to return and a determination to continue his fight for the emir's freedom.

Dupuch was not alone. Daumas, Boissonnet and commissioner of the Var, Citizen Ollivier, were joined by unexpected allies from England. An empathetic William Thackeray composed "*The Caged Hawk*," an elegy to Abd el-Kader, for whom unjust confinement was likened to death. The Earl of Winchelsea of the House of Lords dedicated 6,000 lines of epic doggerel to the emir. The Marquis of Londonderry began an impassioned correspondence on the emir's behalf with the new president, whom he had befriended while Bonaparte was a fugitive in London.

Even that unpredictable force in British politics, public opinion, was solidly with the emir. Abd el-Kader had transformed the popular view of the North Africans as cutthroats and marauders on the high seas to plucky, valiant underdogs. His name soon would be on the lips of tens of thousands of ordinary British. In 1850, against odds of 33-1, the horse that would win the Grand National Steeple Chase an unprecedented two years in a row was named Abd el-Kader, or "Little Ab" as he was affectionately known to the racing public.*

---

* Abd el-Kader was owned and trained by a Joe Osborne of Julianstown, County Meath, Ireland. His time of 9.57 minutes set the benchmark until 1862. The eight-year-old was the smallest horse in the field.

In April, General Bugeaud was permitted to write the emir. It was the war ministry's last attempt to convince the emir of his true interests. Not only France's word was at stake, but its pride. If the emir would only make France his adopted home, then the whole world would understand. France would not have dishonored its word, but simply enabled him to see the light of its superior culture.

"You have experienced great misfortunes and so, too, has Algeria because of you," Bugeaud wrote. "But neither has God spared France. Since you have surrendered to the French army, unprecedented troubles have fallen upon our country. No doubt both your country and ours merited these punishments because God is sovereign and just, and no one can know His designs.

"I must now talk to you with the candor of a true friend. It could be many years before you will see the city of the Prophet, and to carry a vain hope may make you only more miserable." Bugeaud proposed that the emir ask the government to give him an estate that would be his legal property and which could be passed on to his heirs. He could practice his religion as he wished and educate his children in the Muslim faith.

Even if this proposal was in no way enticing to the emir, Bugeaud thought it merited consideration for the sake of his children and companions, who were dying of boredom and inactivity. They could hunt. They would be occupied with good healthy outdoor work, and cultivating the soil, and "their morale would be raised by the invigorating process of transforming nature." Bugeaud concluded: "These are my sincere thoughts, stimulated by my concern for your suffering and respect for the great qualities which God has bestowed upon you."

The emir replied that he wanted only one thing: that France honor its commitments. "I will not release you from your word," he answered Bugeaud. "I would rather die for your dishonor than to give back your word."

Louis-Napoleon had undoubtedly authorized Bugeaud's letter. It was a clever mixture of sincerity and manipulation — an attempted solution to the problem of squaring his sense of honor with domestic politics. Notwithstanding his victory at the polls and his good intentions, the president faced not only the strong opposition of his minister of war, but a stubbornly resistant legislature as well. It had adopted a declaration that the emir, "by commanding the massacre of our prisoners has put himself outside the law." The normal rules of war or honor did not apply in his case, according to the new National Assembly.

Abd el-Kader resigned himself to watch and wait. He counseled resignation to his companions: they must simply wait for circumstances to change and to trust those who believed in Napoleon's good intentions.

Two months later, on June sixth, General Bugeaud died from cholera, at age sixty-five. After hearing the news, Abd el-Kader wrote a letter of condolence to his family. "...This great marshal fought me as a worthy and noble enemy. He taught me to admire the French. The letters he wrote to me, the advice he gave, will always remain with me."

‽

Dupuch's brief on behalf of Abd el-Kader appeared in the summer of 1849, dedicated to President Louis-Napoleon. He forthrightly explained his purpose in the preface of his booklet, *Abd el Kader au Château d'Amboise.*

"I have just returned from Amboise where I spent several days in the most gentle intimacy of an illustrious prisoner. More than many others, I believe I know and appreciate Abd el-Kader 's qualities. But upon my return to Bordeaux, I met everywhere people, otherwise of good judgment, who have a completely false and incomplete idea of this extraordinary man, and this contributes, in ways they do not suspect, to delaying further the day when justice will be done. I believe if people in France knew Abd el-Kader as I do today, that day would be soon...I imagine that it is my duty as a human being, knowing that I can do more, to try to establish the truth regarding certain events... This belief, which I admit I cannot resist, is my best explanation for those into whose hands these few simple conscientious pages fall. They ought to be regarded as an act of true patriotism as well as an act of Christian charity."

The charged political atmosphere of France, the prejudicial stereotypes of Arabs in general — and of the emir in particular — combined with partial truths about the emir's role in the massacre of the French prisoners reduced Dupuch's treatise to addressing one question: the value of the emir's word. It was not Dupuch's intent to argue the emir's case regarding blame for treaties broken, but to give testimonials from different sources that supported the good character of the emir and the sincerity of his word.

Dupuch told the story of how, as the new bishop of Algiers, he had had his first astonishing experience with Abd el-Kader in 1841 when he had sent his vicar, Suchet, with a letter for the emir asking to release a French officer whose wife and daughter had begged the bishop to seek his freedom. The emir's unexpected response had been to reproach him gently for not thinking of the fate of all the prisoners — all the French in his hands and the Arabs in French prisons. Why would a man who had such concern for his prisoners in 1841 commit a criminal act in 1846 against French prisoners in defiance of his own strict rules? Dupuch wondered. Abd el-Kader had stopped "the barbarous but common custom" of decapitating prisoners and bringing their heads back hanging from saddles. Instead of paying his troops for enemy heads, he insisted that his soldiers treat their prisoners humanely.

There was the surprising payment to the European advisors who had been employed by the emir during the Treaty of Tafna to teach his Arabs how to make armaments and to improve the discipline of his regulars. Each had been assured payment of 3,000 francs on completion of their services. When hostilities broke out, the emir paid them all in full, although many had not completed their assignments. Again, the emir surprised the advisors by offering them armed escorts to be sure they returned safely to the French controlled areas. "This I heard from their own mouths," wrote Dupuch.

The emir's scrupulousness was shared by his lieutenants. Dupuch told Napoleon of the much talked about incident of Sidi Embarek Ben Allal, caliph of Miliana. Ben Allal had purchased a horse from Lamoricière and still owed him money when the fighting restarted. At the risk of his life, Ben Allal stole into Lamoricière's Zouave camp at night and left a leather sack hanging from an orange tree containing the sum due.

Blind intolerance and fanaticism were other charges Dupuch had frequently heard leveled against the emir by Frenchmen. He reported the conversation of two Europeans he met in Algiers who had been advising the emir how to train his small regular army. After a day of instruction, they came to the emir's tent and asked to become Muslims. The advisors recalled for Dupuch his response:

"If your wish is sincere, that is good. If it is out of fear or desire to be accepted in your new position, then it is against your conscience, and that is bad. Don't do it. Don't worry. Not a single hair will fall from your head because you are Christians, not with my consent or knowledge. Furthermore, imagine what will happen when you return home as apostates. You will be treated as traitors, or deserters."

"And, if you don't believe me," Dupuch told his readers in summation, "talk to those who fought him and considered him a worthy and noble enemy — Bugeaud, Changarnier, Bedeau, Lamoricière, Cavaignac. Talk with his former prisoners in Africa or his guards in France — Captain Zaragossa at Pau, Daumas, Boissonnet or any of the people at any social level who were in his company and you will hear only the same. He is an honest man of deep and sincere faith, who could forgive almost anything, but not lies and treachery."

Dupuch's modest tract for the new president became another stone on the scales that were slowly tipping in the emir's favor.

༼༽

Conditions began to improve during the year 1850. Lamoricière was gone; so too Rulhière and Shramm, who had been replaced by the more benevolent General Hautpoul as Louis-Napoleon continued to seek a war minister who fitted his politics. In divided post-revolutionary France, a man who controlled the army, but was out of step with the president was a dangerous person. General Daumas was now an aide to war minister Hautpoul, a friend as well as a veteran of the African campaigns. Daumas helped persuade the minister to send 2,000 francs to the emir for his "personal needs."

The emir thanked the minister for the money and went on to ask in a letter if the minister would help him obtain information about his nephew, Mohammed Sadok, the son of his oldest brother, Mohammed Said. He had been taken prisoner by the Moroccans in the last days of the fighting before the surrender. Abd el-Kader had heard that the nephew had escaped and taken refuge in Marrakech. Could the minister help get him out of the country if he managed to get himself to the French consul in Tangier?

A month later the nephew was in Amboise. A great celebration took place at the chateau when the young man rejoined the community, for he was also the fiancé of the emir's daughter, Khadijah.

"Thanks to God, and to you, my nephew is here. May God grant to you the fulfillment of all your wishes in exchange for this great good deed," he wrote to Louis-Napoleon, acknowledging also the helpful role of Hautpoul and Daumas in the transaction. A discreet correspondence with the new president had begun, thanks to the many ears Daumas had now reached. The emir sent Louis-Napoleon a poem of praise, hope and goodwill, celebrating his election.

Abd el-Kader began to loosen his self-imposed chains and take walks in the neatly trimmed gardens on the chateau grounds. He paused often at the gravestones of his companions and family who had already died from pneumonia, or suffering from depression and despair, had lost the will to live. His youngest wife, Embaraka, and two children, Khadijah and Ahmed, were among them, buried next to each other in the chateau park. Nevertheless, the emir still maintained his outward serenity and always addressed himself to France's higher nature. "One must not judge France based on a moment in time, but over the course of years," he said often in discussion with visitors. "If one shows confidence in her, one will be repaid in full, and more."

The debates in the Assembly continued. On November 25, General Fabvier made a motion to free the captive, but was met with hisses, catcalls and counterarguments. It was beyond the comprehension of some of the deputies (for whom all North Africa was simply the Barbary Coast) that "these pirates should be considered as fair adversaries." "He had no right to complain of the hospitality he received in France if he reflected on the fate of the French prisoners," another shouted. General Shramm justified the breach of faith, saying that "it is necessary to destroy the enemy by all means in one's power," but added when objection was taken to his turn of phrase "compatible with the honor of a soldier." The time was still not ripe for the president to act.

In the spring of 1851, the emir left the confines of the chateau grounds for the first time. In May, yet another minister of war, General Randon, sent a cavalry escort to Amboise. Boissonnet had finally persuaded the emir that he should go out into the countryside, not only for his health, but to show his goodwill toward the citizens of Amboise who were anxious to meet him. His first outing was to Chateau Chenonceaux, the residence of Count and Countess of Villeneuve, which became a topic of interest to the local newspaper: "The Emir

Abd el-Kader 's excursion showed his sense of politesse. From the day of his arrival in Amboise, the count and countess had regularly sent the illustrious prisoner flowers and rare fruits that they grew in their hothouses. They had been among the first to visit him."

After Chenonceaux, the emir began to explore more widely the region's chateaux in an open calèche, accompanied by a doctor, selected lieutenants, family members and servants. Typically, they would stop and have mint tea at a local chateau, prearranged by Boissonet, while the younger members of the emir's congregation found other diversions.

Exploring the cobblestoned alleys of Amboise, they were received by the townfolk in a friendly way, a bit too friendly for the emir's strict morality. Reports made their way to the emir that some of his men could be found in the streets, "sightseeing" with women known to be interested in learning more about the fabled sexual appetite of Arabs than conducting cultural tours of the town. Others squatted for hours along the railroad tracks where they waited and watched with stupefied wonder the locomotives that puffed, hissed and whistled into town. They called them Araba esh Sheitan, the Devil's Carriage.

The emir wrote Randon, thanking him for relaxing their restrictions. A few months later, the minister visited the emir incognito, curious to meet the fabled emir. General Randon had served for ten years in Algeria, and while a colonel in the Second Regiment of Chasseurs, his reputation for decisiveness and honorable conduct had been made known to Abd el-Kader. The emir welcomed him, declaring, "for a long time I have heard of you. My eyes were jealous of my ears." Abd el-Kader was greatly pleased to learn from the minister that Boissonnet had been promoted to commander. Touched by the visit of the war minister, he wrote to Daumas thanking him, knowing that he was the silent partner in this unexpected initiative.

Another unexpected visitor had met with Abd el-Kader that year. Lord Londonderry had written Louis-Napoleon soon after his electoral victory to lobby for the emir's cause. He received an encouraging reply from his old friend: "…in your solicitude for him, I recognize the same generous heart that pleaded for the prisoner of Ham…I confess that ever since I was elected, Abd el-Kader 's captivity has constantly been in my thoughts."

The interference of an English lord was not particularly welcome to the powerful war ministry, for whom suspicion of British intentions ran high. Nevertheless, the sponsorship of the president himself eventually resulted in permission being given to Londonderry, his wife and daughter to go to Amboise. The ministry did not capitulate abjectly to the request, however. Measures were taken to make the visit of the Englishman as unwelcoming as possible. First, the trio was treated to a long wait outside the chateau gates before entering the tunnel into the grounds. Once inside, they were made to wait in the cold, wind-blown chapel next to the chateau. Then, they were told to wait some more in a small, dirty storage room that was piled with dusty books and bird cages.

When finally they were led into the "dreary, dismal old chateau," Londonderry recalled his first impression upon entering the emir's chambers in the grand Salle des Étoiles: "His stature is commanding; his gesture, softness and amiability of expression almost inexplicable. Upon my approaching the emir, he held out a large, bony, deep-brown hand. When I grasped it, he turned and led me to the mahogany sofas and arm chairs at the head of a well-appointed room." Throughout their conversation, the emir held Londonderry's hand. When he took his leave, the emir hugged him so hard, the Englishman complained later that his neck and shoulder ached for days.

The marquis had come as both curiosity seeker and moral supporter. A former celebrated cavalry officer himself who had also fought the French and served in the Peninsula Campaign, horses and the smell of gunpowder were a common bond. He had told the emir of England's great sympathy for his struggle and interest in his fate. As always, Abd el-Kader was polite but pressed his visitor to arrange for him an audience with the president. Londonderry doubted that would be possible, but promised to do his best, adding that he had "innate confidence" in Louis-Napoleon to do the right thing.

A few months later, the president tested public opinion by allowing the release of nineteen Arabs from the chateau, most of whom returned to Algeria. There was no public outcry.

❧

Another year passed. 1852 saw the death toll grow, despite the greater freedoms allowed the Arabs. The indefiniteness of their captivity, the false hopes and the clammy, unnatural confinement were leading to a slow form of suffocation. Despair and depression, mixed with frequent bouts of pneumonia, cholera and tuberculosis, were sucking the life out of the weaker souls.

"Liberty, liberty alone will cure me," cried the emir's nephew on his deathbed. Twenty-five gravestones dotted the makeshift Arab cemetery near the chateau in the summer of 1852. Three bore the name Abd el-Kader, two belonging to the sons of servants, and one to his older brother, Mohammed. Three members of the emir's immediate family had died — his youngest wife, Baraka, his sister, Khadijah, and son, Ibrahim. His brother Hossein watched over his daughter, Aicha, as she wasted away from consumption, and his devoted agha, Kara Mohammed, lost his young daughter as well.

On October 16, the emir did not give much attention to the atmosphere of suppressed excitement that seemed to be rippling among the French personnel. Even the normally self-controlled Boissonnet seemed agitated. That afternoon Abd el-Kader was pacing in the arcade enjoying its panoramic view of the Loire when he heard sounds of martial music and cheering crowds below. Ignoring the commotion, he returned to his room. Shortly, Boissonnet appeared at his door smartly turned out in his dress uniform with an announcement: "You have an important visitor."

CHAPTER TWENTY

Liberation

"THE PRINCE-PRESIDENT WISHES TO SEE YOU." A stunned Abd el-Kader silently followed Boissonnet to the gothic salon in the north tower. Dozens of candles from a great multilayered crystal chandelier lit the room, a massive log fire raged in the baronial hearth and there, in the middle of the floor, seated at a table surrounded by a clutch of attentive officers, was a small, pale-faced man, with sad eyes, black hair and a small spade beard on a long face.

Louis-Napoleon rose from his chair and looked inquisitively at the man who had charmed thousands of Frenchmen. "I have come to give you your freedom." Abd el-Kader had caught the word liberté and had already knelt and kissed Napoleon's hand before Boissonnet could read the hand-written proclamation of the president. Controlling his own emotions with some difficulty, Boissonnet read aloud from the piece of paper he had been handed:

"…You will be taken to Bursa in the territory of the Sultan as soon as certain details are settled. The government will provide you with a pension worthy of your former rank. For a long time I have been chagrined by your imprisonment, for it has been a constant reminder that my predecessor government had failed to keep its commitments toward an enemy caught in the grip of misfortune. In my view, it is humiliating for a great nation to have so little confidence in its own power that it breaks its promises. Generosity is always the best councilor, and I am sure that your residence in Turkey will in no way disturb the tranquility of my possessions in Africa.

Your religion, as well as mine, teaches submission to the decrees of Providence. If France is now the mistress of Algeria, it is because that is God's will…You have been the enemy of France; nevertheless, I am ready to render full justice to your courage, your character, and your resignation in suffering.

Consequently, I consider it a point of honor to end your imprisonment and to put my full confidence in your word."

Abd el-Kader was overwhelmed. But before he could call his mother to come and hear the news, the emir was introduced to Napoleon's entourage. Of particular interest to him was the new minister of war, General Saint-Arnaud, the exterminator of Arabs in the Dahra caves and great admirer of Bugeaud. His peaked eyebrows, pointed d'Artagnan beard and air of stiff dignity made him look the very embodiment of the cold, military aristocrat. Yet, he was another officer to whom the emir was henceforth indebted. Saint-Arnaud had been among those working behind the scenes for the emir's freedom.

Surrounded by two of her grandsons, Lalla Zohra shuffled into the salon leaning on her cane. With a rare smile shining below her white haik, she approached Napoleon and kissed his hand. He hadn't been briefed that the correct response to this humble gesture from an Arab queen mother was to withdraw his hand and kiss her forehead. A meal of couscous had been prepared so the President and his staff could sit at the table with Abd el-Kader and his family to celebrate his first meal in freedom.

"Others have knocked me down or imprisoned me, but only Louis-Napoleon has conquered me," Abd el-Kader told his companions after the president had departed.

He gathered his companions to announce the news and to offer thanks to God for their good fortune. The next day, the emir composed letters to thank the many people he knew had been working for his release.

Abd el-Kader had discovered in exile that politics shrinks the spirit, whereas the sacred enlarges it without limit. In his own defeat and the fall of successive French governments, he had witnessed the meaning of that verse in the Koran he knew by heart: *Everything on earth is ephemeral; only the face of your Lord will abide forever, in all its majesty and glory.* Ruination is the inevitable companion of the politics of the sword.

The emir also had experienced the kindness of Christians and the nonreligious alike, understanding that the paths, even if straight and narrow, are also many. Yes, God is infinite, all-embracing and self-sufficient. Yet, His limited creatures can only know and worship Him in part. For Abd el-Kader, the plurality of beliefs was but a reflection of the infinite nature of God and the inexhaustible ways to praise God.

These ideas would be set to paper a few years later, but their roots were planted in the soil of study and reflection, and fertilized by the goodness he could find in a France that had betrayed him. From people of all stations — Dupuch, Daumas, Boissonnet, Ollivier, the Prince-President himself, and the humble coffin maker — he had witnessed the meaning of charity and goodwill in a land he could no longer call, "infidel."

Abd el-Kader wrote to Louis-Napoleon asking permission to come to Paris to "admire the marvels of France and to better understand the spirit and nobility of the French nation."

℘

On the afternoon of October 28, Abd el-Kader was driven through the streets of Paris accompanied by Kara Mohammed, Kaddour Ben Allal and Boissonnet, now Major Boissonnet. An enthusiastic crowd was eagerly waiting to catch a glimpse of the emir as his carriage drew up at the Hotel de la Terrasse on the Rue de Rivoli. The influential daily, *Le Moniteur*, had written approvingly of Louis-Napoleon's action. "The prince has marked the end of his tour of France by a great act of justice and national generosity — he has set Abd el-Kader free. A loyal and generous policy is alone fitting to a great nation." Amboise had been the last stop of the President's procession around the countryside to take the people's pulse — a pulse that showed fatigue with all the political turmoil of the past years and a desire for stability.

Soon after his arrival at the hotel, a message was delivered inviting the emir to attend a special performance of Rossini's *Moses* that same night. Abd el-Kader wanted to plead fatigue, but first asked Boissonnet if the "Sultan" would be there. When he learned that he would, the emir decided that he must go after all, even if he would only see him from a distance.

The emir's carriage joined a stream of broughams, landaus and heavy diligences flowing toward the opera. The Boulevard des Italiens was lined with people as the carriages rolled over freshly sanded cobblestones toward the brilliantly gas-lit opera house that had been decorated with garlands and wreaths. Excitement charged the air. A plebiscite had been announced that would determine if France would again become an empire, this time with the great Napoleon's nephew as emperor. That night, the *beau monde* of Paris was celebrating in anticipation of a new era.

A murmur rippled through the glittering crowd in the auditorium. Word had spread that Abd el-Kader was among the Arabs dressed in simple white burnooses who had entered the loge above. Society women and generals alike craned their heads to see which one might be the emir. Hundreds of lorgnettes and opera glasses searched the figures above. Suddenly a hush fell upon the crowd. Wild applause. The crowd rose to its feet and shouted "Vive l'Empereur!" as a man who was the same age as Abd el-Kader and who had also known imprisonment, entered his red velvet box, embroidered with golden bees topped by an imperial crown.

A special cantata had been composed for Louis-Napoleon between the first and second acts whose aria had the refrain "Empire is peace," a popular slogan he had coined during a stump speech in Bordeaux, which had echoed across France. After the cantata, Abd el-Kader received an invitation to visit the president's box. When the emir bowed to kiss the president's hand, Louis-Napoleon pushed it away and embraced Abd el-Kader, kissing him on the cheek in the European manner. The crowd applauded approvingly the generous spirit of their emperor-to-be.

Louis-Napoleon also had offered to give an official reception at Saint-Cloud for the emir after he returned from two days of hunting. In the meantime, he had instructed his aides to show Abd el-Kader the sites of Paris. First, he was shown the Madeleine, whose mighty Corinthian columns resembled a massive Greek temple. Waiting for him at the top of the steps was the curé, whose arm the emir took affectionately before entering the nave where the two stood together, arm in arm, in front of the alter. An astonished crowd watched as the emir, side by side with the priest, prayed silently in a Christian house of worship. "When I began my terrible struggle with the French, I thought they had no religious feeling," Abd el-Kader told the cure´ as they left the richly decorated nave. "If I had not already been disabused of my prejudices before, I would have been now after seeing the magnificence of this temple."

It is likely the emir didn't know that the Madeleine contained much of the story of France's tortured relationship with God. The foundation stone of the church was laid in 1763 under the reign of Louis XV, but its construction was abandoned in 1891 by the Constituent Assembly that eventually beheaded his slow-witted successor, Louis XVI. Napoleon Bonaparte started to convert the structure into a temple glorifying the French army in 1806 following the battle of Austerlitz, but his debacle in Russia caused a change of heart. A humbled Napoleon reverted to the original idea of glorifying God and ordered that it be a church after all. But by 1852, the Madeleine was empty much of the time; its use was mostly ceremonial.

At Notre-Dame, Abd el-Kader admired the coronation robe of Emperor Napoleon I, then climbed one of the cathedral's towers to view the city. He saw the emerald-green sarcophagus of the great Bonaparte at the Invalides and visited the hospital where veterans sat up as he passed by their beds. The appropriate words always seemed to come to him. "I have touched the sword of Napoleon and seen his tomb. I would leave this place completely happy if it were not for the thought that some of you may be here because you have been wounded by me or my soldiers."

There were trips to the Hippodrome to witness French skill with the new art of ballooning, to the National Artillery Museum and the National Printing Works. Impressed by intricacy and speed of modern presses, Abd el-Kader exclaimed to his hosts: "Yesterday, I saw the batteries of war. Today, I see the batteries of thought."

In between his visits to the monuments of French civilization, the emir entertained a stream of over 300 visitors in his hotel room. Alexander Bellemare, his new interpreter who had replaced the worn out Boissonnet, marveled at the ease with which Abd el-Kader received his guests. "To understand him properly," wrote Bellemare, "one has to see him in the company of all those people who came every morning to pay their respects — to hear him talking tactics with the generals, science with the scholars and of his work as an organizer and a statesman. For each he found a kind word, an answer exactly suited to his own position and that of his guest. This endless sequence of apposite remarks made for two weeks to people whose position could be explained in advance only with a few brief words, revealed one of the most remarkable aspects of a man so remarkable in countless other ways." Gustave Flaubert, Victor Hugo, Bonaparte's aging brother, Jerome, Prince Murat and the Duke of Aumale were among the great, along with the humble, who sought an audience with the emir.

Five French soldiers who had been his prisoners came to see the emir. They wanted to thank him for the kindness showed during their two years of captivity. One was about to be discharged from the Municipal Guard because of ill health and begged him to be allowed to go to Turkey with him as his personal servant. The emir turned to Bellemare after the former prisoners left. "The French are good and just."

Abd el-Kader also received a visit from Courby de Cognord who still believed five years later that Abd el-Kader was personally responsible for the murder of the prisoners.

"The massacre took place against my orders and against my known wishes," the emir explained. "I was far away at the time."

"Then why did you not punish the culprits?"

"I could not do so. My chiefs were in revolt and no longer obeyed me. My soldiers, embittered by defeat, had only a few handfuls of barley to live on. Do not question me further. I do not wish to accuse another."

De Cognord suddenly understood the honorableness of this man who had chosen to shield his own brother-in-law. The Frenchman grasped the emir's hand warmly in his own.

୬୬

As promised, an official reception was given the emir at Saint-Cloud when Louis-Napoleon returned from his hunting expedition. The minister of war, Saint-Arnaud, and his former keeper, Daumas, accompanied the emir and his companions Kaddour Ben Allal and Kara Mohammed on the long ride from his hotel to the suburbs of Paris. This residence of Napoleon I was of special interest to the emir. Not only had he been compared to Napoleon by a number of Frenchmen, he had become a student and admirer of Napoleon's achievements on and off the battlefield, but especially off. He also had with him a document that he wanted to give the president.

He had learned that the French newspapers were saying that when the president released the emir, he had received certain pledges in return. In fact, the emir had not given pledges, though he had considered the idea and rejected it. "I preferred not to do so for his sake and mine," the emir explained to Bellemare. "It would have detracted from his generosity by giving the impression he had imposed conditions on me. For my part, it was repugnant to appear like a Jew buying his freedom for a piece of paper." The emir wanted to give him a written statement of his own free will.

When Louis-Napoleon entered the grand salon at Saint-Cloud, Abd el-Kader wanted to kiss his hand, as was his custom, but was again embraced by the French "Sultan." Abd el-Kader handed him the piece of paper, saying that words are like the wind. Writing alone is permanent.

"I have come to your Highness to thank you for your kindness… You trusted me. You refused to listen to those who doubted. You set me free, thus fulfilling the commitments others made, but failed to keep. I come to swear to you by the Covenant and promises of all the prophets and messengers of God, that I will never do anything to betray your trust. I will never break my word. I will never forget your kindness and I promise never to return to Algeria…"

The president politely acknowledged the document, considering it unimportant, and then proceeded to personally conduct the tour of the palace and its grounds. At the stables, Abd el-Kader admired a beautiful white horse of Arab stock. "It is yours. I hope it will make you forget that you have not ridden for along time. Try him out and ride him in the review that will be held in your honor at Versailles."

November third was the finale of the emir's conquest of Paris. Not only had he taken Paris with his charm, even the army saluted him. Abd el-Kader was brought from his hotel to the Versailles rail station in an opulent salon car accompanied by War Minister Saint-Arnaud, Daumas, Magnan and a handful of other generals. Six regiments from the cream of the army he had tormented for fifteen years were going to pay their respects to a worthy adversary. Trumpets sounded, swords flashed, flags dipped that afternoon on the Sartory Plain as the emir, mounted on his new Arab charger, flanked by Daumas and Magnan, observed thousands of brightly colored cuirassiers, lancers, carabiners, troops of the line and artillery units parade and maneuver for hours. That evening, War Minister Saint-Arnaud hosted a dinner in the emir's honor for eighty guests in the palace of Versailles.

For two weeks Abd el-Kader paid homage to France and official France paid homage to him in a mutual love fest that was summed up by *The Times* of London. "Abd el-Kader is the lion of the day…He is equally at ease in a church, at the opera, receiving visitors or being received, dropping his eyes respectfully when confronted with the admiring gaze of beautiful ladies or lighting up with a fire that is not yet dead within him at the neigh of a charger…"

Since October 16, Lalla Zohra hadn't needed her cane. Back at Amboise, Abd el-Kader found her waiting for him by the door of his room. Bellemare remembered the scene. "He ran toward his mother, embraced her warmly, then threw himself at her feet and smothered them with kisses. Zohra lifted him up and begged him to give her a full account of his visit. He made her sit down while he stood and told her of the receptions he had attended and the things he had seen."

For the first time in years, Lalla Zohra shed tears of joy.

CHAPTER TWENTY-ONE

The Emir's Letter

BEFORE HE LEFT FRANCE, Abd el-Kader showered with letters of gratitude all those who had done him a good turn, however small. Two humble women won a particularly warm spot in the emir's heart and in the hearts of all his entourage.

Natalie and Saint-Maurice (Catholic nuns sometimes take the names of male saints) of the Dominican Sisters of Charity of Tours had been assigned to look after the women and children at the chateau, thanks to Bishop Dupuch. Their piety and wholehearted care for their charges created a bond that extended to all the Arabs. Abd el-Kader spoke for his community in an extravagant letter of appreciation to Sister Natalie, who had virtually lived among the Arabs at Amboise: "… A lady of deep piety, a shining mirror of goodness made from the purest mother of pearl, a marabout known for her noble feelings, this is our gracious, always patient and obliging Natalie. In her, we have seen only a deep attachment to her religion, a perfect intelligence, sense of discretion and breeding…"

The emir's sentiments were echoed in confessions of mutual admiration by the sisters: "Allowing for certain exceptions of a theological nature, there is no Christian virtue that Abd el-Kader does not practice to the highest degree," Sister Natalie wrote in an internal communication to her order. She even wrote that she would have been happy to have devoted the rest of her life serving the emir and his followers.

Above all, Abd el-Kader was in the thrall of Louis-Napoleon. The prince-president's generosity of spirit had, indeed, "conquered" him. He petitioned the mayor of Amboise to allow his Arabs to vote in the upcoming plebiscite that would confirm popular approval of Napoleon's military coup of the previous year. Abd el-Kader offered the thought that they had earned a kind of French citizenship, a "right of soil." The children they had given birth to in France, and the time spent were evidence enough.

In a gesture of goodwill to his liberator, on November 21, 1852, fourteen male votes were cast for Louis-Napoleon's imperial renewal in an urn specially provided for the Arabs of Amboise. President Louis

Napoleon would soon become Emperor Napoleon III. By a curious convergence of the stars, on that same date twenty years earlier, Abd el-Kader had been elected Commander of the Faithful on the Plain of Ghriss.

Abd el-Kader was still Commander of the Faithful on December 21, 1852, as he set sail from Marseille for Turkey. To be sure, his official smala had shriveled to a remnant of family members and followers. Yet, its ranks had become more "catholic," enlarged after his five years of stoic endurance not by adoring Muslims, but by admiring Frenchmen and women. His politess, generosity of spirit, broad-ranging intellect and sincerity in his devotions to the Almighty had seduced all but the most hard-core Arab-haters. Monarchists and republicans, believers and non-believers, the rich and the poor, nobles and commoners counted among his champions: Bishop Dupuch, the Duc d'Aumale, Madame de l'Aire, the wife of Major Boissonnet… Baron James Rothschild who had solicited the emir's autograph at the Gare de Lyon railroad station en route to his final departure from Marseille, the private Escoffier who had asked to have the honor of guarding Abd el-Kader in Pau, General Daumas whom the emir called "the key to all murky situations and a slave to his promises…Ferdinand de Lesseps who had visited him in Pau and would later seek the emir's moral support for the Suez Canal…Emile Ollivier, past republican prefect and future prime minister of Emperor Napoleon III.

The *Labrador*, a private steamer that had belonged to the deceased Marquis de Saint Simon was put at the emir's disposal to take him to Istanbul, accompanied by the devoted Boissonnet and his wife, who had insisted on helping him with the transfer of his family. From there, he would be taken to his new home in Bursa with an ample annual living allowance of 100,000 francs* (the French consul in Turkey received a salary of 5000 fr). The sum was deemed by the emperor as appropri-

---

* This allowance or "pension" was calculated as an annuity when General Randon was war minister under Louis Napoleon. It represented the compensation value over time of his vaste family domains that were expropriated by the French. The annuity was paid by the government to his heirs up until 1954. The amounts paid over time speak millions of the goodwill the emir had earned in France.

ate for a man of Abd el-Kader's stature and having such a large family. Between Louis-Napoleon and Abd el-Kader, a genuine mutual admiration developed. Yet, why Louis-Napoleon's generosity, even affection toward the emir? He was obviously not alone in his admiration. Perhaps he saw in the emir virtues for which he had a nostalgic attachment. Here was a man of a bygone era, chivalrous and generous, stoic in suffering, loyal to his benefactors, honorable toward his enemies, uncorrupted by commercialism and greed, yet also devoted to progress and improving the human condition, while never forgetting his debt to the Almighty. In his mixture of Realpolitik and romanticism, Louis-Napoleon may also have believed a grateful emir could still be useful to France and his pursuit of glory.

But to pursue glory abroad, have prosperity at home and make improvements for the working classes, Louis-Napoleon, now Emperor Napoleon III, had no sure compass to navigate the treacherous crosscurrents of a society deeply divided, wrestling with the new forces of industrialization and demands from the masses for more inclusive government. His dream of restoring France to its position of former greatness converged with a recognition, as he wrote in one of his prison tracts, "that the rule of the classes is over, you can only govern with the masses." This led him into a series of foreign-policy disasters, for he believed that the newly articulate masses thrived on national glory.

There was only one compass for the emir: Islam. Not a narrow sectarian Islam, but an Islam writ large, the Islam of nature and of every living thing that submits to Divine Law. The emir's Islam trusted in a God that is "greater." Greater, that is, than whatever puny man or any of his religions, including Islam, can begin to imagine. "Each person worships and knows Him in certain ways and is ignorant of Him in others." In other words, we are all wrong. Squaring the Oneness of God with the diversity of the ways His creatures worshipped Him was Abd el-Kader's great preoccupation. One of his visitors in Paris had given him a reason to expand on his ideas that had already been incubating in Amboise.

❧

The president of the Asian Society of Paris, Monsieur Reinard, had qualified as one of the few among the many seekers who had the privilege of meeting Abd el-Kader in Paris. On behalf of this international society of scholars and afficionados of the East, he asked the emir if he would write an autobiography. Three years later, he offered up something unexpected — a window to his soul.

It took the form of a philosophy lesson about man's uniqueness among God's creatures. In the Western literature it has become known as *A Letter to the French,* though in reality its audience was universal, as indicated by the original, cumbersome Arabic title: *Brief Notes for Those with Understanding in Order to Draw Attention to Essential Questions.*

He begins modestly, sensing his limited credibility in the eyes of a French public predisposed to look down on Arabs. "First, realize that it is necessary for an intelligent person to reflect on the words that are spoken, not the person who says them. If the words are true, he will accept them whether he who says them is a known truth teller or a liar. One can extract gold from a lump of dirt. Medication from the venom of a snake...For an intelligent person, wisdom is like a lost sheep which is sought, and can be found anywhere and in any individual."

As to man's uniqueness, he proposed in Platonic fashion that the "perfection" of anything in nature is realized when that thing — animal, plant or mineral — fully expresses its particular distinguishing quality. A horse shares with a donkey the ability to carry heavy loads, but its true essence lies as a creature of grace and speed. A horse is truly a horse only when it gallops at full tilt.

And wherein does the emir believe lies man's distinguishing quality among God's creation? Not in the need for food and the ability to reproduce, which he shares with plants. Nor in his mobility or possession of five senses, which he shares with animals. Only his love of knowledge and the pursuit of truth make man distinctively different from the rest of creation. Whereas animals are prisoners of their senses, man's uniqueness and nobility come from a capacity to grasp a reality beyond the senses — to reach truths of mathematics, geometry, philosophy and the moral truths. The natural respect that even "the stupidest among the Turks or the crudest of the Arabs give to their savants and sheikhs," the emir notes tartly, is further proof that "the search for knowledge is man's distinction."

Abd el-Kader's ultimate reference book is nature. And since nature is God's handiwork, it is self-evident that in nature, properly observed, lies much wisdom. Knowledge, like nature, is also hierarchical.

In the first rank is basic knowledge. This category includes knowledge for agriculture, construction, weaving and politics. Food, shelter and clothing are essential for human physical survival, but the practice of politics in the Greek sense — the art of living together — is equally vital. Man is a social animal. People need to cooperate to survive. Harmonious community life assures adequate resources, mutual aid and collective effort. He compares these needs to the roles played by the human heart, brain and liver.

In second position is toolmaking knowledge, such as carding, loom making and metal working — arts needed to support the primary activities. These correspond to organs such as the stomach, arteries and veins, lungs that serve the brain, the heart and the liver. And finally, there is knowledge of the finishing arts — grinding, bread making or wool cleaning. Such knowledge corresponds to the teeth, eyelids and fingernails of the human body. Of the three categories of knowledge, the noblest activities are the basic ones. On their backs, society is built. And the greatest of these activities is politics.

That Abd el-Kader uses human body parts to illustrate a hierarchy of knowledge needed to make life agreeable is not surprising. For him, society is a living organism knit together by structured relationships. If those relationships are good, the parts work together in harmony. If the relationships are bad, the parts war with each other, or stop functioning. Updating the emir's metaphor, perhaps politics is the hormonal system that regulates and balances relationships according to life's circumstances.

Politics, however, requires a "higher degree of perfection than all other forms of knowledge." Why? Because it affects the way people live together. Political life should be governed not by the distortions of ambition and love of power, but by generosity and care — the hormones that build unity and closeness. In Abd el-Kader's view, there is no knowledge more important than that needed for understanding the elements of collective life and guiding human behavior in a just and righteous way.

Yet, politics itself is of two kinds: the politics of the throne, and the politics of religious scholars, or ulema. The former has power over the external aspects of people's lives — taxes, military service, employment — but not over their inner life. The religious scholars have the ability to influence men's interior lives, but they should refrain from the direct exercise of power, which can only corrupt. They do, however, have a duty to speak truth to power and to expose injustice.

The expert, whatever his métier, influences the spirit of the person seeking his knowledge, according to the kind of knowledge being taught — the purpose it serves and the rigor of its arguments. Comparing mathematics to astronomy Abd el-Kader elevates mathematics, as he considers the methods of mathematics more rigorous. Comparing medicine with mathematics, he judges medicine the higher form of knowledge because the purpose of medicine is to save lives, even if its methods are less rigorous. Mathematics is a superior form of knowledge by the force of its reasoning, but Abd el-Kader gives greater importance to goals than to methods. Comparing medical knowledge with religious knowledge, he holds religious knowledge superior. Medical knowledge can achieve, at best, only temporary salvation of the body, while divine knowledge offers salvation for eternity.

So let us now pause for a moment. Here Abd el-Kader's reasoning joins that of other believers, but excludes the nonbelieving, materialistic modern man. The force of his argument assumes what modernists deny: a creator, revelation, an immortal soul and a Judgment Day. The believers among the children of Abraham differ on details of the story, but they accept the premise: our short sojourn on earth is but a preparation for an eternal one.

The only permanent, enduring reality is God. The One. The Universal Soul. The source from which all things flow, and to which they return. God's presence is in all his creation, just as a writer's presence is in his writing, a chef's in his cooking, a parent's presence in its child. Abd el-Kader recognizes that such knowledge is not shared by all believers; in fact, by very a few. Why?

Because we are all spiritually sick, to a greater or lesser degree. Knowledge is effect, not cause. Its cause is *aql*. Man's desire for knowledge proceeds from *aql*, just as light comes from the sun. What is this thing, *aql*, the French translate as ésprit? Whereas English distinguishes between mind and spirit, the French ésprit combines "spirit," as in "Holy Spirit" or "team spirit", and "mind," which includes intelligence, reason and discernment.

The richness of the human spirit varies, the emir reminds us, just as the availability of water in the earth. Water readily gushes forth in some places; in most, it must be dug for, and in others it is nonexistent. Like finding water, most of us have to dig to find our source within. Alas, some of us are dry holes. All men have the ability to acquire a certain degree of knowledge, but that "certain degree" depends on their inner, spiritual reservoir, which is a seedlike potential.

Aql is important for moral reasons. It is one of the four virtues needed for achieving that distinctively human potential — moral improvement. *Aql* makes possible "distinguishing truth from error, promotes memory, good judgment, energy and a discerning eye in situations requiring finesse." But moral perfection demands three other qualities: courage, self-control and just behavior.

Just, or equitable behavior, is free from the emotions of anger, greed, envy and impatience. Courage, in the emir's lexicon, is that quality of the spirit that either directs or restrains anger in order to do what is right — that is, moral courage. Courage carries with it companion qualities of generosity, endurance, firmness, compassion and the spirit of sacrifice. The fourth virtue needed for moral progress is self-control, a requirement to hold in check unruly passions that lead us astray. Which brings us back to justice, that essential glue for social harmony that requires self-control and courage. "Whoever possesses these four mothers of moral virtue deserves to be either a king, or an advisor to kings and men. Those who do not, yet call themselves servants of God, should be banished." Wisdom and virtue are inseparable.

It should be obvious to any healthy spirit, Abd el-Kader tells us, that the *aql* wasn't given to man simply to gather rain water — which is to say, simply the fruits of practical knowledge. Mundane knowledge is constantly changing, or disappearing, as new knowledge is acquired. "Without question, the most worthy knowledge of all is of God the Highest and of the wisdom that is transparent in His creation."

Man gains this higher knowledge not through his senses, but through his spirit. The senses are stimulated only by what is presented to them. They are not "fecund." They lead to believing that the earth is flat. "Without the spirit," Abd el-Kader writes, "the senses can't evaluate the future, assess risk and benefit, draw conclusions that lead to new knowledge or perceive final ends." That is why spirit, or *aql*, is the noblest of man's faculties. It is the part that can see what is invisible to the eye. It is the part that belongs to God.

❦

Abd el-Kader left France deeply impressed by its "spirit of practical application." Nonetheless, he believed the French savants fell short in the "spirit of speculation," which, alone, permits attaining knowledge of God and the wisdom that lies within His creation. No doubt the emir's opinion — not wholly accurate (Pasteur was devout Catholic) — was influenced by the absence in France of a Muslim's reflexive recognition of the Creator's role in one's accomplishments. To not openly acknowledge God is to be ungrateful, like not thanking someone for a gift. To not acknowledge God is to cut oneself off from Divine Wisdom.

And wherein does that wisdom lie? In nature itself, to be sure, but in Divine Law, as transmitted across the ages by His prophets. The Torah, the Psalms, the Gospels and the Koran are all repositories of this prophetic knowledge. Only through a deep understanding of these revelations can men approach moral perfection and become truly healthy spirits. Like Rabbi Hillel,* Abd el-Kader tells us to go forth and study the Word with an open heart. But this knowledge cannot be obtained by the human spirit alone.

The knowledge of Divine Law possessed by the prophets can be acquired only through faith in their teachings, and by obeying them. Thus, obedience is the guardian of all the virtues.

When the body is sick, we turn to doctors and their specialized knowledge. A person with an aching finger might apply an ointment directly on the finger until a doctor, someone with higher knowledge, points out that the ointment should go on the opposite shoulder. The patient might consider this nonsense at first. When the doctor explains the way nerves are distributed in the body, the intelligent patient accepts the doctor's recommendation. He obeys.

The prophets also possess a deeper knowledge, though of a different kind. From Adam to Mohammed, these doctors of the spirit have a special gift that goes beyond mere intelligence and allows them to be vessels of Divine Wisdom. Call it a third eye. With it, they can perceive

---

* Hillel is thought by some to have been a teacher of Jesus. When asked by a pagan to explain Judaism, Hillel replied: "That which is harmful to you, don't do to others. The rest is detail. Go forth and study."

differently and see further. Like the gift of poetry, or music, it is not possessed by most people. The prophets are all equal in their capacity to mediate God's wisdom. Each has a portion of the Divine Wisdom to transmit. Intellectual knowledge is food, but knowledge of Divine Law is the cure for sick spirits. Most people are satisfied with the food, unaware that they are even sick. The cures are found through following God's ordinances.

Some Divine Laws may be difficult to understand, like a doctor's recommendation to put ointment on the shoulder opposite from the painful finger. This merely reflects the weakness of the spirit. A healthy spirit can grasp the reasons when they are explained. Abd el-Kader illustrates using the case of gold and silver.

The Koran prohibits hording gold and silver without giving a portion to the poor. A sensible and just person might object. "I worked hard for my gold and I will do with it what I want. Why should I give some to the poor? I made this money myself."

These seemingly reasonable objections ignore a higher wisdom, says the emir. Gold and silver have no use in themselves. They don't protect a person against the cold, they can't be eaten. These metals were created by God to serve as a universal medium of exchange so people can easily acquire things that are useful without the cumbersome need to barter. Their purpose in life is to circulate from hand to hand. To hoard gold without giving a portion to the poor is unjust. "God didn't create man to live naked and in poverty," the indignant emir exclaims. It is the duty of the rich to help the poor. Those who ignore this rule will be punished, if not in this world, then in the next.

Worse than hoarding is conspicuous consumption, which occurs when gold and silver are used frivolously for plates and cups. Such a misuse of God's creation is like "employing a judge to work as a butcher." To disrespect the distinctive quality of a thing or a person, is to degrade it, to render it "imperfect." Platonically speaking, tableware has only one purpose — to contain food and drink. For this, many other less noble materials, such as clay or bronze, are available.

Lending gold for a price is an offense, as well. It transforms a friendly act — helping someone in need — into a form of subjugation. Abd el-Kader ends his discourse on gold and silver by reminding his reader that generosity and mutual aid are the bonds that hold a society together. At the core of all religions are rules of behavior that promote neighborliness and friendship. True understanding of Divine Law leads to that conclusion.

Nor is there any contradiction between knowledge of Divine Law, as revealed by the prophets, and intellectual knowledge acquired by man. "The prophets," the emir writes, "were not sent to debate with philosophers or argue with scientists over whether the earth is a sphere or made up four of elements." Science, however, should never be used to contradict the oneness of God. "Those who say such and such scientific knowledge contradicts religion or that religion is against such and such knowledge sin against religion." Above all, the prophets remind us to be thankful and to glorify God as Creator of the universe.

❧

Nor do the prophets contradict each other — not, at least, in the fundamentals. They all have a common message: glorify God and show compassion for all his creatures. The laws preached by all the prophets concern respect for the soul, the mind, for property and for the rights of inheritance. Their differences concern the different ways for preserving these laws.

Abd el-Kader understood Divine Revelation as multilayered truth, deposited over time, like geological strata. "The laws dictated by the prophets vary according to the considerations which inspired them at the time. The interests and needs of men change over the ages, and all judgments are just only in terms of the circumstances of the people at the time they are promulgated. Religious law can change for the same reason a doctor may change his prescriptions." Anyway, Abd el-Kader reminds his readers, God can do whatever God wants. He can establish or eliminate a law without justification. His wisdom alone determines the duration of the law and the time of its abrogation.

"The Jews objected to Jesus for annulling their laws, but the teachings of Jesus say nothing about the legal code. He offered instead parables and exhortations. *I come not to change the law, but to fulfill it.* The response of the Christ to the Jews is the same as that of the Muslims to the Christians. The Prophet Mohammed said, in effect, 'I have not come to annul the Gospels or the Law of Moses, but to make them more perfect. The Mosaic Law concerns the external behavior of men generally. The Gospels speak to the hearts of individuals.'

"The wisdom of Moses is based on action, and is concerned with obligations and proscriptions," the emir recapitulates. "The wisdom of the Messiah is concerned with the spirit, inviting renunciation in order to attain higher truths. The wisdom of Mohammed unites both. The prophets only differ in the details of certain rules." Reasoning like the good polygamist he was, Abd el-Kader proposes that "they are like men who have a common father, but each has a different mother."

எ

An arrow in the sky, one among many. So the emir modestly described the manuscript he sent to the president of the Asiatic Society. It landed well. On July 9, 1855, France's main daily newspaper, *Le Moniteur Universel*, published a summary of the emir's essay. It made a strong enough impression on the intellectuals of Paris that one of them, Gustave Dugat, an Arabist of distinction, thought this "arrow in the sky" deserved a full exposition.

Three years later, Dugat explained why in his 1858 introduction to his translation of the full text *(Le Livre d'Abd el-Kader)* published by the Academy of Sciences. Contemporary "Arab philosophy" was little known in France. The work of Abd el-Kader bore clear traces of Greek thought and showed "the marks of a superior mind that knows how to think." Even if the author's ideas were sometimes deficient in details, Dugat praised the emir's points of view as "always elevated and often original."

On the emir's treatment of faith and reason, Dugat was astonished. "He speaks like a theologian at the Sorbonne and is in perfect communion with the Pope, when he says,

'Faith is above reason; but, as they both come from God, there can be no conflict between them, only mutual support.'

"The emir reasons like us regarding revealed religion," Dugat affirmed, "prophecy is above reason, which by itself cannot comprehend the wisdom of the prophets."

Gustave Dugat's effort to rescue from oblivion the moral philosophy of a man who had conquered the Parisian elite six years earlier would have touched the emir's friend, Bishop Antoine-Adolphe Dupuch, if only he had been alive. In 1856, the debt-ridden Dupuch had died a pauper, a victim of man's golden rule. His creditors virtually hounded him to death, while his friends kept him one step away from prison. Yet poverty, his friends said, did not bother Dupuch in the end. Like Abd el-Kader, he had detached himself from the things of this world.

And like the emir, whose greatest difficulties in his struggle against French occupiers were with his own kind, so too Dupuch. Those who opposed most strenuously his calling in Algeria were not Arabs, but anticlerical Frenchmen who, illwilled, or wellmeaning but ignorant, feared that Jesus-loving ministers of God with their crucifixes and statues of the Virgin would offend Muslims. Prisoners of their own anticlerical prejudices, they did not know what the Duke of Rovigo (Commander of the Army of Africa in 1831–32,) had learned when he asked the mufti of Algiers if he could convert one of their mosques into a church. Rather than be insulted, the mufti acted elated: "May God be blessed, may Africa rejoice! The French can no longer be accused of not believing in God. Take whichever mosque suits you the best. The form of worship may change but not the Master, for the God of the Christians is also ours. We are only different in the way we address ourselves to Him."

In exile, the emir echoed the mufti's thoughts differently. "Our God and the God of all the communities different from ours are in reality all one God...He reveals himself to Muslims as beyond all form, to Christians in the person of Jesus Christ and monks...he reveals himself even to pagans who worship objects. For no worshipper of something finite worships the thing for itself. What he worships through this object is the Epiphany of God." At age forty-four, Abd el-Kader's new life in exile seemed set on a course of study, teaching and pious meditation that would lead to a peaceful end in the Almighty's embrace.

Higher Wisdom had a different plan, however. Nature and great power politics were its instruments.

CHAPTER TWENTY-TWO

The Road to Damascus

TURKISH EXILE HAD BEEN a sweet-and-sour experience for the emir. Bursa's population, like its blue and yellow wooden houses, was a colorful mix of Turks, Jews, Armenians and Greeks nestled at the base of the snowcapped mountain the Turks called Uludag — meaning "exhalted," "mighty" and "sublime." The white minarets that lanced the air, the lush gardens, hot springs, plentiful streams and hills covered with vineyards and fruit trees reminded the emir of Tlemcen. Bursa was famous internationally for its textiles, but no less famous locally were its melons, strawberries, raisins, and above all, its peaches. To taste a large, succulent Bursa peach, they said, was to taste the divine.

Living again in a Muslim culture was a tonic for Abd el-Kader. On Fridays, he spent long hours in the red marble baths of Eskikaplica and Yenikaplica, cleaning five years of prison life from his system. He couldn't deny the grandeur of the Ottoman Empire that once was, yet neither could he forgive the Porte for abandoning him in his struggle against France. His hostility toward the Turk was never overt — he was too polite for that, but their apostasy gnawed at him to the end of his days.

Money and lodgings for his Algerians were Abd el-Kader's main preoccupations at first. A huge, dilapidated, two-story caravanserai with courtyards, gardens and baths had been put at the emir's disposal by the sultan, but it required repairs and furniture, which the French government ultimately provided, as well as ten horses that the French had included in his generous exile package. There were more than 100 people following in the emir's wake. In addition to his mother, children, three wives, a dozen nannies and domestic servants, were fourteen other relatives and loyalists and their servants.

Encouraged by Paris to help with the costs of supporting the emir, the Turkish government gave Abd el-Kader 133,000 francs to buy a farm near Bursa, where he exercised his horses and planted barley and fruit trees to provide work for his companions in arms and for other Algerians who might want to join him. His former caliph, Ben Salem, who had surrendered to Bugeaud in 1847 and his former secretary Haj al-Kharroubi, who had been captured during the raid on the emir's smala, followed him to Bursa with their own family retinues. Eventually hundreds, then thousands of Algerians from around the Mediterranean flocked to their emir. Just as Abd el-Kader was considered by the Turks a protégé of the French emperor, so the Algerians became his protégés, forming a quasi-French subcolony within the Ottoman Empire.

In fact, the emir was constantly pressing the Turks or the French for money. Not for himself, but for others. He used no more than half of the allotted 100,000-franc annuity for his own family's needs and distributed the rest to his followers. When the emir learned that hard times had forced the two daughters of the aging Dey Hussein of Algiers to take up a woman's oldest trade, he insisted on taking them under his wing. Abd el-Kader was regularly pleading with French diplomats in Istanbul and in Bursa to arrange free transportation for Algerians stranded in Beirut, Cairo, France or somewhere else around the Mediterranean, who wanted to rejoin their families or to live with him in exile. Women, it seems, were the only exception to Abd el-Kader's life of austere self-denial whose growing harem caused grumbling, and not a little envy, among the diplomats.

If not helping him to resolve various problems affecting his own family or followers, the harried consular staff might have been scurrying around trying to figure out how to pay for this or that request, such as shipping three pureblood Arabians back to Paris for the emperor. In 1853, Louis-Napoleon fulfilled a promise he had made when the emir travelled to Paris to congratulate him for his plebiscite victory. The emperor had delivered to Abd el-Kader a magnificent Damascene sword whose hilt and scabbard was inlaid with arabesque tendrils of lapis lazuli and dotted with emeralds, pearls and rubies. In the Arab world no gift can go unanswered.

A brown bay, a light bay and a chestnut had been carefully selected by Ben Salem after months of searching as far afield as Syria for appropriate specimens. Embroidered in gold thread on the headpiece of their bridles, were a few lines composed by the emir, according to the markings of each horse. "Honor and accept me, for I am a horse of distinction; the whiteness of my feet and face reflect the purity of the heart of him who sent me," waxed the eloquent bay.

Abd el-Kader found the French diplomats in Turkey cool and suspicious compared with the attention and celebrity status he had experienced in Paris under the emperor's patronage. To be sure, he had been treated with appropriate dignity upon his arrival: a twenty-one gun salute as the *Labrador* rounded The Golden Horn, a formal reception by the French ambassador, an audience with the sultan.

The consulate in Bursa was to be "at his service." In reality, this meant that it was to keep an eye on him — Abd el-Kader was not allowed to travel outside the region without the consulate's approval. Some in the Ministry of War still considered him an enemy of France who was quite capable of breaking his word and making trouble. The restriction was an insulting aggravation, for he had imagined that by then he would have been trusted. After all, he was the emperor's friend.

And there was the problem of communication with the local people. The emir spoke no Turkish and the Turks spoke little Arabic, on top of which, he detected an air of indifference on the part of the religious scholars. Or was it jealousy or fear of his influence? After all, the emir was not only a scholar of the law, he had actually wielded a sword in defense of the faith. He was thought to have Arab nationalist leanings and to not much like the Turks.

The emir was pleased, however, that his new interpreter and handler in Turkey was a familiar and welcome face. The twenty-five-year-old George Bullad had been an auxiliary translator for Daumas and Boissonnet during Abd el-Kader's years of imprisonment, and earlier, had been a translator on the Duke of Aumale's staff in 1847 when the emir laid down his arms. The young Bullad came from a branch of a Syrian Christian family of silk merchants who had migrated from Damascus to Cairo in the eighteenth century. The Bullads had offered their services to Bonaparte when he arrived in Egypt with his army and legion of scholars, but lacking in competent translators. When Bonaparte returned precipitously to France, his Syrian translators followed him, knowing they would be considered traitors by the local Arabs. Bullad was born in Marseille in 1827, but his father insisted that he learn Arabic.

Bullad sent daily reports to the war ministry detailing the emir's comings and goings. His mail was read, as well. To Abd el-Kader's great annoyance, his request to make a pilgrimage to Mecca with his mother was refused. Nevertheless, his relationship with George Bullad remained good, even though the emir was chafing under his prisoner-like status. Bullad, like Daumas and Boissonnet before him, was an admirer of the emir and trusted his loyalty to Napoleon. He had been an alternate translator in Toulon and Amboise. Short, a prim, black-goateed bachelor at the beginning of a promising career, Bullad wanted to be Abd el-Kader's confident, which would also help him serve better his government. He began telling the emir about his numerous cousins and the cosmopolitan, intellectually sophisticated atmosphere that the emir would find in Arab-speaking Damascus. The Bullads were also a leading family that had once been masters of the art of making Damascene steel swords, and later, important silk producers. Bullad assured the emir his family was well positioned to introduce him to all the notables of the city.

In the summer of 1855, a massive earthquake struck Bursa, destroying much of the city, though not his own residence. The emir was not one to complain about his lot, but when nature lent a helping hand, he jumped on the opportunity to return to France. His excuse was the World Exhibition in Paris, but his real purpose was to seek permission from the emperor to move to Damascus.

૬૭

France was in a state of frenzied celebration when Abd el-Kader arrived in Marseille on September 8, 1855. The Crimean War had taken a decisive turn. Sebastopol had fallen, thanks to a successful French assault on the Malakov Bastion that ended a year-long siege. France and Britain had played leading roles in a European coalition formed to prevent the Russian bear from taking more bites from the decaying body of the Ottoman Empire.

An emissary of Napoleon was among the first to seek out the emir after his arrival. Did Abd el-Kader wish to attend a victory Mass in Paris? Yes, if it would please the emperor for him to be present, not explaining that he was suffering from cholera — Marseille's pestilential gift to the returning emir. Five days later, a pale and weakened emir moved slowly down the great nave of Notre-Dame Cathedral as heads turned to watch him leaning on the arm of a military officer accompanying him to the front row with the emperor. He stood when the *Te*

Deum was chanted, and afterwards, he was enthusiastically applauded outside the cathedral as his calèche drove him away.

Accompanied by his old friend Boissonet, now a commander, and his brother-in-law, Abd el-Kader went twice to the freshly cleared Champs-Elysees to see the world's newest technical marvels, where they were personally escorted by the exposition's general manager, Monsieur Le Play. The new uses of steam power impressed him, as did the latest sewing and textile machines that did in minutes what had taken him hours and days to do as a young boy who had to make his own clothes. The scholar and book collector in the emir was captivated by the machines at the Imperial Printing House that could spit out texts in different languages. Always the connoisseur of horseflesh, the exhibit on equine anatomy was a favorite, where he engaged in a spirited discussion with the presiding veterinarian. On September 27, Abd el-Kader thanked the general manager for the last time. "This exhibition is a temple of reason and intelligence, animated by the breath of God. Only the Creation itself is superior to your works."

Later, at a reception in the glittering Tuileries Palace across from the Louvre, a well-briefed Napoleon helped the emir when they met.

"Bursa must not be a very agreeable place now. Where would you like to live?"

"That is for you to decide."

"Would Damascus please you?"

"Yes."

"I will arrange for you to go to Damascus and have my frigate, *Tage*, take you from Turkey to Lebanon."

Before leaving Paris, Abd el-Kader wrote to Comte Waleski, minister of foreign affairs, to request that Bullad be assigned as his interpreter in Damascus, calling him a man "wise and intelligent, who speaks and translates Arabic in a very satisfactory way, while being a loyal and zealous servant to his government." The emir knew that interpreters played a double role as ministry informants, yet if they were tactful and intelligent, this didn't prevent him from liking them and forming genuine friendships that could help him in the behind-the-scenes debates over his future as a dependent of France. Bullad had agreed to also act as the emir's personal secretary in Damascus, where he would not only translate for him in his official dealings with the French diplomats, but also translate his extensive personal correspondence with the likes of Eugene Daumas, Leon Roches, Ferdinand de Lesseps and dozens of others whom Abd el-Kader befriended in France or Algeria.

e/ɔ

Negotiations began with the French ambassador as soon as the emir arrived back in Istanbul. Armed with the emperor's offer to transport him to Beirut at the state's expense, Abd el-Kader wanted to get as many of his people as possible onto the boat. Who were his people? It was the same question he had argued with Daumas when his entourage was transferred from Fort Lamalgue in Toulon to Pau. He could make no distinction between family and nonfamily. They were all his.

In the end, his extended family of 111 persons were allowed passage, of which twenty-seven were his immediate blood family. There was the touchy question of the women. They had to occupy quarters inside the ship so they would not be exposed to prying eyes. The men would sleep on the deck. On November 24, the emperor's steamship disgorged Abd el-Kader's retinue in Beirut. Scarcely off the boat and happy to breathe again the air of an Arab land, the emir received an invitation.

The English army officer who had visited him in Bursa two years earlier discovered that they had much in common. Colonel Charles Henry Churchill now wanted him to visit his own Howara estate in Mount Lebanon, as Syria's coastal mountain range was known.

"The approach to Syria from the sea is most striking. The magnificent range of The Lebanon (White Mountain) which salutes the eye, inspires the spectator with astonishment and awe," wrote the emir's future biographer of the mountains that stretched a hundred miles between Sidon and Tripoli. "The lofty chain, rising to an elevation of upwards sixteen hundred fathoms, whether robed in snow or capped with clouds or mingling its clear, cold granite coloring with the deep azure of a summer sky, excites feelings of wonder and admiration. From its cedars, Solomon built his temple, and from its quarries was built the harem of Mecca. Christians glory in it as the land of prophets and saints...By degrees, the villages of the Maronites recede in successive gradations from the sea coast to the topmost acclivities over a range thirty miles wide, while the highest peaks are crowned with white and glittering convents." The impression made on Churchill was of a "vast suburban city."

But why were people living on the edges of rocky precipices struggling to hue out a living in calcareous rock when they had the rich Bekaa Valley to cultivate? The feudal lords who had ruled profitably in the valleys had fled to the mountains, Churchill tells us, because of the terrible Turk and other oppressors.

Churchill didn't shy from casting stones. Biblically literate, and an ardent proponent of Christian civilization, he nevertheless wrote with the air of a skeptic with a keen eye for hogwash, masquerading as religion. "Though all traces of apostolic simplicity and evangelical truth have long been lost among the Christians who now possess it, The Lebanon was ever a resort to fugitives of that denomination that fled from the great Mohammedan invasion; and later for those sectarians exposed to the fury and persecution of the dominant faith and doctrine of Constantinople."*

As for the Maronites, in their eyes "every authority, civil or otherwise, is merged and absorbed in the authority of the priests, and with lynx-eyed vigilance do their priests and bishops in the present day, as indeed of yore, watch every movement, every tendency which may menace their long established dominion." For Turkish rule, Churchill had only naked contempt. "They returned (following an intermezzo of ten years, of which more later) like screeching vultures to their baffled prey. Every kind of appointment was up for auction. Places of trust were filled with men notorious for their cupidity and fanaticism. Justice, which had been purified of her defilements under Egyptian rule, was again contaminated with the offal of corruption."

The corruption that had seeped into the pores of daily life in Lebanon could easily have been forgotten by anyone winding through the painstakingly terraced mountains that led stepwise up to Churchill's domain. In the spring, tulips, lupins, sweet peas, anemones and hyacinth "filled the air with their fragrant exhalations." Mulberry trees and vineyards, fig and olive orchards competed with wild oak and fir for their share of the meager soil that covered sharp, limestone rocks that formed The Lebanon.

---

* The Eastern Orthodox Church was generally more tolerant than the Latin one in the West, yet also known to have had fits of persecution toward nonOrthodox sects, such as Nestorians and Armenians.

When his string of mules, camels and horses approached the vicinity of Howara, the emir broke away with a few companions and a guide to catch up with his cavalcade later as it descended toward the Litani River. The effect of the visit on Abd el-Kader is not known directly, but the outcome was what Churchill wanted. The emir agreed in principle to cooperate with Churchill who wanted to prevent the emir's life from becoming "alms for oblivion." The two men became friends, and four years later, Churchill began his daily, hour-long interviews with the emir that lasted for six months.

They were like celestial twins. They shared the same passions: for horses, love of the hunt, contempt of danger, appreciation for the opposite sex, love of learning and noblesse oblige towards the less fortunate. Like, Abd el-Kader, Churchill was conscious of his genealogy. He was descended from the dukes of Marlborough, one of the most distinguished tribes among England's own Nobility of the Sword. His grandfather, General Henry Churchill, was the nephew of John, the first Duke of Marlborough. His father made his military career in India, married well and left Charles Henry a comfortable fortune.

At nineteen, Churchill entered the 60th Rifle Regiment. No ordinary regiment, the 60th Rifles had its origins in the French and Indian Wars and was later used to fight the colonial militias of their day, skilled at shooting brightly colored "Lobsterbacks" from behind rocks and trees. This ungentlemanly American way of fighting produced a British regiment of "special forces" whose uniforms were dull green. They were lightly equipped, fast-moving sharpshooters who operated semi-independently from mainline units. Not surprisingly, the 60th attracted the unorthodox and the independent-minded. And so it seems was Charles Henry Churchill. Coincidently, both men were born in 1808.

When the thirty-two-year-old Commander of the Faithful was raising the banner of jihad against France in 1840, Churchill was disembarking in Lebanon as a staff officer to General Charles Napier. Napier was commanding a European expeditionary force that had been organized to protect the Ottoman Empire following a crushing Turkish defeat the previous year by Egyptian troops — a defeat that led to aggressive demands on the Porte by the assertive Mehmet Ali. The modernizing Egyptian viceroy whom Abd el-Kader admired as a young man, and emulated as emir, had become powerful enough to rival the sultan for control of the empire.

The man considered the founder of modern Egypt was nominally a subject of the Porte, but he had his own agenda. It included carving out of the Ottoman Empire an Arab kingdom ruled from Cairo, an idea that was obviously threatening to the Turks, but also to the British. Napier's mission, to which Churchill had been attached as a budding Arabist, was to send the Egyptians packing to prevent a premature dismemberment of the Sick Man by Egyptian hands — hands too easily guided by their French rivals.

Greater Syria, the predominately Arab *pashalik* that had come under Mehmet Ali's control, was strategic real estate. Today, it would include Syria, Lebanon, Jordan, Israel, the West Bank and parts of Iraq. While Mehmet Ali was an enlightened, western-minded reformer in French eyes, the apostolic successor to Napoleon Bonaparte in the Middle East, to the British he was merely a cunning and savage brute who had coldly massacred those who brought him to power. France also had historic ties to Syria.

During the crusades, French knights won kingdoms and built castles there. France maintained close ties with catholic Maronites along the coast who had been under its nominal protection since the sixteenth century when Francis I negotiated with Sultan Suleiman "capitulations" that gave French merchants special rights within the Ottoman empire. Stretching from the north southward, the ports of Latakia, Tripoli, Beirut, Sidon and Tyre linked Europe with China, Damascus, Baghdad and India. Syria's silk producers became closely connected with weavers in Lyon who enjoyed their cheap alternative sources of raw material. France could exercise influence either directly or through its friendly relations with Egypt — a legacy of Bonaparte's respectful attitude toward Islam, even acquiring a Muslim bodyguard as he destroyed Mameluke armies.

British interests were above all commercial. Exports to the Ottoman Empire on the eve of the Crimean War had increased eightfold over the previous twenty-five years, giving the United Kingdom a six million pound annual surplus — and a turnover greater than its trade with Russia, Italy, France and Austria together. Of even greater importance was protecting future trade routes that could reduce by as much as a third the time to move goods from the homeland to India and back, goods which otherwise had to sail around Cape Horn. Whether a canal through the Suez, or railroad from Baghdad to Beirut, a Greater Syria under French influence was unwelcome to England. Russian interests centered on the Balkans and control of the Black Sea. British diplomacy favored keeping the Ottoman Empire intact, at least until it was properly positioned to get its proper share of the Sick Man's estate.

உ

Possessing, perhaps, a whiff of Byronic romanticism, Churchill developed strong affections for the Bedouins, and especially the Druze, in their struggle to maintain their cultural identity in the face of Turkish, Egyptian or Christian pressures. He was not merely sympathetic. Churchill had committed the most scandalous sin of all in the eyes of the European community in Damascus. He had gone native.

Identifying with, even liking, those one is trying to dominate was considered apostasy. Such fraternization, it was widely believed, would compromise the representation of one's own national interests, as the Victorian mind was convinced that carrying the White Man's Burden required aloofness and separation from those in need of civilization. Real knowledge of the culture was less important than an air of indomitable superiority.*

Churchill married the daughter of a well-connected Muslim family after serving as British vice-consul in Damascus in 1841. He dressed like a native, spoke Arabic and was known to consistently sympathize with minorities against the decadent Turk. Above all, he admired the Druze. When the Druze and Maronites were slaughtering each other in 1845, Churchill reported to his commanding officer: "Though always inferior to the Maronites in numbers, they are infinitely superior in

---

* In *Peace to End all Peace*, David Fromkin points out that Kitchner's staff in Cairo had considerable expertise on the Muslim world going into World War I. Yet, life in Cairo was provincial and the British community homogenous, its life centering around the Turf Club and going to balls. Many of his staff were competent Arabists, yet their insularity caused some to miss much of the complexity of the Muslim and Arab world. According to Fromkin, Kitchner's experts held two basic misconceptions: the widespread assumption that Islam was an "it," a single entity whose believers obeyed their leaders, and a failure to realize that Arab dissatisfaction with Turkish rule didn't mean they were willing to accept rule by non-Muslims. (pp 93-96)

courage, prudence and judgment both in military as well as political matters."

Churchill was the bête noire of the French diplomats in Syria. His intrigues and plotting were met by French counterplotting that resulted in his forced resignation over a trumped-up scandal that accused him of misbehaving with Muslim women. In fact, no one was sure for whom he really worked. Was it the colonial office, the foreign office, or was he simply motivated by his genuine admiration for the Druze and their Bedouin cousins? It was known that he acted as a military advisor to the various local potentates who populated the region and that he had become a potentate in his own right.

His true colors may have been reflected in his works — investments on the hill slopes of Howara and surrounding areas. Churchill created agricultural enterprises on his own estate using the latest irrigation methods and terracing techniques. He planted mulberry forests — the feedstock of the silkworm — for supplying silk to the local textile producers, and built roads and bridges to strengthen the economy and promote the movement of goods. Like Abd el-Kader, he wanted to uplift and regenerate the Arabs. He differed with the emir about the means. Churchill could only imagine uplifting occurring through British benevolence, but with Lebanon as part of a British sphere of influence following the Ottoman collapse. Egypt and Syria, he was sure, would follow. His job was to help assure that outcome by cultivating the Druze to offset French influence among the Maronites.

From Churchill's palatial manor in The Lebanon the emir descended into the Bekaa valley and back up through the Anti-Lebanon, a parallel range only fifteen miles from Damascus. Midway, his caravan was greeted by the sounds of gunfire, and then from the surrounding heights, by the sight of hundreds of Druze cavalry galloping in tight formation to welcome their Islamic hero, Abd el-Kader. His reputation had preceded him. Now, there were effusive salutations, kissing of his hands and robes, and excitement at seeing the man who had been so long admired from afar; another invitation to be feted and sheltered as their guest for a night by fellow Arabs. For hours, the Druze chieftains interrogated the emir about the one topic that most interested them — his campaigns against the French. The next day the sheiks escorted the emir to the edges of their territory. "May God keep us always united,"

Abd el-Kader called out to his hosts. "May God grant it and may we see you again," they replied.

☙

"Not since the days of Saladin had anyone received such a triumphal welcome," wrote Churchill. A few miles from Damascus, government and religious dignitaries greeted the emir and escorted him into the city at the head of a Turkish military band that marched smartly in embroidered blue vests, baggy red pantaloons and white spats. Closer to the city, the route was lined with men, women and children of all ranks, festively turned out to welcome their Islamic hero, a welcome that may not have been entirely spontaneous.

Abd el-Kader's unofficial advance man and former caliph, the loyal Ben Salem, had also received permission to move to Damascus along with hundreds of other Algerians previously in Bursa. To an Arab population already restless under the Turk, the Algerians' stories of Abd el-Kader's resistance to the most powerful army in the world (so it was widely thought) aroused a ready enthusiasm and would become a symbol many would try to use for their various agendas, agendas that were either anti-Turkish or pro-Arab nationalism.

The true direction of the emir's mind was revealed when he surprised the Turkish dignitaries by his first request after entering Damascus. It was not to see the famous Omayed Mosque or to pay a courtesy call on the Turkish governor, but rather to visit the Ibn Arabi Mosque and pay homage to the great teacher whose writings had shaped his own Islam. Muhi al-Din Abu Bakr Muhammed ibn 'Ali ibn al 'Arabi had not always been honored with a tomb inside a mosque built in his honor.

The man whose teachings left deep traces on the emir's own spirit was born in Muslim Andalusia in 1165 in the town of Murcia. Like Abd el-Kader, Ibn Arabi was a prodigy whose potential was soon recognized by his father who gave his son both a religious and worldly education. By the age of eight, Ibn Arabi had begun the study of the Hadith, Koranic commentary and recitation. In Seville, he studied literature, poetry, the physical sciences and associated with Sufi masters as well as distinguished female spiritual figures. At age thirty-six, after both his parents had died, Ibn Arabi began a peripatetic life of prayer, study and seeking wisdom throughout the Arab world until he finally was persuaded by the governor of Damascus to make that city his home.

But in Damascus he made enemies among the religious elite — notably, theologians and scholars jealous of the good graces he enjoyed with the ruling class and upset because of his very public condemnation of their love of money. He could not abide religious scholars who sold their knowledge and lived in luxury.

Ibn Arabi died in 1240, beaten to death, it was said, by an angry mob whose imam he had berated during a sermon for his money-loving ways. He was respectfully buried in the Kurdish hill town of Salihiyyah, outside the walled Damascus, but the slighted scholars later got their revenge. His gravesite was used as a garbage dump. Three hundred years later, the Ottoman warrior-sultan, Selim The Resolute, conquered Damascus. His first act was to find the master's burial site. It is said he wept when he saw it; then he ordered a tomb to be built on it and a mosque to be built around the tomb.

Known to his followers as the master of love, Ibn Arabi left posterity these telltale lines:

> *My heart is capable of wearing all forms*
> *It is pasture for gazelles and a monastery for monks,*
> *A temple for idols and the Kaaba for the pilgrim.*
> *It is the tablets of the Torah and it is the book of the Koran*
> *I profess the religion of love, wherever the destination of its*
> *caravans may be.*
> *Love is my law and my faith.*

Just as there is no place where God is not, Ibn Arabi believed there is no place where saintliness cannot be found. *He is with you wherever you are.* "Perfection," the master wrote, "does not come from withdrawal, but through living together in society…The best do not flee their condition, rather their condition flees them." Seclusion, he taught, was like a hospital for the sick at heart, useful for treating a temporary condition. Perfecting one's humanity comes through living with others. "The lesser war against the enemy without does not divert them from the more important struggle against the enemy within. Their lives unite the affairs of this world with those of eternity." So it was with the emir, though few European diplomats understood.

With time and help from the French government, Abd el-Kader acquired farms to earn money that would support his Algerians. He came to own large agricultural enterprises as far west as the Sea of Galilee, promoted road construction between Damascus and Beirut, and built a toll bridge in partnership with James Rothschild. His worldly activity notwithstanding, the emir's heart was with his books, his students and his pious devotions. To the Arabs he wore a triple crown: descendant of the Prophet, religious scholar and warrior-prince.

Turkish officialdom viewed him suspiciously. He and his Algerians lived under the protective wing of mighty France and their official status wasn't even clear. Were they to be treated as French nationals, Ottoman subjects or simply privileged guests of state? The emir had quietly transformed himself into a political eunuch, yet Arab admiration for him still carried a political message to the insecure Turkish government wary of a brewing Arab nationalism.

***

The Crimean War officially ended in the spring of 1856. Abd el-Kader was settling into his thirty room, two-story residence in the Armara district, once occupied by his master, Ibn Arabi. Its façade — three homes that had been made one — was the length of a soccer field, with three entrances on the narrow Nekib Allée. The guest entrance had its own mounting block recessed into the outer wall next to the door, and led into an airy, marble-floored reception room lined with divans and surrounded by walls painted with blue and green arabesques, which, in turn, opened onto a courtyard echoing with the murmur of splashing water from an alabaster fountain. Here the emir would receive visitors from all walks of life for almost thirty more years.

The location was well chosen. It was a short walk to the Christian quarter where the French, American and other consulates were located, but also close by the great Omayed Mosque where the body of Saladin was buried, and, it is said, the head of John the Baptist. There he taught every day, holding classes following midday prayer and often attended by prominent local scholars, which made him unpopular with the dimmer lights among the religious teachers and imams who were losing students to the popular Algerian.

While the great power doctors were absorbed in the diplomatic wrestling match that produced the Treaty of Paris on March 30, the emir was wrestling with his students' questions about the teachings of his Sufi master, questions that ultimately produced fifteen hundred pages of commentary on the works of Ibn Arabi. Like the great powers, Ibn Arabi was concerned with order — only his order began within.

To encounter Ibn Arabi is to begin to know Abd el-Kader. The Andalusian master writes in his *Divine Governance of the Human Kingdom* that a human being has an interior city and this interior city must itself be properly ordered to bring order to the exterior world. "As man is created central to the universe as God's deputy on earth and is the microcosm of the macrocosm, so the soul is central to the human being and is the deputy of the Lord within us." The soul is not created, rather it is a direct extension of God, a divine influence within to guide His deputy toward the truth.

And where does the soul reside? Ibn Arabi is confident it is in the heart, though he admits the location of the soul is disputed. *The Lord looks neither at your face or your riches but at your heart and your deeds.* He likens the heart to a small piece of meat in the body of man — if it is clean and righteous, the whole being is clean; if it is rotten, the whole being is rotten.

There is another precinct in the human realm where the daughter of God's deputy lives. Her name is Personality and her address is Selfhood or Ego. Here we find contradictions. Here, both God's commands and His prohibitions are kept. Selfhood is a place of order and enlightenment when it heeds the soul's prime minister, intellect. However, the self is a Jekyll and Hyde, easily tempted into disobedience by the Evil-Commanding Hyde-Self. Transformed by succumbing to temptations, self becomes impure. When intellect and self start fighting the whole human kingdom is disturbed. *If in a single nation men swear allegiance to two rulers, eliminate one of them.* But there is a rub. Ibn Arabi wisely notes that in the country of our warring self, one is liable to mistakenly eliminate the intellect, leaving the kingdom in the hands of the Evil-Commanding Self.

Only obedience to a benevolent influence from without can save the human realm from self-inflicted wounds. That influence is Divine Law, transmitted through the prophets. The reason God gives man Divine Law is to reduce disorder and promote harmony. Yet, acknowledges Ibn Arabi, no government is ready to rule by it.

❧

Certainly not the diplomats negotiating in Paris in the spring of 1856. Their worldly selves were in full control as they sought to do what their essential nature required — to seek advantage for their nations, clothed in noble rhetoric. The war had been waged as a European crusade to check despotism, more specifically Russian despotism. To Britain, especially, it seemed that Tsar Nicolas was pushing to the head of the queue in dismembering the Ottoman Empire.

The dispute that produced the war that nobody wanted had a nimbus of religiosity about it. Ostensibly, it was over control of the keys to shrines in the Holy Land: the Church of Bethlehem, the tomb of the Virgin Mary, the Holy Sepluchre and the Grotto of the Nativity, among others. Napoleon III did not give a wit about such things, but wanted to buttress the legitimacy of his 1852 coup d'état by currying favor with the Catholic church.

Like his uncle, Napoleon Bonaparte, Louis-Napoleon was pragmatic about religion. Both believed in its utility as a foundation for moral order in society, and viewed the church as a useful political ally. The Porte yielded to French pressure to restore rights to the Latin monks that had been ceded over time (from simple neglect by a distracted France) to the Orthodox monks. Russia responded to this turnaround in the fortunes of its Orthodox guardians by sending an overbearing diplomat to Istanbul to demand recognition of the Tsar's protectorate over all the sultan's orthodox subjects. With British advisors at his elbow, the sultan repeatedly rejected the Russian demands until an exasperated Tsar Nicholas finally sent troops into the Turkish Danubian Principalities of Moldavia and Wallachia.

March 30, 1856, after two years of carnage and the allies' logistical incompetence on the Crimean Peninsula, a peace treaty was signed in Paris. The treaty left the Black Sea closed to the warships of all countries, the Danubian Principalities restored to the Turk and offered noble declarations by France, Britain, Prussia and Austria to guarantee and respect the independence and the integrity of the Ottoman Empire that became officially a member of the Concert of Europe. The emir's new friend Churchill considered the Paris treaty the equivalent of getting the Turks to put a knife to their own throat. The knife was the package of reforms the Porte promulgated a month before the Treaty of Paris was concluded.

The sultan's reform edict of February18, known as *Hatti Humayun*, was hailed in Britain as a "Magna Carta" for the eastern Christians. The final treaty language approvingly took note of the edict while repudiating the "right to interfere either collectively or separately" in the internal affairs of Turkey. Yet, this was precisely what the European powers wanted to do and *Hatti Humayun* was their tool.

The different Christians minorities used the European powers to promote their interests against the Turk, but were also used by the powers as constituents to advance their agendas and justify their interventions. The French saw themselves as protectors of the Christians in Syria, especially the Latin Maronites and Greek Melkites, who followed Rome; Russia was the long-standing protector of Orthodox Christians, especially in the neighboring Balkans; Johnny-come-lately Great Britain, low and behold, had become protector of the Turks and Druze, if only to hold off its competitors. To the increasingly insecure Turks, these client relationships between the Christians and their European protectors gave the Christian communities the odor of a fifth column.

The reforms would give new rights to non-Muslim minorities and reinforce old reforms that had affected all subjects. Arbitrary confiscation of property, the use of torture to force confessions, killing and robbing with impunity by pashas were past malpractices already addressed with some good effect by earlier reforms. The newer ones in 1856 focused attention on minorities and promised them equality before the law. Yet, the proposed change of the legal status of Christians and Jews was in itself an affront to Muslims. The *dhimma*, derived from the Prophet words, already held them by faith to respect and protect minorities, especially, the People of the Book.

What did Abd el-Kader think about the reforms? His apolitical persona didn't allow him to pronounce his views publicly about the reforms. Nevertheless, one may surmise that his respect for tradition and his natural Islamic instincts made him protective of Islamic law. Yet, Bullad's report to the ministry in March of 1856 implied that the emir begrudgingly recognized the need for change. "It's not possible to know exactly what he thinks," Bullad wrote, "but I presume that if in his heart he is against putting Christians and Jews on the same legal footing as the Muslims, he also understands that necessity is what makes law. Knowing his religious sensibilities, I suppose he sighs when he thinks about the future of Islamism so long as it insists on remaining as in the seventh century. He often says 'Islam is dying from a lack of Muslims, true Muslims.'"

The proposed reforms would allow Christians and Jews to testify in Muslim courts and give them equal access to all government positions, including, and especially, the army. Having the right to serve in the army would relieve Jews and Christians of the special tax paid in lieu of military service, about which they often complained to their respective European sponsors, even when there was no real desire to serve. Announcing edicts was one thing. In the decentralized Ottoman Empire, enforcement was another.

ↄ

Unrest in Lebanon had become acute by the spring of 1860. The Porte had announced its reforms in 1856, but little had been done in the four years that had lapsed. The Turkish government was caught between European pressure to modernize its laws to conform with their new status as a member of the Concert of Europe, and the hostility of local notables to abolishing the dhimma, and with it, a source of revenue. European badgering and superciliousness only fueled the anger. Istanbul left the whole business to the notables who were traditionally responsible for governing the *pashaliks*, and whose behavior could be disavowed if the Europeans protested. The emirs, aghas and pashas in Lebanon acted no differently than in other parts of the empire — they ignored the edict.

Emboldened by the reform edict of February 1856 and the allied victory in defense of Turkey, the Maronites in Lebanon stopped paying the poll tax. They began demanding jobs once off limits. Confident of their European sponsors support, the Christians showed an unseemly arrogance. They loudly proclaimed during the Crimean War that the empire was finished and would soon be carved into pieces by the great powers. Their idea was right, only the timing was wrong.

Angry Turkish authorities didn't appreciate that the uppity Christians were not paying their taxes. They had no need for Christians in the army. They wanted their annual ten shillings per head. The Christians would have to be "corrected." The Christians knew well the meaning of this Oriental euphemism, one that applied to Christians and Muslims alike.

In Lebanon, the Turks used the Druze to do their "correcting."

CHAPTER TWENTY-THREE

All for One

T HE RUMORS WERE UGLY. There were few details, but when the word on the street reached him, the emir was horrified. The Christians were going to get their comeuppance — soon. On March 5, 1860, the governor of Damascus, Ahmed Pasha, had invited various local leaders to a meeting at his palace. The agenda, it was later reported, was to neuter the reforms that would abolish the dhimma. Among his accomplices were two Druze chiefs — Said Bey Jumblat and Ould el-Atrach — as well as the mufti of Damascus. The Druze would carry out the first phase in Lebanon, where clashes between Muslims and Christians were already occurring daily over taxes and the new equal-rights reforms. Ahmed Pasha would take care of Damascus. Once trouble started in Damascus, they believed the "correcting" would spread spontaneously to Homs, Aleppo, Latakia and other places with Christian communities.

Abd el-Kader called on Lanusse, the acting French consul. Lanusse was an Arabist and a member of the unofficial "Kaderian Party" of French admirers. He trusted the emir well enough to call a meeting of fellow consuls. They decided to talk directly with Ahmed Pasha about the reports circulating. The smooth governor received them graciously, and reassured them that there was no basis to the rumors. They could count on his troops to protect them. There was nothing to worry about. The diplomats left reassured, and Amed Pasha immediately sent messages to his Druze conspirators to delay action until further notice.

In early May, Abd el-Kader received new information that the conspiracy against Christians was again in motion. This time his sources were his own Algerians, some of whom had been asked to join in the plot. He told them to play along and keep him informed. The emir went to Lanusse again. With some difficulty, Lanusse convened his colleagues again to discuss the revived threat of a massacre. They were reluctant to call on the governor a second time. It would be insulting to question his good faith. Certainly the plot, if there was one, had been already compromised, they argued. But what if they were wrong and something did happen, countered Lanusse? He could be in error, but the embarrassment of a second visit to the governor would be a small thing compared to the eternal shame they would carry if his warning were proven true. The Frenchman's argument carried the day and a second meeting was arranged. The suave Ahmed Pasha tranquillized the diplomats one more time with his convincing reassurances. He again sent word to the plotters to defer action.

Abd el-Kader circulated a letter to the Druze leaders urging calm and caution, following reports that Druze cavalry had been pillaging Christians living outside of Damascus. "These actions," he wrote, "are unworthy of a community known for its good sense and wisdom." The emir acknowledged the long-standing animosity between Druze and Christians and imagined that the government would not hold them entirely responsible for misdeeds in Lebanon. As for Damascus, he warned: "If you are to commit aggressions against the inhabitants of a town with whom you have never been in a state of hostility, we fear this will lead to a serious rupture with the Turkish government. We are anxious for your well-being and that of your compatriots…The wise calculate the consequences before taking the first step." The emir sent other letters to the ulema in Damascus and to Muslim notables, urging them to use their influence to prevent harm to innocents, reminding them of their obligations to protect minorities, especially People of the Book.

At the end of May, the emir came a third time to Lanusse with information. An explosion was imminent. He had precise details this time. It had been reported that Ahmed Pasha had tried once already to raise a revolt against the Christians in Damascus, but had been blocked by opposition from local leaders. The Christians, it was reported, would be "rescued" by the Turks and taken to the citadel for "protection" where they would be slaughtered by Druze conspirators. The Frenchman's diplomatic colleagues would have nothing to do with yet another demarche to the governor. Lanusse, nevertheless, took the emir's newest information seriously enough to put his own career at risk.

French diplomats at that time were allowed to draw on an unlimited credit line for unanticipated situations of the "gravest order." Lanusse agreed with Abd el-Kader to arm a thousand of his Algerians, even without the approval of his ambassador in Istanbul, whose advisors were skeptical of arming men believed to be "motivated as much by hatred of the French as devotion for their emir." Seven hundred Algerians living outside Damascus would come into the city in small groups to join the 300 already living there. Confident of the emir's trustworthiness, Lanusse authorized him to acquire, in the strictest secrecy, all the weapons possible.

The French consul met once again with the governor, this time alone. Lanusse made it clear by what he intimated that he knew what was about to happen and that Ahmed Pasha would be held responsible by the European powers. The conversation had a sobering effect on the Turk. He immediately sent another message to Ould el-Atrach and Said Bey Jumblat countermanding the conspiracy, but too late. The two chiefs had already launched their plot.

Ahmed Pasha performed his part three weeks later on July 8. Some Muslim boys had drawn images of crosses and mitres on the pavement of Straight Street bordering the Christian quarter of Damascus, only to spit and then throw garbage on the drawings. For publicly insulting Christianity, Ahmed Pasha chose a diabolical punishment — one that would provide evidence to the watchful Europeans of the respect demanded of Muslims for their Christian brothers, as required by the reforms, yet certain to arouse the rage of Muslims already indignant over European interference in their affairs.

On July 9, the culprits, mere props in a scenario planned by Amed Pasha, were ordered to be publicly beaten, then forced on their hands and knees to wash the streets they had slopped with garbage. Provocateurs did the rest.

℘

The American vice consul was running for his life. Eyewitnesses saw the rotund, sixty-year-old Michael Mechaga save himself by throwing coins on the pavement each time his pursuers got too close for comfort. Nor was he alone among the European diplomats whose embassies and residences were the first targets of the mob's wrath.

But Mechaga wasn't actually an American. This Lebanese pastor had become a close friend and supporter of American Protestant missionaries in Syria. He had been born into the Greek Catholic church, but soured on its bigotry and corruption. At age forty-eight, Mechaga converted to Protestantism and became known as the "Luther of the Orient" for his disgust with the Latin Church. Diplomats and politicians valued his linguistic knowledge and good relations with leaders of all the different communities — the Druze, Alawites, Jews, Armenians, Shiites, Zoroastrians, Copts, and even some of the Greek and Latin Christians. Thanks to his good reputation and wide knowledge, the Americans asked him to serve in the consulate. The honor almost cost him his life.

Mechaga had fled when the mobs broke into his home, and like many European diplomats who knew the emir, he ran for his residence, which bordered the Christian quarter. Mechaga and Abd el–Kader had become friends during the previous five years. The two shared many interests and had a similar large outlook on matters of faith and reason and the diversity of God's ways. Like the emir, Mechaga was also a man of wide knowledge — medical doctor, religious scholar, mathematican, musician and amateur astronomer. He banged desperately on the door, but it didn't open fast enough. A sickle sliced his ear as he was pulled inside by one of the emir's servants. Mechaga found the emir's wife, Kheira, in the courtyard where she was calmly tending to her desperate, frightened flock as though they were guests at a tea party — only they were being served cucumbers and bread.

But where was Abd el-Kader on the morning of July 9? At dawn the previous day, the emir had ridden out of town to his Hochblass estate and had not responded to urgent messages to return to Damascus. Why would he leave town just when tensions were rising and his presence was most needed?

Simply bad timing? A nefarious conspiracy with the French that would mean sacrificing some innocent lives, as some later suggested? Both seem unlikely. Churchill provides a plausible explanation for his absence. Abd el-Kader had learned that the rumored plot to slaughter Christians taken to the citadel under the pretext of protecting them was, indeed, true. Informed that Druze cavalry was already headed toward Damascus, the emir rode out with his sons, Mohammed and Hachem, to dissuade them from their impious acts. From his farm at Hochblass, near Sehnaya, he had a better chance of intercepting them before it was too late. At nearby Ashrafia, the emir found the Druze sheiks waiting for a signal from Ahmed Pasha to enter the city. Protracted discussions ended when the Druze leaders turned away from their grisly mission. It is not hard to imagine the emir using on the Druze the same weapons he would use soon again at his own portals: his superior knowledge of Divine Law and of the entrance requirements to Paradise.

☙

Once back in Damascus the afternoon of the tenth, Abd el-Kader rode first to the French embassy in the Christian quarter. His agha, Kara Mohammed, and forty-odd Algerians were already protecting Lanusse and his staff, as prearranged in the event of an emergency. Satisfied that his French patrons were safe, the emir then called on the mufti of Damascus to persuade him in the name of their faith to carry out his obligations to protect the Christians. "He is sleeping and can't be disturbed," the emir was told.

Abd el-Kader soon learned that the Turkish troops assigned to protect the populace had been ordered into the citadel or were lackadaisically watching as rioters were running amok, burning homes and slaughtering Christians. When he returned to the French consulate and saw that the crowd had grown larger and more threatening, Abd el-Kader offered to take responsibility for Lanusse's safety.

"You have always said, 'Where the French flag is, is France.' Bring your flag with you and plant it on top of my home. My home will be France. You and your staff will be my guests and I can then use my soldiers who are protecting you here to save other Christians." Lanusse arrived to find himself joining Russian, American, Dutch and Greek diplomats, some of whom had made him the butt of jokes for his repeated efforts to intervene with the governor, impelled by his faith in the emir's street intelligence.

All afternoon of July 10, Abd el-Kader plunged into the chaos of the Christian quarter with his two sons shouting: "Christians, come with me! I am Abd el-Kader, son of Muhi al-Din, the Algerian…Trust me. I will protect you." For several hours his Algerians led hesitant Christians to his fortresslike home in the Nekib Allée, whose two-story interior and large courtyards would become a refuge for the desperate victims.

"As night advanced fresh hordes of marauders — Kurds, Arabs, Druzes — entered the quarter and swelled the furious mob, who, glutted with spoil, began to cry for blood. Men and boys of all ages were forced to apostatize and were then circumcised on the spot… Women were raped or hurried away to distant parts of the country where were put in harems or married instantly to Mohammedans," wrote

297

Churchill of the events. "To say that the Turks took no means to stay this huge deluge of massacre and fire would be superfluous. They connived at it, they instigated it, they shared in it. Abd el-Kader alone stood between the living and the dead." At the Franciscan monastery near the Thomas Gate, all the rhetorical powers of the emir were for naught. He couldn't convince the nine monks who had barricaded themselves inside to entrust themselves to his Algerians. Fearing treachery, the Franciscans wouldn't leave. Abd el-Kader finally left them to their fate to save another Christian community particularly dear to him for their work with children.

The Lazarists had been overlooked during the initial outbreak of bloodletting, apparently because they were located outside the Christian quarter. The emir's friend, Father Leroy, ran a school for 400 orphans. The children, the six priests and eleven Sisters of Charity were hustled through a maze of alleys strewn with blood and dead animals, shielded at the head by the emir himself and his veteran mudjahideen. The fate of the untrusting Franciscans was less happy. They were burned alive in their building.

News spread among the rioters that the emir was protecting the Christians. The next day an angry crowd gathered at his door to protest. They were prepared to tolerate his harboring diplomats, but demanded that he hand over the local Christians under his protection. As the mob got larger and more unruly, the emir came to the door.

"Give us the Christians," the crowd shouted after he had quieted it by his silent presence.

"My brothers, your behavior violates the law of God. What makes you think you have a right to go around killing innocent people? Have you sunk so low that you are slaughtering women and children? Didn't God say in our holy book, *Whoever kills a man who has never committed murder or created disorder in the land will be regarded as a murderer of all humanity?*

"Give us the Christians! We want the Christians!"

"Didn't God say there should be no constraint in religion?" the emir vainly replied.

"Oh holy warrior," cried out one of the leaders of the mob. "We don't want your advice. Why do you stick you nose in our business?"

"You have killed Christians yourself, " shouted another. "How can you oppose us for avenging their insults. You are like the infidels yourself — hand over those you are protecting in your home, or you will be punished the same as those you are hiding."

"You are fools! The Christians I killed were invaders and occupiers who were ravaging our country. If acting against God's law doesn't frighten you, then think about the punishment you will receive from men…It will be terrible, I promise. If you will not listen to me, then God didn't provide you with reason — you are like animals who are aroused only by the sight of grass and water."

"You can keep the diplomats. Give us the Christians!" shouted the mob, sounding more and more like Romans in the Coloseum.

"As long as one of my soldiers is still standing, you will not touch them. They are my guests. Murderers of women and children, you sons of sin, try to take one of these Christians and you will learn how well my soldiers fight." The emir turned to Kara Mohammed. "Get my weapons, my horse. We will fight for a just cause, just as the one we fought for before."

"God is great," his men shouted, brandishing their guns and swords. Faced with the emir's battle-hardened veterans, the crowd melted away bravely hurling insults.

৩

The North Africans, as the Algerians were called by the locals, continued searching the streets for Christians until over a thousand refugees had been brought to the emir's residence. The mansion became so crammed there was no space for people to lie down or sit. Lack of water and the risk of dysentery or plague breaking out in the unsanitary conditions made the situation impossible to maintain. After consulting with the diplomats, the emir decided to send a deputation to talk with Amed Pasha about moving the refugees to the citadel.

The governor admitted that his troops were of low reliability — many were recently released prisoners — and was coaxed into allowing the Algerians to bring Christians to the citadel under their protection. The decision brought no relief to those crowed in the Nekib Allée. On the contrary, they howled when they learned of the decision: "Kill us now yourselves! Have pity on us! Don't hand us over to our executioners alive!"

The first group of 100 stubbornly wouldn't leave, but were finally persuaded after the Russian consul agreed to go along as a guarantee of their safety. When it was learned the first arrivals were safe, the others began to cooperate. "Despite all that I had already done for them, they still believed I was capable of sending them to these butchers," the emir sadly admitted to a French officer after the events.

The residence was finally emptied out and cleaned. Abd el-Kader then circulated word that a reward of fifty piasters would be paid for each Christian brought to his home. For five days, the emir rarely slept, and when he did, it was on a straw mat in the foyer of his residence where he dispensed reward money from a sack he kept by his side. As soon as 100 refugees were collected, his Algerians escorted them to the citadel.

Some of the Christian "notables" stayed on in the emir's home for weeks while they figured out where to go. The emir and his Algerians eventually accompanied a caravan of 3,000 Christians to Beirut, among them were members of the Bullad family who had been the emir's guests during the massacres.

George Bullad was not among them. He had asked the ministry to recall him in 1857, when he felt he had lost the confidence of Abd el-Kader. A certain coolness had entered into their relationship. It is not known exactly what passed between them. Abd el-Kader may have simply tired of being handled by Bullad and wanted to deal directly with his French interlocutors at the consulate. Nor was he cut from the same cloth as Daumas and Boissonnet, who had known the smell of gunpowder in Africa. Nevertheless, Bullad maintained a high opinion of the emir, even if he thought he had begun to put on holy airs and affected a careless disdain for money when supplicants came to him.

The tornado of violence that bloodied the Christian quarter for five days left thousands dead. Estimates of how many died vary widely. Some as few as five hundred, others as many as ten thousand.* Lanusse reported to his ministry that there were nineteen thousand Christians living in Damascus at the time of the outbreak, including five thousand refugees who had fled from Lebanon in the spring. Most of them

---

* The lowest number is based on the French estimate of dead as of July 13, when the worst of the rioting ended; the higher number includes those who died in the aftermath from wounds, exposure and sickness.

would have been living in villages outside the walls of the old city. Space was limited and rents high in the inner city Christian quarter that was home to eight or ten thousand, mostly Greek Christians. How many lives did the emir save? No one was keeping count. How many others were inspired by his example? Abd el-Kader's friend, Lanusse, credits him with saving the lives of eleven thousand people, virtually every Christian in the inner city, and then some.

∽

The horrifying news first hit the French public on July eighteenth. From an earlier dispatch sent by the French naval commander in the Levant, *Le Moniteur* reported that "the attack on Christians began in Damascus on the afternoon of the ninth. By that evening large numbers of men had been killed and women carried off to harems....While the Turkish authorities were inexplicably lethargic in the face of immanent danger, the emir had actively tried to warn the ulema and notables of the threat to Christians ...Throughout the crisis, the emir's behavior was admirable. Day and night, he looked after the general safety of the population, giving clear proof of his devotion to humanity and self-sacrifice."

More articles appeared in August, all unanimous in their praise of the emir's conduct. *Le Gazette de France* was positively dithyrambic. "The emir Abd el-Kader has immortalized himself by the courageous protection he has given the Syrian Christians. One of the most beautiful pages of the history of the 19th century will be devoted to him." *Le Pays, Journal de l'Empire* quoted the Lazaristes: "When the carnage was at its worst, the emir appeared in the streets, as if sent by God." And so it went from the French press. By October 20 enough information had worked its way back to the United States for the *New York Times* to add its own accolade.

"Twenty years ago the Arab Emir was an enemy of Christendom, hunted through the ranges of his native hills...Today, the Christian world unites to honor the dethroned Prince of Islam, the most unselfish of knightly warriors, risking limb and life to rescue his ancient foes, his conquerors and the conquerors of his race and religion, from outrage and from death...For Abd-el-Kader* this is indeed a chapter of glory,

---

* This was the *New York Times'* spelling of his name. There is no agreed upon standard spelling of the emir's name in any language.

and of the truest glory. It is no light thing for history to record that the most uncompromising soldier of Mohammedan independence became the most intrepid guardian of Christian lives and Christian honor in the days of his political downfall and in the decline of his people. The defeats which surrendered Algiers to the Frank have been strangely and nobly avenged."

But why did he do it? Many wondered. Some people were amazed that this former head of the resistance hadn't used the situation to avenge the suffering inflicted by France on him and his country. Some Muslims saw his behavior as pandering to France, that in fact he had become more French than Arab. The emir's own explanation reported by *Le Pays* in October gave two simple reasons: he was doing God's will in saving innocents and his humanity demanded it. "These motives amounted to a sacred duty," the emir concluded. "I was simply an instrument. Sing your praises to Him who directed me — to your Sultan, as well as mine."

Others thought that the emir's intervention was a *cri du coeur* on behalf of his own religion. Hadn't Bullad reported that the emir often lamented that Islam was dying for "lack of real Muslims." Perhaps, by example, he could show Muslims what it meant to be a true Muslim. His reply to a letter of gratitude from Bishop Louis-Antoine Pavy, Dupuch's successor in Algiers, said as much between the lines. The emir often revealed his truest self when writing to other ministers of the Lord.

"…That which we did for the Christians, we did to be faithful to Islamic law and out of respect for human rights. All creatures are part of God's family and those most loved by God are those who do the most good for his family. All the religions of the book rest on two principles — to praise God and to have compassion for his creatures…The law of Mohammed places the greatest importance on compassion and mercy, and on all that which preserves social cohesion and protects us from division. But those who belong to the religion of Mohammed have corrupted it, which is why they are now like lost sheep. Thank you for your prayers and good will toward me…"

An avalanche of honors descended on the emir after the press reports appeared. The French government awarded him the Legion of Honor and diverse distinctions came from Russia, Spain, Sardinia,

Prussia, Great Britain, the Papacy, the Turkish sultan and President Lincoln. Lincoln, on the eve of his own national disaster, sent the emir a quintessentially American form of recognition: a pair of finely engraved custom made colt pistols, delivered in a box of bird's eye maple bearing the inscription: "From the President of the United States, to his Excellency, Lord Abdelkader, 1860."

However, the most valued of all the accolades Abd el-Kader received was a letter from fellow Muslim freedom fighter, Mohammed Shamil, the Islamic hero of Chechnya. He too was exiled, but in Moscow, after years of struggle against Russian imperialism.

"May God be praised who clothed His servant with power and faith… Abd el-Kader the Just. Greetings. May the laurels of distinction and honor always bear fruit for you." Shamil's themes: chagrin and shame toward fellow Muslims who had behaved so detestably toward Christians, and dishonored their faith. "I was stupefied by the blindness of the functionaries who committed these excesses, forgetting the words of the Prophet: *Whoever is unjust toward a protégé, whoever commits a wrong against him, or takes something from him without his consent — let him know I will be his accuser on the day of judgment…* You have put into practice the words of the Prophet…and set yourself apart from those who reject his example…May God protect us from those who transgress his laws." The emir recognized in Shamil a fellow Muslim cut from the same cloth. His response repeated what he wrote to Bishop Pavy and had said often to George Bullad.

"…What I did was merely obedience to our sacred law and to the precepts of humanity," he wrote Shamil. "…Vice is condemned in all the religions, for to be led by vice is to swallow a poison that contaminates your body…When we think about how rare are the real champions of truth, and when one sees ignorant people who imagine that Islamism is about severity, hardness, excess and barbarism — it is time to repeat these words: patience is godliness, trust in God."

ෞ

The massacres had provided France the opportunity to press its case that the Ottoman Christians needed European protection. A French force of 6,000 was on its way to Beirut, estimated to arrive in mid August.

A week after the killing had subsided, on July 25, the outraged European powers agreed to have a Franco-European expeditionary force sent to Lebanon, capable of marching inland to Damascus. Under the command of another old adversary of the emir from the Algerian struggle, General Beaufort Hautpoul's mission was to satisfy "humanistic imperatives." Before the French could arrive, Fouad Pasha, the Ottoman minister of foreign affairs, a strong proponent of reform and a favorite of Great Britain, was ordered immediately to Damascus from Lebanon with 3,000 troops to identify and punish the malefactors, and deprive the French of a pretext to penetrate into the interior.

Fouad Pasha consulted with his military officers, with Abd el-Kader, the European consuls and met with the local notables, before creating an Extraordinary Tribunal. The tribunal asked the surviving Christians to draw up a list of perpetrators, when in fact, most of the Christians had no idea who had attacked them. The living knew the faces of only those who had saved them. Fouad Pasha then told the precinct officers in the Muslim quarters to present lists of inhabitants they had seen armed during the mayhem.

On August 3, the governing council of Damascus, together with other Muslim leaders, met with Fouad Pasha to review the names in order to confirm or reject the candidates for punishment. The gates of the city were closed throughout the precedings, except for deliveries of food and other necessities. The tribunal arrested 350 people from 4,600 names that had been presented. Many of those on the list had fled; others were exculpated or simply released for lack of witnesses. Of the 350, all but twelve were found guilty of "instigation, murder, arson or pillage." Of the 338 men found guilty, 181 were shot or hung and 157 were exiled. Among those shot was the governor, Ahmed Pasha. Six of Mechaga's attackers were hung, as well as the precinct officer of his quarter.

Eighty-two of the condemned were from Turkish paramilitary groups. Sixty-four were identified as recent arrivals in Damascus. One hundred and twenty-three were identified by occupation, including shopkeepers, craftsmen, peasants and members of elite families. But whose hand was really behind the whole affair? Fingers were pointed in every direction.

The French consul pointed at the British, noting that theirs was the only European embassy not looted and burned (later, it too had been protected by the emir's Algerians). And then there was the curious story about the murderer of the English Reverend Graham who pleaded to his accusers that he had made a mistake. Others suspected a French hand in the matter. France was known to be looking for an excuse to occupy Syria and to install its own silk producers to eliminate the local middlemen. In his correspondence with his ambassador in Istanbul, the British consul in Damascus accused Abd el-Kader of collusion with the vice-consul Lanusse, rekindling a tradition of paranoia about French designs going back to 1840, when the British consul in Damascus, Richard Wood, had suspected France of intrigue with Egypt. Such were a few of the "greedy foreign hand" theories.

The actual facts, such as they are, make Churchill's explanation the obvious one: the desire to "correct" the arrogant Christians produced a plot born of resentment and anger stoked by antireform Muslims. Mechaga takes Churchill a step further, asserting that the plot was hatched in Istanbul. The Christians were in bad odor for their disrespectful arrogance and disobedience of the law, but so too were the Muslims of Damascus, most of whom were restless Arabs and Kurds. Their past behavior also needed correcting for such offenses as failing to pay back taxes and assassinating imperial viziers. Disrespect was everywhere. "Therefore," wrote the worldly-wise Mechaga, "the empire strove to incite the Muslims against the Christians and so have its revenge on both of them."

What is known is that mobs entered through the Thomas Gate to attack first the Russian Embassy and then the rest of the European embassies in the Christian quarter of Khamarieh. The Jewish quarter was untouched. Mechaga reported that some Jews were seen providing sugarcane-flavored ice to the Turkish militia men and bought loot from the pillagers at bargain-basement prices. Interestingly, the mixed Christian-Muslim quarter of Maydan was not touched by violence. The Maydan quarter of Damascus had few silk weavers and was known for its large number of grain merchants. The minority Christians in Maydan had taken pains to maintain good relations with their Muslim neighbors over the years. They were polite, deferential to the local authorities and had not arrogantly gloated over their new rights.

The murdering and pillaging was confined to the exclusively Christian Khamarieh quarter, which happened to be where the more technologically efficient Christian silk weavers worked. Added to the competitive inferiority of Muslim silk weavers who didn't have access to the modern Jacquard looms, were other gnawing grievances. Many Muslims were in debt to Europeans and the working class was suffering from high food prices caused by a severe grain shortage that summer. Mix these elements of discontent with a generalized resentment over the reforms instigated by the Europeans, and all the tinder was at hand to ignite a collective impulse to "correct" impudent, disobedient infidels.

Yet, collective mass impulses usually produce messy results. The blast of fury unleashed on July 9 was surprisingly concentrated — limited to the small, one-third-of-a-mile square, Christian neighborhood of Khamarieh. The large number of militiamen and outsiders punished in the aftermath would indicate a provocation executed by hired help with no personal ties to the victims, but who were encouraged by angry locals until a little pillaging erupted into a raging massacre. It would make sense for the conspirators to direct the outsiders to a place where attacking Christians could be done easily, without confusing them with Muslims.

In the mixed neighborhoods of Maydan and Shughar, Muslims were praised by the investigators for restraining violence and protecting their Christian neighbors. Abd el-Kader's conduct was exemplary, though the praise he would receive eventually overshadowed the heroism of many other Muslims who, like the emir, risked the wrath of the mob for harboring their Christian neighbors. In his colorful memoir *Murder, Mayhem, Pillage and Plunder* Mechaga calls out other outstanding Muslims of Damascus who followed their religious law to protect Christians: Sheikh Salim Attar, a well-respected member of the ulema, and in the mixed Maydan quarter, Salih Agha al-Mahayini, Said Agha al-Nuri, Umar Agha al-Abid and others. The emir may have been the boldest and most dramatic savior of Christians, but not the only one.

And what was Abd el-Kader's view of the events when asked by the investigating commission? Ever discrete, he would only say that the Christian quarter could have been spared "if the governor had wanted it." He refused to elaborate. A year later, a famous French archeologist and Orientalist, the Comte de Vogüe, called on Abd el-Kader, whose address had become an obligatory visit for European travelers. During the meeting, the Frenchman wrested from the emir his view of the Damascenes' behavior. Abd el-Kader's answer surprised his visitors. "They were wrong to use their right as they did, but their right to punish the Christians was unquestionable. The Christians had refused to pay the exemption tax." The emir might have added, but did not, that as former leader of an embattled Arab federation, he knew all too well the importance of raising taxes and the need to enforce their collection.

The law was perfectly clear to Abd el-Kader. The Christians were protected people, yet they still were obliged to respect the law. The Christians were in the wrong for disobeying the law. They were in rebellion and deserved punishment. The Muslims were in the wrong for the indiscriminately savage manner in which "correction" was applied.

The emir was certainly au courant. The reforms pressed on the Porte by the Europeans had eliminated officially their djimmi status. The djimmi poll tax lifted, it had been replaced by a universal exemption tax that both Muslims and Christians had to pay to stay out of military service. The Christians and Turks were now equal. The Christians were required to do military service, though it was generally understood that they detested the very notion of serving the Ottoman Empire. Nor did the Turks want Christians to serve. But, whereas the Christians only had to pay fifty liras per head, the Muslims had to pay 100 liras. The Christians still refused to pay, thinking that if they offered themselves to serve, the Turks would reject them and they would escape having to pay the tax.

The French visitors were surprised by the emir's stern orthodoxy and, most likely, unaware of the new complexities brought on by the reforms. In France, Abd el-Kader had been transformed by his many admirers into a "liberal"; however, had Comte de Vogüe spoken with the emir's Protestant friend and victim of the rioting, Michael Mechaga, he would have heard the same.

Mechaga was known locally as the "Luther of the Orient" for a good reason. Luther's revolutionary doctrine of the "priesthood of all believers" had contributed to the chaos in the German lands of the Holy Roman Empire: let every man, no matter how untutored, be his own priest; no intermediaries are required between man and God. Horrified at how his doctrines were being misused, Luther became a staunch defender of secular authority. Better a bad ruler than anarchy was the lesson he drew, and found support for, in the writings of Saint Paul to the Romans.

Like Luther 300 years earlier, Mechaga witnessed personally a torrent of bloodshed unleashed by rebellious spirits — Christian and Muslim. His extended memoir warned those who denied the necessity of obeying the constituted authorities. "My sole intention was to illustrate the results of disobedience to orders of one's overlords and to explain the causes…for we have never seen yet a state wreak vengeance on obedient subjects." Mechaga, like Luther, referred often to Romans 13: *Let every soul be subject to the governing authorities. For there is no authority except from God.…Rulers are not a terror to good works, but to evil…therefore you must pay taxes, for rulers are God's ministers tending to this very thing. Render, therefore, to all their due…Owe no one anything except to love one another…*

☙

A sixteen-page brochure was circulating in Paris in the fall of 1860 under the title *Abd el-Kader, empereur d'Arabie*. The brochure spoke of the need of the Arabs to have a true leader of quality, and championed Abd el-Kader for the throne of the Arab orient — Greater Syria. He would teach the West and the Muslims, it said, "the true interpretations of the maxims of the Koran and how a true believer ought to interpret them." Its anonymous authorship suggested some kind of straw in the wind.

But did it come from French or from Arab sources? French diplomats in Istanbul had suspected that local notables were in league with Ahmed Pasha. Proto-nationalist intrigue had been in the air. Had the Arab notables of Damascus, tired of the oppressive Turk, but as fellow Muslims flying the flag of "correction," conspired with Ahmed Pasha to instigate disorder with the intent of liberating Syria from all foreign control. Yes, Ahmed Pasha had been told in clear terms by Lanusse that mistreatment of Christians would bring French intervention, the expulsion of the Ottomans and unification of Syria with Egypt under French influence. Yet the notables also knew that the British would not permit French or Egyptian control over Syria.

Nevertheless, notables often conspired to improve their own positions in local power struggles by exploiting factional divisions and popular discontent. When accounts were settled in the fall of 1860, the representation on the city council of two powerful families — the Maydanis and Azms — had been radically altered. The Maydani faction had considerably increased its influence while all but two members of the Azm faction were exiled to waste away their days in the Magusa fortress in Cyprus.

Alternatively, Louis-Napoleon had controversial ideas of creating a quasi-independent Arab Kingdom in Algeria that would respect and protect the indigenous culture from French greed and "civilization." The bellowing protests of the colonists at the very hint of such an absurd notion scotched its further incubation. Not only was the name Abd el-Kader anathema to the Europeans in Algeria, Abd el-Kader had also given his word never to return to Algeria. But Syria was a different matter.

After the July events, the emir's prestige had reached new heights within the "civilized world" and his candidacy to lead a movement to win Syrian independence might be acceptable to both the British and the French who were striving for harmonious competition. Certain of their representatives had exchanged such thoughts even before the horrors of 1860.

Bullad's regular taking of the emir's political temperature following the sultan's unpopular *Hatti Humayun* reform edicts had been reassuring. He confirmed in his reports to the French embassy that the emir was a devoted loyalist toward France and to Emperor Louis-Napoleon, yet Bullad also was apprehensive. In 1857 he had written to his minister that Abd el-Kader might harbor ambitions to regenerate the Arabs by doing in the Middle East what he had failed to accomplish in Algeria. "His name still has great prestige in the Orient especially in fanatical circles who hate the Turks. We must not forget that the son of Muhi al-Din has always dreamed of an Arab nationality. The emir no longer considers the Ottoman empire viable, despite Europe's efforts to keep it alive." After warning his minister not to take the emir's benevolence toward France as a reason for complacency, Bullad also suggested that it could be advantageous for France to have a man such as Abd el-Kader as an ally or as a "weight in the balance that would determine the fate of the Ottoman Empire."

The bloody events of July left France and Britain with the question of what to do next. Though competitors in the Middle East, the two nations had a common interest in arrangements that would yield no clear advantage to the other. Practically, this meant supporting the integrity of the Ottoman Empire, while trying to reorganize Syria to assure adequate protection of the Christian minorities. The British candidate for the new governor of the *pashalik* was their reform-friendly foreign minister, Fouad Pasha, who had so efficiently and swiftly laid the ax to a large number of presumed conspirators and scattered others into exile, thus precluding a French occupation of Damascus. Certain Frenchmen had Abd el-Kader on their mind as a future governor, even though the British had made it clear that they considered him unacceptable to the Turks, and therefore they would be opposed.

In September, the Minister of War, Marshal Randon, another former adversary of the emir, asked General Hautpol's opinion of the emir's suitability as a candidate to govern Syria. Hautpol, still commanding the expeditionary force sent to Lebanon in the summer, did not think the European powers would agree to the emir governing all Syria, though possibly Damascus, the territory of Acre, and Judea as well. Eventually, the emir's government might stretch from Baghdad west to the Litani River in south Lebanon. Lebanon itself would never tolerate a Muslim ruler, even of the stature of Abd el-Kader, Hautpol concluded.

On October 23, Hautpol was stood up by the emir. Abd el-Kader never appeared at a meeting intended to explore with the general the different political schemes circulating.

"I was told he was afraid of compromising himself at a time when the Turks were silently hostile toward him and the Muslims in Damascus hated him," Hautpol wrote his minister afterward. "Nevertheless, it would be good to push for an autonomous Lebanon and to obtain for Abd el-Kader some kind of political power."

There was one big problem with all these speculations. No one had bothered to ask the emir's permission to put his name in play. In December of 1860, a French journalist visiting Damascus finally asked him the question.

"Your name has been mentioned in French newspapers as a possible governor of Syria. Have you heard?"

"Yes, and that, if I am not mistaken, is one of the main reasons the Turks are angry with me. But Turkey can rest assured. My career in politics is over. I have no ambition for worldly glory. From now on, I want only the sweet pleasures of family, prayer and peace."

One of those pleasures was to take his aged mother in his arms every day, and carry her up the steps to the rooftop terrace to breathe fresh air and watch the sun set on the Djebel Kaysun. Lalla Zohra was approaching 100 years and rarely left her bed. The emir's font of wisdom and compassion would die during the following year.

გა

While General Hautpol was fancifully planning the emir's future, in Paris a committee of the French Masonic Lodge, "Henry IV", was carefully editing a letter to the emir and selecting a piece of jewelry with an appropriate inscription. On November 16, after a month of editing, a letter was finally put in the mail to "the most illustrious emir" Abd el-Kader, accompanied by a green-enameled medallion covered with Masonic symbolism. A circle surrounded a double square, forming an octagon that emanated rays of light, in the center of which was inscribed a square rule with Pythagorean formulas streaming from it like bird shot.

The Lodge introduced itself to the emir, explaining the qualities that made one suitable to become a Free Mason. "Wherever tolerance and humanity have been protected and glorified, masons seek to recognize those who, at great sacrifice, do God's work on earth and lend a disinterested hand to the oppressed and needy." The authors then compared Abd el-Kader to other great Muslim personalities, and finally in a crescendo of acclaim: "Free Masonry, which believes in the existence of a moral God, the immortality of the soul…the practice of tolerance and universal brotherly love, cannot observe without emotion the great example you have given the world. It recognizes and claims as one of its own a man who practiced so well its noble motto, 'One for All.'" The letter's grand finale was an invitation to become a mason, for "there are hearts that beat in unison with yours, brothers who love you already as one of them and who would be proud if closer bonds would permit them to count you as one of the adepts of our institution."

Free Masonry in the mid-nineteenth century was an international brotherhood of distinguished and accomplished minds dedicated to building solidarity and harmony with their fellow man. Its roots were in the medieval guild system, when guilds educated initiates according to various rites, rules and trade-knowledge. But professional knowledge was always presumed to be both a divine gift and a divine obligation — to serve God by serving others. Their world, like the emir's, admitted no separation between secular and divine knowledge. For most guilds, the rights of members to organize and protect their craft was restricted to a specific locality and entailed the payment of a tax. The free masons were exempted from these restrictions.

More than any other, their guild was religious in its bones. Monks and clerics were themselves often masons. Masons were obligated to be men of faith, a faith they expressed in stone. Their first obligation was to be faithful to God and to the church and "to flee from heresy and error." They were obligated to undertake charitable works and assure the good moral education of its members. Nor was their craft education a matter of simply learning construction techniques in stone and wood. A mason's education was designed to enable him to express universal truths. He needed to be an architect, mason, carpenter and sculptor. His instruction required learning geometry, theology, art and philosophy. The medieval mason's education differed little from Abd el-Kader's. God's presence was seamless.

The church needed the masons for glorifying God, building its churches, cathedrals and monasteries. The church also had enough moral authority to liberate masons from the local restrictions that bound other guilds. Under the church's writ, masons paid no taxes and could travel freely, providing them a unique possibility to fraternize with like spirits and to create associations where knowledge and ideas could be exchanged — within the intellectual boundaries defined by their rule.

By 1815, the order had evolved from being strictly Christian to being Deist. A member no longer had to accept Christian dogmas, but rather acknowledge a Creator and a moral law. "A mason is required to obey the moral law...among men he should best understand that God sees differently than man, because man sees the exterior of things, but God sees the heart. Whatever a man's religion or his manner of worshipping God, he will not be excluded so long as he believes in the glorious Architect of heaven and earth and practices his moral obligations towards his fellow man."

The evolution of the masons had followed a path of tolerance not much different from the reasoning of the emir himself, though Abd el-Kader's acceptance of even paganism, as divine epiphany, might have been more than most masons could have digested in 1860.

In 1864, the emir was named honorary grand master of the Syrian Masonic Lodge in Damascus. A year later, during a visit to France, Abd el-Kader was inducted into the French Lodge, "Henry IV," joining Benjamin Franklin, Laplace, Lafayette, Voltaire, Soult, Monge, Talleyrand, Proudhon and other distinguished minds for whom nature, reason and moral law were compatible manifestations of one Divine Architect. *

---

* Because of a widespread but mistaken belief among Muslims today that the Masons were a quasi-Zionist organization at the time, the emir's affiliation with the Masons is perplexing to many Muslims, or considered a stain on his reputation and hotly disputed by members of his family. In reality, there were hardly any Jews in the Masonic Lodges of his day, nor did they have a Zionist agenda. (More in the chapter notes.)

CHAPTER TWENTY-FOUR

Distinguished Misfits

ABD EL-KADER'S NEW FAME as a great humanitarian and protector of the Christians turned his residence in the Nekib Allée into one of the most sought after addresses in Damascus, especially for Europeans, who, in the manner of bird-watchers, had come with a "people-of-interest" checklist. The French government had raised the emir's pension from 100,000 to 150,000 francs after his heroics. In 1865, an act of the Senate gave him and his fellow Algerians French nationality.* On his way to Paris and London that same year, Abd el-Kader used his new aura of holiness and piety to plead (in Istanbul) for the early release of those Damascene "notables" who had been sent into exile by the Extraordinary Tribunal of 1860 that investigated the massacres. The emir petitioned Louis-Napoleon to intervene with Tsar Alexander on behalf of Emir Shamil, a request he repeated again in London during an audience with Queen Victoria. After an appropriate interval, Shamil was allowed to return to the Caucasus.

On November 17, 1869, the emir sat in the grand pavilion with Napoleon's wife, the Empress Eugénie, Archduke Victor of Austria, the king of Hungary and ambassadors and dignitaries from all over the world to inaugurate the opening of the Suez Canal. Also there was the Emir Shamil who had been released from house arrest by Alexander II and allowed to make a pilgrimage to Mecca.

Abd el-Kader had played no small part in helping the Frenchman, Ferdinand de Lesseps, realize his dream of joining the seas of the East with the West. Lesseps needed the emir's freshly reminted prestige to convince a skeptical Egyptian khedive, Ismail Pasha, that his project was not only feasible, but would benefit the Arabs as well as the Europeans. The emir had many reasons to play the part asked of him. Lesseps was a persuasive and passionate believer in his project. Its realization would create not only jobs for Arabs and more cultivatable land, but benefit the region and world commerce.

---

* French nationality, however, did not carry with it the full rights of French citizenship. French Algerians, like black Americans, remained second-class citizens.

Abd el-Kader believed in projects that could improve lives. He also had a sympathy for its French sponsorship, especially since his friend Napoleon III had given his support to the venture. But there was an appealing sense of fraternity being heralded by the promoters of the canal. Many were Saint Simonians and Free Masons whose local lodges unfurled identifying banners with names such as "Sincere Friendship," "Love and Truth," and "Union of Seas."

The operative word at the inauguration was "union": union of the Mediterranean and Red seas, of the Atlantic and Indian oceans, of East and West, of Christianity and Islam. The inauguration was trumpeted in optimistic tones of friendship and the brotherhood of all people — Saint Simonian, Masonic ideals that merged with Abd el-Kader's own desire to be a bridge between Christians and Muslims and to leaven European materialism with Islamic spirituality. It was, possibly, the main reason he officially joined the Masonic Lodge, "Henry IV," during his trip to Paris four years earlier. (The emir's membership with the Masons lasted until 1877, when atheists were admitted to the society. For him, it was the final and unacceptable step of a society whose members had followed a path from Christian exclusivity to Deism and finally to accepting a godless humanism.)

It was inevitable in the small world of Damascus society that Abd el-Kader and the new British consul soon would meet. It was less inevitable that the great Muslim believer would become an admirer of a man who professed the gospel of "Doubt and Denial." A friend called Richard Burton a "Spiritualist without the Spirits."

಄

Grubby, litter-filled alleyways and dilapidated, pealing exteriors hid elegantly tiled courtyards, lushly planted interior gardens and magnificent rooftop terraces in a city where all signs of wealth were (and still are) discreetly concealed from the tax collector or the thief (generally viewed as the same). One of the more frequented terraces of the Damascene intelligentsia belonged to the Burtons. Another was the emir's summer villa in Dummar on the banks of the Barada River, a short distance from the old city.

Britain's swashbuckling explorer of the Nile, daring pilgrim to forbidden Muslim holy places and master of twenty-five languages decided from the outset that he wasn't going to live cooped up within the walls of the Damascus whose thirteen gates were locked each night. He chose, instead, to live in hilly Salihiyyah, a dilapidated Kurdish suburb of some 10,000 souls planted along the base of the Djebel Kaysun southwest of the city. The name meant "of the saints," but the local wags called it El Talihiyyah, "of the sinners." Salihiyyah at the time was considered the most dangerous and crime-infested part of Damascus. At night servants would go home armed and in groups. Residents from the city would only come visit in daytime, and then scurry home through the orange and lemon groves before sunset.

After Burton had hosted his weekly open house that was truly "open" to people of all creeds, colors and classes, and other guests had hurried home past the emir's villa in the Barada Valley to beat the nightfall, Abd el-Kader would frequently linger on their mat- and cushion-covered roof-top terrace that surrounded a courtyard filled with the fragrance of orange, lemon and jasmine trees and the cooling patter of a lapping fountain. Well into the night, they (Isabel did not speak Arabic) swapped stories about their adventures and talked of their common love for the East, its myths and legends, its past and future.

Superficially, Burton was everything the emir was not. Burton was a social and cultural misfit in his own land. He was not comfortable in his skin, whose complexion looked more Arab than English. He had served seven years in the Indian Army where he mingled in disguise with the natives, predicted the Sepoy rebellion of 1857* and showed an un-English affinity for the local cultures that earned him the title of "The White Nigger." He was an ambiguous creature, some would say the product of a recessive gene from some Arab ancestor who had sown his seed on his way to Poitiers.

Burton relished administering shock therapy to Victorian society. He was known to throw Indian scalps across a dinner table, give clinical descriptions of female circumcision practices, defend loudly polygamy and sing the praises of Islam. Unlike the emir, Burton was not known for patience, diplomacy or conciliation. He was a man who did right but too often in the wrong way. "Honor, not honors" was his motto.

---

* Muslim and Hindu natives serving in the British Indian Army whose mutiny was triggered when rumors spread that the cartridges of their Lee-Enfield rifles, which they had to bite off before loading, were greased in pig fat or beef tallow.

The new British consul soon started making enemies in Damascus in his blunt, imperious way. A system of government that he called "despotism tempered by assassination" didn't take kindly to someone who was flagrantly incorruptible, a rare and fearful virtue to those accustomed to the practice. Burton was known to physically hustle from his office those who came bearing "gifts." Jewish moneylenders, who claimed the rights of British protection, were furious to learn of the unflattering reports Burton was sending to London, complaining of the extortionist interest rates (as much as sixty percent) they were charging the Arabs. Missionaries detested Burton who, in turn, loathed their cant and hypocrisies. He was unsupportive of their dreams of converting the Muslim faithful, particularly in the volatile, sectarian tinderbox of Damascus.

In 1870, responding to unsettling signs of a possible renewal of violence, Burton questioned two young Jewish boys accused of drawing crosses in a privy attached to a mosque, a blasphemous act reminiscent of the provocation that incinerated the Christian quarter ten years earlier. Offended Jews spread rumors that he had tortured the boys. Muslim fanatics suspected his catholic wife, Isabel, of proselytizing for the Catholic Church. Between his high-handed wife and his own autocratic self, the Burtons made enemies.

His penchant for adhering to his own sense of justice also made him many friends, but not always in the right places. With influential Christian missionaries and Jewish bankers, the rabbi of London, the philanthropist, Moses Montefiore, the Turkish governor, Rashid Pasha, and others clamoring for his dismissal, the simmering Shazli affair finally eroded the last remnants of his support in the Foreign Office.

The Shazlis were an order of Dervishes thought to be lukewarm in their acceptance of the Prophet as the last word of divine revelation. They were a Muslim species of Unitarians who believed in the oneness of God without being unquestioningly wedded to a specific religious path to spiritual knowledge.* They were continually seeking. Truth for them was not static. During one of their gatherings, a Shazli adept fell

---

* They believed God is in all things and all things are in God. In the mixed Muslim-Christian quarter of Shugar where the Shazlis were concentrated, their reasoning may well have been responsible for the absence of any Christian deaths during the rampage of 1860.

into an ecstatic trance. He claimed afterward to have had a vision of a venerable old man with a white beard who would lead them all on a better path to truth and righteousness. A bit later, the Shazli visionary encountered in the flesh the venerable old man in his vision. The venerable old man was Fray Emmanuel Förner, a Spanish monk, living in a nearby Franciscan monastery.

Burton was intrigued by the monk's story of his meeting with this member of the Shazli who had asked Fray Förner to shepherd them to the Truth. He attended the Shazli rituals in disguise and observed their rapt attention while the monk explained his faith. Their interest seemed genuine. Burton, no stranger to mysticism himself, became convinced of the sincerity of the Shazlis' spiritual transports. Urged on by his wife Isabel's natural enthusiasm for winning souls for the true faith, and his own spiritual restlessness, Burton came to believe something momentous was happening. Saul of Tarsus, after all, had been converted to Christianity in this same land. By the beginning of 1871, there had been 250 conversions and more were expected.

Before long, Shazli leaders were jailed. Their property was confiscated. Emmanual Förner died mysteriously. Burton saw the hand of his Turkish enemy, Rashid Pasha, at work. He confronted the wali, flew into one of his famous rages, and claimed the British government's right to protect the Shazlis. He wrote the Foreign Office suggesting there might be 25,000 Shazlis ready to be baptized, and proposed different ways to protect them. One was for him to buy some land where the Shazlis could practice their religion freely under the protection of the British flag. Syria was rocked by the conversions. The bazaars hummed with talk of the Shazlis, and Burton's enemies found ways to read into it whatever evil intent they wished to lay at his feet.

On August 16 1871, Burton was summarily fired. The Shazli affair had frightened the British Foreign Office. Burton's letter in favor of enabling the baptism of thousands of prospective converts from Islam had persuaded Lord Grenville that he had lost his senses. Hatti Humuyun was one thing, but British conniving in support of a mass defection might easily have resulted in a new religious war.

In the aftermath of the Shazli conversions, Abd el-Kader was asked to serve on a tribunal of legal scholars to reconsider the death sentence given to fourteen Shazlis by the local authorities, a punishment intended to chill their enthusiasm for Christianity. Since the introduction of the reforms pressed by the European powers, religious freedom had become law of the empire. Thus, the official charge against the men had been evasion of military service. The tribunal met in the Nekib Allée at Abd el-Kader's residence, assembled in response to the British outcry at the severity of the punishment. The tribunal had to reconcile the real Shazli crime of apostasy and the Koran's first principal: there should be no constraint in religion.

There is no record of the arguments among tribunal members, but Isabel Burton, who took a close interest in the Shazlis fate, reported in her memoirs that Abd el-Kader and Sheik Abd el-Ghani argued against the death penalty for the fourteen Shazlis chosen for exemplary punishment. It is not hard to imagine the emir arguing that one's religion should not be turned into an ideology. Perhaps he did, and changed minds, as he had done forty years earlier as a young man at his father's council when they were considering Bey Hassan's request for protection. In the end, the condemned Shazlis were spared their lives and sent into exile.

A flood of letters expressing moral support for her husband were collected by Isabel while she organized the logistics of departure. Abd el-Kader's tribute waxed characteristically poetic: "You have left us the sweet perfume of charity and noble conduct in befriending the poor and supporting the weak, O wader in the seas of knowledge, O well of learning about our world, who transcended his time." Isabel left her home unobtrusively in the early dawn on September 13, 1871. Only two people from her social circle saw her off as she headed with her considerable baggage train toward Beirut where her husband was licking his wounds — Jane Digby and Abd el-Kader. Isabel called them "the two most interesting people in Damascus, who never knew what fear meant."

છ૦

Jane Digby was another rare bird on foreign visitors' watch list. Abd el-Kader met her soon after his arrival in Damascus in 1855, when she was already bravely married to a Bedouin chieftain, having ignored the dire warnings of the British consul and other Europeans who were certain such a marriage could only come to a bad end. Astonishing the naysayers, she actually had found genuine happiness, after leaving behind a trail of countless lovers and six marriages that stretched from London, via Paris, Munich and Athens to Syria.

Digby had also become a favorite of the aging emir who kept a youthful appearance with his carefully dyed black hair. She was a regular visitor in the Nekib Allée, and in the summer, often seen among the guests drinking the emir's famous mint tea at his villa overlooking the Barada River. Under the terms she had negotiated with her husband, Medjuel el-Merzag, she could live a European life style for six months a year in Damascus. The other six months she devoted herself to living in a goat skin tent in the desert as a Bedouin woman, going barefoot, wearing the traditional blue robe and yashmak, living apart with the other women of the camp and humbly serving her husband.

In the best tradition of the daughters of English nobility, she had been tutored in Greek, Latin and French, eventually adding Italian, German, Russian and Arabic. Digby was also an accomplished horsewoman, a talented painter and sketch artist. A good shot, too. Like Burton, she was also an outcast in her own country — married, Society whispered, to a "nigger."

Her marriage to Medjuel el-Mezrag had sealed a spectacular love-career that had made Digby one of England's most notorious black sheep. Jane's happiness and sincere embrace of her husband's culture was evident to all with eyes in their heads. She was older than her husband, and a Christian, though not particularly devout. Her husband was a deeply religious Muslim. Each had no difficulty respecting the faith of the other.

For Digby and Burton, England was a prison of staid convention and cramped Victorian primness. She was attracted to the same things as Burton — the space, the wildness, the freedom and the adventure of the East. Unlike the tempestuous, aggressive Burton, hers was a diffident, airy brilliance that made her a pleasing, unthreatening conversationalist. Lady Jane was widely read and witty — refined qualities that didn't prevent her from being a desert Amazon. She could ride as hard as any man and do her part in a razzia. She was loyal and courageous.

Abd el-Kader knew of these qualities. As the bloody events of July 1860 unfolded, Abd el-Kader had sent one of his sons to Jane's home in the mixed Maydan quarter outside the walls of the old city, inviting her to stay in his residence. She insisted she was safe in her husband's house, explaining that she had Christian servants, and didn't want to abandon them. Jane took in terrified Christians banging at their gate for help, despite Medjuel's warning that the mobs might return at night to storm houses sheltering Christians.

When the carnage was over, she put on her bedouin clothing and entered the Christian quarter to find out how she could help the victims. For days she dispensed unleavened bread and medications, encountering in her work "mutilated bodies, half devoured by dogs, and filling the air with all the elements of plague and cholera." Her firmness, compassion and spirit of self-sacrifice — Abd el-Kader's "companions" of courage — showed themselves on the killing fields during those gruesome July days. Jane Digby el-Mezrag undoubtedly endeared herself to the emir well beyond what her natural charm and intelligence had already accomplished.

She once had the privilege of visiting Abd el-Kader's fabled harem. It was rumored that the emir took a new wife each year, mostly Circassian girls no older than fifteen. But Jane reported that unless he had divorced most of them, the rumor was untrue. She counted only five wives,* still one too many according to Islamic law. His senior and most valued wife, Kheira, Digby described as "massively fat and physically ugly. Yet, she presided over the harem with stately dignity and calm authority."

During her last twenty years, she remained a loyal and loving wife to an Arab chieftain. Jane Digby el-Mezrag was as unique in the East as she was in the West. She, like Burton, was a law unto herself — she upset all preconceived notions.

ço

Abd el-Kader was a friend and admirer of two of England's great cultural rebels. One, a free-thinking iconoclast and misfit who aided and abetted the conversion of Muslims to Christianity, whose special topics for parlor entertainment included nymphomania, prostitution

---

* There is no way of knowing how accurate was Digby's wifecount or whether she mistook a concubine for a wife. There is talk among some descendents of the emir living in Damascus of his having taken a young Circassian wife and one of them does believe he had five wives at one point. It would not have been characteristic of the emir to violate the limit of four wives permitted in the Koran, yet neither was he perfect.

and techniques of castration. The other, a supposedly immoral, self-absorbed, scandalous woman who had even abandoned a child in pursuit of amorous adventure.

Yet, was not Abd el-Kader, a strict constructionist Islamist, a man of puritanical simplicity and abstinence — save the pleasures of the harem — also a rebel who upset old ways? Not by virtue of his own caprice or disregard of the law or of tradition, but by virtue of his deep knowledge and rigorous, unselective application of the Law — condemning popular customs that violated, or were confused with, Koranically correct behavior? He forced tribes to pay war taxes in times of peace. Unheard of. He forbade the age-old practice of decapitating prisoners on the battlefield. He insisted on humane treatment of French prisoners taken into captivity.* The emir rescued innocent Christians from bloodthirsty Muslims, which in the eyes of some less-enlightened Muslims, made him despised as a French lackey and an infidel.

Laying down arms because God doesn't approve of useless suffering, Abd el-Kader preferred to trust the word of French generals to that of a weak, treacherous Moroccan sultan. What could be a more politically scandalous decision for a Muslim warrior? That his decision was accepted that rainy December night in 1847 was a measure of the respect with which he was held, even by his die-hard lieutenants who wanted to continue to fight as desert outlaws. Yet, his greatest heresy as a warrior-saint had been to violate customary tribal hierarchies and traditions. Much of the old douad warrior aristocracy, represented by his nemesis, Ben Ismail, couldn't abide a young marabout who so often put religious knowledge and moral character ahead of blood ties and seniority.

Burton and Digby, uncomfortable in their English identities, were seeking new ones. Abd el-Kader was confident of his identity in Islam, yet was not he also seeking a higher identity, one that would not exclude others by their non-Islam? In the eyes of some Muslims, that made him an oddball. He seemed to recognize this himself in a letter he wrote to

---

* Abd el-Kader's humanitarianism, and specifically, his rules for the treatment of prisoners anticipated Geneva Code of 1949 codified human rights and prisoners' rights. The emir's humanitarian accomplishments were the subject of an international conference at The Place of Nations in Geneva sponsored by the United Nations in April 2006: *Emir Abdelkader, forerunner of human rights and champion of interreligious dialogue.*

his friend the Swiss banker and Saint Simonian, Charles Eynard: ..."I have become so tolerant that I respect all men whatever their religion and beliefs...I try not to harm any man, but rather do him good. God created men to be His servants, not the servants of other men."

The words of Simon Peter, which the emir surely had read during his years of Bible study in France, could have been written by the emir... *add to your faith virtue, to virtue knowledge, to knowledge self-control, to self-control perseverance, to perseverance godliness, and to godliness brotherly kindness and love*...Abd el-Kader's Islam was not a safety belt that he clung to for security, but a platform from which to plumb the depths and meaning of God's diverse creation. He was a unifier, not a separator. Knowledge and virtue were his tools.

Abd el-Kader's spirit had become like that of a scientist seeking a unified-field theory, with Ibn Arabi as his guide. On the 25th of May of 1883, failing kidneys and its toxic companion, uremic poisoning, carried him to the ultimate ecstatic state: he was reunited to his Source through slow starvation and delirium. The emir was finally laid to rest, as requested — next to his master in the Ibn Arabi Mosque on the hills of Salihiyya, a short, dusty walk from Sir Richard Burton's villa.

℘

Curiously, the death of the emir had been anticipated exactly three months earlier with an encomium from the *New York Times*. In summarizing his career in an 800 word pre-obituary, it passed its magisterial judgment.

"One of the ablest rulers and most brilliant captains of the century, if the estimates made of him by his enemies is correct, is now, in all probability approaching the end of his stormy career. Abd-El-Kader is dangerously ill, and his advanced age and hardships of sixteen years of campaign life leave little room for believing he will long survive...The nobility of his character, no less than the brilliancy of his exploits in the field, long ago won him the admiration of the world...Great men are not so abundant that we can afford to lose them without a word. If to be an ardent patriot, a soldier whose genius is unquestioned, whose honor is stainless; a statesman who could weld the wild tribes of Africa into a formidable enemy, a hero who could accept defeat and disaster without a murmur — if all these constitutes a great man, Abd-El-Kader deserves to be ranked among the foremost of the few great men of the century."

The Emir's family at Fort Lamalgue
Engraving by Valentin. Location; B. Etienne

Amboise Chateau
Lithograph unknown artist. Location; St. Louis Foundation

Liberation at Amboise.
Zohra kissing the hand of
Louis Napoleon
Ange Tissier,
Location; Chateau Versailles

Portrait of Emir displaying his
medals
anonymous, 1868, based on
photo by Abdoullah Bros. 1865,
Location; Museum of the
Masonic Lodge, Grand Orient

Colt Pistols from President Abraham Lincoln
Army Museum, Algiers

Emir Abd-el-Kader with three of his aghas and General MacMahon on his left,
future President of the French Republic. 1867.

Christian quarter in Damascus after the massacre of 1860

Photograph. Location; unknown

Group picture at Port Said, c. 1860s
Emir standing center, Viceroy Ismail Pasha left, Emir Shamil in chair

Photograph. Location; unknown

I N ALGERIA, I OWE A SPECIAL THANKS to Mochtar Darrar, the former mayor and deputy-mayor for culture in Mascara, who guided me to locations where events described in the story took place. He shared not only his knowledge of the emir's life and local history, but the hospitality of a home warmed by the generous cuisine of his Polish wife. To Nouredine Rehab, Mascara's town librarian and an Abd el-Kader connoisseur, I am most grateful for his constant readiness to answer questions and provide materials. Bishop Henry Teissier opened up his personal library and shared with me new and useful materials I might have never discovered. He also was responsible for introducing me to Mohammed Ben Allal, a direct descendant of one of the emir's most devoted and feared caliphs. Mohammed provided valuable information about his ancestor's character and tribal traditions. Thanks to Waciny Laredj and to Fouad Gouni for your insights and advice.

I am indebted to Nabil Kuwatly, Elias Bullad and Princess Badira for their gift of time spent with me, their introductions and specialized areas of knowledge while I was in Syria, and to Jafar Jazairy for taking me on a tour of the emir's residences in and around Damascus. No one should do research on Abd el-Kader today without consulting Professor Bruno Etienne in Aix en Provence. He generously shared bits and pieces of his encyclopaedic knowledge of the emir's life, as well as documentary sources and answers to a multitude of questions. I am also grateful to Bruno Etienne's collaborator, Francois Pouillon, for helping me sort through the politics and confusion of portraits and photographic images of Abd el-Kader. To the specialists at the Army Museum in Paris, my thanks for the fine points of uniforms and weaponry.

A big thank you to the Center for Advanced Studies in Culture at the University of Virginia for a research grant, and to the Virginia Center for the Creative Arts for an opportunity to retire into a writer's cocoon in the my final days of editing the manuscript. Thanks also for support from the Matheson Trust (UK) which promotes the comparative study of religion. My deep appreciation to Ed and Ruth Olson for introducing me to the Clayton County Archives in Elkader, Iowa where the emir's legacy to America continues to be nurtured. Many people read, critiqued and improved the manuscript before it fell into the good hands of Paul Cohen and Peter Lewis, my editors at Monkfish Publishing. I especially want to thank Carol Edwards, Zoe Rosenberg, Beth György, Julie Portman, Tony Kiser, Anne Kiser, Sarge Cheever, Pat Curry, Al Fairchild, Scott Willis, Gay Barclay, Mohammed Khan Nasir, Reza Shah-Kazemi, Idriss Jazairy and Mireille Luc-Keith. Mireille was also my indispensable research assistant without whom I would have been overwhelmed by the voluminous French literature. Finally, I am profoundly thankful to my wife, Pam, for understanding that writing requires monkish and often anti-social ways.

1492	Spanish capture Granada, drive out last of Arabs and Jews	
1576	Regency of Algiers established under the protection of the Ottoman Empire	French explorers arrive in North America
1779		Colonies declare independence from Britain
1789	Beginning of the French Revolution, formation of National Assembly	US Constitutional Convention in Philadelphia
1793	The Terror instituted to defend the Revolution	
1798	Turks recapture Oran from Spain	US "federalist" Congress passes Alien & Sedition Acts permitting deportation of non citizens, criminalizes "false or malicious" criticism of the US government
1799	Napoleon Bonaparte invades Egypt and Syria	
1801	Napoleon crowns himself emperor at Notre-Dame	The Louisiana Purchase concluded by Thomas Jefferson
1804	Napoleonic Code revolutionizes French and European societies	
1808	Birth of Abd el-Kader	Tecumseh leads revitalization movement among Shawnees

1815	Defeat of Napoleon at Waterloo	Creek Indian war breaks out in US; Spain sells territories east of the Mississippi
1827	Dey Hussein strikes French consul with fly whisk	
1830	General de Bourmont leads punitive expedition to capture Algiers, abdication of Charles X in favor of Louis-Philippe	US Congress passes Indian Removal Act, enabling forced deportation of Indians west of the Mississippi River
1831	Oran falls to French, Muhi al-Din, father of Abd el-Kader becomes reluctant leader of jihad	
1832	Muhi al-Din cedes leadership of jihad to Abd el-Kader, seven tribes vow loyalty	Seminole Indian Wars; Andrew Jackson vs. Chief Osceola; Scorched-earth tactics practiced by US Army followed by forced relocation of Seminoles to Oklahoma
1834	Demichels Treaty makes the emir an ally	
1835	Battle of Machta	Cherokees forced to leave territory, many perished on "Trail of Tears"
1837	Treaty of Tafna	First "Afghan War" British troops are massacred in retreat from Kabul; Victoria becomes queen of Great Britain

1839	Jihad resumes	First "opium war" forces Chinese to allow British to use ports; cede Hong Kong
1841	Bugeaud named governor of Algeria	International force under General Napier pushes Egyptians out of Syria
1843	Duke of Aumale captures emir's smala, Abd el-Kader becomes a fugitive under Moroccan protection	British troops conquer Sindh region of India
1845	France pressures Moroccan sultan to deny Abd el-Kader asylum	British troops conquer Sikh region of India; President James Polk champions "Manifest Destiny"
1846	French prisoners massacred by Mustafa Ben Thami	US declares war on Mexico, seizes New Mexico and California
1847	Abd el-Kader surrenders to General Lamoricière and the Duke of Aumale	Navaho wars begin in American southwest; Mexico city captured
1848	Abd el-Kader and entourage imprisoned at Toulon, moved to Pau again transferred to Amboise	California Gold Rush; British annex Punjab
1852	Abd el-Kader liberated by Louis-Napoleon	British go into Burma

1853	Abd el-Kader settles in Bursa, Turkey	
1855	Abd el-Kader takes up permanent residence in Damascus	Hostilities involving Teton Sioux, retaliatory massacres on both sides
1860	Abd el-Kader intervenes to rescue Christians living in Damascus	Apaches go on warpath in Arizona South Carolina secedes from the Union
1863	Abd el-Kader goes on pilgrimage to Mecca and Medina, ending with a visit to Alexandria where he meets with Masonic Lodge "Pyramides"	Indian uprisings in Minnesota Navajo Indians' "long walk" to Bosco Redondo
1869	Opening of Suez Canal, Abd el-Kader among dignitaries	
1870	French defeated by Prussians at Sedan, ending the second Empire and image of French invincibility among Algerians	Nez Perce Indian Wars; defeat of Chief Joseph
1883	Death of Abd el-Kader	

Chapter One: A General in the Dock

The general's remarks are excerpts from a much longer self-defense presented in Dupuch's treatise, *Abdelkader au Amboise* (pp. 72-79) that includes heated exchanges between deputies over the treatment of their famous prisoner. For Lamoricière's comparison of the religious sentiment with the principal of legitimacy in prerevolutionary France, see Churchill, Chapter twenty, p. 273 of French version. Also Aouli, Redjala, Zoummeroff (*Islam-Occident: les voies du respect, de l'entente, de la concorde* p. 398) referencing Zoummeroff's private collection of documents.

An abbreviated portrait of Lamoricière can be found in *Islam-Occident: les voies du respect, de l'entente, de la concorde*, by Georges Hirtz (PSR edition, 1998). This concise volume presents snapshots of four figures from 19th-century Algeria who demonstrated through attitude and behavior how Christians and Muslims can live in harmony with each other. They include emir Abd el-Kader, General Lamoricière and a fascinating Christian-Muslim couple, Aurelie Picard and Sheik Ahmed Tidjani, head of the Tidjani Brotherhood that was centered at the zawiya of Ain Madhi (besieged by Abd el-Kader in 1838). Aurelie Picard never gave up her Christian faith nor did she ever wear a veil during her long marriage, consecrated in Algiers in 1872 by Cardinal Lavigerie in a civil ceremony.

Chapter Two: Lords of the Tent

This chapter draws heavily from three sources: the French version (which is more readily available) of Churchill's, *The Life of Abd el Kader (ex Sultan of Algeria)*; General Melchior Joseph Eugene Daumas, *The Horses of the Sahara* and *Ways of the Desert*, both of which have been translated into English by Sheila Ohlendorf; and Professor Bruno Etienne's *Abdelkader*.

The description of Abd el-Kader's birth and dialogues with his parents and teachers are drawn from Part I, pp. 21-103 of *Abdelkader*. Prof. Etienne is married to an Algerian, is steeped in Algerian culture, a fluent Arabist and has made Abd el-Kader a life work. I have incorporated his mixture of original research, which includes making use of an oral tradition still alive in the regions where Abd el-Kader is a favorite son, his deep knowledge of the culture and his well-grounded imagination that has rightly stressed the importance of Abd el-Kader's upbringing and close relationship with his parents based on the principles of obedience, hierarchy and Divine Law.

General Daumas approached the subject of the Arab horse and way of life as a culturally engaged intelligence officer and a practical cavalry commander looking for remounts and ways to improve the endurance of French horses in the field. *Horses of the Sahara* has gone through nine editions and is a classic of its genre. His long friendship with Abd el-Kader, which began in 1833 as a French representative to Abd el-Kader's court and embryonic nation state in Mascara following the Desmichels Treaty, continued for over thirty years. Abd el-Kader, was the source of much of his information.

The description of Abd el-Kader's youth, his love of hunting, his family and his education come from the emir's recollections provided to Col. Charles Henry Churchill (chapter one), and are the basis for embellishments by other biographers of the emir.

Chapter Three: Unity and Complexity

The story of Abd el-Kader's defence of the honor of his cousin and future wife, Kheira, is retold in many books and is based in the oral tradition recorded and used by Etienne. Churchill (chapter two) and Etienne (Part I, chapter two) are the principal sources for the description of his pilgrimage with his father, Muhi al-Din. Highlights of the teachings of Abd el-Kader al-Jilani (also a Muslim patron saint of travelers) were drawn from al-Jilani's own work, *The Secret of Secrets* (Islamic Texts Society, Golden Palm Series), translated by Shayk Tosun Bayrak al-Jerrahi al-Halveti.

Al-Jilani was born in 1077 in a region of present day Iran called al-Jil. It seems he had an unusual youth, marked by a mystical experience: an angel in the form of a beautiful young man accompanied him everyday to school and walked him back home. To this angelic companion, al-Jilani attributed his remarkable memory and ability to learn in a day what other students did in a week. Finally, one day plowing a field behind an ox, he reported that the ox turned its head and spoke: 'You are not created for this.' He ran to his widowed mother and asked her to send him to Baghdad where he could follow the path of truth and 'acquire knowledge, to be with the wise and to those close to Allah.' (Such people in Islam are called "friends of God" because, like Christian saints, they are considered faithful mirrors of Divine Will who can inspire less worthy believers.) His teachings, especially chapters four (On Knowledge) and ten (On Veils of Light and Darkness) have a strong bearing on Abd el-Kader's writings and theory of knowledge expressed in his Letter to the French written in 1855. When asked one day what he had received from God, al-Jilani answered: "Good conduct and knowledge."

Chapter Four: Arrival of the Infidels

Descriptions of the French adventure are drawn from the memoirs of Pellissier de Reynaud, a French officer who participated in the invasion and a prolific memoirist. Also useful was Churchill (chapter two); chapters seven and eight in *Abd el-Kader* (Aouli Rejala and Zoummeroff), and for good general background, Larbi Icheboudene's *Alger*.

Drawing on numerous contemporary sources — French and Arab — Icheboudene makes convincingly clear that the popular French schoolboy explanation for the attack (a reprisal for a diplomatic insult) doesn't hold up under scrutiny. Charles X was in serious political trouble at home and needed a diversion. According to Hamdan Khodja *(le Miroir)*, who was an eyewitness in the court of Dey Hussein, the insult delivered by Deval was an intentional provocation. In contrast to the official valuation of forty-eight million francs given the French government, Hamdan Khodja estimates the treasury's true value at 150-700 million francs.

Chapter Five: The Obedient Son

Yale University's Jennifer Pitts has rendered a great service by translating de Tocqueville's insightful essays on France's divisive and bumbling occupation of Algeria (*Writings on Empire and Slavery*, pp 17, 25). Churchill remains the principal source for all authors (chapters 2-3), embellished by Col. Azan in Vista Clayton's 1975 lively book, *The Phantom Caravan*. Clayton's book is the sole popularization of the emir's life written by an American, while Raphael Danziger's *Abd al-Qadir and the Algerians* (written for a PhD thesis) might be the preferred source for scholarly researchers.

The emir's own autobiography, contains the dialogue attributed to his father when Muhi al-Din abdicates in favor of his son. It reads like a disjointed stream of consciousness, intelligible only to someone very familiar with the details of his campaigns and life.

Churchill's description of the phases of Abd el-Kader's "enthronement" is generally accepted, but is disputed by Mochtar Darrar, the former mayor of Mascara and local historian. Though he believes the plebiscite by the tribes held in the valley occurred on November 21, before the homage given by local leaders in the beylicat, I have stayed with the traditional narrative. Thanks to Darrar's insights, however, I have omitted a detail in Churchill usually retained by other authors. It describes Abd el-Kader receiving his homage seated in a gilded Spanish chair (booty from the recapture of Oran in 1792). This seems an unlikely prop, given his Bedouin culture and ascetic nature.

Rouina. Like the Mongols and the jerky they ate on horseback, the Arab horseman's ability to live for days on *rouina* gave them the enormous advantage of speed over the heavily weighted French soldier and his cumbersome baggage train. As Napoleon brilliantly demonstrated, generalship and speed can compensate for smaller mass, confirmed in basic physics by the formula: F(force) =M(mass) x (V)velocity.

Chapter Six: France's New Ally, 1834

Adolph V. Dinesen was a Danish artillery officer serving in the French army in the late 1830s. Thanks to a translation undertaken by Editions ANEP and The Abd el-Kader Foundation in 2001, Dinesen's memoir, published in Danish in 1840, was made available to the Francophone world. His work, *Abd el-Kader et les relations entre les francais et les Arabs en Afrique du Nord*, was a useful source for this chapter, especially the description of the festivities following the conclusion of the Desmichels Treaty. Pages 57-60 provide an extensive excerpt from commander de Torigny's report of his trip accompanying the emir back to Mascara with one hundred rifles and a thousand pounds of gunpowder. Dinesen also provides additional details about the emir's puritanism, legal rulings and private life (pp. 80-82).

In *L'Emir Abdelkader* by Abdelaziz Ferrah, the author uses an imaginary dialogue with the emir as a device for getting inside his head. He makes it clear that the emir deeply regretted what happened (pp. 61-62). Ben Tahar was the cadi of Arzew, a much-respected scholar and friend of Muhi al-Din. His undoing was his failure to repent and repudiate his commitments to Boyer. According to an Arab source (*Tulu'saad as suud*, by Ismail el-Mazari) this was the first instance of eye gouging being used to torture a person, and the practice was never allowed by the emir, though what the Koran does permit would itself qualify as torture by most lights.

Abd el-Kader's autobiography makes clear that dissension among the tribes was a greater problem than fighting the French. His tribal enemies were constantly spreading rumors that he was acting in bad faith, could not be trusted and had no authority.

Chapter Seven: Building an Islamic Nation

Dinesen is a useful source (pp. 61-84) on the organization of the emir's nation building efforts and makes reference to his brother Mustafa's opposition to his leadership. Denisen's Danish memoir was discovered by the Algerian ambassador to Denmark in 19— and translated by The Abdelkader Foundation in Algiers, at the urging of Idriss Jazairy, then president of the Foundation.

According to Denisen and Lamoricière (Emerit p.182), the rebellion against the emir by members of his own family was based on their hostility to his peace treaty with the Christians, bearing in mind that Arabs considered all Europeans, whether believers or not, to be Roumi — hence Christians. The Arab word for a Christian originates from the confounding of Romans and Christians following the conversion of Emperor Constantine to Christianity. After the fall of Rome, the Roman association with Christianity was maintained by the Holy Roman Empire, which gave rise to the claim of moral supremacy by the Papacy under Pope Gregory VII (1073-1085). The so-called Holy Roman Empire was created by disgruntled lords and clerics to reform a Catholic Church which had fallen into an appalling state of fragmentation, chaos and debauchery (R.R.Palmer, p.33-34; *History of the Modern World*).

Quoting Palmer: "In this world people have no nationality, they do not live in a state; they live in a church. Society itself is a great religious community (Umma-like). Its leaders are clergy to which all educated people belong…all are living in the religious community and preparing their souls for eternal life." Gregory's ideal was not a "world state" rather a "spiritual counterpart under the discipline of a centralized, morally reformed Papacy that would judge and guide human actions." Indeed, the consciousness of medieval Europe modeled Islamic consciousness before the intrusion of European concepts of nationality in the 19th century.

Churchill, chapter five, p.94 (of French version), quotes the emir's discourse to the Beni Amer chiefs in the mosque after signing Desmichels treaty. The number of 15,000 horseman comes from Churchill, and represents about the maximum the emir ever fielded at once. For excerpts of letters from the emir to the Comte d'Erlon, see Aouli et. al. (chapter nine).

For more details on the organization of the emir's army, his *Autobiography* pp. 76-80 reveals more details than those in found in Churchill.

Chapter Eight: The Wheel Turns

For the battle of Machta and the aftermath, Denisen pp. 90-93. There is a considerable discrepancy between Dinesen and Churchill about the number of troops involved on both sides. Churchill cites 5,000 French infantry versus the 2,500 mentioned by Dinesen. Dinesen credits Abd el-Kader with having 10,000 cavalry and 2,000 infantry at the start of the three-day battle that began in the Moulay Forest, whereas Churchill reports only 2,000 cavalry and 800 regular infantry. It is likely the discrepancy arises from Dinesen using French sources, which would be prone to exaggerate the size of the opposing forces, and in Churchill, the emir doing likewise in overestimating the size of the French forces.

Dinesen did not begin his service with the French until 1837, two years after the battle, though many of his sources must have come from French soldiers who served at the time, as his memoir was published twenty years before Churchill's. It is unfortunate that his book (in the translated version) does not contain any bibliography. His memoir was especially appreciated by The Abdelkader Foundation located in Algiers, in large measure because it lacked the sneering attitude of many French writers toward Arabs and Arab culture. The author's admiration of the emir was untainted by the condescension and incomprehension often found in the French writings. French authors, even those admiring of the emir's generalship, had difficulty imagining a leader who was not only devoutly and sincerely immersed in his faith, but for whom defending that faith was the equivalent of a Frenchman defending his country. To a Frenchman and most Europeans and Americans, then and still today, to die for one's religion is "fanaticism," while to die for one's country is noble patriotism.

The scene of the piles of French heads and the emir's reaction is described in Churchill (p. 104). Churchill and Pellissier de Reynaud are the main sources for details of Clauzel's punitive expedition to Mascara and subsequent occupation of Tlemcen.

Chapter Nine: "He Looked Like Jesus Christ"

Dinesen is believed to have been among those soldiers mustered for the ceremony at Tafna. His tour with the French Army of Africa was from 1837 to 1839. His account of the encounter between the emir and Bugeaud (*Abd-el-Kader*, pp. 134-137) is one of the most detailed with only minor differences from that of Azan and Churchill. Dinesen's description of the emir appears to be based on Bugeaud's own report to the Minister of War. Unlike many of the French accounts of this event, Dinesen describes the encounter as the birth of a nation. To some Algerians, this makes him an ally of those who see the emir as a proto-nationalist, prefiguring a secular state. Others would argue that he was foremost an Islamic Arab nationalist whom today would be called an "Islamist," which is what the emir would likely call himself as well. Organizing his revived Arab nation according to the dictates of Islamic law was certainly a given, regardless of the label contemporary partisans of the debate assign to the emir.

Chapter Ten: An Uneasy Peace

Marcel Emerit gives us the most thorough account of the Menonville-Zaccar episode (pp. 155-167 in *l'Algérie à l'Epoche d'Abd-el-Kader*). By adopting the mantle of Commander of the Faithful, the emir's authority was rooted in confrontation with the infidel invaders. Azan, Warnier and others saw this as the flaw in the emir's authority. (Yet, what other mantle was there for a marabout?) Peace was problematic because it required the emir to punish other Muslims in the name of an authority which was not accepted by those who did not want to be part of the emir's new state, did not believe in his divine calling, or simply saw no reason for paying taxes in peacetime. The emir saw treaties as intervals of French weakness that gave him an opportunity to strengthen his nascent confederation and prepare for new hostilities.

Chapter Eleven: The Emir's Frenchman

Leon Roche's account of his years living with the emir is thought by many to be a self-serving and unreliable source, as he wrote his memoirs after being employed as Gen. Bugeaud's trusted secretary and interpreter. Was he actually a spy as Ben Allal, one of the emir's caliphs believed immediately, or was he a romantic adventurer and rogue? He may well have been both. He had worked as a translator for the French army to quench his heart, inflamed by the loss of Khadija. It is not impossible to imagine that his obsession with Khadija became known within the army, as he undoubtedly talked about his loss with colleagues. This may have led to his being recruited to serve French interests while engaged in his quixotic escapade. If he was in fact a spy, the secret was well kept among the French officer corps who viewed him suspiciously long after he crossed back into French lines and had proven himself useful to Bugeaud.

It is assumed his memoir was self serving (they all are), yet it also reflected a deep respect for the emir, one that continued well after Abd el-Kader was released from prison. There is no question that his experience living tooth by jowl with the emir yielded highly valuable knowledge for the French military, but his two-volume memoir should be labeled: "Use with Caution."

Chapter Twelve: Jihad, 1839-1840

Emerit, Roches, Churchill provide the principal sources for this chapter. Marcel Emerit (*L'Algérie à l'epoche...*) is particularly useful, as his work is actually an edited collection of original documents, most of them reports from French officers to their superiors. The description of the meeting between Commander de Salles and the emir to obtain his approval of the agreement signed by his minister Miloud Ben Arrach is drawn from in his report to Marshal Valée (pp. 168-172). Pellissier de Reynaud (pp. 366-67) *Annales*, Livre xxix, is the source for the emir's response to Valee's appeal to keep the peace after sending a column through the disputed territory.

Chapter Thirteen: Total War

The best source for the account of the prisoner exchange and the meeting between abbé Suchet and the emir can be found in *Annales de la Propagation de la Foi*, vol. 14 (pp. 81-111) published in 1842 in Lyon. It contains a letter of September 10, 1841, from Suchet to the vicar-general of Algiers that is a fascinating piece of cultural reportage from a man who was protected only by his cleric's robes and the emir's aman as he roamed about in territory that was officially hostile. It has been now been issued as a reprint and is readily available in the bishopric's library in Algiers. Suchet's *Lettres curieuses et édifiantes*

sur l'Algérie (Cahier no. 3, reprinted in diocesan bimonthly *Rencontres* July/
Aug, 2002) with the Centre d'Etudes Diocésain d'Alger is full of fascinating
first hand descriptions of the country and people by this hardy man of God.

Adrien Berbrugger's memoir published under the title *Négotiations entre
Mgr l'évêque d'Alger et Abd-el-Kader pour l'échange des prisonniers* (Delahaye,
Paris, 1844) provides a detailed description of the first negotiation to exchange
prisoners between the emir's caliph, Mohammed Ben Allal Sidi Embarek and
Bishop Dupuch in Boufarik. Bugeaud's philosophy of warfare required to
achieve victory and lasting benefit for France is contained in *Par L'Epée et Par
le Charrue, écrits et Discours de Bugeaud* (esp. no. 27). These writings can be
found in a collection entitled *Colonies et Empires*, les classiques de la colonization, published under the direction of Ch-André Julien in 1948, by Presses
Universitaires de France.

Chapter Fourteen: Trail of Tears, 1843

There are many accounts of the capture of the smala, but perhaps the most
complete, from the French point of view, is contained in Edmound Jouhaud's
book *Yousouf* (Editions Robert Lafont, pp. 94-110), the celebrated Mamelouk
slave who rose to be a general in the French Army of Africa. Aside from
Lamoricière, Yusuf was the emir's most-dangerous opponent in this war of
rapid movement and cultural savoir faire. I am grateful to Mohammed Ben
Allal for drawing my attention to Mustafa Lacheraf's book, *L'Algérie: Nation
et Sociétié* (Editions Francois Maspero, 1965), which contains excerpts from
General Changarnier's memoirs citing the failed attempts of the French to
pry away Ben Allal from the emir (pp.104-105). Mohammed Ben Allal, a
direct descendent of the caliph, is the family historian and today lives in his
ancestral villa in Kolea.

Chapter Fifteen: Mischief Makers, 1844-1847

Correspondence between the emir and his caliph, Ben Salem, is found in
Churchill (pp. 250-253 of French version). Churchill's chapter eighteen describes the Bou Maza phenomenon and its fallout. Perhaps the best material
on Lieutenant Col. Montagnac, his unauthorized sortie that led to the French
setback at *Sidi Brahim,* the disagreements between Ben Thami and Bou
Hamidi and subsequent massacre of French prisoners is found in Paul Azan's
monograph, *Sidi Brahim,* published by Horizons de France, Paris, 1945. The
exchange between an indignant Bugeaud and a worldly-wise emir is found
in Aouli, Redjala and Zoummeroff (p. 377). The Bou Maza phenomenon is
taken from Wilfrid Blunt, *The Caged Hawk*, chapter eighteen.

Chapter Sixteen: Men of Honor

Aouli, Redjala, Zoummeroff provided the curious detail about Ben Salem's son, Cherif, who was studying in France and persuaded his father to quit the fight (p. 378). The same authors give a more detailed accounts (pp. 379-383) of the emir's relationship with Sultan Abderrahman; also the tenacious resistance of the Beni Amer, who having defected to the sultan, later sided again with the emir, and the Abd el-Kader's stunning victory against a much larger Moroccan force on the Moulouya River (reminiscent of Bugeaud's victory at Isly against much larger forces). Churchill, chapter twenty, provides the basis for virtually all other accounts of the encounter with Lamoricière, Montauban and the Duc d'Aumale at Djemaa Ghazaouet.

Chapter Seventeen: Betrayal

Vista Clayton (*The Phantom Caravan* pp. 240-49), drawing upon Azan, describes the family members and companions of the emir, as well as the crossing to Toulon, Daumas' attempts to bribe the emir to release France from the agreement made with the Duc d'Aumale. Julien provides the detail about the Europeans who were married to Arabs in the Emir's entourage (*Histoire de l'Algérie Contemporaine*, p. 207) surprising Col MacMahon. Bruno Etienne (pp. 221-229) and Aouli et. al. (pp. 389-407) provide additional details about their reception at Fort Lamalgue. Charles Poncey's account of his visit with the emir in Toulon is found in *le Bulletin Trimestriel de la Société des Sciences, Belles Lettres et Arts* of the department of the Var, 1850, no. 4. In his preamble, Poncey reports the emir having three wives when he arrived in Toulon (Kheira, Baraka, Aicha) and acknowledges that the emir's brother-in-law, Ben-Thami was the executioner of the French prisoners.

Chapter Eighteen: The View Is Most Magnificent

The reactions of the locals to the news that their cherished Chateau Pau would have the Arab prisoners living in it came from the archives of the Chateau Pau museum. Many details of his occupation were also presented in documents compiled for a colloquium about the emir in 2004. One of the documents was a transcription of Madame la Marechale de Grouchy's note about her visit to the chateau to see the famous prisoner and his family.

Chapter Nineteen: A Prison Fit for a King

Etienne is good at weaving in the emir's spiritual state of mind (pp. 228-244) during his captivity, bringing out the intense religious dialogue with Christians that he carries on; Aouli, Redjala, Zoummeroff (pp. 409-424).

The visit, and politics thereof, of the Marquis of Londonderry's meeting with the emir is in Wilfrid Blunt, *The Caged Hawk* (pp. 244-47). The journal, *La Semaine,* (no.4, February, 2004) provides an accounting of the emir's entourage and list of all who died at Amboise, as well as general conditions at the chateau — mostly derived from Charles Gabeau, one of the team of military interpreters and admirer of the emir.

Chapter Twenty: Liberation

Churchill and Alexander Bellemare, the emir's new interpreter in Paris, provide the primary sources for most of the standard narrative. Etienne and Aouli add various embellishments.

Chapter Twenty-One: The Emir's Letter

The excerpt of emir's letter of gratitude to Sister Natalie was found in the brochure *L'Emir Abd El-Kader à Amboise*, prepared by J-L Sureau and A. Feulvarc'h for the archives of the Dominicans of the Grande Bretèche in Tours. His more philosophical letter, known as *Lettre aux Francais*, has been republished most recently (2007) by Phébus with a preface by Antoine Sfeir, a well-known French specialist on Middle Eastern politics, and introduction by René Khawam, the translator of the letter.

Chapter Twenty-Two: The Road to Damascus

Mount Lebanon: A Ten Year's Residence from 1842-1852 Vol.I, is very instructive of both the local culture complexities and Churchill's own personality, which reflects in equal measure his learned and colorfully opinioned views. *The Balkans Since 1453* (Holt Reinhardt, 1961) by L.S. Stavrianos is a useful textbook, especially for the post Crimean War period and the interplay of European and local interests in the Middle East (chapter seventeen, p. 320, for British trade data). Again, C-H Churchill, chapter twenty-three, on "correcting" and Syrian Christian gloating in the aftermath of the Treaty of Paris.

Chapter Twenty-Three: One For All

Bellemare (*Abd-el-Kader*, pp. 222-230) provides one of the most detailed accounts of the emir's role in the events of July (and that of his sons and fellow Algerians) and Lanusse's confidence in his warnings despite the skepticism of his peers and smooth denials of the governor. On the aftershock, punishments and causes, M. Mechaga's memoir (*Murder, Mayhem...*pp. 244-270, translated by W.Thackston) was very useful as a source of insight into the political climate and motives of different actors in the drama. Also *New York*

Times on-line archives yielded copies of stories it published in the 1860s until the emir's death.

The controversial (among Muslims) subject of Abd el-Kader's membership in the Masons (Grand Orient de France, or GODF) can be resolved to a large extent, I believe, by clarifying what "membership" entailed. It is clear that the emir was not a regular participant at lodge meetings whether in Cairo or in Damascus, or anywhere. He enjoyed intellectual exchange with other Masons which took place most often on the comfortable divans at his residence in Damascus. Even if his membership was purely "honorific," it was still real. He is officially inscribed in the registers of the GODF in Paris and its affiliate in Damascus. He is listed in the book *Ten Thousand Famous Masons* (Macoy Publishing & Masonic Supply Co, with a Foreword by Harry S Truman, 1957) compiled by William Denslow and can be found on line. There were few Jews and no Zionist agenda at the time of the emir's recruitment into the society. Educated Muslims (outside the emir's family) I have spoken with, including Algerians, acknowledge that members of Masonic Lodges in the Middle East generally constituted an intellectual elite who could freely exchange ideas in confidence, nor are they shocked at the idea of the emir belonging to a lodge. The issue is mainly one of contemporary politics and "image." (See T. Zarcone, *Mystiques, Philosophes et Francs-Macons en Islam*, p. 232.)

Chapter Twenty-Four: Distinguished Misfits

Portraits of Sir Richard Burton and Lady Jane Digby rely on Byron Farwell's *Burton* and Fawn Brodie's *The Devil Drives* for the former, and Leslie Blanch's *The Wilder Shores of Love* for the latter. Isabel Burton's memoir, *The Inner Life of Syria*, was the main source for contextual flavor as well as the close relationship between Digby and Abd el-Kader.

According to Setty Simon-Khedis, the emir had five wives at the time of his death — Khadijah, mother of Omar; Aicha, mother of Sakina; Shafika, mother of Abdelmalek; Mabroukah (an Ethiopian or Sudanese), mother of Abdallah and Kheira, his cousin and favorite wife.

Abd al-Qadir al-Jilani. *The Secret of Secrets*. Translated by Shaykh Tosun Bayrak al-Jerrahi al-Halveti. Cambridge, UK: Islamic Texts Society, 1992.

Abd el-Kader. *Autobiographie*. 1855. Reprint. Translated by Hacène Benmansour. Paris: Dialogues Éditions, 1999.

Abd el-Kader. *Lettre aux Francais*. Translated by René R. Khawam. Algiers: Éditions ENAP, 2005.

Ammi, Kemir M. *Abd el-Kader*. Paris: Presses de la Renaissance, 2004.

Aouli, Smaïl, Ramdane Redjala and Philippe Zoummerof. *Abd el Kader*. Paris: Fayard, 1994.

Azan, Paul. *L'Émir Abd el Kader. Paris: Hachette*, 1925.

Bardin, Pierre. *Algeriens et Tunisiens dans l'Empire Ottoman de 1848 a 1914*. Paris: Editions du Centre de la Recherche Scientifique, 1979.

Bellemare, Alexandre. *Abd-el-Kader: Sa Vie Politique et Militaire*. Paris: Editions Bouchene, 2003 (originally published in 1863).

Bencherif, Osman. *The Image of Algeria in Anglo-American Writings*. Lanham, MD: University Press of America, 1997.

Benhamed, Amed Kouidir (Col Nabil): *la Bataille de la Machta* — juin 1835. Algiers: Editions Dar El Gharb, 2004.

Berbrugger, Adrien. *Negociations entre Mgr l'eveque d'Alger et Abd-el-Kader pour l' Échange des Prisonniers*. Paris: Delahaye, 1844.

Bertherand, E.L. *Medecine et Hygiene chez les Arabs*. Paris: Germer Bailliere, 1885.

Blanch, Leslie. *The Wilder Shores of Love*. New York: Lesley & Graff, 1993.

Blunt, Wilfrid. *Desert Hawk*. London: Methuen, 1974.

Bouamrane, Cheikh. *L'Émir Abd-el-kader, Resistant et Humaniste*. Algiers: Éditions Hammouda, 2001.

Boualmane, Bessaïh. *De l'Émir Abd el-Kader à l'Imam Chamyl*. Algiers: Dahalb, 1997.

Boutaleb, Abdelkader. *L'Émir Abd-el-Kader et la Formation de la Nation Algerienne*. Algiers: Dahalb, 1990.

Brodie, Fawn M. *The Devil Drives, the Life of Richard Burton*. New York: Norton, 1967.

Bugeaud, Thomas. "Par l'Epée et par la Charrue" (écrits et discours de Bugeaud) in *Colonies et Empires, Collection Internationale de Documentation Coloniale*. Paris: Presses Universitaires de France, 1948.

Burton, Isabel. *The Inner Life of Syria, Palestine and The Holy Land*. London: C. Kegan Paul & Co. 1879.

Clayton, Vista. *The Phantom Caravan*. Hicksville: Exposition Press, 1975.

Chodkiewicz, Michel. *Écrits spirituals,* Paris: Seuil, 1982.

Churchill, Charles Henry. *The Druzes and the Maronites Under the Turkish Rule from 1840 to 1860*. London: Bernard Quarich, 1862.

____. *Mount Lebanon*. London: Saunders and Otley, 1853.

____. *La Vie d'Abd el Kader*. Algiers: SNED (original English published in 1869).

Civry, Eugène de. *Napoléon III et Abd-el-Kader*. Paris: Martinon, 1853.

Danziger, Raphael. *Abd al-Qadir and the Algerians.* New York: Holmes & Meier, 1977.

Daumas, Eugene. *The Ways of the Desert.* Austin: University of Texas Press, 1971.

_____. *Horses of the Sahara.* Austin: University of Texas Press, 1968.

Dinesen, Adolph V. *Abd el-Kader.* Translated by Fondation Emir Abdelkader. Algiers: Éditions ENAP, 2001.

Dupuch, Mgr. Antoine-Adolphe. *Abd el Kader au Chateau d'Amboise.* Paris: Ibis Press, 2002 (originally published in 1849).

Estailleur-Chanteraine, Philippe d'. *L'Émir Magnanime, Abd-el-Kader le Croyant.* Paris: Fayard, 1959.

Étienne, Bruno. *Abdelkader.* Paris: Hachette, 1995.

Étienne, Bruno and François Pouillon. *Abd el-Kader le Magnanime.* Paris: Découvertes Gallimard, Institut du Monde Arabe Historie, 2003.

Emerit, Marcel. *L'Algérie à l'Époque d'Abd-el-Kader.* Paris: Éditions Bouchene, 2002.

Ferrah, Abdélaziz. *L'Émir Abdelkader.* Algiers: Marinoor, 1999.

France, M.A. de. *Les Prisonniers d'Abd-el-Kader, vols. 1&2.* Paris: L. Desessart, 1837.

Hirtz, Georges. *Islam-Occident: Le Voies du Respect, de L'entente, de la Concorde.* La Roche-Rigault, France: PSR Éditions, 1998.
Hardy, Madelaine. *Antoine-Adolph Dupuch, Premier Evêque d'Alger.* Bordeaux: Self-published, 2004.

Ibn 'Arabi. *Divine Governance of the Human Kingdom.* Translated by Shaykh Tosun Bayrak al-Jerrahi al-Halveti. Louisville: Fons Vitae, 1997.

Icheboudene, Larbi. *Algiers: Histoire et Capitale de Destin National.* Algiers: Casbah Éditions, 1997.

Jouhaud, Edmond. *Yousouf, Esclave, Mamelouk et General de l'Armée d'Afrique.* Paris: Editions Robert Laffont, 1980

Julien, Charles-André. *Histoire de L'Algérie Contemporaine. Vol 1.* Paris: Presses Universitaires de France, 1979.

Keller, E. *Le general de La Moricière.* Paris: J. Dumaine, 1874.

Khodja, Hamdan. *Le Miror: Aperçu Historique sur la Régence d'Algiers.* 1833. Reprint Algiers: Éditions ANEP, 2005.

Lataillade, Louis. *Abd-el-Kader, Adversaire et Ami de la France.* Paris: Pygmalion, 1984.

P. Lory, D. Rivet, H. Teissier, M. Lagarde, B. Etienne, K. Bentounes (collection of texts). *L'emir Abd el-Kader, Temoin et Visionnaire,* Paris: Ibis Press, 2004.

Laredj, Waciny. *Le Livre de l'Emir.* Paris: Sinbad/Actes Sud, 2005.

Legras, Joseph. *Abd el Kader.* Paris: Berger-Levrault, 1929.

Levallois, Michel. *Ismaÿl Urbain: une autre conquête de Algérie.* Paris: Masonneuve et Larose, 2001.

Maspero, François. *L'Honneur de Saint-Arnaud.* Algiers: Casbah Éditions, 2004.
M'Hamsadji, Kaddour. *La Jeunesse de l'Émir Abd el Kader.* Algiers: Office des Publications Universitaires, 2004.

Mishāqa, Mikhayil. *Murder, Mayhem, Pillage, and Plunder. 1873.* Memoir translated by Anne Royal and W.M. Thackston, Jr. Albany: State University of New York Press, 1988.

Montagnon, Pierre. *Histoire de l'Algérie.* Paris: Pygmalion, 1998.

Naudon, Paul. *La Franc-Maconnerie.* Paris: Presses Universitaires de France, 2006.

Palmer, R.R., *Twelve Who Ruled.* Princeton, NJ: Princeton University Press, 1970.

Péan, Pierre. *Main Basse sur Algiers.* Algiers: Chihab Éditions, 2005.

Pioneau, Abbé E. *Vie du Mgr. Dupuch, premier evêque d'Alger.* Bordeaux: Paul Chemmes, 1865.

Reynaud, E. Pellissier de. *Annales Algériennes.* Paris: Libraire Militaire, 1854.

Roches, Léon. *Trente-deux Ans à Travers l'Islam.* Paris: Firmen-Didot, 1887.

Sahli, Mohamed Chérif. *Abdelkader, Chevalier de la Foi.* Algiers: Éditions ENAP, 1984.

Schilcher, Linda. *Families in Politics: Damascene Factions and Estates in the 18th and 19th Centuries.* Stuttgart: Franz Steiner Verlag, 1985.

Sulayman, A. D. Ashrati. *The Emir Abd al-Qadir.* (3 vols. in Arabic). Algiers: Editions Dar el Gharb, 1998.

Teissier, Henri. *L'Eglise en Islam.* Paris: Le Centurion, 1984.

Tocqueville, Alexis de. *Writings in Empire and Slavery.* Translated & edited by Jennifer Pitts. Baltimore: Johns Hopkins University Press, 2002.

Yacine, Kateb. *Abdelkader et l'Independence Algérienne.* Algiers: Société Nationale d'Édition et de Diffusion, 1983.

Zarcone, Thierry. *Mystiques, Philosophes et Francs-Macons en Islam.* Paris: Editions Jean Maisonneuve, 1993.

MISCELLANEOUS PAPERS, BROCHURES, ARTICLES

Boulad, Elias. "Les évènements de 1860 au Liban et à Damas: sont-ils une sedition religieuse ou un complot politique fermenté par l'occident?" Damascus: *unpublished paper,* 1985.

Free Masonry Documents Treasury. Damascus: Al-Watha'eq House, 2004.

Le Grand Orient de France (brochure listing members). Paris: EDIMAF, 1979.

Paillat-Flitti, Bernadette. "L'organization medicale et sanitaire dans le Smala." Paris: *unpublished paper,* 2004.

Poncey, Charles. "Une Visite à Abd-el-Kader," *Bulletin Trimesteriel de la Societie des Sciences, Belles Lettres et Arts du Department du Var.* Toulon: Imprimerie de L. Laurent, 1850.

Sureau, Jean-Louis and Alexis Feulvarc'h. *L'Émir Abd el-Kader à Amboise, 8 Novembre 1848 – 11 Décembre 1852.* Tours, France: Archives Générales Dominicaines de la Présentation la Grande Bretèche, 2004.

Suchet, M. *Lettres édifantes et curieuses sur l'Algérie* (cahier III). Tours, France: 1840.

_____ . "Lettre à M. Samatan". *Annales de la Propagation de la Foi* 14(81), Reprint. Lyon: Chez l'editeur des annales, 1842.

Teissier, H. "L'Émir Abdelkader et les chrétiens à l'époque de son combat en Algérie et son exil en France." Paper presented at Colloque International sur l'Émir Abdelkader, 24-26 November, 1997.

_____."À Pau, l'amitie de l'Émir Abdelkader et de l'Evêque D'Alger." Paper presented at Colloque au Musée du Château de Pau, 6-7 June, 1998.

_____. "L'Émir et l'Evêque". Paper presented at Colloque de la Fondation Émir Abdelkader, Algiers, 22-23 November, 2000.

_____. "L'Émir, homme de dialogue." Paper presented at Centre Culturel Algérien, Paris, 22 September, 2001.